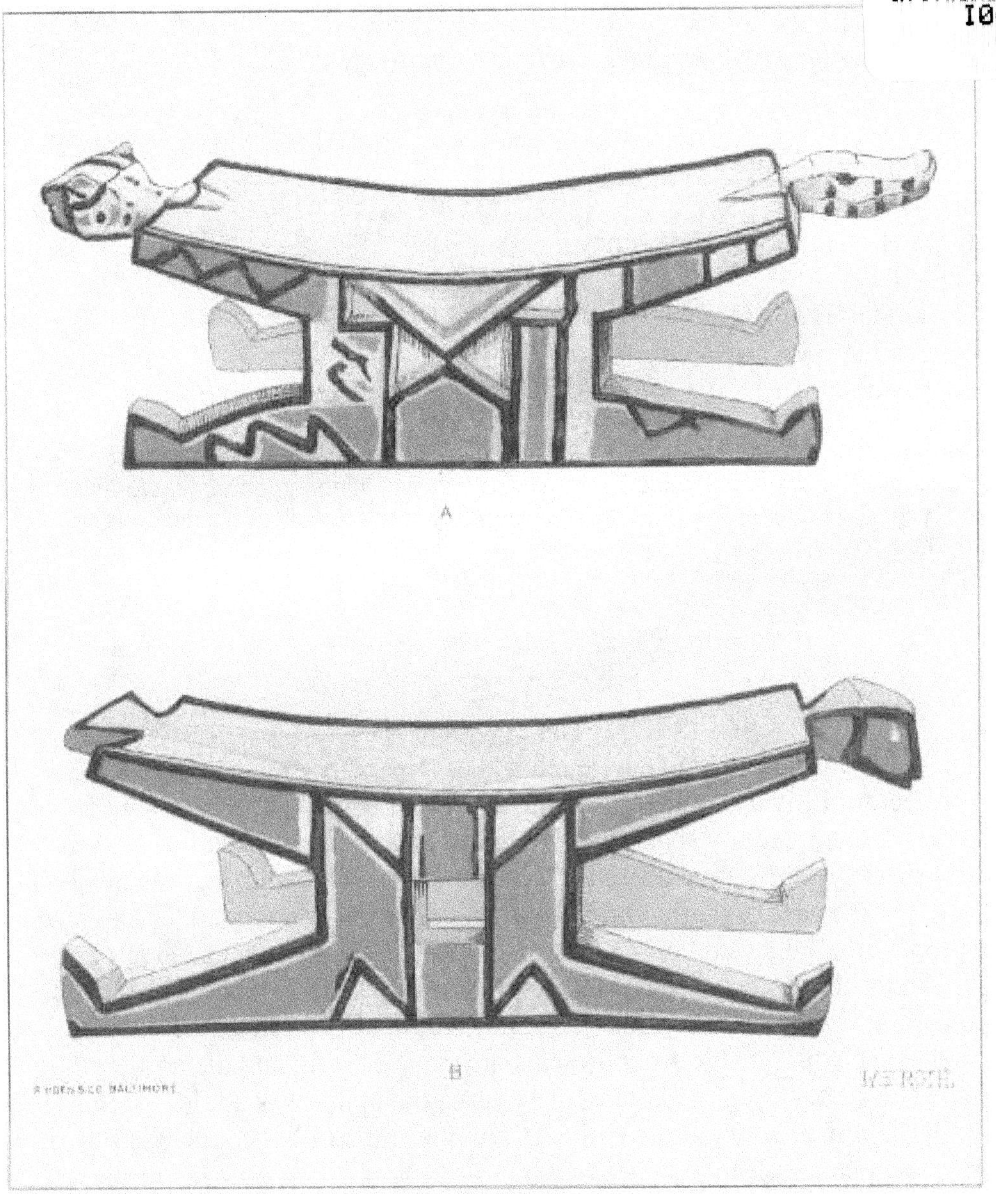

AN INQUIRY INTO THE
ANIMISM AND FOLK-LORE OF THE
GUIANA INDIANS

BY

WALTER E. ROTH

*Commissioner of the Pomeroon District, British Guiana; late Chief Protector of
Aboriginals, Queensland; late Royal Commissioner appointed to inquire*

into the condition of the natives of Western Australia;
Corresponding Member of the Anthropological Societies of Berlin and Florence;
Author of "North Queensland Ethnography," etc.

To
two of my oldest friends
CHARLES HEDLEY
Curator of the Australian Museum, Sydney
and
TOMMASO TITTONI
Italian Ambassador at Paris
I dedicate this Memoir

PREFACE

When, some seven years ago, I took up the duties of stipendiary magistrate, medical officer, and protector of Indians in this mosquito-cursed district of the Pomeroon, I determined upon devoting all my spare time—and there has been plenty of it—to an ethnographical survey of the native tribes of British Guiana, somewhat on the lines I had already followed in the case of North Queensland. As the work progressed, I recognized that, for the proper comprehension of my subject, it was necessary to make inquiry concerning the Indians of Venezuela, Surinam, and Cayenne, with the result that the area to be reviewed comprised practically that portion of the South American continent bounded, roughly speaking, by the Atlantic seaboard, the Orinoco, and the northern limits of the watershed of the Rio Negro, and the lower Amazon; and it was not long before I realized that for the proper study of the Arawaks and the Caribs I had to include that of the now almost extinct Antilleans.

In the course of my ethnographical work, I collected sufficient material in the way of myth, legend, and fable to warrant the publication of a separate volume on Animism and Folk-lore, and so the following pages have come to be written. The legends collected have been drawn mainly from Arawak, Carib, and Warrau sources, and are initialed (A), (C), and (W), respectively.

WALTER E. ROTH.

Pomeroon River, British Guiana, June, 1913.

CONTENTS

WORKS OF REFERENCE

(NOTE.—The following list of publications is not presented as a complete bibliography, but as indicating those authors to whom, directly or indirectly, I find myself indebted. The titles of works from which excerpts have been taken are initialed. As most of these publications are in foreign languages, the excerpts, here given in English, are necessarily translations, many of them being paraphrased to some extent in order that they may be best adjusted with the context.

Throughout the memoir authorities are cited by the initials used below, respectively; in connection with these, roman numerals indicate the volume numbers and arabic figures the page numbers.—W. E. R.)

Ac   ACUÑA, CHRISTOPHER. Relation of the great River of Amazons in South America. London, 1698.

A   ALEXANDER, J. E. Transatlantic sketches. 2 vols. London. 1833.

     APPUN, C. F. Unter den Tropen. Jena, 1871.

Ba   BANCROFT, EDWARD. An essay on the natural history of Guiana. London, 1769.

PBa BARRERE, PIERRE. Nouvelle relation de la France équinoxiale. Paris, 1743.

HWB BATES, HENRY WALTER. The naturalist on the Amazon. London, 1892.

     BECHAMEL. *See* GRILLET.

     BELLIN [JACQUES NICOLAS]. Description géographique de la Guyane. Paris, 1763.

     BENOIT, P. J. Voyage à Surinam. Bruxelles, 1839.

Be   BERNAU, J. H. Missionary labours in British Guiana. London, 1847.

     BIET, A. Voyage de la France équinoxiale en l'Isle de Cayenne, en l'année 1652. Paris, 1664.

BW   BODDAM-WHETHAM, J. W. Roraima and British Guiana. London, 1879.

Bol BOLINGBROKE, HENRY. A voyage to the Demerary. Norwich, 1807.

BBR BORDE, FR. DE LA. History of the origin, customs, religion, wars, and travels of the Caribs. *Timehri*, V, pt. 2, Demerara, 1886. Translated from the French, and condensed, by G. J. A. Bosch-Reitz.

     BOSCH-REITZ. *See* BORDE.

Br   BRETT, W. H. The Indian tribes of Guiana. London, 1868.

BrA — Mission work among the Indian tribes, etc. London (n. d.).

BrB — Legends and myths. London (n. d.).

Bri BRINTON, DANIEL G. The American race. New York, 1891.

Bro BROWN, C.B. Canoe and camp life in British Guiana. 2d ed., London, 1877.

     — *and* LIDSTONE, W. Fifteen thousand miles on the Amazon, etc. London,

1878.

LaC CASAS, BARTOLOMÉ DE LAS. An account of the first voyages and discoveries made by the Spaniards in America. London, 1699.

CASTELNAU, FRANCIS DE. Expédition dans les parties centrales de l'Amérique du Sud. 4 vols. Paris, 1850-57.

CC CATALOGUE OF CONTRIBUTIONS transmitted from British Guiana to the London International Exhibition, 1862. Georgetown, 1862.

GC CATLIN, GEORGE. Life among the Indians. London (n. d.).

DAC CHANCA, DIEGO ALVAREZ: The letter of, dated 1494, relating to the second voyage of Columbus to America, by A. M. Fernandez de Ybarra. *Smithsonian Misc. Coll.*, No. 1698, pp. 428-457, 1907.

Cou COUDREAU, H. A. La France équinoxiale. 2 vols. Paris, 1887.

Cr CRÉVAUX, J. Voyages dans l'Amérique du Sud. Paris, 1883.

DALTON, HENRY G. The history of British Guiana. 2 vols. London, 1855.

Da DANCE, CHAS. DANIEL. Chapters from a Guianese log-book. Demerara, 1881.

[DAVIES]. The History of the Caribby Islands . . . 1666. [For the original work see ROCHEFORT.]

FD DEPONS, F. Travels in parts of South America, during the years 1801, 1802, 1803, 1804. London, 1806. (In Phillips, Coll. of Modern Voyages, vol. IV, London, 1806.)

DIXON, GEO. G. Four months of travel in British Guiana. *Geographical Journal*, April, 1895.

DRAKE. Sir Francis Drake Revised: etc. 1626.

Df DUFF, ROBT. British Guiana. Glasgow, 1866.

PE EHRENREICH, PAUL. Die Mythen und Legenden der südamerikanischen Urvölker. Berlin, 1905.

Fe FERMIN, PHILIPPE. Description générale, historique, géographique et physique de la Colonie de Surinam. 2 vols. Amsterdam, 1769.

WF FEWKES, J. WALTER. An Antillean statuette, with notes on West Indian religious beliefs. *Amer. Anthr.*, n. s., XI, pp. 348-358, 1909.

GF FRIEDERICI, GEORG. Scalping in America. *Smithsonian Rep. for 1906*, pp. 423-438, 1907.

GALARD-TERRAUBE. Neue Reise nach Cayenne. Leipzig, 1799.

GILI, F. S. Saggio di storia Americana.

Go   DE GOEJE, C. H. Beiträge zur Völkerkunde von Surinam. *Int. Archiv für Ethnographie*, Bd. XIX, Heft i-ii, pp. 1-34, Leiden, 1908.

GB   GRILLET, JOHN, and BECHAMEL, FRANCIS. A journal of the travels of . . . . . into Guiana. London, 1698.

G   GUMILLA, JOSEPH. Historia natural . . . . del Rio Orinoco. 2 vols. Barcelona, 1791.

HARCOURT, ROBERT. A relation of a voyage to Guiana. London, 1613.

HA   HARTSINCK, J. J. Beschryving van Guiana of de wilde Kust in Zuid-America . . . . . Amsterdam, 1770.

HERRERA, ANTONIO DE. Historia general de los Hechos de los Castellanos en las islas, etc. Second edition. Madrid, 1730.

HiA   HILHOUSE, WILLIAM. Journal of a voyage up the Massaroony in 1831. *Jour. Roy. Geog. Soc.*, IV, pp. 25-40, 1834.

HiB   — The Warow land of British Guiana. Ibid., pp. 321-333.

HiC   — Notices of the Indians settled in the interior of British Guiana. Ibid., II, pp. 227-249, 1832.

AVH   HUMBOLDT, ALEXANDER VON. Personal narrative of travels to the equinoctial regions of America. 3 vols. London, 1852-53.

IT   IM THURN, EVERARD F. Among the Indiana of Guiana. London, 1883.

WI   IRVING, WASHINGTON. Companions of Columbus. London, 1884.

Je   JENMAN, G. S. To Kaieteur [in 1881]. Georgetown, 1907.

WJ   JOEST, W. Ethnographisches und Verwandtes aus Guayana. Leiden, 1893.

JUAN Y SANTACILIA, JORGE, *and* ULLOA, ANTONIO DE. A voyage to South America. 2 vols. London, 1760.

AK   KAPPLER, A. Sechs Jahre in Surinam. Stuttgart, 1854.

KEYE, O. Kurtzer Entwur von Neu-Niederland und Guajana. Leipzig, 1672.

Ki   KIRKE, HENRY. Twenty-five years in British Guiana. London, 1898.

KG   KOCH-GRÜNBERG, THEODOR. Zwei Jahre unter den Indianern. Reisen in Nordwest Brasilien, 1903-5. 2 vols. Berlin, 1910.

KUNIKE, HUGO. Das Sogenannte "Männerkindbett." *Zeitschrift für Ethnologie,* Heft III-IV, pp. 546-563, 1911.

LABAT, J. B. Nouveau voyage aux isles de l'Amérique. 6 vols. Paris, 1722.

— Voyage du Chevalier des Marchais en Guinée, Isles Voisines, et à Cayenne, en 1725-27. Amsterdam, 1731.

LA CONDAMINE, CHARLES MARIE DE. Relation abrégée d'un voyage fait dans l'interieur de l'Amérique méridionale. Maestricht, 1778.

LAFITAU. Mœurs des sauvages amériquains. 2 vols. Paris, 1724.

LAS CASAS. *See* CASAS.

LIDSTONE. *See* BROWN.

MARTIUS. *See* SPIX.

Nor   NORDENSKIOLD, ERLAND. Indianerleben. El Gran Chaco (Sudamerika). Leipzig, 1912.

PATERSON, J. D. British Guiana local guide 1843 [from notes of].

PENARD, F. P. *and* A. P. De Menschetende Aanbidders der Zonneslang. Paramaribo, 1907.

NIEUHOFF, J. Voyages and travels into Brasil. 1707.

Pnk   PINCKARD, GEORGE. Notes on the West Indians. 2 vols. London, 1816.

LAP   PITOU, L. A. Voyage à Cayenne. 2 vols. Paris, 1807.

PREUSS, K. TH. Die Opferblutschale der alten Mexikaner erläutert nach den Angaben der Cora-Indianer. *Zeitschrift für Ethnologie*, XLIII, pp. 293-306, 1911.

QUANDT, C. Nachricht von Suriname und seinen Einwohnern, etc. Görlitz, 1807.

RoP   ROCHEFORT, C. DE, *and* POINCY, L. DE. Histoire naturelle et morale des iles Antilles de l'Amérique. Rotterdam, 1665.

AR   ROJAS, ARISTIDES. Obras escogidas. Paris, 1907.

StC   ST. CLAIR, T. STAUNTON. A residence in the West Indies and America. 2 vols. London, 1834.

ScO   SCHOMBURGK, O. A. Reisen in Guiana und am Orinoko. Leipzig, 1841.

ScR   SCHOMBURGK, RICHARD. Reisen in Britisch Guiana. 2 vols. Leipzig, 1847-48.

ScA   SCHOMBURGK, ROBERT HERMANN. Diary of an ascent of the river Berbice. *Jour. Roy. Geog. Soc.*, VII, pp. 302-350, 1837.

ScB — Expedition to the lower parts of the Barima and Guiania rivers. Ibid., XII, pp. 169-178, 1842.

ScBc — Excursion up the Barima and Cuyuni rivers. Ibid., pp. 178-196.

ScC — Diary of an ascent of the River Corentyn. Ibid., VII, pp. 285-301, 1837.

ScD — A description of British Guiana. London, 1840.

ScE — Journey to the sources of the Essequibo, etc. *Jour. Roy. Geog. Soc.*, X, pp. 159-190, 1841.

ScF — Journey from Fort San Joaquim to Roraima. Ibid., pp. 191-247.

ScG — Report of an expedition into the interior of British Guayana. Ibid., VI, pp. 224-284, 1836.

ScH — Journey from Esmeralda to San Carlos. Ibid., X, pp. 248-267, 1841.

p. 116

SCT SCHOMBURGK, ROBERT HERMANN. Visit to the sources of the Takutu. Ibid., XIII, pp. 18-75. London, 1843.

— On the religious traditions of the Macusi Indians who inhabit the upper Mahu and a portion of the Mocaraima Mountains. Read before the Society of Antiquaries Nov. 17th, 1836. [Thus far I have be unable to trace the publication of this address.—W. E. R.]

AS SIMSON, ALFRED. Travels in the wilds of Ecuador. London, 1886.

SM SPIX *and* MARTIUS. Reise in Brasilien. 3 vols. Munich, 1823-31.

St STEDMAN, J. G. Narrative of a five years' expedition against the revolted negroes of Surinam. 2 vols. London, 1806.

VDS VON DEN STEINEN. Durch Zentralbrasilien. Leipzig, 1886.

— Unter dem naturvölkern Zentralbrasiliens. Berlin, 1893.

DU TERTRE, JEAN BAPTISTE. Histoire générale des Antilles habitées par des Français. 4 vols. Paris, 1667-71.

Ti TIMEHRI. Journal of the Royal Agricultural and Commercial Society of British Guiana. See various volumes cited.

ULLOA. *See* JUAN Y SANTACILIA.

ARW WALLACE, A. R. A narrative of travels on the Amazon and Rio Negro. London, New York, and Melbourne, 1889.

W WATERTON, CHAS. Wanderings in South America. London, 1891.

WICKHAM, H. A. Rough note of a journey from Trinidad to Para via the Orinoco and Rio Negro. London, 1872.

YBARRA, FERNANDEZ DE. See CHANCA.

AN INQUIRY INTO THE ANIMISM AND FOLK-LORE OF THE GUIANA INDIANS

By WALTER E. ROTH

CHAPTER I
NO EVIDENCE OF BELIEF IN A SUPREME BEING

Originally, Indians had no terms expressive of the conception of a Supreme Being; such terms as they now possess have been framed to suit civilized, especially missionary, requirements (*1*).[1] On the other hand, traditions of certain Tribal Heroes have been unconsciously assumed as indicative of the existence among the natives of the knowledge of a God (*2*).

1.*Careful investigation forces one to the conclusion that, on the evidence, the native tribes of Guiana had no idea of a Supreme Being in the modern conception of the term. This contention is confirmed in a way by Gumilla (II, 7),[2] one of the early missionary fathers on the Orinoco, who writes as follows:

> In three nations which will be mentioned directly they have a word indicative, after their fashion, of God: we trust that time and labor will also reveal, in other tribes, a name which until now they have furnished no sign of recognizing either by word or expression. Even in the said nations no outward ceremony of divine worship or adoration has been observed. Nor are the terms which express God in the different languages so particularized and indubitable as to convince us of their sure and certain signification. The Caribs call God Quiyumocón, *i. e.*, Our Big Father, but it is not sufficiently clear whether they mean by this expression the First Cause or the most ancient of their ancestors. The Salivas say that Púru made all that is good; that he lives in the expanse of the sky . . . The Betoyes, before their conversion, used to say that the Sun was God, and in their language, they speak of both God and Sun as Theos.

The nations of the upper Orinoco, the Atabapo, and the Inirida, as Humboldt records, have no worship other than that of the powers of Nature: they call the good principle Cachimana; it is the Manito, the Great Spirit, that regulates the seasons and favors the harvests (AVH, II, 362). In Cayenne there is the similar evidence of the Jesuits Grillet and

Bechamel (25): "The Nouragues and the Acoquas, in Matters of Religion, are the same with the Galibis. They acknowledge there is a God, but do not worship him. They say he dwells in Heaven, without knowing whether he is a Spirit or no, but rather seem to believe he has a body. . . The Nouragues and the Acoquas call him Maire, and never talk of him but in fabulous stories." They p. 118have not even in their language any suitable term to express the Divinity, still less the homage and respect due to him (PBa, 218). The present-day British Guiana Carib name for God is identical with that just given, Tamosi-Kabutana, Old Man-Sky [Kabu = the Sun], figuratively The Ancient of Heaven, or simply Tamosi, without particularizing. But this word is undoubtedly the same as *tamuchi*, the Cayenne Carib term for the head-man or chief of a tribe; it serves also to designate a grandfather (PBa, 218). The same remark perhaps may be applicable to *theos*, the word given by Gumilla as the Betoya word for the Divine Person, recognizable in the terms *tuchao* (Cr, 372) and *tushaúa* (HWB, 241, 244), the name given to the chief, head-man, of the tribe or nation, in the upper and lower Amazons, respectively. Koch-Grünberg (II, 82) talks of Tuschaua as being Lingoa Geral. Wallace (348), too, says that the Indians of the Amazon appear to have no definite idea of a God. The Arawak terms for the Christian deity also show signs that they have been adapted to express a conception to which they could have been introduced only within modern times, a statement which is made advisedly, because in none of the Arawak myths and legends relative to the Creation, even in those published by clerics, is there a single reference to the All-Maker (Br, 58) under the term of Wa'chinachi, Our Father, Wa'murretakuon(na)chi, Our Maker, or even Aiomun Kondi, Dweller on High. It is very noteworthy that the same discrepancy as to the alleged word for God is at once apparent in almost all the Creation myths of the other tribes that so far I have managed to unearth: for example, the Warrau word (ScR, II, 515) *kwarisabarote*, really intended for *kwaresa ba-arautu*, meaning literally 'on-top belonging-to.' The only exception perhaps would seem to be the Warrau Kanonatu, Our Maker (IT, 366), referred to by Brett in his Warrau story of the origin of the Caribs (BrB, 62), where its introduction is certainly suspicious. "Some [of the Orinoco] tribes, Father Caulin tells us, considered the Sun as the Supreme Being and First Cause; it was to him that they attributed the productions of the earth, scanty or copious rains, and all other temporal blessings; others, on the contrary, believed that everything depended on the influence of the moon, and conceived, when she suffered an eclipse, that she was angry with them." (FD, 51.) It is known that the Chaimas, Cumanagotos, Tamanacs, and other original tribes of the Carib people, worshipped (*adoraban*) the Sun and Moon (AR, 185). For perhaps the most extraordinary conception met with, however, concerning ideas of a Supreme Being, I would quote the reply given to Acuña (97) by a cacique of one of the Amazon tribes: "He told me himself was God, and begotten by the Sun, affirming that his Soul went every night into Heaven to give orders for the succeeding Day, and to regulate the Government of the Universe!" The Tupi language, at least, as taught by the old Jesuits, has a word, *tupána*, signifying God (HWB, 259). And so p. 119 it happened that the little china dolls which Koch-Grünberg (I, 184) presented to the women and children on the Aiary River (Rio Negro) were generally called *tupána*: the people took them for figures of saints from missionary times.

2.* Conversely, it is interesting to note how both travellers and missionaries have assumed almost unconsciously the Indian traditions of certain mythic Heroes to be more or less indicative of the view no doubt *a priori* conscientiously held by the former that the native was not without the knowledge of a God. Thus, Hilhouse (HiC, 244) writing in 1832, makes the statement, blindly followed, strangely enough, by Schomburgk (ScR, II, 319) in 1848, that "The Indians acknowledge the existence of a superior divinity, the universal creator; and most tribes, also, believe in a subservient power, whose particular province is the protection of their nation. Amongst the Arawaaks, Aluberi is the supreme being, and Kururumanny the god or patron (*Schutz gott*) of the Arawaak nation," etc. With regard to the former there is a very probable reference to him under the name of Hubuiri, some three centuries previously, in the *Archivos de Indias: Patronato* (quoted by Rodway in *Timehri* for 1895, p. 9), where, in an account of the Provinces and Nations of the Aruacas [Arawaks] by Rodrigo de Navarrete, the latter says: "From those whom I have frequently kept in my house, I have understood that their belief and object of adoration is the firmament or heavens, because they say that in the greater heaven there is a powerful lord and a great lady . . . when they die, their souls will go with Hubuiri, as they call the great and powerful lord in heaven." This same Alubiri, or Hubuiri, is still recognizable as Haburi (Sect. *9*) in the stories related by me, and as Abore, the Warrau "Father of Inventions" in the legend told by Brett (BrB, 76). In his Arawak vocabulary the name for God is given by Schomburgk (SCR, II, 515) as Kururumanni: Brett (Br, 58), however, is more correct in saying. that it is the Warraus who "sometimes use the word 'Korroromana' when speaking of God; but it is doubtful what ideas some of them attach to that name." As a matter of fact, both of these would-be deities, Alubiri (Sect. *3*) and Kororomanna (Sect. *19*), were Arawak and Warrau Tribal Heroes, respectively. Similar remarks may be made of Makunaima and Pia (Sects. *29-41*), and of Amalivaca (Sect. *42*). The name Amalivaca is spread over a region of more than five thousand square leagues.

> He is found designated as "the father of mankind," or "our great grandfather," as far as to the Carribbee nations. . . . *Amalivaca* is not originally the *Great Spirit*, the *Aged of Heaven*, the invisible being, whose worship springs from that of the powers of nature, when nations rise insensibly to the consciousness of the unity of these powers; he is rather a personage of the heroic times, a man, who, coming from afar, lived in the land of the Tamanacs and the Caribs, sculptured symbolic figures upon the rocks, and disappeared by going back to the country he had previously inhabited beyond the ocean. [AVH, II, 474.]

Footnotes

1 This and similar reference numbers correspond to section numbers, which appear in bold-face type.

2 See Note under WORKS OF REFERENCE (p. 113) as to the system employed in this memoir in the citation of authorities.

CHAPTER II
TRIBAL HEROES

3.* Some of the mythic Heroes have a history peculiarly their own, of which it is now proposed to give a few particulars.

I will begin with Alubiri, or Hubuiri, for whom Hilhouse, as already stated (Sect. 2), found a place in the Arawak cosmogony, a view which Schomburgk indorsed, with a reference to him, however, as one "who does not trouble himself about men." In Brett's time, however, and at the present day, throughout the Pomeroon district the Hero seemingly appears only under the name Haburi. The Pomeroon Warrau now claim Haburi as their particular Hero, in just the same way as Brett (BrB, 76) did for them under the name Abore. For my own part I suspect that the term Alubiri is but another form of the name Oruperi, the mythical Carib snake (Sect. 235), which gave rise to all the hunting binas, and that Haburi has some philological connection with Yaperi-Kuli, the Hero (Sect. 45) of the Siusi branch of the Arawak stock. It is only for the reason that an old Arawak friend identified Hariwali (cf. Arawanili, Sec. 185) with Haburi—an identity which I admittedly can neither confirm nor challenge—that I propose beginning with these mythic Heroes by introducing the story of—

*HARIWALI AND THE WONDERFUL TREE (A)

Hariwali was a clever, painstaking piai, who spent most of his time in clearing the field for his two wives. These two women, their children, and his brother lived with him at his house. While felling the timber, the wives undertook, turn and turn about, to bring their husband some cassiri daily. It happened now that while carrying the usual refreshment one of the wives was met by the brother-in-law, who was bringing in some itiriti strands to weave baskets with. "Hullo!" he said, "where are you going?" to which he received reply, "I am taking cassiri to my husband; the field.—But I like you. Do you like me?" "No, I don't," he answered, "and even if I did, my brother, being a medicine-man, would find it out very soon." She tried him again, and tempted him sorely, and then she threw her arms round him. He was but mortal. . . . She assured him that her husband would never find out what had happened, and both went their respective ways. Before she reached the field, however, she broke the calabash; then with a pointed stick she cut her knee, causing it to bleed. When Hariwali saw her coming slowly along with a limp carrying the broken calabash, he asked her what had happened. All she could do was to point to the scratch and blood on her lame knee, and tell him that she had p. 121 had an accident, having fallen on a stump. He was a shrewd piai, however, and knew exactly what had happened, and though he said nothing then, he determined not only upon getting rid of her, but of his other wife also; he just then, however, directed her to return home.

4.* Next morning he bade both the women accompany him, as he intended fishing in the pond, and he merely wanted them to do the cooking and make the fire. When fire had been made, he brought them a turtle, which they put on the hot ashes without killing it, so it promptly crawled out; they pushed it on again, but with the same result. It was the omen betokening their death. The semi-chichi [medicine-man] had bewitched them and they thought they had already killed the turtle. What they imagined was that the fire was not hot enough, and so the faithless spouse went to look for more dry wood. Now, as she was breaking up the timber she found it very hard work, and exclaimed Tata—Ketaiaba (lit. hard—to break), but no sooner were the words out of her mouth, than she flew away as a hawk, the "bul-tata," which can often be heard crying bul-tata-tata-tata. . . . Of course it was her husband who had done this. The other wife said she felt hot and would bathe her skin; no sooner had she ducked into the pond, than her husband turned her into a porpoise—she was the very first porpoise that ever swam in these waters.

5.* Hariwali thus punished his wives, and now pondered over what he should do with his brother. While returning home, he met the very man with bow and arrows starting out to hunt, but neither spoke. That same afternoon the brother, who had never missed a bird before, made a bad shot every time now, the arrow invariably flying absurdly wide of its mark. This was really all Hariwali's doing. At last the brother did manage to hit a bird, but only just hard enough to knock a few feathers off, nothing more. "Don't do that again," said the bird, "and now look behind you." And when he did so, there was a large sheet of water, and he realized that he was upon an island. But how to escape? Round and round he wandered, until he finally found a path; no ordinary path, but a Yawahu's path leading to the Spirit's house. Arrived at the house, the Yawahu caught him, and took all his bones out except those of his fingers; this was done only out of kindness, so that he could not escape, the Yawahu putting him into a hammock and paying him every care and attention.1 The bones themselves were tied up in a bundle under the roof (as bundles are kept by many other Indian tribes). The Yawahu was quite a family man, with plenty of youngsters who were always practising with their bows and arrows; when their arrows got blunted they had only to go up to the captive's hammock and sharpen them on his bony finger tips. All this time, Hariwali's mother would cry regularly every night over her absent son, whose whereabouts and condition she was absolutely igorant of. So at last the piai's heart became softened, and he determined on going to fetch his brother home again. It was all due to his "medicine" that his brother fell into the clutches of the Spirits. He told the old woman to pack up everything, because when he returned with his brother they and all their family would have to leave the place forever.

6.* The night previous to their departure, he "played the shak-shak" (i. e., called up his Spirit friends with the rattle), and next morning hosts of parrots were passing overhead. His children called his attention to them; so he went out and asked the birds to throw down a seed of a certain tree the bark of which he used medicinally. This they did, and though the youngeters saw the seed falling, directly it touched ground the father put his foot on it, and look as much as they could, the children could not find it. As he did not want them to know what he was doing, he told them that nothing had fallen, that they must be mistaken, and that they must run away now. Young folk are not allowed to see what the old medicine-men practise. When left alone, Hariwali planted the identical seed just where it had fallen, and that same evening p. 122repeated the performance with the rattle; by next morning a stately tree had grown from that one seed. He told his mother to tie all the things which she had packed up, on the branches of this tree (Sect. 286), and to await his and his brother's return.

7.* It was not long before he reached the Yawahu's place, where, the family being away, he had no difficulty in releasing the captive, untying the bones from the roof, and making good his escape. Unfortunately the Spirit returned earlier than was expected, and seeing the empty hammock and no parcel of bones, was not long in concluding what had happened. He recognized the fresh tracks, and put his dogs on the scent. Poor Hariwali and his brother! They heard the barking of the dogs and the whistling of the Spirit, and barely had time to crawl into an armadillo hole. They just managed to get out of sight when Yawahu came up, threatening that if they did not come out, he would drive a stick into them; the fugitives laid low, and said nothing. Yawahu then shoved a stick in, but Hariwali touched it with his hand, and changed it into a bush-master snake. (This is why, even to the present day, a bush-master snake is always found in an armadillo hole.) At any rate, Yawahu on seeing the serpent thought he must have been mistaken in folowing the tracks and retraced his steps. Having put the bones back into his brother's skin, and waiting till the coast was clear, Hariwali led the way home.

8.* And how glad their mother was to see them! She had everything packed away in and among the branches of the big tree, and she herself, her daughter, and the grandchildren were all prepared for a long journey. As night fell, they all, big and little, climbed up into the lower branches, finding shelter among the leaves while Hariwali made his way up to the very summit and began again the shak-shak performance. This continued till quite into the middle of the night, when all of a sudden, the family below felt the tree shaking, and heard rumbling noises, followed by a quivering, and experienced a sensation of the trunk being rooted out of the sand, and starting to fly up into the air. Now, it was just about the moment when they were off on their proposed journey that the old woman's daughter, the piai's sister, felt a bit chilly, and casting her eyes downward, remembered that she had left her apron behind in the house. All she could do was to shout out to her brother above, Dekeweyo-daiba (lit. "my apron back"), "I have forgotten my apron," and he told her to slip down quickly and fetch it. But by the time she had reached the old home, she was changed into a wicissi-duck (Anas autumnalis), which even yet can always be heard saying dekeweyo-daiba, but as it only whistles these two words, they do not sound so distinctly as if they were spoken slowly. As to the rest of the family—well, we know that the wonderful tree flew away somewhere, but we have never heard anything more about the people who were on it.

*THE STORY OF HABURI (W)

9.* Long ago, there were two sisters minding themselves; they had no man to look after them. One day they cut down an ite tree (Mauritia), from which they commenced to manufacture flour. It was now late, so they left their work and went home. Next morning when they went back, the starch was lying there all ready prepared, and they were much puzzled to know how this came to be so. Next day, the same thing happened—all the ite starch was found ready; and this happened again, and often. So one night they watched, and about the middle of the night they saw one of the leaves of the neighboring manicole tree (Euterpe sp.) bend gradually over and over until it touched the cut which they had made in the trunk of the ite palm lying beneath. As soon as the leaf actually touched, both sisters rushed up and caught hold of it, begging it earnestly to turn into a man. It refused at first; but as they begged so earnestly it did so. His name was Mayara-kóto. The big (elder) sister was now happy and by-and-bye she had a beautiful baby boy, called Haburi.

10.* The two women had their hunting ground near two ponds; one of these ponds belonged to Tiger, but the other one was their own, in which they therefore used to fish. And they told Mayara-kóto not to go to Tiger's pond. The man, however, said, "Our pond has very few fish in it, but Tiger's has plenty. I am going to fish in his." He did so, but Tiger came along and caught and killed him for stealing his fish. Tiger then took Mayara-kóto's shape and form, and returned to the spot where the two women were camped. It was very late when he came and quite dark. With him he brought not only Mayara-kóto's waiyarri (a temporary openwork basket made of palm-leaf) but in it the fish the latter had stolen before being killed. Tiger put down the waiyarri, as is customary, before coming into the house, and after telling them good-night (lit. "I am come"), said he had brought some fish. Both women were astonished at the coarse, rough voice. He then said he was much tired, and would lie down in his hammock, telling them that he would nurse Haburi, who was accordingly brought to him. He told them also that he was going to sleep, and that they must bring up the fish and cook it, but not to mind him. The women cooked the fish. When cooked, and while the women were eating it, the man fell asleep and began to snore very curiously and loudly—indeed, so loud that you could have heard him on the other side of the river. And while snoring, he called the father's name—Mayara-kóto. The two women looked at each other, and they listened. They said "Our husband never snored like that; he never called his own name before." They therefore stopped eating at once, and told each other that this man could not possibly be their husband. And they pondered as to how they were going to get Haburi out of the man's arms where he was resting. Making a bundle of a particular kind of bark, they slipped it under the child and so got him away; then they quickly made off with him while the man was still snoring. With them they also took a wax light and a bundle of firewood.

11.* While going along, they heard Wau-uta singing. Wau-uta was a woman in those days, indeed she was a piai woman, and she was just then singing with her shak-shak (rattle). The two women went on and on, quickly too, for they knew that once they arrived at Wau-uta's place they would be safe. In the meantime, the Tiger-man woke up and found the bark bundle in his arms instead of little Haburi, and both the sisters gone. So he got angry; he changed back into his animal shape, and hurried after them. The women heard him coming and hurried still more. They called out "Wau-uta! open the door." "Who is there?" said Wau-uta, to which she received reply "It is we; the two sisters." But Wau-uta would not open the door. So the mother pinched little Haburi's ears and made him cry. Directly Wau-uta heard it She shouted out, "What child is that? Is it a girl or a boy?" "It is my Haburi, a boy," was the mother's reply, upon which Wau-uta opened the door immediately and said, "Come in! Come in!" Just after they had all got in, Tiger arrived and, calling out to Wau-uta, asked her where the two women and the baby had gone. But Wau-uta lied, telling that she had not seen them, that she had seen no one. Tiger, however, could tell by the scent that they were there, so he waited outside, and refused to go away. This vexed Wau-uta, who became very angry, and told him that he might just put his head in, and have a look round, and if he saw them, he could eat them if he liked. But the door was covered with pimplers (thorns) and as soon as silly Tiger put his head in, the old woman closed it, and so killed him. The two sisters remained there, and cried much; they grieved for their husband. They cried so much indeed that Wau-uta told them to go into the field, gather some cassava, and make a big drink. They accordingly got ready to go, and were about to take Haburi with them, but Wau-uta said, "No. I am quite able to look after the child in your absence." So they did as they were told and went away to the field.

12.* In the meantime Wau-uta made the child grow all at once into a youth, and gave him the harri-harri to blow and the arrows to shoot. As the mother and aunt p. 124 were returning with the cassava, they heard the music playing and said to themselves, "There was no man or boy there when we left the house; who can it be? It must be a man playing." And though ashamed they went in and saw the youth blowing the harri-harri. As soon as they had taken the quakes (baskets) from off their backs and placed them on the ground, they asked after Haburi, but Wau-uta said that as soon as they had left for the field, the child had run after them, and she had thought it was still with them. Of course all this was a lie. Old Wau-uta was desirous of making Haburi grow quickly, with the intention of making him ultimately her lover. She still further deceived the two sisters by pretending to assist in the search which was then undertaken in the surrounding bush, but she took good care to get back to her house first, and told Haburi to say she, Wau-uta, was his mother, and gave him full directions as to how he must treat her.

13.* Haburi was a splendid shot—no bird could escape his arrow—and Wau-uta directed him to give to her all the big birds that he killed, and to his mother and aunt all the little ones, which he had to pollute first by fouling them. The object of this was to make the two sisters so vexed and angry that they would leave the place: but this they would not do; they continued searching the neighborhood for their little child. This sort of thing went on for many days, big birds and dirtied little birds being presented by Haburi to Wau-uta and the two women, respectively. Haburi, however, did one day miss a bird for the first time, his arrow sticking into a branch overhanging a creek where his uncles, the water-dogs, used to come and feed. It was a nice cleared space, and here Haburi eased himself, covering the dung with leaves. He next climbed the tree to dislodge the arrow, but just then the water-dogs arrived, and, scenting the air, exclaimed, "What smell is this? That worthless nephew of ours, Haburi, must be somewhere about." So they looked around, and down, and up, and finally discovering him on the tree branch, ordered him to come down. They then sat him on a bench, and told him he was leading a bad life, that the old woman was not his mother, but that the two younger ones were his mother and aunt, respectively; they furthermore impressed upon him that it was very wicked of him to divide the birds so unfairly, and that in future he must do exactly the opposite, giving his real mother, the bigger of the two sisters, the larger birds. They told him also to let his real mother know that the way he had hitherto treated her was due entirely to ignorance on his part, and that he was sorry.

14.* So when Haburi got home that day, he carried out the instructions given him by the water-dogs, handing the dirtied little birds to Wau-uta, and making a clean breast of it to his mother. She, poor thing, felt very strange that day, and could not bring herself to speak to him as "my son" all at once, but when he explained that it was only Wau-uta who had made him a man quite suddenly, she believed him, and became quite comforted. Old Wau-uta, on hearing all this, worked herself into a great passion, and, seizing Haburi by the neck, blew into his face (Sect. 85), and told him he must be mad; so angered and upset was she that she could eat nothing at all. She spent all that day and night in nagging him, and telling him he had left his senses. Haburi went away next morning as usual, returning late in the afternoon, when he again gave the big birds which he had shot to his real mother and the dirtied little ones to Wau-uta. The latter, as might have been expected, gave him no peace.

15.* Haburi, therefore, made up his mind to get out. So telling his mother that they must all three arrange to get away together, he made a little corial (a dugout canoe) of bees'-wax, and when completed, he left it at the water-side; but, by next morning a black duck had taken it away. He therefore made another little clay corial, but this was stolen by another kind of duck. In the meantime he cut a large field, and cleared it so quickly that the women with their planting could never keep up with him. They required plenty of cassava for their proposed journey. At any rate, while the women planted, Haburi would often slip away and make a boat, always of a different kind of wood and of varying shape, and just as regularly would a different p. 125species of duck come and steal it. At last he happened to make one out of the silk-cotten tree and this particular one was not stolen. It was thus Haburi who first made a boat and taught the ducks to float on the surface of the water because it was with his boats that they managed to do it; indeed, we Warraus say that each duck has its own particular kind of boat.

16.* But what was more curious, the last boat to be manufactured was found next morning to be very much bigger than it was the night before. Haburi told his mother and her sister to collect all the provisions and put them aboard in anticipation of their long journey. He himself returned to the field, bringing the cassava cuttings for old Wau-uta to plant in their respective holes, and so they both continued working hard. By and bye, he slipped away, went back to the house, took his arrows and ax, and proceeded down to the water-side. But before he left the house, he told the posts not to talk, for in those days the posts of a house could speak (Sect. 169), and if the owner were absent a visitor could thus find out his whereabouts. There was a parrot, however, in the house, and Haburi quite forgot to warn him to keep silent. So when the old woman after a time found herself alone, she went back to the house, and seeing no Haburi, asked the posts whither he had gone; they remained silent. The parrot, however, could not help talking, and told her.

17.* Wau-uta thereupon rushed down to the landing, arriving there just in time to see Haburi stepping into the boat to join his mother and aunt. She seized hold of the craft, screaming "My son! My son! you must not leave me so. I am your mother," and though they all repeatedly struck her fingers with their paddles, and almost smashed them to pieces on the gunwale, she would not let go her hold. So poor Haburi had perforce to land again and with old Wau-uta proceeded to a large hollow tree wherein the bees had built their nest. Cutting down the tree, Haburi made a small hole in the trunk, and told the old lady to get in and suck the honey. She was very fond of honey, and though crying very hard all the time at the thought of losing Haburi, crawled through the little opening which he immediately closed in upon her. And there she is to be found to the present day, the Wau-uta frog which is heard only in hollow trees. And if you look carefully, you will see how swollen her fingers are from the way in which they were bashed by the paddles when she tried to hold on to the gunwale. If you listen, you can also hear her lamenting for her lost lover; she still cries Wang! Wang! Wang!

18.* The tree-frog above referred to is probably the kono(bo)-aru, or rain-frog, the name given to the old woman in the Carib version of the story (Sect. 35). The croaking of this creature (Hyla venulosa Daud.) is an absolutely sure sign of rain. This frog lives only in the trunk of the Bodelschwingia macrophylla Klotzsch, a tree found on the Pomeroon and Barama (ScR, II, 419). Though the Warraus are believed to have been the first of the Guiana Indians to use boats, the invention of the sail has been credited to the Caribs. A modern addition to the above version of the story is that Haburi sailed away, found new lands, and taught the white people all their arts and manufactures, all about guns and ships, and for many years used to send his old Warrau friends certain presents annually, but they never come now—an unscrupulous Government detains them in Georgetown!

19.* With regard to Koroiomanna, or Kururumanni, the same remarks concerning his tribal origin apply as in the case of Haburi. Hilhouse and Schomburgk (ScR, II, 319) seemingly would have him an Arawak, but Brett undoubtedly makes him a Warrau, the view which p. 126 is held by the present-day Warraus and Arawaks on the Pomeroon. He is said to be the creator of the male portion of mankind, another Spirit, Kulimina,1 being responsible for the female. Uri-Kaddo and Emeshi are his two wives, one name signifying 'darkness-people,' 'a worker in darkness,' and the other a large red ant that burrows in the earth; "together, they are typical of the creation of all things out of the earth in the dark" (HiC, 244). Kororomanna would seem to have experienced a remarkable number and variety of adventures some of which are given here.

*THE ADVENTURES OF KOROROMANNA (W)

Kororomanna went out hunting and shot a "baboon" (Mycetes), but as it was already late in the afternoon, in trying to make his way home he lost his way in the darkness. And there he had to make his banab, and to lie down, with the baboon beside him. But where he lay was a Hebu road; you can always distinguish a Spirit road from any other pathway in the forest because the Hebus occupying the trees that lie alongside it are always, especially at night, striking the branches and trunks, and so producing short sharp crackling noises (Sect. 104). It was not pleasant for poor Kororomanna, especially as the baboon's body was now beginning to swell with all the noxious humors inside; lest the Hebus should steal it from him, he was obliged to keep the carcass alongside and watch over it with a stick. At last he fell asleep, but in the middle of the night the Hebus, what with the knocking on the trees, aroused him from his slumbers. Now that he was awake, he mimicked the Spirits, blow for blow, and as they struck the limb of a tree, Kororomanna would strike the belly of the baboon. But what with the air inside, each time he struck the animal, there came a resonant Boom! Boom! just like the beating of a drum.2 The Hebu leader heard the curious sound, and became a bit frightened: "What can it be? When before I knocked a tree, it never made a noise like that." To make sure, however, he struck the tree hard again, and Boom! came once more from the carcass. Hebu was really frightened now, and began to search all around to find out where the extraordinary noise could possibly come from; at last he recognized the little manicole banab, and saw Kororomanna laughing. Indeed, the latter could not help laughing, considering that it was the first time he had heard such a funny sound come out of any animal.

20.* Hebu then said to him, "Who are you? Show me your hand," to which Kororomanna replied, "I am Warrau, and here is my hand," but instead of putting out his own, he shoved forward one of the baboon's, and then held forward the animal's other hand, and finally both feet. Hebu was much puzzled and said he had never seen before a Warrau with so black a hand, and would not be satisfied until he saw the face. Kororomanna accordingly deceived him again and held out the monkey's, which caused Hebu to make the same remark about his face as he had done about his hands and feet.

21.* The Spirit became more frightened than ever, but his curiosity exceeded his fear, because he next wanted to know where all that Boom! Boom! sound had come from. And when he learnt its source of origin (breaking wind), he regretted that he had not been made like ordinary mortals, he and all his family having no proper posteriors, but just a red spot (Sect. 99). He thereupon begged Kororomanna to make for him a posterior which would allow of his producing a similar sound. So with his bow Kororomanna split the Spirit's hind quarters, and completed the task p. 127by impaling him, but so rough was he in his methods, that the weapon transfixed the whole body even piercing the unfortunate Hebu's head. The Hebu cursed Kororomanna for having killed him, and threatened that the other Spirits would avenge his death; he then disappeared.

22.* Our hero, becoming a bit anxious on his own account, and, recognizing by the gradually increasing hullaballoo in the trees that swarms of Hebus were approaching the scene of the outrage, now climbed the manicole tree sheltering his banab, leaving the baboon's corpse inside. The Spirits then entered the banab, and believing the dead animal to be Kororomanna, began hitting it with their sticks, and with each blow, there came Boom! Our friend up the tree, whence he could watch their every movement, and their surprise at the acoustic results of the flogging, could not refrain from cracking a smile, which soon gave way to a hearty laugh. The Spirits, unfortunately for him, heard it, and looking at the dead baboon, said, "This cannot be the person who is laughing at us." They looked all around, but could see nothing, until one of them stood on his head, and peeped up into the tree.1 And there, sure enough, he saw Kororomanna laughing at them. All the others then put themselves in the same posture around the tree, and had a good look at him. The question they next had to decide was how to catch him. This they concluded could most easily be managed by hewing down the tree. They accordingly started with their axes on the trunk, but since the implements were but water-turtle shells, it was not long before they broke.2 They then sent for their knives, but as these were merely the seed-pods of the buari tree, they also soon broke.3 The Hebus then sent for a rope, but what they called a rope was really a snake. At any rate, as the serpent made its way farther and farther up the tree, and finally came within reach, Kororomanna cut its head off; the animal fell to the ground again, and the Hebus cried "Our rope has burst." Another consultation was held, and it was decided that one of their number should climb the tree, seize the man, and throw him down, and that those below might be ready to receive him when dislodged, the Hebu was to shout out, when throwing him down, the following signal: Tura-buna-sé mahara-ko na-kai.4 The biggest of the Spirits being chosen to carry the project into execution, he started on his climb, but head downward of course, so as to be able to see where he was going. Kororomanna, however, was on the alert, and, waiting for him, killed him in the same peculiar manner as that in which he had despatched the other Spirit just a little while before; more than this, having heard them fix upon the preconcerted signal, he hurled the dead Spirit's body down with the cry of Tura-buna-sé mahara-ko na-kai! The Hebus below were quite prepared, and as soon as the body tell to the ground, clubbed it to pieces. Kororomanna then slipped down and helped in the dissolution. "Wait a bit," he said to the Spirits; "I am just going in the bush, but will soon return." It was not very long, however, before the Spirits saw that they had been tricked, and yelled with rage on finding that they had really destroyed one of themselves; they hunted high and low for their man, but with approaching daylight were reluctantly compelled to give up the chase.

23.* In the meantime, Kororomanna had no sooner got out of their sight than he started running at topmost speed, and finally found shelter in a hollow tree. Here he discovered a woman (she was not old either), so he told her that he would remain with her till "the day cleaned" (i. e., till dawn broke). But she said, "No! No! my p. 128 man is Snake and he will be back before the dawn. If he were to find you here, he would certainly kill you." But her visitor was not to be frightened, and he stayed where he was. True enough, before dawn, Snake came wending his way home, and as he crawled into the tree, he was heard to exclaim, "Hallo! I can smell some one." Kororomanna was indeed frightened now, and was at his wits' end to know what to do. Just then dawn broke, and they heard a hummingbird. "That is my uncle," said our hero. They then heard the doroquarra: "That also is an uncle of mine," he added.1 He purposely told Snake all this to make him believe that, if he killed and swallowed his visitor, all the other hummingbirds and doroquarras would come and avenge his death. But Snake said, "I am not afraid of either of your uncles, but will gobble them up." Just then, a chicken-hawk (Urubitinga) flew along, which made Snake ask whether that also was an uncle of his.

"To be sure" was the reply, "and when I am dead, he also will come and search for me." It was now Snake's turn to be frightened, because Chicken-hawk used always to get the better of him; so he let Kororomanna go in peace, who ran out of that hollow tree pretty quick.

24.* It was full daylight now, but this made little odds, because he had still lost his way, and knew not how to find the road home. After wandering on and on, he at last came across a track, recognizable by the footprints in it: following this up, he came upon a hollow tree that had fallen across the path, and inside the trunk he saw a baby. This being a Hebu's child, he slaughtered it, but he had no sooner done so than he heard approaching footsteps, which caused him promptly to climb a neighboring tree and await developments. These were not long in coming, for the mother soon put in her appearance; as soon as she recognized her dead infant, she was much angered, and, looking around, carefully examined the fresh tracks, and said, "This is the man who has killed my child." Her next move was to dig up a bit of the soil marked by one of the fresh footprints, wrap it up in a leaf tied with bush-rope, and hang it on a branch while she went for firewood. Directly her back was turned, Kororomanna slid down from his hiding place, undid the bundle, and threw away the contents, substituting a footprint of the Spirit woman. Then, tying up the parcel as before, he hung it where it had been left, and hid himself once more. When the woman returned with the firewood, she made a big fire, and threw the bundle into the flames, saying as she did so: "Curse the person whose footprint I now burn. May the owner fall into this fire also!" She thought that if she burnt the "foot-mark" so would the person's shadow be drawn to the fire. But no one came, and she felt that her own shadow was being impelled. "Oh! It seems that I am hurting myself; the fire is drawing me near," she exclaimed. Twice was she thus dragged toward it against her will, and yet she succeeded in resisting. But on the third occasion she could not draw back; she fell in, and was burnt to ashes; she "roasted herself dead."2

25.* Kororomanna was again free to travel, but which direction to follow was the puzzle; he had still lost his way home. All he could do was to walk more or less aimlessly on, passing creek after creek and back into the bush again, until he emerged on a beautiful, clean roadway. But no sooner had he put his foot on it, than it stuck there, just like a fish caught in a spring-trap. And this is exactly what the trap really was, save that it had been set by the Hebus. He pulled and he tugged and he twisted, but try as he might, he could not get away. He fouled himself over completely, and then lay quite still, pretending to be dead. The flies gathered on him and these were followed by the worms, but he continued to lie quite still. By and by two of the Spirits came along, and one of them said, "Hallo! I have luck today. My spring-trap has caught a fish at last," but when he got closer, he added, "Oh! I p. 129have left it too long. It stinks." However, they let loose their fish, as they thought it was, and carried it down to the riverside to wash and clean it. After they had washed it, one of the Hebus said, "Let us slit its belly now, and remove the entrails," but the other one remarked, "No, let us make a waiyarri (basket) first, to put the flesh in." This was very fortunate for Kororomanna, who, seizing the opportunity while they went collecting strands to plait with, rolled down the river bank into the water and so made good his escape. But when he succeeded in landing on the other side, he was, in a sense, just as badly off as before, not knowing how to get home.

26.* Kororomanna next came across a man's skull lying on the ground, and what must he do but go and jerk his arrow into its eye-ball? Now this skull, Kwa-muhu, was a Hebu, who thereupon called out: "You must not do that. But now that you have injured me, you will have to carry me." So Kororomanna had to get a strip of bark, the same kind which our women employ for fastening on their field quakes, and carry the skull wherever he went, and feed it too. If he shot bird or beast, he always had to give a bit to Kwa-muhu, with the result that the latter soon became gradually and inconveniently heavier, until one day he became so great a dead weight as to break the bark-strip support. The accident occurred not very far from a creek, and Kororomanna told Kwa-muhu to stay still while he went to look for a stronger strip of bark. Of course this was only an excuse, because directly he had put the skull on the ground, he ran as fast as he could toward the creek, overtaking on the way a deer that was running in exactly the same direction, swam across, and rested himself on the opposite side. In the meantime Kwa-muhu, suspecting that he was about to be forsaken, ran after Kororomanna, and seeing but the deer in front of him, mistook it for his man and killed it just as it reached the water. On examining the carcass, the Hebu exclaimed, when he got to its toes (Sect. 126): "Well, that is indeed very strange. You have only two fingers;" and though he reckoned again and again, he could make no more—"but the man I am after had five fingers, and a long nose. You must be somebody else."1 Now Kororomanna, who was squatting just over on the opposite bank, heard all this, and burst out laughing. This enraged Kwa-muhu, who left the deer, and made a move as if to leap across the creek, but, having no legs, he could not jump properly, and hence fell into the water and was drowned. All the ants then came out of his skull.2

27.* Poor Kororomanna was still as badly off as before; he was unable to find his way home. But he bravely kept on his way and at last came upon an old man bailing water out of a pond. The latter was really a Hebu, whose name was Huta-Kurakura, 'Red-back' (Sect. 99). Huta-Kurakura, being anxious to get the fish, was bailing away at the water side as hard as he could go, but having no calabash had to make use of his purse [scrotum], which was very large. And while thus bending down, he was so preoccupied that he did not hear the footfall of Kororomanna coming up behind. The latter, not knowing what sort of a creature it was, stuck him twice in the back with an arrow, but Huta-Kurakura, thinking it to be a cow-fly (Tabanus), just slapped the spot where he felt it. When, however, he found himself stuck a third time, he turned round and, seeing who it was, became so enraged that he seized the wanderer and hurled him into a piece of wood with such force that only his eye projected from out the timber. Anxious to be freed from his unenviable position Kororomanna offered everything he could think of—crystals, rattles, paiwarri, women, etc., but the Spirit wanted none of them, As a last chance, he offered tobacco, and this the Hebu eagerly accepted, the result being that they fast became good friends. They then both emptied the pond and collected a heap of fish, much too large for p. 130Kororomanna to carry home. So the Spirit in some peculiar way bound them all up into quite a small bundle, small enough for Kororomanna to carry in his hand.

28.* Kororomanna now soon managed to find the right path home, because each and every animal that he met gave him news of his mother. One after the other, he met a rat with a potato, an acouri with cassava root, a labba with a yam, a deer with a cassava leaf, a kushi-ant with a similar leaf on its head, and a bush-cow (tapir) eating a pineapple. And as he asked each in turn whence it had come, the animal said, "I have been to your mother, and have begged potato, cassava, yam, and other things from her." When at length he reached home, and his wife and mother asked what he had brought, he told them a lot of fish, and they laughed right heartily at what they thought was his little joke. So he bade them open the parcel, and as they opened it, sure enough out came fish after fish, small and large, fish of all kinds, so many in fact that the house speedily became filled, and the occupants had to shift outside. [Cf. Sect. 303.]

28A.* [Note.—In a Carib version of the story the hero's name is given as Kere-Kere′-miyu-au, and he finds his way back home to his mother's place through the help of a butterfly. When I happened to mention to the narrator that this was the first time I had ever heard a "Nancy" story about this insect, he told me that the butterfly was always a good friend of the Caribs. "Does it not," he added, "come and drink of the washings from the cassiri jar, and remain stuck in the mess?" (i. e., "Does it not come and join in our feasts, and get so drunk that it can not fly away?").—W. E. R.

29.* Makunaima, or Makonaima, the alleged God (ScR, II, 225, 515) or Supreme Being (IT, 365) of the Akawais, the Maker of Heaven and Earth (ScR, II, 319) of the Makusis, was one of the twin children of the Sun—in this particular all the traditions concerning him are in agreement. He and his brother Pia may be regarded as both Akawai and Makusi heroes. The name itself, Makunaima, signifies "one that works in the dark" (HiC, 244); the Being working in opposition to him, according to Makusi beliefs, is Epel (ScR, loc. cit.). I am fortunately able to give three versions of the tradition of these Heroes—from Warrau, Carib, and Makusi sources, respectively.

*THE SUN, THE FROG, AND THE FIRESTICKS (W)

Nahakoboni (lit., the one who eats plenty) was an old man who, never having had a daughter, was beginning to feel anxious about his declining years, for, unlike the other old people around, he of course had no son-in-law to care for him. He therefore carved a daughter for himself out of a plum tree, and being a medicine-man, so skilfully did he cut and carve the timber that by the time the task was completed there was indeed a woman lovely to gaze upon. Her name was Usi-diu (lit., seed-tree) and her physical charms were almost, but, as we shall presently see, not quite, perfect. So attractive was she that all the animals, bird and beast, came from far to court her, but the old man liked none of them, and when they asked him for her as wife he gave them a curt refusal. The old man had a very poor opinion of the abilities of these prospective sons-in-law. But when Yar, the Sun himself, stopped on his journey, and paid the old man a visit, it was quite clear what his purpose was, and proof was not long in coming that his advances would meet with encouragement.

30.* Nahakoboni thought he would try Yar's mettle, and see what stuff he was made of. He told Yar to feed him, and made him fetch along all the barbecued meat that he had brought with him on his journey, and had left at the edge of the bush. He ate very heartily, as might have been expected from the name given him, leaving only a quarter of the meat for his visitor. He next told Yar to give him drink; the latter emptied a big jugful down his throat. His next order to Yar was to bring p. 131 him water to bathe with, and for this purpose gave him a quake.1 But when the poor fellow put the quake into the water-hole, and pulled it out again, the water of course all escaped; he tried many times, but it continued to escape. Just then he heard a rushing sound proceeding from the bush, and there appeared a Hebu: when the latter learned what he was trying to do, he offered his assistance, and made the water remain in the quake. The would-be bridegroom carried it to his prospective father-in-law, and bathed him. The old man then told Yar to shoot some fish for him; that he would find the corial at the waterside, a bench for it under the roots of a particular tree, and an arrow lying in the shade of another. It is true the corial was at the waterside; it was really lying under water and was a very heavy one—but the young man managed to haul it up at last, and then bail it out. Proceeding to the particular tree indicated, and looking in and among the roots he was surprised and frightened at seeing an alligator there; he held on to its neck, and it changed into a bench which fitted the boat.2 In the shade of the other tree he was similarly taken aback when a big snake came into view; he seized its neck, however, and it changed into a fish-arrow. The old man now joined him; they got into the corial and paddled down the stream. "I want some kwabaihi3 fish," said the old man, "but you must not look into the water. Shoot up into the air." His companion did as he was told, and so skilful was he with the bow that the arrow pierced the fish and killed it. So big was the fish that when hauled in it almost sunk the corial; they managed to get it home, however.

31.* The old man was now thoroughly satisfied with Yar's worth, and gave him his plum-tree daughter, Usidiu. Next morning the young couple went out hunting in the bush.4 When they returned late in the afternoon, father and daughter had a long and earnest conversation of a private and somewhat delicate nature, the outcome of which was that the old man learnt for the first time that the masterpiece upon which he had expended so much time, skill, and cunning, was not quite perfect. Her husband had found fault with her. Hunting was resumed the following day; a private conversation was again held in the late afternoon, the result of which showed clearly that the fault complained of still remained. The distracted father could only assure her that he could do nothing further to render her acceptable to his son-in-law. When the latter heard this, he consulted a bú-nia bird (Opistho comus), whom he brought back with him next day. While being nursed and fed in the girl's lap, the wretched bird forcibly took a very mean advantage of her innocence, and then flew away. This outrage having been brought to the knowledge of the father, he determined upon giving his daughter one more trial, with the result that he succeeded in removing a snake ex parte questa personæ eius. The difficulty was now remedied and the young woman went once more to join her husband. The following afternoon, on their return from the usual hunt, father and daughter met again in private conversation. Happy girl!—her husband was quite satisfied with her, having no complaint whatever to make.

32.* Now although the old man purposely evinced no signs of ill-will, he was greatly displeased with his son-in-law, not only for expressing discontent with the piece of sculpture when it first came into his possession, but also for having allowed the bunia bird to tinker with it. He bided his time, waiting for his revenge to come when the young man should complete the customary marriage tasks—the cutting of a field, and the building of a house for him. It was not long before Yar commenced cutting the field: he worked at it early, he worked at it late, and at last told his wife to let her father know that it was ready for his inspection. The old man went to have a p. 132look and on his return home told his daughter that he found fault with it. The young couple then went off to inspect the field on their own account; they were much surprised to see all the trees and bushes standing there, just as luxuriant as before, little dreaming that Nahakoboni by means of his "medicine" had caused this rapid growth to take place only the night before. Yar had therefore to cut another and a bigger field, and just the same thing happened as before, the old father again expressing himself in terms of strong disapproval. "How is this?" said Yar to his wife. "I have cut a field twice, and yet the old man is not satisfied with it." She thereupon advised him to cut a third field, but on this occasion suggested, in addition, his pulling out all the stumps by their roots. Having cut the third field, he started pulling up the stumps; it is true that he started on many, but he did not succeed in pulling out one! He fell down exhausted. By and by, his old friend the Hebu put in an appearance, and seeing his distress, offered to do the job for him, advising him to return home at once and to tell his wife that the field was now thoroughly cleared. Nahakoboni went next morning to inspect, and planted the field with cassava, plantains, and all other useful plants; he returned in the evening, but spake never a word. This made Yar suspicious, so getting up early the following day, he was much surprised to find in place of an empty field, a beautiful crop of ripe cassava, plantains, and all the other good things that his belly might yearn for. But anger still rankled in the old man's breast, so that when his son-in-law started on and completed his other marriage task, the building of a house, the old man again found fault, pulled it down, and said he wanted it built stronger. Yar accordingly rebuilt it with purple-heart—the hardest timber he could find. Nahakoboni, pleased at last, took charge of the house, and lived there.

33.* Yar, the Sun, was now free to look after his own domestic affairs, and being well satisfied with his wife, they lived very, very happily together. One day he told her he proposed taking a journey to the westward, but that as she was now pregnant, she had better travel at her leisure; she would not be able to keep pace with him. He would start first, and she must follow his tracks; she must always take the right-hand track; he would scatter feathers on the left so that she could make no mistake. Accordingly, next morning when she commenced her journey, there was no difficulty in finding her way, by avoiding the feathers, but by and by she arrived at a spot where the wind had blown them away, and then the trouble began.1 What was the poor woman to do now that she had lost her way? Her very motherhood proved her salvation, because her unborn babe began talking, and told her which path to follow. And as she wandered on and ever on, her child told her to pluck the pretty flowers whose little heads bobbed here and there over the roadway.2 She had picked some of the red and yellow ones, when a marabunta (wasp) happened to sting her below the waist; in trying to kill it she missed the insect and struck herself. The unborn baby, however, misinterpreted her action, and thinking that it was being smacked, became vexed and refused any longer to show its mother which direction to pursue. The result was that the poor woman got hopelessly astray, and at last more dead than alive found herself in front of a very large house whose only occupant was Nanyobo (lit. a big kind of frog), a very old and very big woman. Saying "how day" to each other, the visitor was asked her business. She was trying to find her husband the Sun, but she had lost the road, and she was so very weary. Nanyobo, the Frog, therefore bade the woman welcome, and giving her to eat and drink and telling her to be seated, squatted on the ground close, and asked her to clean her host's head "But mind," continued the old woman, "don't put the insects into your mouth, because they will poison you." Our wanderer, however, overcome with fatigue p. 133and anxiety, forgot all about the injunction, and picking out a louse, placed it, as is customary with the Indians, between her teeth. But no sooner had she done so, than she fell dead.1

34.* Old Nanyobo thereupon slashed open the mother, and extracted not one child, but two; a pair of beautiful boys, Makunaima and Pia. Nanyobo proved a dear, kind foster-mother and minded them well. As the babies grew larger, they commenced shooting birds; when still bigger they went to the waterside and shot fish and game. On each occasion when they shot fish, the old woman would say, "You must dry your fish in the sun, and never over a fire;" but what was curious was that she would invariably send them to fetch firewood, and by the time that they had returned with it, there would be the fish all nicely cooked and ready for them. As a matter of fact, she would vomit fire out of her mouth, do her cooking, and lick the fire up again before the lads' return; she apparently never had a fire burning for them to see.2 The repetition of this sort of thing day after day made the boys suspicious; they could not understand how the old lady made her fire, and accordingly determined to find out. On the next occasion that they were despatched to bring firewood, one of them, when at a safe distance from the house, changed himself into a lizard, and turning back, ran up into the roof whence he could get a good view of everything that was going on. What did he see? He not only saw the old woman vomit out fire, use it, and lick it up again, but he watched her scratch her neck, whence flowed something like balata (Mimusops balata) milk, out of which she prepared starch. Sufficiently satisfied with what he had witnessed, he came down, and ran after his brother. They discussed the matter carefully, the result of their deliberations being summarized in the somewhat terse expression, "What old woman do, no good. Kill old woman." This sentiment was carried into execution. Clearing a large field, they left in its very center a fine tree, to which they tied her; then, surrounding her on all sides with stacks of timber, the boys set them on fire. As the old woman gradually became consumed, the fire which used to be within her passed into the surrounding fagots. These fagots happened to be hima-heru wood, and whenevep we rub together two sticks of this same timber we can get fire.

35.* The Carib version of the tradition is noteworthy mainly in that the Hero ultimately finds a place among the stars.

*THE SUN, THE FROG, AND THE FIRESTICKS (C)

A long time ago; there was a woman who had become pregnant by the Sun, with twin children, Pia and Makunaima. One day the as-yet-unborn Pia said to his mother: "Let us go and see our father. We will show you the way, and as you travel along pick for us any pretty flowers that you may come across." She accordingly went westward to meet her husband, and plucking flowers here and there on the pathway, accidentally stumbled, fell down, and hurt herself; she blamed her two unborn children as the cause.3 They became vexed at this, and when she next asked them which road she was to follow, they refused to tell her, and thus it was that she took the wrong direction, and finally arrived, foot-sore and weary, at a curious house. This belonged to Tiger's mother, Kono(bo)-aru, the Rain-frog, and when the exhausted traveler discovered where she was, she told the old woman she was very sorry she had come, because she had often heard how cruel her son was. But p. 134the house-mistress took pity on her, and telling her not to be afraid, hid her in the big cassiri jar, and popped on the cover. When Tiger got home that night, he sniffed up and down, and said, "Mother, I can smell somebody! Whom have you here?" And though she denied having anybody on the premises, Tiger was not satisfied, but had a good look round on his own account, and peeping into the cassiri jar, discovered the frightened creature.

36.* On killing the poor woman, Tiger found the two as-yet-unborn children, and showed them to his mother, who said that he must now mind and cherish them. So he put them in a bundle of cotton to keep them warm, and noticed next morning that they had already begun to creep. The next day, they had grown much bigger, and with this daily increase in about a month's time they had reached man's size. Tiger's mother told them that they were now fit to use the bow and arrow, with which they must go and shoot the Powis (Crax) because it was this bird which had killed their own mother. Pia and Makunaima therefore went next day and shot Powis, and these birds they continued shooting day after day. When they were about to let fly the arrow at the last bird, the Powis told them that it was none of his tribe who had killed their mother, but Tiger himself, giving them both full particulars as to how he had encompassed her death. The two boys were very angry on hearing this, spared the bird, and coming home empty-handed, informed the old woman that the Powis had taken their arrows away from them. Of course this was not true, but only an excuse; they had themselves hidden their arrows in the bush, and wanted the chance of making new and stronger weapons. These completed, they built a staging up against a tree, and when Tiger passed below, they shot and killed him. And when they reached home, they slaughtered his mother also.

37.* The two lads now proceeded on their way and arrived at last at a clump of cotton-trees in the center of which was a house occupied by a very old woman, really a frog, and with her they took up their quarters. They went out hunting each day, and on their return invariably found some cassava that their hostess had baked. "That's very strange," remarked Pia to his brother, "there is no field anywhere about, and yet look at the quantity of cassava which the old woman gives us. We must watch her." So next morning, instead of going into the forest to hunt, they went only a little distance away, and hid themselves behind a tree whence they could see everything that took place at the house. They noticed that the old frog had a white spot on her shoulders: they saw her bend down and pick at this spot, and observed the cassava-starch fall. On their return home they refused to eat the usual cake, having now discovered its source. Next morning they picked a quantity of cotton from the neighboring trees, and teased it out on the floor. When the old woman asked what they were doing, they told her that they were making something nice and soft for her to lie upon. Much pleased at this, she promptly sat upon it, but no sooner had she done so than the two lads set fire to it; thereupon her skin was scorched so dreadfully as to give it the wrinkled and rough appearance which it now bears.

38.* Pia and Makunaima next continued their travels to meet their father, and soon arrived at the house of a Maipuri (tapir), where they spent three days. On the third evening Maipuri returned, looking very sleek and fat. Wanting to know what she had been feeding on, the boys followed her tracks, which they traced to a plum-tree; this they shook and shook so violently as to make all the fruit, both ripe and unripe, fall to the ground, where it remained scattered. When Maipuri next morning went to feed, she was disgusted to see all her food thus wasted, and in a very angry mood quickly returned home, beat both boys, and cleared out into the bush. The boys started in pursuit, tracked her for many a long day, and at last caught up with her. Pia now told Makunaima to wheel round in front and drive the creature back to him, and as she passed, let fly a harpoon-arrow into her; the rope, however, got in the way of Makunaima as he was passing in front, and p. 135cut his leg off. On a clear night you can still see them up among the clouds: there is Maipuri (Hyades), there Makunaima (Pleiades), and below is his severed leg (Orion's Belt.). [Cf. Sect. 211.]

39.* In the story as told by a Makusi (Da, 339), there are but a few main variations from the particulars given by the Warraus (Sect. 29). These variations are as follows:

The Sun, finding his fish-ponds too frequently robbed, set Yamuru, the water-lizard, to watch them. Yamuru, not being sufficiently vigilant and deprivations continuing, Alligator was appointed watchman. Alligator, the depredator, continued his old trade while employed as a watchman, and at last was detected by the Sun, who slashed him with a cutlass within an inch of his life, every cut forming a scale (Sect. 141). Alligator begged piteously for his life, and to propitiate the Sun offered him his beautiful daughter in marriage. But he had no daughter. He therefore sculptured the form of a woman from a wild plum tree. He then exposed her to the Sun's influence, and fearing ultimate detection of the fraud, hid himself in the water, peering at the Sun; and this habit Alligator has continued to the present time. The woman was imperfectly formed, but a woodpecker, in quest of food, pecked at her body atque genitalia preparavit. The Sun left her and she, grieving for his desertion, said that she would seek him. [Then follows the incident of her advent at old Mother Toad's house, the sickness caused by eating the poisonous head-lice, the death of the woman, as in the Carib version, caused by Tiger, and the discovery of the two unborn children, who subsequently became the two Heroes.]

40.* Pia's first work was to slay Tiger and take out of his carcass the parts ot the body of his mother, who became whole and alive. [Next comes a repetition of the Warrau legend concerning the old toad guarding her fire-making secret.] But Makunaima had an appetite for fire-eating, and invariably devoured the live coals. The toad remonstrated, and Makunaima in anger prepared to leave and to travel throughout the land. To attain his purpose he dug a large canal, into which flowed water; and having made a corial, the first of its kind, he persuaded his mother and Pia to go with him. It was from Crane that the brothers learned the art of fire-making when he struck his bill against a flint and the friction produced fire. The brothers placed huge rocks in all the rivers to detain the fishes: the rocks thus placed caused the great waterfalls. Crane was at first accustomed to catch his own fish, but finding Pia and Makunaima more successful fishermen after the rivers had been dammed, kept near to them and took away their fish. Pia consequently quarreled with Crane, who, becoming angry, took up Makunaima (who had taken part with him against his brother) and flew away with him to Spanish Guiana.

41.* Pia and his mother, thus deserted, continued their daily employment of traveling together, fishing, and seeking fruits. But at last one day the mother complained of weariness and Pia conveyed her to the heights of Roraima, these to be her abiding place of rest. Then came a change of occupation for Pia. He abandoned the hunt as the sole or principal occupation of his life, and traveled from place to place, teaching the Indians many useful and good things. By him and his teachings we have the Piai men. Thus did Pia pursue his course of benevolence until he disappeared finally from men and remained awhile with his mother on Roraima. And when his time of departure from her had arrived, he told her that whatever of good she desired she would obtain if she would bow her head and cover her face with her hands (Sect. 256) while she expressed her wish. This she does in her need to the present hour. Whenever the mother of these two heroes of our race is sorrowful, there arises a storm on the mountain, and it is her tears that run down in streams from the heights of Roraima (Da, 342).

p. 136

Mount Zabang, the Olympus of the Makusis, is the dwelling their great Spirit Makunaima (ScR, II, 188).

42.* Amalivaca (Sect. 2), venerated by the Caribs and more especially by the Tamanacs, is said to have arrived in a bark, during the subsidence of the great waters, and carved the sculptures now seen high on the perpendicular faces of the rocks which border the great rivers (Br, 387). He has a brother Vochi—together, they created the world. While making the Orinoco they had a long consultation about causing the stream to flow up and down at one and the same time, so as to ease the paddlers as much as possible. Amalivaca had daughters who were very fond of gadding about, so he broke their legs to render them sedentary, and force them to people the land of the Tamanacs. He also did many other things. He made the earth sufficiently level for people to dwell on. He seems to have known music. His house, consisting of some blocks of stone piled one on another, forming a sort of cavern, may still be seen on the plains of Maita, and near it is a large stone which the Indians say "was an instrument of music, the drum of Amalivaca" (AVH, II, 473). Strange to say, I can obtain no information first-hand from the Pomeroon District Caribs concerning this Amalivaca; even the name appears to be now unknown here.

Footnotes

p. 121

1 Compare Kon, the boneless Tribal Hero of the Yunka Indians of Peru (PE, 29, 41).—W. E. R.

p. 126

1 A name I have been unable to trace.—W. E. R.

2 One end of the drum is commonly closed with baboon hide.

p. 127

1 The Hebus of the Warraus are believed to possess eye-brows so prominent that it is possible for them to look directly upward only when in this upside-down position. [Sect. 99.]

2 On the Amazons, before the advent of Europeans, we have Acuña's authority for stating that all the tools which the Indians employed for making their canoes, huts, etc., were axes and hatchets made of tortoise-shell (Ac, 90).

3 The seed-pod in question is about 10 in. long, much flattened, hard-shelled, with a curved surface, so that when the halves are split asunder, each bears a somewhat fanciful resemblance to a cutlass.

4 The first word is in Spirit language, i. e., not understood by the Warraus, who tell me that it is nothing more than a watch-word; the second means "to kill with the arm;" the third indicates "to fall down."—W.E.R.

p. 128

1 This bird is the Odontophorus Guianensis. "The notes of this bird, from which it takes its name, are usually the first heard In the morning, and frequently before dawn" (BW, 183).

2 Present-day cursing, the hó-a of the Warraus and Arawaks, is done on somewhat different lines, usually by medicine-men or by very old people only.

p. 129

1 The account given of Kororomanna's doings in this paragraph forms the complete story of an unnamed Indian, as related by the Caribs, who give the name Pupombo to the Skull Spirit.

2 Ehrenreich refers to the many examples of such individual giant heads or skulls in the North American legends (PE, 71).

p. 131

1 It would seem to be an invariable practice with the Indians to bathe after a meal.

2 A very common form of house-bench is one in the shape of this reptile.

3 The name of a big species of lukunanni (Cicllia ocellaris).

4 Previous to the advent of civllizing influences among the Indians, the jus connubii was usually exercised during the waking hours.

p. 132

1 In Sect. 223 there is mentioned a connection between certain feathers and loss of memory.

2 Dance (p. 340) In connection with the Makusi, says, "she plucked pretty leaves and flowers and placed them in her girdle . . . the same as we do now when our pregnant wives travel with us."

p. 133

1 For further reference to head-lice in legendary lore, see PE, 78, 82.

2 I find it to be well known among the Indians that certain kinds of frogs, after dark, can be made to swallow glowing embers, which are then probably mistaken for various luminous insects.—W. E. R.

3 When I suggested to the narrator that the woman went eastward to meet the sun, he emphatically contradicted me, explaining that site went to meet him where he would fall to the earth again, at the distant horizon.—W. E. R.

CHAPTER III
TRACES OF SPIRIT, IDOL, AND FETISH CULT

Evidence very scarce, but recognizable in Familiar Spirits, and in the kickshaws of the Medicine-man (43); Dancing with noisy instruments in front of Idols (44); the Sacred Trumpets or Flutes (45); Frogs and Toads as divinities (46); Snakes (47). On the Amazons: Idols (48); Other objects, of obscure signification, recorded from within (49) and without (50) the Guianas, can hardly be regarded as Idols or Fetishes.

43.* It must be admitted that the positive evidence of idol or fetish worship among the Guiana Indians is very scarce, even Schomburgk recording (ScR, II, 321) that he never found the slightest trace of idolatry or of supplication to a fetish. And yet, in view of the historical records that the people living to the north, the west, and the south of them, did certainly have something akin to an idol or fetish cult leads one to the belief that the Guiana natives, at some not very remote period of their history, may possibly have pursued similar practices. Their northern neighbors, living on the islands, apparently worshiped Cemi, or so-called familiar spirits, a cult still traceable, as I propose showing (Sect. 93), in certain kickshaws of the mainland medicine-man.

44.* Among their western tribesmen a religious rite performed by some of the Orinoco tribes "was that of dancing to the sound of very noisy instruments, before two small idols, to which they paid reverence by chanting extemporaneous couplets" (FD, 52).

45.* This reference to noisy instruments suggests the sacred trumpet, or botuto, which was an object of veneration on the upper reaches of the Orinoco, the Atabapo, and the Inirida. It was sounded under the palm trees that they might bear abundance of fruit. Humboldt says that, to be initiated into the mysteries of the botuto, it is requisite to be of pure morals and to have lived single. The initiated are subjected to flagellations, fastings, and other painful exercises. There is but a small number of these sacred trumpets. The most anciently celebrated is that upon a hill near the confluence of the Tomo and the Guainia. Father Cereso assured us, continues the celebrated traveler, that the Indians speak of the Botuto of Tomo as an object of worship common to many surrounding tribes. Fruit and intoxicating liquor are placed beside the sacred trumpet. Sometimes the Great Spirit himself makes the botuto resound; sometimes he is content to manifest his will through him to whom the keeping of the instrument is entrusted. "Women are not permitted to see this marvelous instrument, and are excluded from all the ceremonies of this worship" (AVH, II, 363), at the risk of life.

Wallace (348) also refers to similar instruments among the Uapes River Indians, upper Rio Negro, which are used at their festivals to produce the Jurupari, or Forest-Spirit, music. He says that—

These instruments, however, are with them such a mystery that no woman must ever see them, on pain of death. They are always kept in some igaripé' [water-chanel] at a distance from the malocca, whence they are brought on particular occasions: when the sound of them is heard approaching, every woman retires into the woods, or into some adjoining shed which they generally have near, and remains invisible till after the ceremony is over, when the instruments are taken away to their hiding-place, and the women come out of their concealment. Should any female be supposed to have seen them, either by accident or design, she is invariably executed, generally by poison, and a father will not hesitate to sacrifice his daughter, or a husband his wife, on such an occasion.

Koch-Grünberg (I, 186-187) speaks of these "Devil" flutes on the Aiary River (Rio Negro) among the Siusi, an Arawak tribe. He says that these are sounded in honor of Ko-ai, the son of Yaperi´kuli, their tribal Hero; that the festival at which they are used is held at the time of ripening of the fruit of the manicole (Euterpe oleracea) and turu (Œnocarpus bacaba); that on the same occasion there is mutual flagellation with whips. The flutes have to be carefully guarded from the gaze of women, and when not in use are hidden under water, etc. They take their name from that of the spirit in whose honor they are sounded. Elsewhere (KG, I, 314-316) he speaks of the dance as having magic powers; it can dispel sickness and even heal big wounds. Granted that the whipping is part and parcel of the festival, and the object of the festival is to ensure abundance of fruit, the following extract from Gumilla is worth consideration: When the time arrives for clearing the open plains with a view to sowing their corn, yucca, plantains, etc., they [the Salivas] place the young men, some separated from the others, in lines, and a certain number of old men provide themselves with whips and rough thongs made of twisted agave (pita). As soon as intimation is given that it is time to commence work, the whipping of these young men takes place, and notwithstanding the cuts and marks which their bodies receive, neither groan nor complaint escapes them (G, I, 188). It is true that the missionary was told that they received the whipping to cure them of their laziness, but I am strongly inclined to the view, corroborated as it is by the examples already given, that flagellation is a propitiation for favors already received or expected, that the object of the whole festival in fact is comparable with that met with in connection with the cassava plant (Sects. 165, 166). The flagellations inflicted at the burial ceremonies (Sect. 75) would seem to have a different origin.

46.* "Some other tribes of Indians, who likewise dwelt upon the banks of the river Oronoka, paid to toads the honours due to the divinity [Sect. 342]. Far from injuring these animals, they carefully p. 139 kept them under pots, in order to obtain rain or fine weather; and so fully persuaded were they of their power in this respect, that they scourged them as often as their petitions were not answered." (FD, 52.) It is known that for the Chaimas, Cumanagotos, Tamanacs, and other original tribes of the Caribs, the frog was the god of the waters (cf. Sect. 18): Ruiz Blanco (Conversion de Piritu) says that the Cumanagotos never killed a frog, but kept one like a domestic animal, beating it when the rain did not fall (AR, 185). There is an intimate connection between frogs, toads, and certain other animals, and success in the chase (Sect. 349).

47.* Beyond the mention of certain snake dances, I can find nothing akin to actual worship and similar ceremonies in connection with these creatures, notwithstanding the very deep-rooted belief in the relationship of the serpent to sexual matters (Sect. 347). At Maroa, River Guainia, (upper Rio Negro), Humboldt (II, 386) talks of "that ancient dance of serpents, the Queti, in which these wily animals are represented as issuing from the forests, and coming to drink with the men in order to deceive them, and carry off the women." So also Wallace (204) records in connection with a snake dance among the Uaupes River Indians, participated in by men and boys, "two huge artificial snakes of twigs and bushes bound together with sipós, from thirty to forty feet long, and about a foot in diameter. . . . They divided themselves into two parties of twelve or fifteen each, and lifting the snakes on their shoulders, began dancing."

48.* South of the Guianas, there is the evidence of Acuña (92) from the Amazons, in 1639:

The Religion of these barbarous People is much alike: they all worship Idols which they make with their own hands; to one of them they ascribe the authority of governing the waters, and put a fish in his hand in token of his power; they choose others to preside over their seed time, and others to inspire them with courage in their Battles; they say these gods came down from Heaven on purpose to dwell with them and to show them kindness. They do not signify their Adoration of these Idols by any outward ceremonies, but on the contrary seem to have forgotten them as soon as they have made them, and putting them in a case let them lie, without taking any notice of them so long as they imagine they have no occasion for their Help; but when they are ready to march out to war, they set up the Idol in which they have placed the hopes of their Victories, at the Prow of their Canoes (Cf. Sect. 84): so, when they go a fishing, they take that Idol with them to which they attribute the government of the waters.

49.* On the other hand, there are a few accounts of the existence of various cult objects, the actual signification of which has so far not been satisfactorily explained; lest these should ever be claimed as examples of a fetish cult, it would be well to mention them here. In the Catalogue of Contributions transmitted from British Guiana to the London International Exhibition of 1862 there is a record (p. 52) of "Figures of Clay, made by an Indian of the Caribisi tribe, p. 140and representing human beings and an armadillo. From Massaruni River. Contributed by H. C. Whitlock and Geo. Dennis. These are the only specimens of Indian plastic art ever seen by the Contributors." I myself have obtained children's whistles in the shape of frogs and turtles made of clay by the Moruca River Caribs. Among the Caribs of the Parou River, French Guiana, Crévaux (262) speaks of meeting with a young woman who was modeling a tapir in black wax. From the upper Aiary (Rio Negro) Koch-Grünberg (I, 125) figures several wax objects modeled by little boys, and wooden fishes employed in the death ceremonies (KG, II, 154). In our own colony, Schomburgk states (ScR, II, 471) that at a Maopityan settlement under the cone-shaped shelter raised on top of the giant huts, were several flat pieces of wood, cut into all kinds of figures, which swayed to and fro with the wind. Among the Monikos and Sokorikos, branches of the Carib race inhabiting the districts on both sides of the Cotinga, "a very marked feature in all their houses," says J. J. Quelch (Ti, 1895, pp. 144-5), "are the rude imitations birds, chiefly of the herons, the negrocop [Mycteria], the muscovy duck, and the swallow-tailed hawk, which are made from cotton thread, corn-cobs and sticks, and are suspended high up under the roofs of the houses, in the positions occupied during flight." These are probably identical with the targets met with on the Aiary River (Rio Negro). Targets of artificial birds, made of maize-cobs and their coverings, hang as decorations from the crossbeams of the houses: the boys blow at them with nonpoisoned arrows (KG, I, 102; II, 244).

50.* Outside of the Guianas to the westward, among the Carijonas of the upper Yapura, Crévaux (361) speaks of a bench with rough carvings representing a bird of prey; also of the wooden figure of a man with legs wide apart. To the southward, Acuña (142) makes mention of the Capunas and Zurinas on the south side of the Amazon, near its junction with the Rio Negro:

They will cut a raised figure so much to the life and so exactly upon any coarse piece of wood that many of our Carvers might take pattern by them. It is not only to gratify their own fancies, and for their own use that they make these pieces of work, but also for the Profit it brings them: for they hereby maintain a trade with their neighbours, and truck their work with them for any necessaries to serve their occasion.

CHAPTER IV
CREATION OF MAN, PLANTS, AND ANIMALS

Man was either brought here from Cloud-land, etc. (51), or was created here (52); in the latter case, from Animals, as Tigers (53), Snakes (54-56), from Plants (57), or from Rocks and Stones (58).
Certain Plants were derived from human beings or Bush Spirits (59), or grew upon a Wonderful Tree (60-61). Some animals arose from the Spirits of Mortal Men (62).

51.* Certain tribes believe that man, already made, reached this world from elsewhere, while others claim that he developed here, where he either merely grew into being or was indebted to some Master Spirit for coming into existence at all. His presence on the planet, however, would not seem to give rise on his part to claims superior to those of various animals, including birds.

In those cases where Man, already created, reached this "vale of tears" from elsewhere, his place of origin appears to have been Cloud-land, the Skies, and countries beyond them, according to views held by Caribs, Arawaks, and Warraus.

The first-mentioned hold that mankind descended from on high . . . unfortunately, the clouds which had brought them down receded and so left them behind. Being hungry, they were forced to eat earth, which they baked into cakes, and followed the beasts and birds to see what wild fruits they were accustomed to devour, and so learned to help themselves (BrB, 103). According to the Island Caribs, "Louquo was the first man and a Carib. He was not made of any other body; he descended from the sky and lived a long time on earth;" in fact it was he who made it. "He had a large nostril from which, as also from an incision in his thighs, he produced the first men (BBR, 226-7). Bolingbroke talks of Longwo as being the first man, in the Indian belief of the "central parts" of Guiana: "Certain vapors, or spirits, to which the savages ascribe thunders and fevers, are the objects of their fear and propitiatory worship. They do not ascribe a human form to these divinities, but conceive them to have brought hither the first man,whom they call Longwo" (Bol, 371). The Korobohána, one of the many group-divisions of the Arawaks . . . believe that they originally came from above the clouds. The weight of a heavy woman broke the rope by which they were descending: and communication was thus cut off between those who had reached the ground and those remaining above. The Great Spirit, pitying the latter, supplied them with wings and plumage; and they came down to colonize the trees above the heads of their p. 142 brethren—still privileged to live near, and to converse with them, though changed into kuriaka parrots (BrB, 179).

The Warrau version of their own origin is very similar. Okonoróté one day went hunting for a rare bird—in those times the Warraus lived up above the sky and the only creatures they knew of were birds—and it was many a long day before he succeeded in locating it, though he did so at last. Letting fly an arrow he transfixed it, but on rushing up to the place where it had fallen, there was nothing visible but a big hole in the ground through which he could see the deer, peccary, and other animals disporting themselves on the green plains below. With the help of a cotton rope he descended to earth, and saw jaguars, snakes, and wild beasts devouring their prey. He shot a young deer, cooked the flesh, and finding how sweet it tasted, took some of the flesh back with him on his ascent up the rope, home again. Needless to say, all the Warraus were only too eager to accompany him when he repeated his descent, which they did in safety, one after the other until the very last—and this happened to be a woman who got wedged in the aperture, and could neither get up nor down. The hole being thus filled up, the Warraus have never been able to reach their old home again (BrB, 55). The name of this woman who thus stuck half-way is Okona-kura, the Warraus still recognizing her as the Morning Star.

Certain of the Salivas did not hesitate to proclaim themselves children of the Sun (G, I, 113).

52.* In those cases where man, as such, put in his first appearance on this world's stage (i. e., as in many other places was created on the earth) there is no evidence available pointing to the existence of any belief that his creation took place out of nothing, either spontaneously or at the instance of some Master Spirit, or some person, or thing. Indeed, the two or three examples which might be claimed in support of the existence of such evidence are very dubious. Schomburgk notes an Arawak tradition, which I can not find elsewhere, that man was created by Kururumanni, and woman by Kulimina (Sect. 19); he mentions also that the former was subservient to Aluberi, the Supreme Spirit (ScR, II, 319). Among the Maipures of the Orinoco, however, it was the Supreme Being Purrunaminari who created man, but the traveler just cited admits that the above tradition, among others reported by Gili, shows a seemingly evident admixture of Christian ideas (ScR, II, 320). So also does the alleged Akawai legend that Makunaima, admittedly the Supreme Being, put his son, the first man, in charge of all the other animals that he had just made (BrB, 126). On the other hand, the Indian seemingly can conceive of man's origin only from something already existing in the world of nature immediately surrounding him. And so, in considering the reputed origins p. 143of the various tribes, the belief becomes more and more prominent that Mankind—and by Mankind each Indian means the original ancestors of his own people—was originally derived, with or without the assistance of pre-existing agencies, from various animals and plants, from rocks, stones, and rivers.

53.* Among various animal forms, "tigers" (jaguars) and snakes constitute the commonest sources from which peoples claiming an animal pedigree have been derived.

Carib history furnishes excellent examples in this respect, because we have records not only of what they themselves thought about their own origin, but of what other peoples also believed concerning it. Thus the Achagua maintain that the Caribs are legitimate descendants of tigers . . . chavi in their language signifies a tiger, whence they deduce chavinavi, "arising from a tiger," which is their term for a Carib. Other branches of the Achagua explain the term more satisfactorily thus: chavi in their language is a tiger, and chavina is the spear, lance, pike, pole, and from these two words, "tiger" and "pike," they derive the word chavinavi, as being the children of tigers with pikes (G, I, 112).

54.* The Salivas say that the son of Puru conquered and put to death a horrible snake that had been destroying and devouring the nations of the Orinoco; but that as soon as the monster began to putrefy, certain large worms began to develop in her entrails, and that from each worm there finally arose a Carib Indian and his woman; and that in the same way that the snake was so bloody an enemy of all those nations, so her children were savage, inhuman, and cruel (G, I, 111).

55.* The Warrau version, like that recorded by Brett in his Legend of Korobona (BrB, 64) refers to a special water-snake, and the account which I now give is almost word for word as related to me:

*THE ORIGIN OF THE CARIBS (W)

A Warrau man warned his sister not to bathe in a certain neighboring pond at those regular periods when she happened to be unwell (Sect. 188). For a long time she obeyed his instructions, but after a time, forgetting all about them, she went to bathe at the forbidden spot and time, and was caught by a large snake, the water-camudi Uamma. By and by she became pregnant. Now it was during the bullet-tree (Mimusops belata) season, when the Indians used to cut down the trees to secure the seed, which are excellent eating, and it was noticed that this same woman, although she took no ax away with her in the morning, invariably returned with a large quantity of the delicious seed in the afternoon. The brother, thereupon becoming suspicious, watched her. Unobserved himself, he followed her next day, saw her approach a huge bullet-tree, and saw the Uamma snake (Sect. 244) exeuntem ex corpore feminæ, coil around the tree, and make his way up into the topmost branches. There the snake changed into a man, who shook the boughs for the woman, thus causing the seeds to fall to the ground, where she gathered them. Having done this, the Uamma, reverting to his original form, descended the tree, and iterum corpus p. 144feminæ intravit. Thereupon the brother said, "There is something wrong here; this will not do: Soror mea probabiliter serpentem in corpore suo habet." So told his friends who, in company with him, watched his sister the next day, when the same thing took place, Uamma exeuns sub corpore feminæ, climbing the tree, changing into human form, shaking the seeds down, and then becoming a snake again. But just as Uamma was about to reach the ground, the watchers rushed up and cut him into thousands of pieces. The woman grieved sorely, but collected all the fragments under a heap of mold and leaves, each piece of which by and by grew into a Carib. Many years passed; the Caribs growing strong and numerous, became a nation. They lived in harmony with the Warraus, so much so that when one tribe caught some game or other dainty, they would send a child with a piece of it over to the Warraus. The latter would then return the compliment and send a child of theirs with food to the Caribs. This lasted a long time, until one day the original mother of the Caribs—a very old woman now—told them to kill the child which the Warraus had sent to them; this was in revenge for the way the Warraus had slain her snake lover years before. As might have been expected, the Warraus on the next occasion slaughtered the Carib child, and thus a blood feud arose between the two nations, the Caribs finally overwhelming the Warraus.

56.* The Carib version of the story was told me on the upper Pomeroon, by probably one of the oldest local survivors of the tribe, who spoke somewhat as follows:

The water-camudi had an Indian woman for a sweetheart. During the day he took the form of a snake; at night, he was "a people" like myself. The couple used to meet at the water side, and hence the girl's parents knew nothing about their being so fond of each other. After she became pregnant, a baby camudi was born. The little one used to appear when she reached the river bank, swim about, and after a time return to its nesting place. Now, as she stayed so long each time at the water side, the old father said to his two sons, "What is the matter with your sister? Why does she take so long to bathe?" Accordingly, the brothers, watching her go down to the stream, videt serpentem parvam exire atque serpentem magnam intrare. They saw also the huge camudi bring his infant son something to eat and saw the baby take the father's place when the latter left. When they reached home, the sons complained to the old man about what they had seen: he told them to kill both the snakes. So on the next occasion they killed the huge camudi, and seizing the baby serpent, carried it far away back into the bush, where they chopped it up into many small pieces. Some months afterward when hunting in the neighborhood, the brothers heard a great noise and the sound of voices coming from the very same direction, and going to ascertain the cause, found four houses in the identical spot where they had cut up the baby camudi, all occupied by Indians who had grown out of the fragments of the snake. In the first hut the house-master said he was glad to welcome his two uncles, but in the other three the occupants wanted to kill them for having destroyed their sister's child from which they had all sprung. But the first house-master said: "No, don't do that, because these two visitors are uncles to all of you, and you must not have a bad mind toward them." And thus it happened that the two brothers got away without further molestation, and on arrival at home told their old father how the snake fragments had grown into people. And when he expressed a wish to see his grandchildren, his two sons led the way into the bush, and he was right glad to see his numerous progeny, with whom he made good friends, and they all drank paiwarri. And thus the Carib nation arose from a water-camudi.

57.* The vegetable world takes a share of the responsibility for the derivation of man. There is either a story of some fabulous Tree of Life, or reference to certain well-known plants, as the silk-cotton tree p. 145 (Bombax) or ité palm (Mauritia). The Akawai and Makusi idea of creation is that, co-eval with Makunaima, there was a large tree, and that, having mounted this tree, with a stone ax he cut pieces of wood which, having been thrown into the river, became animated beings (HiC, 244; ScR, II, 319). The Arawaks hold that from his seat on the silk-cotton tree, the Mighty One scattered twigs and bark in the air, on the land, and in the water, and that from these pieces arose the birds, beasts, reptiles, fish, and also men and women. The sire of the Arawaks was Wadili (BrB, 7). Some of the Salivas affirmed that certain trees used to bear men and women for fruit, and that these people were their ancestors (G, I, 113). The Maipures and, according to Humboldt similarly the Tamanacs, say that in early days the whole earth was submerged in water, only two people, a man and a woman, saving themselves on the top of the high mountain Tamanaku; that as they wandered around the mountain in deep distress over the loss of their friends, they heard a voice which told them to throw the fruits of the Mauritia behind them over their shoulders, and that as they did so, the fruit which the man threw became men, and that which the woman threw, women (ScR, II, 320). Certain of the Achagua Indians pretend that they are the children of tree-trunks and from this allusion call themselves Aycuba-verrenais (G, I, 114). Loku-daia is the mythic Indian tree, growing out of a grave, which is said by some Indians to have been the root from which they sprang. When it was cut down, it was transformed into a rapid, whence the name of one of the Demerara River rapids (Da, 195).

According to the idea current among the Trios, people were originally like wood, stone, etc., and had no faces (Go, 12). The manufacture of a woman out of a plum tree (Sect. 29), and the tree changing into a man (Sect. 9), should also be noted here.

58.* Not a few legends (Sect. 158) connected with the origin of the tribes contain curious examples of animism relative to earth, rocks, and stones (Sect. 171). The Mapoyas, the Salivas, and the Otomacs, all three of them Orinoco tribes, had beliefs of this nature (G, I, 113). The last-mentioned used to say that a stone made up of three parts, arranged in the form of a pyramid upon the summit of a rock called Barraguan, was their earliest ancestress; and that another monstrous rock, which served as the summit of another pinnacle, two leagues distant, was their first ancestor. Being consistent, they believed that all the rocks and stones of which the said Barraguan (a high promontory of large rocks, bearing hardly a particle of earth) was formed, were each of them one of their predecessors. Although these Otomacs buried their dead, they dug up the skulls at the end of a year, and placed them in and among the crevices and holes between the rocks and stones constituting the promontory mentioned, p. 146where they expected them in their turn to change into stone. The Mapoyas would call such a stone as that serving for the summit of the pinnacle just mentioned, Uruana, describing it as the source of their tribe, and would be delighted at any one speaking of them as Uruanayes in allusion to this fact. These tombs, caverns filled with bones, in the strait of Barraguan, are again referred to by Humboldt (II, 487). Some of the Salivas would declare that they were children of the soil, and that in former times the earth used to breed men and women in the same way that it now produces thorns and hidden rocks (G, I, 113). According to the Makusi tradition, Makunaima sent great waters: only one man escaped . . . this one man who survived the flood threw stones behind him, and thus peopled the earth anew (ScR, II, 320). Those of the Achaguas who believed in their origin from rivers distinguished themselves from the the tree-trunk ones (Sect. 57) by the name Uni-verrenais (G, I, 114).

59.* The Yahuna Indians of the Apaporis River have a belief in certain palm trees having been derived from the ashes of a human being (Sect. 163A). The Arawaks and Caribs hold similar views as to the origin of certain cultivated plants. In an Arawak story it is one of the Bush Spirits which supplies man with the first fruit plants, whereas the Carib version gives a wonderful tree itself as the source (Sect. 60). The following is the Arawak story:

*THE FIRST FRUIT TREES (A)

There were three sisters alone in the house, preparing drink; the men-folk were away at a party. Early in the afternoon a young man came along, bringing a powis with him. He was not what he appeared to be, a friend, but an Adda-kuyuha (Tree Spirit). (Sect. 96.) The girls, however, did not know this. They asked him inside and offered him pepper-pot and Cassiri. He refused the former, saying it did not agree with him, and putting to his mouth the calabash which contained the latter, he broke the vessel. This made the girl who handed it to him laugh. (Sect. 125.) She was the youngest of the three; he told her on taking his departure that he would pay her another visit later in the evening. The afternoon wore on, and night fell, when, sure enough, the young man appeared again, as arranged. The elder sister took a good look at him, and recognized that, though bearing a great resemblance, he was not identical with the person who had visited them in the afternoon. She went into the adjoining room and conveyed her suspicions to the second sister. They both kept watch. He proceeded to get into the hammock where the youngest sister was lying, and began caressing her, whereupon she said she was displeased with his actions. But as he continued troubling her, she said, "What do you want with me?" With this, he slipped his arm round her neck, and broke her "neck-bone," thus killing her. He then began eating her body and finished all except the head, by early dawn. He belched and said: "Yes! I am indeed satisfied. My mother told me to bring her the head, so I must spare it for her." Holding up the head by its beautiful long hair, he carried it away. Now, the sisters who had been keeping their eyes on him all night, watched well where he carried it; they saw him bear it far away into the bush, where he disappeared with it in a hollow tree, of which they, following him, took note. When they got back home again, their men-folk had returned from the party, and among them was a piai. They told p. 147 these people exactly what had happened to their young sister, how she had laughed at the Tukuyuha, and how she had been killed (Sect. 125) and eaten by him. The piai told them to collect plenty of firewood, and to bring it to the hollow tree, which the sisters were able to show them. This wood they piled up in plenty around the tree, and then started to fire it. It burned right merrily, and in amidst the din of the cracking timber, enveloped in smoke and flame, you could hear the whole Tukuyuha family screaming, and the old grandmother reviling her wicked grandson for having brought so much trouble on them. It did not take very long for the hollow tree and the whole family of spirits to be reduced to ashes. From the ashes grew the first fruit trees of our forefathers—the plantain, the pineapple, and the cocoanut, with all the others. But the piai had to taste the fruit before the others were allowed to touch it.

60.* The statement has been already made, on Carib authority (Sect. 51), that mankind learned from the beasts and birds what wild fruits to devour. But it was the Bunia bird which taught the Carib folk all about the cultivated plants, which originally grew upon a certain wonderful tree, and it happened in this way:

Time was when the Indians had no cassava to eat; they all starved. Animals and birds also had nothing to eat; they likewise starved. It was the Maipuri alone who, going out regularly every morning and returning home of an evening, always appeared sleek and fat. The others, noticing his droppings—banana-skins, cane strips, etc., talked to one another after this manner: "Maipuri must have found a good place to get food. Let us watch him." So next morning they sent the bush-rat to dog his footsteps, and find out how he managed to keep in such good condition. The bush-rat did what he was told and followed Maipuri a long, long way into the bush, when he saw him pause under the shade of an immense tree and gather the fruit that had fallen. This tree was the Allepántepo, and very wonderful, in that everything you could wish for grew upon its branches—plantains, cassava, yams, plume, pines, and all the other fruits that Caribs love. As soon as Maipuri had had his fill the bush-rat climbed the tree, and picked upon the corn to satisfy his hunger; when he could eat no more, he came down and brought with him a grain in order to show the others what he had succeeded in finding. The Indians thereupon followed the rat who led the way back to the tree, and by the time they reached it, many plantains, pines, and other things had fallen on the ground. After they had cleaned up everything, they tried to climb the tree to get more, but it was too big and smooth, so they all agreed to cut it down. They made a staging around the trunk, and began hacking with their stone axes, and they cut away there for ten days, but it would not fall—so big was Allepántepo. They cut away for another ten days and still it would not fall. By this time their work had made them thirsty, so the Indians gave calabahes to all the animals except the Maipuri, to go fetch water; to the Maipuri they gave a sifter. When they all reached the waterside, they of course drank out of their vessels, except Maipuri out of whose sifter the water poured as fast as it was poured in: this was part of his punishment for being so greedy in keeping the secret of the bountiful tree all to himself. At the expiration of another ten days, cutting continuously, the tree at last fell. The Indians took away as their share all the cassava, cane, yams, plantains, potatoes, bananas, pumpkins, and watermelons, while the acouri (Dasypwata), labba (Cœlogenys), and other creatures crept in among the branches to pick out all they wanted. By the time the Maipuri had got back to the tree from the waterside only the plums were left for him, and with these he has had to remain content even to the present day. What the Indians took they brought home with them and planted in their provision fields. But it was the Bunia bird who spoke to them and explained how each was to be propagated and cooked, and how some, like the bitter cassava juice, had to be boiled before drinking, while others could be eaten raw.

61.* The above is the tradition, almost word for word as it was told to me by an old Carib, but no explanation was forthcoming as to the origin of the tree itself. Brett however ascribes it to Tamosi (BrB, 103-114) in the same way that he gives Makunaima credit (BrB, 126) for the similarly wonderful Akawai tree. In the latter case the immediately preceding sentence, however, shows an undoubted bias due to Christian influences: "Makunaima made all the beasts and birds, all of one speech, bade them live in unity, and put his Son, the first man, in charge of them." The same author gives also an addition to the story as above narrated, by the mention of a fountain or swelling waters in the stump, or under the roots, of this wonderful tree, the overflowing of which is temporarily checked by means of a rugged rock (Carib) or an inverted basket (Akawai). Owing to the reputed wickedness of the people in the one case, and the mischief of a howling monkey in the other, the waters are let loose, and a flood occurs, which overwhelms nearly everything, most of the people being destroyed." Some try to escape by climbing a high kokerite palm whose top reached the heavens, but a poor woman not in a condition to climb led the way, and halfway up was turned into stone by terror and exhaustion: none could help her and none could pass over her, and all who tried to do so became rocks likewise. A few survivors then climbed a komoo palm and so saved themselves" (BrB, 106).

62.* Among the mainland Indians, I can find no explanations current concerning the origin of the first birds and beasts. Brett's statement that Makunaima made them (BrB, 126) appears to lack confirmation. The Island Caribs had a tradition that Louquo, their first man (Sect. 51), "made fishes out of scrapings and fragments of cassava, which he threw into the water" (BBR, 227). Many an animal has been derived from the spirit (Sects. 69, 161) of mortal men.

Next
Sacred-Texts Native American South American Index Previous Next

p. 149
CHAPTER V
THE BODY AND ITS ASSOCIATED SPIRITS

The Body: Originally considered immortal (63); renovated by change of skin (64), or by Fountain of Youth (65); its immortality put to the test (66), and assured by its transformation into stone (67).

The Spirits: Several in each body; Shadow Spirits; Head, Heart, and Pulse-beat, Blood, Spittle, Footprint, and Bone Spirits, possessed by both men (68-69) and animals (70): become associated with Dream, Familiar, Forest, Mountain, Sky, and Water, Spirits (71).

Stages in Conception of Spirit Immortality shown in disposal and treatment of corpse: attitude in which buried, etc. (72); flattery and adulation, festivals and feasts (73-74); furnishing dead with means of capturing assailant (75); supplying dead with dogs, women, ornaments, hunting and fighting weapons, and food (76); eating his flesh and bones (77); exhuming his remains for witchcraft and prophecy (78); abandonment of place of sepulture, etc. (79); doubtful animistic indications of other burial customs (80).

Where spirits take on anthropomorphic forms, they reach their final destination direct (81) or only after certain trials and ordeals (82), but the idea of a future existence dependent on present conduct is very probably a borrowed one (83).

Spirits are Good or Bad according as they help or harm the Indian, and not according to the bodies whence they have been derived; the latter conception is an error into which many missionaries and travelers have fallen—e. g., the Maboya Spirit (84).

Individuals can be relieved of the presence of undesirable Spirits by use of rattle, by blowing (85).

63.* As with many another savage people, there are traces among the Guiana Indians of an idea of perpetual existence of both body and its contained spirits. On the upper Yary River, Cayenne, when a Roucouyenne piai is buried, the flesh (matière) and spirit remain in the grave, to be visited by medicine-men and others, as well as by beasts, for the purpose of being consulted (Cr, 298). The following is a curious case from Surinam reported by de Goeje (22): "An Ojana woman asked me, when I came again, to bring her a teremopüilatop which literally means 'die-never implement-for,' so that her little son might be blessed with everlasting life. When I told her there was no such thing, and that everybody had to die, I met with the same extraordinary unbelief that Von den Steinen records in his 'Unter den Naturvölkern' (p. 348)." So also on the upper Rio Negro Koch-Grünberg (I, 197) was applied to for a panacea (Universalsmittel) against death.

64.* Other phases of this idea of an immortal body are met with in the myths relative to changed skins: the Indian belief is that those creatures which undergo ecdysis live forever. After Amalivaca had lived a long while with the Tamanacas, he took his corial to reach the other side of the salt water whence he had come. Just as he was taking his departure he sang out to them, "You will change your p. 150 skins," (i. e., "You will always be young," like snakes, etc.), but one doubting old dame called out "Oh!" which annoyed Amalivaca so much that he now said "You shall die!" (ScR, II, 320). When Kururumanni [Kororomanna] came to earth to see what the Arawaks were doing, he found them so bad that he wished to destroy them, on which account he took away their everlasting life and bestowed it on those creatures who cast their skins—snakes, lizard and cockroaches (ScR, II, 319).

64A.* There are several examples of this taking-off and putting-on of skins and consequent continuous existence, to be met with in the Guiana folk-lore (e. g., Sects. 64B, 137, 162), therefore I can only conclude that all of these are stages in the conception of the same idea of living forever.

*THE MAN WITH A BAD TEMPER (W)

A man and woman once caught a girl monkey and "minded" her: she became quite tame, and when the old people would have to go away for a while, they would often leave the monkey in charge. One day when they had thus gone away on a visit to some friends, the monkey took off her skin, threw it over one of the house-beams, and replaced it with the apron-belt and other ornaments that the household had left behind. She then started with the cassava, which she cooked and ate; finally she put on her skin again. When the house-folk returned, they looked for the cassava, but could find none, and though they were puzzled a good deal, they never suspected the monkey. On the next occasion that they had to leave the place, a young man remained behind, though hidden, to watch lest any one should steal the cassava a second time. After a while the monkey took off her skin, dressed herself as before, and commenced baking the cassava: the young man rushed up and seized her, and a hard struggle took place. "No," said the girl, "I am not fit to be your wife." "But I want you badly" was the rejoinder. "That's all very well," added the girl, "but you will ill-treat me and knock me about." And when he assured her that he would never ill-treat her, she at last consented, and so soon as she agreed to yield to his desires, he pulled the monkey skin down from the beam and threw it into the fire. They remained together a long time. By and by she bore him a little boy. And now her troubles indeed again commenced, because, getting tired of her, he began "lashing" her and kept calling her "Monkey," and annoying her in every way he could. Suffering so much, at last she said to herself, "I can bear this treatment no longer; I will return to my people." Taking a calabash and some ité-starch, she told her husband that she was going to bathe in the pond, but instead of doing so, she really went far away into the bush. Her husband waited long, long, for her to return, and finally followed in search. By this time she was limping along with the help of a stick: she was trying to get back into her original style of walking on four legs, and was just contriving to resume her old habit of jumping from tree to tree; her little boy also was beginning to imitate her movements. And when the husband reached the spot where she had been, there he saw her with the baby jumping from the top of one tree to the top of another. "Come back home!" he kept on shouting, but his wife took no heed; only his child, who felt sorry for his father, threw down the spiders and insects for him to eat. Now, though monkeys eat such things, men can not eat them, and so he had to proceed hungry. "Come back home!" he again called out to her, as he tried to follow her through the bushes below, but looking down upon him, she said, "No! I have had quite enough punishment from you already." And thus they proceeded on and on, the father running along on the ground below, the mother and child jumping from the topmost branches of tree to tree. At last they came to a wide river, and here the monkey cried out to her people Katanni-tóri (i. e. "Come and fetch us!"). And they made the p. 151 wind to blow so strongly that it caused the opposite shore to come close over to the tree where the monkey was, so close that the trees on both sides of the stream touched; by this means the mother and her child jumped across, and once across, the opposite shore with its bushes drew back to their original position. As the separation took place, the monkey called out to the man, "You must swim after us if you want us!" and the little boy, who was really fond of his father, shouted, "Good-bye—I am going!" But the mother would say nothing further. The man was thus left on the nearer shore, and got home again much vexed. He destroyed everything that had belonged to the woman: he cut up her hammock, broke her calabash, and smashed her goblets. What a bad temper he must have had!

64B.* Another example is to be met in the story which I am adapting here from Brett (BrB, 177).

*THE SORCERER'S DAUGHTER

The daughter of a piai fell in love with a brave young hunter, who did not seemingly pay her any too much attention. She begged her father to make her like one of the young man's dogs so that she might always be with him. He put a magic skin over her shoulders and she became a dog. Thus it came about that each time the youth went out hunting with his four dogs, one always ran back home and would never join in the fray; more than this, he found that whenever he got home in the afternoon, there was the fire buming, the cassava ready, and all neat and clean. He thought this was due to some of his neighbors, and went to thank them, but they denied all knowledge. On the next occasion, therefore, as soon as he missed one of his dogs, he tied the three up to a tree, and returned home without making the slightest sound. Taking an advantageous position, he saw a lovely maiden there making casaava, and doing other things, while at one side there hung the charmed skin. He swiftly rushed in, seized the skin, and threw it on the already lighted fire. He then claimed the girl from her father for his wife.

65.* It was owing to a myth relative to the fountain of perennial youth that Florida came to be discovered just four centuries ago. Some old Island Indians, presumably of the Arawak stock, assured Ponce de Leon that—

Far to the north there existed a land abounding in gold and in all manner of delights; but above all, possessing a river of such wonderful virtue that whoever bathed in it would be restored to youth! They added, that in times past, before the arrival of the Spaniards, a large party of the natives of Cuba had departed northward in search of this happy land and this River of Life, and, having never returned, it was concluded that they were flourishing in renovated youth, detained by the pleasure of that enchanting country. [WI, 788.]

66.* Another interesting example of the existence of this idea of immortality is connected with the Arawak stock in Porto Rico:

Many of the most hardy and daring (of the Indians) proposed a general insurrection, and a massacre of their oppressors; the great mass, however, were deterred by the belief that the Spaniards were Supernatural Beings and could not be killed. A shrewd and sceptical cacique, named Brayoan, determined to put their immortality to the test. Hearing that a young Spaniard named Salzedo was passing through his lands, he sent a party of his subjects to escort him, giving them secret instructions how they were to act. On coming to a river, they took Salzedo on their shoulders to carry him across, but, when in the midst of the stream, they let him fall and throwing themselves upon him, pressed him under water until he was drowned. Then dragging his body to the shore, and still doubting his being dead, they wept and howled p. 152over him, making a thousand apologies for having fallen upon him, and kept him so long below the surface. The cacique Brayaon came to examine the body and pronounced it lifeless; but the Indians still fearing it might possess lurking immortality and ultimately revive, kept watch over it for three days, until it showed incontestable signs of putrefaction. Being now convinced that the strangers were mortal men like themselves, they readily entered into a general conspiracy to destroy them. [WI, 779.]

67.* Certain of the Indians (e. g., Otomacs) seemingly held the view that, after death, the body or skeleton itself turned into stone, reverted to the very material from which some of them believed it to have originally sprung (Sect. 58). The Atorais regard certain enormous blocks of granite as some of their local warriors who, after death, have been changed into stone (Cou, II, 346). Hence we must not be surprised to find cases where bowlders (Sect. 171 et seq.) and bones (Sects. 26, 91) possess a more or less independent animate existence of their own. The transformation of people into rocks and stones by way of punishment, or for other reasons, may be a development of the same belief. Thus, a long time ago, the Caribs came up to the Kirinampo Rocks, upper Rupununi, in order to surprise the Makusi and destroy them from off the face of the earth; but the good Spirit who in those days lived among the Makusis took pity on them, and changed their enemies into these stones (ScR, I, 375).

68.* Having reached a higher stage of belief, and realized that the material body does indeed undergo dissolution at death, the Indians are convinced of a Spirit or Something, one or more, being set free at the time of its occurrence. I purposely say "one or more" because it would seem that originally, not only the shadow, but also the heart, the head, and the more perceptible of all the parts of the body where there is a pulsation of arteries, as well as perhaps the blood (Sect. 240A), the spittle (Sect. 112), the footprint (Sect. 24), and the bone (Sect. 69) were each regarded in the light of a Spirit or Something that was part and parcel of the body, and took its departure at the material death. The Arawak present-day conception of this Something is connected with the person's shadow (Sect. 253); their terms for a dead person's spirit and a person's shadow are (h)iyaloko and (h)iyá, respectively. With these same people according as this spirit helps or harms them, they may qualify the designation by satu-(h)iyaloko when doing good, or wakaiatu-(h)iyaloko when doing evil. The hiyaloko, strange to say, does not appear any further in the folk-lore collected by me, unless indeed it is identical with Iya-imi and so with Hyorokon, Yolok, etc., the word for a bush spirit, a term which, as I propose showing (Sect. 94), is met with throughout the extent of the Guianas, from the Orinoco to the Amazon.

69.* The mainland Caribs term a person's shadow ai-akaru, and the spirit resident in his head, his Dream Spirit, aka or akari (Sect. 86); but after the latter leaves the body for the forest permanently, it is p. 153 known as aka-tomba. The Warrau expression for the shadow is amého-ko-i, while ak-óbi is their word for 'heart' or for the heart's Spirit which, leaving the body at death, becomes their Hebu, or Bush Spirit (Sect. 99). The Island Caribs applied the word akamboüe [cf. mainland Carib akatomba] to the spirit of a person whatever it might be like, the women speaking of it as opoyem (RoP, 471); unfortunately no information is given as to the particular part of the body (head, heart, pulse, etc.) whence it was supposed to have emanated. It was these same islanders, however, who held strong beliefs in a connection between spirits and an individual's heart- and pulse-beats: "they talked of the latter as the Spirit of the Hand [RoP, 452]; they spoke of the Spirit-something near the heart as Gonanni or Lanichi" (BBR, 237). This one at the heart was the principal one, which after death went to the sky in company with its Ichĕiri, or Chemin (Sect. 89), to live there with other Familiar Spirits (RoP, 484), and change into a young and new body (BBR, 237). They do not regard the spirit as being so immaterial as it is invisible. As to their other Spirits which have nothing to do with the heart, they believe that some go after death to make their home on the seashore, and that it is they who make the boats tack—these are known as Oumekou; they believe that others go and live in the woods and forests—these they term Maboyas (RoP, 484), or they become changed into beasts. All these Spirits are of different sexes and multiply (BBR, 237). Koch-Grünberg (II, 153) makes the interesting suggestion that certain procedures connected with some of the death festivals point to a belief in the bones constituting the real and final resting-place of the Spirit after the dismemberment (Zersetzung) of the body.

70.* The possession of a Body Spirit, or spirits, was not, however, the prerogative solely of man, but, as will be subsequently shown, there was a widespread belief in the association of spirits with animal life. Survivals of this cult, in part or in its entirety, are still recognizable in the folk-stories, in certain omens and tokens, charms or talismans, in the observance of certain tabus with regard to food, in blood-atonement and the treatment of disease, and perhaps in the application of family group-names. So also, there are similarly many traces of a corresponding association of spirits with plant-life (Chap. X).

71.* The general mainland belief in a Something (singular or plural) emanating, disintegrating, separating, etc., from the dead body of an individual, or an animal, and either remaining in the immediate neighborhood or pursuing various courses, hence becomes quite intelligible. Thus it may associate itself with some other person, to become his spirit friend and adviser as it were, or else may become intimately connected with the bush, forest, fields, and trees, sometimes with stones, rocks, mountains, underground caverns, and occasionally with stars, clouds, lightning, with rain, river, or sea. Thus, associated p. 154 with spirits already there; we can speak collectively of Dream (Sect. 86), Familiar (Sect. 89), Forest (Sect. 94), Mountain (Sect. 171), Water (Sect. 178), and Sky (Sect. 195) Spirits. I have met with no example of a freed spirit associating itself with a person's shadow, and hence purposely omit the term Shadow Spirits (Sect. 68) from this category. The important thing to remember is that two or more different kinds of spirits may have been derived from one and the same body. The old Spanish Fathers used the word demonio as a generic term for these Beings, in the same way that some of the present-day Creoles employ the name Devil; there are, however, too many diverse opinions held concerning the abstract and concrete nature of the latter to permit of the term being profitably employed for comparative purposes. Others of the Creoles as well as the "civilized" Indians often employ the word "Mother," or Máma (e. g., the Mother of Powis, the Water-Mama). I propose using the term "Spirit" throughout the following pages. Another matter to be borne in mind, however, before proceeding further, is that these Spirits of the Forest, Waters, etc., did not all have a human or an animal origin. Unfortunately the evidence at present available is insufficient to demonstrate with certainty how, or along what lines, many of them thus closely associated with the chief physical characteristics of nature, came to have an existence at all. Certain of them (e. g., Mountain Spirits) would seem to have been derived on a principle somewhat analogous to that of choosing a picture to suit the frame; in other cases, they may perhaps have been due to foreign introduction, while I doubt not that a few, like Topsy, "growed" on their own account.

72.* The extent or degree of the spirit's immortality, if such an expression may be used, varies from the primitive idea of its hovering around the place of sepulture to the advanced view of its translation, with or without apparent zoomorphic or anthropomorphic reincarnation, to less defined realms of happiness and bliss. There is nothing to prevent the several spirits of the one body pursuing different courses. Indications of some of these primitive ideas are to be found in certain of the procedures followed with the corpse, namely, the position in which it is laid to rest, its propitiation and address, the objects buried with it, the eating of the flesh, the abandonment of the place of death, and other customs. "McClintock . . . says that the . . . Akawoio races like to bury their dead in a standing position, assigning this reason,—'Although my brother be in appearance dead, he (i. e., his soul) is still alive.' Therefore, to maintain an outward sign this belief in immortality, some of them bury their dead erect, which they say represents life, whereas lying down represents death. Others bury their dead in a sitting posture, assigning the same reason" (Br, 356). Certainly on the Pomeroon, with the Arawaks, if a person should step over another lying down, the latter p. 155would be mortally offended, and would say, "You can cross me only when I am dead. I am not dead yet." This is of interest in connection with the procedure described by Schomburgk (ScR, I, 421) at the burial of a Makusi woman: all the relatives next surrounded the grave, and each one jumped over it in the direction whence he had come. Even the barely twelve-week old orphan was taken in the arms and made to jump over it. So also at the anniversary of the death of a captain among the Guahiba of the Vichada River (Orinoco) the pyre is jumped over by the piai, the men, and women, at the same time that they blow with full force (Sect. 85) in the direction of the country occupied by the Piaroa, their terrible neighbors who make them die through throwing spells over them (Cr, 548).

73.* However beloved or despised during life, the spirit of the dead is always an object of dread, and is to be propitiated by kind and flattering expressions, by festivals and feasts. At York Hill, near Tinadu Creek, Demerara, says Dance (256), an Indian child had taken to the habit of eating sand, which contributed to its early death. While the dead body of the child lay in the open coffin, which his father had procured from a Creole carpenter in the neighborhood, and just before the interment, the grandmother of the child stood over it and in wailing tones said:

My child, I always told you not to eat sand. I never gave you any, for I knew it was not good for you; you always sought it yourself. I told you that it was bad. Now, see, it has killed you. Don't trouble me, for it was your own doing; some evil thing put it into your head (mind) to eat it. Look, I put your arrow and bow by your side that you may amuse yourself. I was always kind to you; be good and don't trouble me.

Then the mother came up crying, and said as in a chant:

My child, I brought you into the world to see and enjoy all the good things. This breast [and she exposed it, or rather held it up, for it was already exposed] nourished you as long as you were willing to take it. I made your laps and pretty shirts. I took care of you and fed you, and played with you, and never beat you. You must be good and not bring evil upon me.

The father of the dead child likewise approached and said:

My boy, when I told you that the sand would kill you, you would not listen to me, and now see, you are dead. I went out and got a beautiful coffin for you. I shall have to work to pay for it. I made your grave in a pleasant spot where you loved to play. I shall place you comfortably, and put some sand for you to eat, for now it can not harm you, and I know that you like it. You must not bring bad luck to me; but look for him who made you eat the sand.

This was a family of Christian Arawaks, but the roots of inbred traditional beliefs could not at once be eradicated.

74.* At the burial of a Makusi woman at Nappi, upper Essequibo: Surrounding the hammock in which the corpse lay, in and between the wailing, the women were chanting eulogiums upon the deceased—one had lost her best friend; another praised the fine cotton thread that she had woven; another, the various objects that she had possessed. p. 156When the last article had passed out of the door, in came the piai: he proceeded to the head of the corpse, bent down to the left ear, and shouted several words into it, when he retired. The piai came back with a bundle of hair, and bending down, exposed the corpse's face from beneath the laths, spat on it; then plugged the hair into the ears and mouth, while he continued spitting; then, addressing it in a harsh tone, he retired (ScR, I, 421). So again, at the death of a Makusi female from the effects of a snake bite, all the women of the village gathered in the hut and shouted unintelligible words into the corpse's ears (ScR, II, 269).1

On the Moruca River, the Warrau women sit in a circle round the grave, and break out ever anew with their song of mourning, which is approximately as follows: "Why have you left your wife, children, and friends who loved you so dearly? Why have you left your home and field, where yams and cassava were thriving so well? . . . Who will catch agouti, monkey, fish, and turtle for us now?" (ScR, II, 446.) "Why are you dead? Were you tired of life? Did you not have cassava enough?" are among the expressions addressed by the Island Carib women to the corpse (BBR, 252). So with their fellow tribeswomen in Cayenne where, on a death, the men, women, friends, and children assemble and weep, or rather sing; the singing is done mostly by the nearest female relatives who, sitting on their heels, slowly pass both hands over the corpse from head to foot, while reproaching him for having let himself die. "Is it because you were not happy with us?" say some. "What have we done for you to leave us like this?" say others. They add: "You were such a good hunter, too! You caught fish and crabs so well! You knew how to make a proper provision-field," etc. (PBa, 228). On the Orinoco the Saliva mourners, on finally eulogizing the deceased would say, "What an excellent fisherman we have lost!" "What a clever archer has died; he never missed his mark!" (G, I, 197). Among the special feasts and festivals in honor, or rather in propitiation, of the dead, I would mention the Arawak Makuari (Mora-Kuyuha, Sect. 75) and Hauyari dances for deceased males and females, respectively. In the far western Guianas, the object of the Mask dances is to propitiate the spirit of the dead, so that he will not come back again to fetch one of the survivors (KG, 138).

75.* When the death of any member of that tribe [Akawai] is supposed to have been brought about by unfair means, the knife of the deceased is buried with him, that he may have the means of avenging himself in the world of spirits. The Warraus, in similar circumstances, place a bow and arrows by the side of the dead man, that he may by means of those weapons keep off malignant spirits in his passage to the other world. (Br, 356.)

At the burial of a male Makusi at Pirari, not only the dead man's knife but several thongs were buried with him. The thongs were put into the grave for the purpose of enabling him to tie to a tree the kanaima who had caused his death (ScR, I, 468). Such thongs are to be seen also at some of the funeral dances of other tribes. Thus, among the Roucouyenne of Cayenne, at the pono, or first of the two festivals in honor of the dead, one man alone stands up, holding in his hand a whip eight meters long. With a swirling motion he cracks it with a report like that of a pistol; each one in turn gets up and cracks the whip (Cr, 258). At their corresponding festival the Arawaks use whips upon each other, often inflicting terrible wounds. To receive their flagellation, the performers put their legs forward as does the white crane or stork (Mycteria sp.), the wooden effigy of which the masters-of-ceremony carry, this particular dance as well as the whips being thus named, after the bird, morakúyuha: this Arawak word, corrupted now into macquarrie, makuari, etc., is seemingly of Tupi origin, the creature being known on the lower Amazon as magoary (HWB, 146, 316).

76.* Future provision may be made for the deceased by burying with him his dog, his women, or his slaves, some food, his hunting and fighting implements, and his ornaments. Examples of these procedures are plentiful in the old records.

His faithful hunting dog was killed and placed with him, and the grave closed in [Warraus, ScR, II, 446].

His dog is also buried to guard him, and watch those that caused him in die. . . .

If the deceased owned a negro, the latter is killed in order to serve his master in the other world. [Island Caribs, BBR, 252.]

They imagine that the Spirit lives the same life as the man lives below; and this is why they still kill the slaves when they can catch those who were in the service of the deceased, so as to serve him in the other world [Island Caribs, RoP, 484].

There are buried . . . on one side of the deceased his bow, arrows, club, and shield; on the other they place one of his wives to look after and accompany him [Orinoco Caribs, G, I, 201].

On the upper Amazon, when a mother dies, her young infant may be buried alive with her [Sect. 284].

Little bits of bone, fruits, bread, etc., were strewn on the corpse in the grave [Makusi, ScR, I, 421]: fruits, bones . . . and a flask filled with water . . . and a drinking cup [Makusi, ibid., 468]: bread, fruit, and dried fish [Warraus, ibid., II, 446]; at the side we find a vessel which . . . contained the couria to stimulate the deceased on his travels in the other world . . . cassava, bananas [Piaroas, of the Orinoco, Cr, 544-548].

It is almost universal amongst these Orinoco nations either to bury with deceased his arms and ornaments, or to burn them [G, I, 207]. Buried in a sitting attitude . . . and all his implements of war and hunting by his side [St, I, 399]. They place at its side . . . a blow-pipe and a quiver full of arrows dipped in curare [Piaroas, Cr, 548].

The dead are almost always buried in the houses with their bracelets, tobacco-bag, and other trinkets upon them [Uaupes, Rio Negro, ARW, 346].

The deceased is clothed in his finest ornaments; a crown of bright colored feathers on his head: to his neck are attached his collars, his wooden comb, and his deer-bone flutes; the arms and legs are covered with bracelets [Roucouyenne cremation, Yary River, Cayenne, Cr, 120].

Many of the Indian tribes, but chiefly the Caribs, Makusi, and Akawai have the custom of burying their dead either in the hut where they lived, or, if a case of death should happen during a journey, a shed covered with palm leaves is built over the grave to prevent the weather from incommoding the person who rests beneath (ScG, 271). For the alleged reason of making doubly sure of giving the spirit or spirits no cause for wishing to come out of the grave, certain of the present-day Pomeroon Arawaks are said either to plant cassava, or to place a cassava-squeezer, upon the top of it.

77.* The eating of the corpse's flesh or the drinking of a preparation made therefrom, except in those cases in which cannibalism was indulged in rather by reason of vengeance with the object of inspiring terror in their enemies (PBa, 171), was but the expression of another link in the chain of ideas which culminated in a belief in spirit immortality. There yet remained in the flesh and bones of the deceased certain qualities, somethings, spirits, etc., which could be detached, separated, and transferred to the living by means of ingestion. There is abundant evidence among these Guiana Indians of a belief in the transference of individual (animal or human) peculiarities through this agency (Sects. 250, 280). Thus in order to strengthen their own courage and contempt for death, the Caribs of the upper Pomeroon would cut out the heart of the person slain, dry it over the fire, powder it, and then mix the powder in their drink (ScR, II, 430).

The Tariánas and Tucános (of the Uaupes River) and some other tribes, about a month after the funeral, disinter the corpse which is then much decomposed, and put it in a great pan, or oven, over the fire, till all the volatile parts are driven off with a most horrible odour, leaving only a black carbonaceous mass, which is pounded into a fine powder, and mixed in several large couchés (vats made of hollowed trees) of caxiri: this is drunk by the assembled company till all is finished; they believe that thus the virtues of the deceased will be transmitted to the drinkers. [ARW, 346.]

The Salivas on the Orinoco also pursued the practice of digging up the bones, burning them, and then collecting the ashes to mix with their drinking water (Bri, 267).

On the other hand, in the lands back [of Cayenne] there are nations who disinter the bones when they consider the body is putrid enough, and after calcining them, drink the ashes which they mix with their vicou, believing that by this means they are giving the defunct a more honorable burial than by leaving them a prey to worms and corruption (PBa, 231).1

78.* Surely it is not unreasonable to suppose, granted certain spirits and other agencies were believed to be contained in the corpses, that the bones of the deceased distributed among friends and acquaintances, or slung up in their houses, must have served a purpose other p. 159than that of an every-day gift or ordinary ornament. The Island Caribs certainly used the bones of their friends for purposes of witchcraft and prophecy (Sect. 91). The practice of exhuming the remains after longer or shorter intervals, although not direct evidence, may nevertheless indicate the existence in former times of a similar use for the bones among the Mainland Caribs and other tribes. Thus, at the expiration of the year, the decomposed body is dug up and the bones are distributed to all the friends and acquaintances (St, I, 399). The bones, having been cleaned by the fish, are packed according to size in a basket already provided, worked with glass beads of various colors; care is taken that the skull of the deceased forms the lid of the basket. The basket is then hung up to the roof of their houses (among the Warraus of the Orinoco) along with the many other baskets containing the bones of their forefathers (G, I, 199). The women (among the Caribs of the upper Pomeroon) who prepare the bones are considered unclean for several months (ScR, II, 431-2).

79.* With regard to the abandonment by the Indians of the locality where death has taken place, nothing can conquer their fear lest the deceased's spirit, located somewhere in the immediate neighborhood, should do them harm. On the Orinoco the practice of rooting up the fields which deceased has planted, so soon as his widow or widows have buried him, is also almost universal: They said they do it to destroy all memory of the deceased (G, I, 207).1 With the Anabali and other tribes of this same river, when anyone dies they bury him in the place where he had his hearth and, covering the grave with many mats, they forsake the village and all their fields, and build and sow at 12 or 15 leagues' distance. They say that when death has once entered their village they can not live in security. But when these people subsequently advanced to a settled life—as soon as the sick person died they broke up his home and burnt everything which the deceased possessed (ibid., 206). One of the chief's wives had died; and in consequence, although the settlement was quite new, the houses most comfortable, the cassava still in the field, every man had abandoned it, and left this poor Indian to look after the crops (Rupununi River, ScG, 238). In an Ojana village (Tuwoli's) on the Tapanahoni (Surinam) three people died in 1907—Tuwoli's adult son Paleku, and two others. One house of Tuwoli and one of Paleku were burned. A month later, the village was deserted—the survivors had established themselves in another one (Go, 15). Among the Roucouyennes on the upper Parou, Cayenne, the common laity must not make the slightest noise, or approach anywhere near the grave of a piai, for fear of meeting his fellow-colleague, p. 160the Tiger medicine-man who guards the corpse, but the spirits of the distinguished dead may be visited by "doctors," by the common crowd, and by animals for the special purpose of consultation (Cr, 298).

80.* Of other obscure burial customs—obscure in the sense that their real signification has been only approximately, if at all, determined—may be mentioned that of the Island Caribs (BBR, 252) who place two weights on the eyes of the deceased, so that he may not see his parents and thus make them ill (Sect. 253). Most extraordinary of all, however, would seem to be the procedure followed by the Warraus at the mouth of the Orinoco:

On the death of a woman, the husband lies down in front of her. He remains there a few minutes, weeping and singing, and then makes way for each and all who have ever had connection with the deceased. As no Indian will willingly act contrary to the established usages of his tribe . . . such a custom seems calculated to prove a check upon persons who are not desirous of having their actions exposed to public notoriety. [Cr, 612.]

81.* While certain of the Indians appear to hold advanced views respecting the immortality of that particular spirit which, on its departure from the body, takes on an anthropomorphic form, they are not in agreement as to the place of translation. This may be identical for the spirits of "good" and of "bad" people, as is the belief of the Warraus and the Makusi, or at all events the places may not be very far apart (e. g., the Caribs of the Yary River, Cayenne). According to the views of these people, the spirits of the "good" and "bad" [within certain limitations to be immediately discussed in this and succeeding paragraphs] rise after death toward the skies, which they call Capoun.1 The former travel high, very high, above the clouds where they find pretty women; they dance every night; they drink cassiri, and do not work in the clearings (provision-fields). The wicked remain below the clouds where they are always roaming without any hope of getting higher. If the body is burned immediately after death, this is done in order that the spirit may ascend with the smoke (Cr, 298). There are interesting records left to us concerning the Island Caribs: (a) Some hold that the most valiant of their nation are carried after death to the Fortunate Isles, where they have everything they can wish for, and that the Arawaks are their slaves; that they swim without being tired, in the wide and large rivers; and live delightfully and pass the time happily in dances, games, and feasts, in a country which produces all kinds of good fruits without being cultivated. (b) On the contrary those who have been cowardly and timid in going to war against their enemies, have, after death, to serve the Arawaks, who inhabit desert and sterile countries which are beyond the mountains. (c) But others, the most brutal, do not trouble about what takes place p. 161 after death: they neither dream not talk about it (RoP, 484-485). The Arawaks maintain that the spirits of "evil" people wander continually around an uninhabited desolate, barren place, while those of the "good" occupy the air above their former huts and settlements, but the conceptions of these Indians as to "good" and "bad" are not identical with modern European views. For instance, if an Arawak by any action of his proves himself a coward or faint-hearted, or succumbs too frequently to excesses in drink, he is called mako-burokwa ['one who forgets'], a man without sense, while one who shows a blameless disposition and has remained a stranger to continual intoxication, is named a kaka-burokwa, or brave man (ScR, II, 497): the spirits of two such people will be separated on the lines just indicated. It must not be forgotten, however, that these Arawaks, of all the Guiana Indians, have been longest in contact with civilizing influences, and that this idea of a future existence dependent on present conduct may be but a borrowed one. Speaking generally, the trend of opinion among the so-called unsophisticated Indians is that certain of the spirits of people departed hasten to a place where they will have all they want, and meet their friends who have gone before. The prevalent neglect of the South American natives of the sick and the want of love in dealing with them can become intelligible, in Schomburgk's opinion (ScR, II, 318), only on the assumption of their belief in some such religious tradition as this.

82.* Certain Venezuelan Indians believed that the spirit retires to certain lakes and is swallowed by monstrous serpents, which transport it to a paradise where its time is occupied in constant dancing and drinking (FD, 52). The Otomacs declare that peoples' souls all speed toward the West to a place where without trouble or toil they live at ease, but before they reach it, they are met by a big bird called Tigtitig, which seizes upon and swallows them, unless they valorously fight it (ScR, II, 318). Humboldt (II, 249) speaks of this fabulous bird as Tikitiki and makes it responsible for the deformities of new-born children (Sect. 279). In the province of Curoana are several lofty mountains, the highest of which is Tumeriquiri.

In this mountain is situated the cavern of Guacharo, which is so celebrated among the Indians. It is very extensive, and serves as a habitation to an immense number of nocturnal birds, especially a new species of the Caprimulgus, Linn., from the fat of which is procured the oil of Guacharo. Its situation is commanding, and ornamented by the most luxuriant vegetation. From this cavern issues a river of considerable size, and in the interior is heard the doleful cry of the birds which the Indians attribute to the souls of the deceased, which according to them, must of necessity pass through this place in order to enter the other world. This privilege they immediately obtain when their conduct has been irreproachable throughout life. In the contrary case they are confined for a longer or shorter time in the cavern, according to the magnitude of their offences. It is this dark and dreary abode that forces from them those groans and lamentations which are heard without. The Indians are so fully persuaded of the truth of this tradition, . . . that immediately on the death of any of their relations p. 162or friends, they repair to the mouth of the cavern, in order to ascertain whether their souls have encountered any obstacles, or been allowed to pass. . . . Whatever the fate of the defunct's soul they give themselves up to the same excesses [drink], making no difference but in the nature of the dance. [FD, 129-130.]

The superstitions connected with this cavern are recorded also by Humboldt (I, 258).

83.* It has been mentioned (Sect. 81) that in the case of a spirit taking on an anthropomorphic form there were indications showing that its future state may sometimes depend on the character of the individual whence it had been derived. But mainly for the reason that the more complex ideas on this subject, as will have been recognized from even the few illustrations already given, are to be met with among those of the tribes which have been longest in contact with European influences, I am inclined to the opinion that the belief in a future condition directly dependent on present conduct is not only of comparatively late introduction, but is a borrowed one; the purgatorial nature of the ordeals to be successfully undergone by the spirits (Sect. 82) certainly savors strongly of Roman Catholic influences. In a sense this opinion is strengthened by a study of the Orinoco Indians, whose original beliefs have been preserved through the careful investigations of Father Gumilla, one of the very first of the missionaries to labor among them. I have searched his writings in vain for any reference to the doctrine of conditional future reward or punishment, or to that of a purgatory. In the same manner, on the Aiary (Rio Negro), the Siusi Indians, an Arawak group which has been but little in contact with civilizing influences, apparently make no distinction between good and bad spirits, all the members of the tribes after death finding their way to a forest upon high mountains on the upper Içana (KG, I, 166).

84.* So again there does not appear to be sufficient warrant for many of the old travelers and missionaries making that arbitrary distinction of "good" and "bad" spirits (according to the bodies whence they have been derived) which has led to so many disastrous misconceptions. The Indian's idea of these comparative virtues is, as might have been expected, simplicity itself, in that a spirit is good or bad according as it is for or against him, that is, inclined to help or to harm him; it is only from this point of view that he concerns himself with the spirit at all. A spirit may be good as judged by its source of origin (e. g., a brave man), but bad as regards the evil which it happens to inflict upon the person concerned. Thus it was among the Carib Islanders, that the good Familiar Spirits, the Chemin or Icheiri, (Sect. 67) were sent by their human associates as messengers to carry sickness and evil to their enemies (RoP, 472). As a matter of fact, the above-mentioned misconception of the Indian's point of view affords an excellent illustration of the error into which certain authors have fallen in failing to recognize the very wide p. 163distinction existing between the Evil Spirit, or Maboya, of the Carib Islanders, and their Good Spirit, or Chemin, when pursuing evil courses. It will be convenient to rectify this error, as far as possible, here. Maboya, or Maboia, was undoubtedly of human origin. Thus, of the several spirits which the body possesses (Sect. 69) some "remain on earth changed into beasts or into Maboia" (BBR, 237): they go and live in the woods and forests and are called Maboyas (RoP, 484). That is to say, in the same way that others of the body's spirits attach themselves to the waters, mountains, skies, etc., and remain there, so the Maboya attaches itself to the bush and forest. Indeed, there can be no doubt that the Maboya of the Antilleans corresponds in every sense with the mainland Spirit of the Forest, that is, the Yawahu, Hebu, Yurokon, etc. (Sect. 94). The Mainland Caribs of Cayenne actually used the identical term Maboya (PBa, 206). The people never invoke Maboya, as some imagine (RoP, 472): notwithstanding the extent to which he or it may be feared, and in spite of the brutality of the treatment received at his hands, the folk do not honor him with offerings, prayers, adoration, or sacrifice (ibid., 476). When the proverbial "pain and anguish wring the brow," Indians believe that these are due to the Familiar Spirits of some of their enemies by whom they have been sent (ibid., 473). When a person is sick, the offerings (anacri, Sect. 89) laid on the little table (matutu) are not for the Maboya, as (incorrectly) stated in one passage by

Rochefort and Poincy (ibid., 563), but for that Familiar Spirit which had been instructed to convey the sickness, or for that Familiar Spirit which had played an important part in effecting the cure, as (correctly) mentioned by the same authors in another passage (ibid., 472). It is known also that the Island, as well as the Mainland, Caribs painted or carved a hideous figure of this spirit in front of their canoes, not only to frighten their enemies, but in order that the spirit's contemplation of its own likeness might divert its attention into other channels. This figure was said to be Maboia (e. g., BBR, 236), but as it would be ridiculous to assume the existence of Bush or Forest Spirits upon the bosom of the waters, I am forced to the conclusion that it represented a Chemin, or Familiar Spirit, capable of course of committing good or evil according to its "master's" instructions (cf. Sect. 48).

85.* Individuals can be relieved of the presence of undesirable spirits by means of the piai-rattle (Sect. 289), as well as by so-called "kissing" and "blowing." It is this latter method that I propose discussing here. While one writer talks of kissing being "unknown among Indians" (IT, 193), another speaks of these people expressing tenderness by kissing, not on the lips, but on all parts of the body (Cr, 175). If osculation is to be regarded as a sign of amativeness, the former is an error, because certainly among Caribs, Akawai, p. 164Warraus, and Arawaks, this is expressed by man or woman, in the protrusion of the tip of the tongue between the loosely closed lips. What can also be considered a form of kissing is the custom of one individual blowing upon another under particular circumstances. The object of this blowing is explained by Schomburgk (ScR, II, 254) on the principle that both by the Indians "and the Orientals, the breath is regarded as an emanation of the most inward spiritual and mental vigor." A far more satisfactory explanation, however, would seem to lie in the fact that the blowing is intended to drive away an attached Evil Spirit, etc., as is indeed the belief among the Galibi piai (Sect. 310) and elsewhere (Sects. 14, 59, 72, 246, 319) a view which is only strengthened by the particular circumstances, above referred to, under which it is practised, namely, in sickness, or in absence of adequate protecting influences. On the way to Roraima, the Serekong "women brought us several of their sick children for us to breathe upon their faces, and so restore them to health" (ScR, II, 253). At Curasawaka streamlet, "a pretty-looking Makusi mother insisted upon my blowing in the face of her sickly infant, which she believed would act as a charm, and restore her child to health" (ScE, 177). "Before we left, she [the old Indian woman] made the entire party [on our way to Roraima] blow three times on her back for good luck, but whether the luck was for her or for us we never found out" (BW, 217).

[At Taiepong Village, upper Potaro] when on the point of leaving, a woman stepped forward to an old Indian in one of our canoes, and held up her head. He tapped her forehead with his fingers, muttered a few words, and then blew on her temple. This was done to charm away a pain in the head, the old fellow being a peaiman, and capable of effecting such cures. On our arrival at villages I have sometimes seen a woman carry her infant round to one after another of the Indians of my party, each man as she passed stooping down and blowing gently on the face of the child. [Bro, 202.]

Among the Arawak and the Warrau, when the child cries, or when father or mother leave it to set out on the chase, to work in the field, etc., they will blow either on the child's face or hand; but they do nothing of the sort on their return. It is a Makusi custom for the infant to be blown upon (angeblasen) by the relatives, before its parents take to their hammocks (ScR, II, 314) to keep the couvade. With the same tribe, the piai will blow upon the girl after the menstruation ceremony with the object of disenchanting her (Sect. 267).

Footnotes

p. 156

1 In these last two examples there is difficulty in interpreting the real signification of the shouting into the ears—whether it is the deceased or the mischievous spirit causing the death (Sect. 310) that is being addressed. In North Queensland I have observed a similar custom. There, the seat of intelligence, life, etc., is located in the ear; and at death these escape through this exit: hence, by shouting into the deceased's ears his friends are trying to restore these essentials to their proper place.—W. E. R.

p. 158

1 This was practically the identical reason given me by a North Queensland aboriginal native when I asked her why she had eaten her little child's body instead of burying it.—W. E. R.

p. 159

1 The more probable reason, by analogy elsewhere in the Gulanas, is for the purpose of supplying the necessary drink at the funeral festivities.

p. 160

1 Kabu, Carib term for 'sun.'—W. E. R.

CHAPTER VI
DREAMS; IDIOCY

Head Spirits are the causes of Dreams (86); the Unreality and Reality of Dream-life (87). Idiocy (88).

86.* From Mainland Caribs, those on the Pomeroon and Moruca Rivers, I have learned that the Aka, or Akari, Spirit (Sect. 69) resides in the head. Yurokon, their Bush Spirit (Sect. 94), comes along when the person is asleep, seizes the Akari, and takes it with him into the forest; this causes people to dream, but sometimes Yurokon forgets, and does not bring it back, with the consequence that the individual dies. In dreaming, the Indians say that the spirit is paying a visit to the world to come (KG, I, 167) or has gone for a walk, etc. (ibid., II, 151).

87.* While Coudreau (II, 198) seems emphatic in his remark concerning the Uaupes River Indians, that they have the correct idea of a dream, and do not take for reality the visions of sleep, im Thurn would seem to have an equally positive opinion to the contrary. The latter (344-345) tells us how—

One morning when it was important for me to get away . . . I found that one of the invalids, a young Macusi, though better in health, was so enraged against me that he refused to stir, for he declared that, with great want of consideration for his weak health, I had taken him out during the night and had made him haul the canoe up a series of difficult cataracts. Nothing could persuade him that this was but a dream, and it was some time before he was so far pacified as to throw himself sulkily into the bottom of the canoe. . . . More than once, the men declared in the morning that some absent man, whom they named, had come during the night, and had beaten or otherwise maltreated them; and they insisted upon much rubbing of the bruised parts of their bodies.

Laborde records similar expences from the Island Caribs: "At night, I have heard them, sometimes two at once, complain, cry, wake with a start, and tell me that the devil wanted to beat them. They went on screaming when quite awake," etc. (BBR, 236). Rochefort and Poincy confirm this for the same people: the Caribs are also subject to other ills which they say come from Maboya, and often complain that he is hitting them, especially during sleep (RoP, 474). The medicine-men appear generally to have enjoyed a great reputation as dreamers (Sects. 264, 300). More than this, dreams were sometimes interpreted as omens and auguries; thus, in token of the missionary coming to visit them, and a sign of his approach, a certain cacique told Gumilla that he had dreamed that his lands sown with seed were very dry, and that the rain had fallen just in the nick of time (G, I, 311).

88.* In connection with the idea of at least one of the individual's Spirits being located in his head, it is of interest to record Schomburgk's observations among the Wapisiana on the Takutu River with regard to idiocy: imbeciles are regarded with awe by the Indians, for according to their traditions, these are in close intimacy with good Spirits, and hence their words and actions are regarded as signs of divinity (ScR, II, 54); their doings and sayings are considered oracular (ScT, 44). True it is also that imbeciles are regarded as "uncanny" and that they will often carry out with impunity and success many a deed which people in their right senses would not even attempt. Here is a case in point, from the Warraus.

*THE IDIOT WHO WANTED TO FLY (W)

A man was blessed with a sister and mother, but unfortunately was without good sense, and for this reason he was known as Wabassi (lit., a sickly person). His sister had a dog called Warribisi (lit., a wasp). One day Wabassi went down to the seashore to catch big bunari crabs, and just as he was about to step out of the boat, an immense tiger approached; thinking it was his sister's dog, he exclaimed: "Warribisi! Warribisi! Come on! What are you doing here?" And as the creature trotted up quite close, he seized it round the waist, and tried to pull it into the boat. Of course the tiger growled, but all Wabassi said was, "Don't bite me, Warribisi," and as the animal was too heavy and clumsy to be dragged in, he lost his temper and said: "Stupid Warribisi. Stay where you are, then, and may Tiger come and eat you!" When Wabassi got home, he told his sister that he had seen her dog. She said: "No, you did not. You can not be in your right senses. Warribisi has been here with me all the time." On another occasion Wabassi joined some friends and relatives on a hunting expedition: they came across a herd of bush-hog, and Wabassi shot one. By and by, his friends collected into one big heap all the hogs that they had shot, and Wabassi came to have a look at their spoil, leaving his own quarry behind. "Oh!" said he, "my bush-hog is different from these. Mine has a mark on his head, and a flat nose." So the other hunters told him to go and fetch it and let them have a look. When they saw it, they were much surprised to recognize a tiger, and still more so to learn that his captor had not even met with a scratch. Next day after they reached home. Wabassi dressed himself like a bird, with a feather (representing the tail) stuck into his belt behind; he climbed a high tree and jumped from limb to limb three times; on the fourth occasion he alighted on a dry limb, which broke, and he fell to earth. "How splendidly I can fly!" he remarked, when he picked himself up.

88A.* The picking up, or handling of, certain birds' feathers conduces to loss of memory and to insanity (Sect. 223).

CHAPTER VII
FAMILIAR SPIRITS

The cult of Familiar Spirits reached a high development among the Island Carib folk (89). Though presented with offerings and other things, these Spirits could be invoked only by the Medicine-man (90), and, being more or less intimately associated with human bones, were often called into requisition for purposes of Witchcraft and Prophecy (91). The Island Arawak people also had similar Familiar Spirits (92), the belief in whose existence is even yet traceable on the Guiana mainland (93). Familiar Spirits and Couvade (93A).

89.* The cult of the Familiar Spirit would appear to have reached a high stage of development among the island tribes; at any rate, it is from these people that comparatively complete records of its existence have come down to us. Thus with the Carib Islanders: "The good spirits which are their gods are more particularly expressed as Ichĕiri (by men) and Chemin (by women): They believe that these good spirits, or these gods, are in great numbers, and in this plurality each person believes he has a special one for himself—his own particular spirit, his own familiar: They say that these gods reside in the sky, but do not know what they do there, and they themselves show no signs of recognizing them as the creators of the world and of things that are" (RoP, 471). The precise source or origin of these Familiar Spirits is unfortunately nowhere given, beyond the statement that they leave the human body at death in company with the particular spirit connected with the deceased's heart (ibid., 484). Again: The Island Caribs dedicated no temples or altars to their divinities, these Icheiri or Chemin: they made them no sacrifices. They simply made them offerings of cassava, and their first fruits. Above all, when they believed that they had been cured by them of some illness, they had a feast in their honor and offered them cassava and oüicou. All these offerings are known as *anacri* [*alakri*]: they place these at one end of the hut in vessels, according to the nature of the thing, on one or several *matutus*, or small tables plaited of rushes and palm leaves. Each one in the hut can make these offerings to his [Familiar] Spirit; but such offerings are not accompanied by any adoration or prayer, and consist only of the actual presentation of the gifts (ibid., 472).

90.* To invoke them, however, requires the Boyé (medicine-man), together with incantations and tobacco smoke. This is the case chiefly on four occasions: (*a*) to be revenged on some one who has done them harm, and so draw punishment on him; (*b*) to get cured of some illness and learn the results of it; (*c*) to consult them on the ₚ. 168 issues of their wars; (*d*) and to hunt away the Evil Spirit, Maboya (loc. cit.). When the Boyé has made his Familiar Spirit appear (Sect. *314*), the latter is heard to reply clearly to the questions put to him: he is heard to click his jaws as if eating and drinking the anacri, but next morning they find that he has not touched it. These temporal viands which have been soiled by these unfortunate spirits are deemed so sacred by the magician and the people whom they have abused that it is only the old men and the most illustrious among them who are free to partake of them, and even then they dare not taste them unless they have a certain cleanliness of person (RoP, 473). "They have asked me," says Father de la Borde, "sometimes to drink of it, and I have done so just to try and change their superstitious ideas, one of which is to drink of this oüicou before eating, otherwise you die, and purposely I ate first before drinking; another is to keep the cup straight so as not to spill the contents, otherwise the eyes would run water everlastingly. I purposely spilt some, and held the cup crooked" (BBR, 235).

91.*These Familiar Spirits [Icheiri or Chemin] often nestle themselves inside bones taken from a grave, which are wrapped up with cotton into grotesque figures, and so give oracles: they say it is the Spirit of the Dead that talks (RoP, 473, 479). "They sometimes put the hairs, or some bones, of their deceased parents into a calabash. They keep these in their huts, and use them for some sorcery. They say that the spirit of the dead one speaks through these, and forewarns them of the designs of their enemies" (BBR, 236). More than this, bones prepared with cotton, as above mentioned, are used for bewitching their enemies, and for this purpose the sorcerers wrap them up with something that belongs to their enemy (RoP, 473).

These Familiar Spirits also enter into the bodies of females and speak through them (loc. cit.). In order to turn aside the vials of their wrath and to divert the anger of these Spirits, tobacco leaves are smoked in their honor through the agency of the Boyés, their hideous likenesses are painted on the canoes, or the Indians carry slung around their necks a small embossed effigy representing one of these cursèd spirits in the ugliest position in which it had ever put in an appearance (RoP, 479).

92.* The Island Arawak also had a belief in certain supernatural beings or spirits, and possessed effigies of them; both the spirit and its effigy were known to these folk as Cemi or Zemi. Thus, in his account of the aborigines of Haiti (Santo Domingo), Columbus says:

> But also in all the other islands and on the mainland [Cuba?] each has a house apart from the village in which there is nothing except some wooden images carved in relief which are called Cemis; nor is there anything done in such a house for any other object or service except for these Cemis, by means of a kind of ceremony and prayer p. 169which they go to make in it as we go to churches. In this house they have a finely-wrought table, round like a wooden disk, in which is some powder which is placed by them on the heads of these Cemis in performing a certain ceremony; then with a cane that has two branches which they place in their nostrils they snuff up this dust. The words that they say none of our people understand. [WF, 352.]

In early writings, zemis are repeatedly called "messengers" and were in fact subordinates of the great gods; being possessed like them of magic power to make the yucca grow, to facilitate childbirth, and to cure the sick (ibid., 356).

93.* These Cemi of the Island Arawaks were identical with the Chemin of the island Carib-owned women who, for very intelligible reasons, spoke an Arawak dialect. Still more interesting is the fact that, on the Guiana mainland, the Arawak designation both of the piai and of the various kickshaws and apparatus employed in the pursuit of his craft is Semi-tchihi, or Semi-sihi. Indeed, it is in the cult of the piai where traces of this belief in Familiar Spirits must be sought among the mainland tribes, and it is here where I have been fortunate enough to find some. Thus, the effigy of the Familiar Spirit of the islanders has its representative in the so-called doll (Sect. *290*) and neck-ornament (Sect. *292*) of the Mainland Arawak and Warrau medicine-man, as well as in the "devil"-figure of the Galibi piai (Sect. *311*) and possibly in the maize-straw figure described by Crévaux (Sect. 311). The Spirit itself is met with in the beings invoked by the Mainland Carib doctor when called upon to treat a patient (Sect. *309*): it is indeed not so very improbable that the actual Island Carib term Icheiri (Sect. 89) may be identical with the Mainland Carib word Iakai-a used today on the Pomeroon.

93A.*While frankly admitting that I have no actual proof from the literature or from my own field-work, as to any relationship of the Familiar Spirit with the little Baby Spirit, on whose account the various forms of couvade are practised (Sects. *281-283*), I am nevertheless very much inclined to believe in their identity. I look on the Familiar Spirit as an early stage in the idea of the Conscious Self, the "Ego."

CHAPTER VIII
THE SPIRITS OF THE BUSH
NATURAL HISTORY

Various names applied (94); the Yàwahu—Tukuyuha, Dai-dai, etc., general appearance (95), and special association with the silk-cotton tree (96); Ekkekuli and Mansinskiri (97); an unusual form of Bush Spirit (98); the Hebu (99); the Immawari (100); the Yurokon, etc. (101). But Bush Spirits may be zoomorphic—able to change into animals, as Tigers, Goat-suckers (102, 103). They can be recognized by Sound (104) or by Smell (105).

They are very shrewd; can bring the dead to life, and render themselves invisible (106); may occasionally do kindnesses to people (107), but generally prefer mischief, though this may be due to the Indians' own fault (108); they cause all the mishaps and accidents of daily life (109)—damage crops, raise disputes, bring death and sickness, produce transformations (110-115); they are excellent hunters (116).

They are fond of women, human flesh, and children at the breast (117-120), and of tobacco (121-122); are usually of abnormally large size (123); shrink from exposure of all descriptions; as to daylight, or in connection with name or origin (124); can not endure being mimicked or chaffed (125).

It is best to leave these Bush Spirits strictly to themselves, as they bring only harm in the long run (126-128); if circumstances force one into their company, measures can be taken to rid the house and neighborhood of them (129); also the road when one is traveling (130).

94.* Those Spirits which, emanating from the human corpse, ultimately find a resting place in the tree, field, forest, or bush, are known collectively as Forest Spirits or Bush Spirits. But let us not forget that certain of the Bush Spirits may arise from the dead bodies of animals and birds, and may even develop spontaneously. The generic term applied to them varies with the tribes: thus, in Cayenne there is Hyorokon (Galibi) or Hyrouca (LAP, II, 223), Amignao and Anaanh (Arroua), Maboya (Carib) (PBa, 206) and Yolok (Carib); in British Guiana, Yawahu (Arawak), Hebo or Hebu (Warrau), Yurokon (Carib), and Immawari (Akawai); on the upper Orinoco, the Atabapo, Inirida, and Guainia (i. e., upper Rio Negro), it is Iolok-iamo (AVH, II, 362, 385); on the Aiary River, Iya-imi (Siusi) (KG, I, 113); on the Orinoco, Tanasimi (Achagua), Memelü (Betoyes, Jiraras), and Duati (Guajivas) (G, II, 24); on the Amazons, Caypor (HwB, 279), Curupari (ibid., 36), and Jurupari (ibid., 381), but this word is said to be Lingoa Geral (KG, I, 113). It will be noticed how the term Yurokon, in the form of Hyorokon, Hyrouca, Yolok, Iolok-iamo, Iya-imi, is spread throughout the extent of the Guianas, while in the form of Juluca (Sect. 216) it is met with on the islands, as the personification of the Rainbow. I have also p. 171 shown the probability of its identity with the Shadow Spirit (Sect. 68).

Equally striking is its resemblance to the word Huracan, the name given by the Aztecs to the autumnal equinox. (Cordonazo de San Francisco). Huracan means the Spirit (corazon) of the Sea, the Spirit of Heaven and Earth: the Nahuas were unable to conceive of the author of the universe except in a cataclysm. Cyclone, Hurricane, or Cordonazo de San Francisco are names of the same phenomenon. Hurakan of the Quiche myths is the Kukulcan of the Maya, the Quetzalcouatl (morning-star) of Mexican mythology. Yawahu, the Arawak generic term, includes the Tu-kuyuha, the Ekkekuli or Manahau, and the Mansinskiri Spirits, the Tu-kuyuha being subdivided into Konoko-(Tu)kuyuha and Adda-(Tu)kuyuha, according as they are more specially associated with the bush and forest, or trees, respectively.

95.* Each tribe seems to exhibit variations in the ideas held as to the form, shape, and peculiarities assumed by its respective Bush Spirits. Of some of these I am able to furnish the following particulars: Starting with the Arawak Yawahus, there are the Tukuyuhas, the Konoko variety of which are spoken of by the Akawai as Arai-dai or Dai-Dai, and by the creoles of the Colony as "Bush devils." An Arawak woman told me that such Spirits are hairy people having so much hair that one can not see their faces. They live underground in the forest; they may be men or women; they are met with suddenly, but may often give a premonitory sign or token of their coming. The token varies greatly, and even when taken note of is usually recognized only after the event of which it has given warning has taken place (Sect. 220 et seq.). Having no bows and arrows, these Spirits are accustomed to fight only with their limbs, so that when an Indian has been attacked and returns home, where he is sure to die shortly after, no marks will be found on his body. Sometimes the Konoko-(Tu)kuyuha will not even allow the victim to return alive, but will eat him, causing him to disappear totally; the friends and relatives never see any further signs of him. The attack may be made at any time, day or night. Now, because these beings (Sect. 331) have no bows, or rather what bows they have are broken, the old-time Arawak people used to call them Shimarabu-akaradáni (lit., bows-broken), and when returning home from some hunting or trading expedition, would sing out that name before reaching their houses, with the view of preventing these undesirable Spirits making an entry (Sect. 129).

96.* The Adda variety of Tukuyuha Spirits, particularly associated with trees, are sometimes in the shape of birds: among such notable trees are the silk-cotton (Bombax sp.) and the kofa (Clusia grandiflora). In Cayenne it would seem that the Hyrouca [Yurokon] was specially attached to a tree known as panacoco (LAP, II, 223), p. 172 which thus far I have not been able to identify. The Indian guide breaks his arrow and asks pardon from the Spirit for his European visitor having touched the timber with unclean victims—a fish and an agouti.1

97.* When perceptible to human eyes, the Ekkekuli or Manahau have the appearance of black people (negroes): they are of a savage nature, killing Indians, and abducting children. If anywhere in the neighboring caves and gullies and their names be loudly called in the forest, they will materialize. The Mansinskiri (Arawak), or Maihisikiri (Warrau) is a particular Yawahu wandering about the bush, and in and among the trees, of which the native women, subsequent to certain regular occasions, have to be especially careful. Such Spirits can assume the identical material appearance of their real husbands or lovers, but woe betide those poor women who yield to their solicitations, for they will surely die in a few days. On the other hand, provided the woman is shrewd enough, she can invariably tell whether she is dealing with the real man or not—she has only to look at the left foot; in the case of a spirit wooer, this is always minus the big toe. During February, 1910, an Indian came and gave me particulars of his wife's death, with details as to name, place, and surrounding circumstances. The wife had been out getting firewood in the bush, and had unexpectedly met what she had believed to be her husband. When she got home there was her husband lying in his hammock; she expressed surprise at seeing him, still more so when he assured her that he had not been away from the house that day. Like a good wife, she told him what had happened to her. Within the week the woman died.

97A.* THE MAIHISIKIRI CHANGES THE WOMAN INTO A BUSH SPIRIT (W)

A man went out hunting, leaving his wife behind by herself. It was then that a Maihisikiri appeared, and believing it to be her husband, the woman allowed him to act like one, but he went away shortly before the time for her real husband to arrive. The same thing happened on a second and a third occasion, but on the last visit, knowing that her husband had gone to a distant locality, she expressed her doubts by asking Maihisikiri, "How can you be my husband? he is gone far away." It was only then that he admitted who he really was, a Bush Spirit in her husband's likeness, and he told her to come away with him. When the real husband returned, the house was empty, and no wife visible, but he could hear her laughing in the distance, and approaching the spot found her prostrate, still laughing. She was laughing because the Maihisikiri was sporting with her: her husband of course could not see the Spirit for the reason that he was invisible to the male sex. Now, when he seized his wife's arm to drag her home, it was all soft, with no bones in it, and then feeling her all over realized that she had not a single bone in her body, which was all soft. Returning home, he waited a while, and then returned a second time to fetch her; but she was still all flesh and skin, and so he left her severly alone. All she could say to him was: p. 173"I do not really want to leave you, husband, but the Maihisikiri is too strong for me, I am now a Bush Spirit. And though you must not be sorry for me, I am indeed sorry for you, for you will have to die before you can become one."

98.* An unusual form of Arawak Bush Spirit is that of the scrub-turkey (Tinamus sp.)—a woman's leg: there are several references, however, to a leg in the folk-lore (Sects. 38, 208, 362). The connection between this astral limb and the bird under consideration is that when the "leg" is above the horizon just before daybreak, then will the scrub-turkey's "call" be heard.1

*THE MAN WHO ALWAYS HUNTED SCRUB-TURKEY (A)

There was a man celebrated for his skill in hunting "maam" (Tinamus sp.); he would regularly bring home four or five of these scrub-turkeys, and people warned him that if he continued in this way he would get into trouble with the maam's "mother," (i. e., Spirit), for killing so many or her brood (Sect. 242). But he did not care, and went on destroying the birds in the same wasteful manner. On one occasion he stayed out later thau usual, waiting to see on which particular trees the maams were going to roost. He could hear their peculiar call in all directions around; indeed, the birds were so plentiful about, that he was somewhat at a loss to know which particular one to follow. However, he proceeded to track one, but the farther he went, the farther off sounded the note, until at last he found himself deep in the forest. As night was beginning to fall, he had to hurry home, not daring to remain out in the dark for fear of the Yawahu (Spirit of the Bush) catching him. The same thing happened next day; he heard many birds calling, and, following one, again found himself deep in the forest, but this time he succeeded finally in coming up with the quarry. Locating the tree, he peered in among the branches to see where the bird was "hollo"-ing, but could see only a woman's leg. Recognizing this to be the Arch Spirit of the maams (Sect. 210), he took careful aim, and shot an arrow right into the center of the foot. The leg fell down, and directly it touched ground, changed into an extraordinarily big scrub-turkey, which he immediately killed and carried home. There his friends knew it at once to be the maam's "mother" (Spirit), and advised him to cook and eat the whole of it himself, and not give away even the smallest particle of it. He did what was advised, and in subsequently hunting for maam he was invariably even more successful than before. And now that he had destroyed the maam-Spirit, he was not afraid of killing as many birds as he liked.

99.* The Hebus are more or less hairy beings, recognizable in a near view by the absence of buttocks, their place being taken by a fire-hearth, with glowing embers, giving rise to the name Huta-kurakura, "Red-back," which is often applied to these folk (Sects. 21, 27). Another peculiarity they possess is the extraordinary prominence of the eye-brows (supra-orbital region), which prevents them having a look at the skies except when standing on their heads (Sect. 22). Perhaps this conception is a survival of the custom of artificial head-compression which certainly used to be practised in the Guianas. As is the case with the Yurokons, Hebus may sometimes appear in the form of skulls or skeletons (Sect. 26). Like all other Forest Spirits they have strong patriarchal tendencies. They seem to be specially digtinguished by the size of their purses [scrotums].

*THE SHREWD LITTLE BOY AND THE HEBU (W)

A woman, having to go to make starch out of the ite (Mauritia) tree, left her little children, two girls, behind the house. While she was away Kau-nassa, a Bush Spirit came along, disguised as their old grandmother, and said, "Come along, my little girls. I will take you to your mother." But instead of doing that, the Hebu led them away far into the bush, till they reached a creek where the old woman sat down and made a basket. When it was completed, she told the youngsters to get inside; once they were in, she closed the top, and threw it into the water, where the children were soon drowned. Kau-nassa then went to another house, where a little boy and girl had been left in charge during their parents' absence and, similarly disguised as their grandmother, repeated her story. She led the children as before to the creek, where she proposed making another basket, and they started playing around her. "You children," she said, "must not play behind my back. Play in front of me where I can see you." Now the very fact of being told not to go behind her made the boy all the more anxious to do what had been forbidden. So while playing in front with his sister, he made an excuse to slip away behind, and then he saw the lower part of the old woman's back, which was all aglow with the fire that she carried there. He now knew that she was a Hebu, and getting back to his little sister, carried her home But before going he called out, Kau-nassa! Kau-nassa! So angered and dismayed was the Spirit at being discovered and hearing her name called (Sect. 124) that she burst into wind and flame and flew away.

100.* Of the Immawari I can not get much information, there being few reliable old Akawai in my district: on the authority of Warraus, however, these Spirits have two immense teeth protruding from their stomachs. Had elephants roamed the country within recent geological periods, one could perhaps have obtained an insight into the origin of so extraordinary a belief: on the other hand it is possible that it may be an idea borrowed from the African (Sect. 113).

101.* So also with the Yurokons. All I can glean is that, in common with the other Forest Spirits, the face, body, and limbs are covered with a luxuriant growth of hair. As to the Caypor, a kind of sylvan deity similar to the Curupira, the belief in this being seems to be common to all the tribes of the Tupi stock: according to the figure they dressed up at Ega (upper Amazon) he is a bulky misshapen monster with red skin and long shaggy red hair hanging halfway down his back (RWB, 279). The Curupari (Jurupari, or Demon) is a mysterious being whose attributes are uncertain, for they vary according to locality: sometimes he is described as a kind of orang-outang, covered with long shaggy hair and living in trees; at others he is said to have cloven feet and a bright-red face . . . he sometimes comes down to the rocas to steal the mandioca (HWB, 36) on the upper Aiary River (Rio Negro) the bad forest demon is a bearded dwarf: he jeers the hunters and drives away the quarry from right under their very noses. At times, he kills people with his poisoned arrows (KG, I, 137).

102.* But the Spirits of the Forest need not necessarily be anthropomorphic. They may take the likeness of animals (e. g., "tigers," birds), an especially favored feathered form being the goat-sucker p. 175 (Caprimulgus). These physical attributes of some particular creature or other they may permanently retain, or on occasion discard, as when playing the rôle of a kanaima, or blood-avenger. At the head of the Arapu River near Roraima "in traversing the country between Waetipu and Ipelemouta . . . we were startled by a most singular prolonged cry. . . . The Indians . . . said that the sound must have proceeded from some Arecuna who, having killed one of his own people, had been turned into a wild animal" (Bro, 123). Among the Trios of Surinam certain of these Spirits are Akalamano, the carrion-vulture (Sarcorhamphus); Soni, a kind of vulture or falcon, etc. As with animals, so in the case of birds, those of them which are Bush Spirits bent on inflicting punishment, in the way of blood revenge or otherwise, upon poor mortal man, may be killed by him with impunity. "One small bird which in the early morning and in the evening flits, with a peculiar and shrill whistle, over the savannahs and some times approaches the Indian settlements, is looked upon with especial distrust. When one of these is shot, the Indians suppose that they have one enemy less, and they burn it, taking great care that not even a single feather escapes to be blown about by the wind; on a windy day on the savannahs I have seen upwards of a dozen men and women eagerly chasing single floating feathers of these birds" (IT, 332). On the other hand, there are certain birds—owls, goat-suckers, and others (undoubtedly Bush Spirits in the sense that they have been derived from human beings)—which must not be killed under any pretence whatever. Such birds do not wish to injure "we Indians," but they often come to give us a warning or token. "You will never persuade the negro to destroy these birds [goat-suckers], or get the Indian to let fly his arrow at them. . . . They are receptacles for departed souls, who come back again to earth; unable to rest for crimes done in their days of nature; or they are expressly sent by Jumbo, or Yabahou [Yawahu], to haunt cruel and hard-hearted masters, and retaliate injuries received from them. . . . If it be heard close to the negro's or Indian's hut, from that night misfortune sits brooding over it; and they await the event in terrible suspense" (W, 177). Reference has already been made to the "souls" of people departed being changed into goat-suckers in the cavern of Guacharo (Sect. 82).

103.* The following legend, current among both Caribs and Arawaks is of special interest in that the bird in question is derived from the head of the Spirit itself:

*THE SPIRIT'S BRAIN AND THE GOAT-SUCKER (A)

A man went out hunting for land crab, and was waiting for the rain to fall, because it is only under this condition that the animal creeps out of its hole into the swamps. Now, when the rain fell, it wet his hair; to protect himself, the huntsman, using his p. 176calabash like a cap, pressed it firmly down upon his head, so that but a little of the hair projected from beneath its circumference. Just then a Konoko-kuyuha put in an appearance, and seeing the man in this guise, and not knowing what it was, could not help exelaiming, "What a fine smooth head you have! How did you manage to get it?"1 The man told him that he had just taken a knife and cut his head all the way round, and that if he wished he would gladly do the same for him. The Spirit was delighted, and allowed the skin all round his head to be cut, and peppers to be rubbed over the raw surface to make it heal the quicker; the latter process, however, caused him to groan in pain, but by this time the huntsman had quietly slipped out of sight.2 A long time afterward, many years in fact, the same man, going out into the bush close to the neighborhood where the above event had occurred, met the same Konoko-kuyuha, whom he recognized by the peppers on his head, which had grown into big bushes. The recognition was mutual, and the Spirit reproached him after this manner: "You are the man who peeled off my head. I will kill you." But the man replied: "No. You are mistaken. The person who really did it has been dead a long time. Come with me and I will show you his bones." And he led him to a place where there was a stack of deer bones. These the spirit took up and threw one by one into his waiyarri. He then said to the man, "Let us dance, and make his bones rattle." Whereupon they both started dancing, and while dancing they sang; the song of the Spirit was "Bassana! Bassana! [lit. meaning unknown.] It was you that peeled my head. It was you that punished me. How do you like to hear your own bones rattling for music?" After a time, the man remarked, "This is not a good place to dance. Come over there where I can see a fine flat baking-stone that will suit better." So they shifted their quarters, and the Spirit recommenced dancing on the flat stone. "Bend your head lower," said the man, "you are not doing the figure properly." So the Spirit bent his head lower, but his companion told him that even this was not low enough; so he tried again, and directly he had bent his head quite close to the stone upon which he was dancing, the man suddenly crushed it thereon. The Spirit's brains thus were scattered, and from each piece there 'grew' a wokorai-yu (goat-sucker). This is why we Indians always dread these birds, and leave them severely alone; they come from the Spirits of the Bush, and give us warning of evil—a token that we may expect trouble of various sorts.3

104.* Speaking generally, the Spirits of the Forest can be recognized, even when invisible, by means of the whistling sound which they make. "The first night after leaving Peaimah [Mazaruni River] we heard a long, loud, and most melancholy whistle, proceeding from the direction of the depths of the forest, at which some of the men exclaimed, in an awed tone of voice, 'The Didi' [Dai-dai]. Two or three times the whistle was repeated, sounding like that made by a human being, beginning in a high key, and dying slowly and gradually away in a low one" (Bro, 87). But instead of a whistle (Sect. 118) they may indicate their presence by a noise somewhat like the neighing of a horse, in places where horses are known not to exist. p. 177 They are then described as Kawaiho-Kuyuha, evidently so called from the corrupted Spanish form caballo, and with anthropophagous tastes have unconquerable attraction toward infant at the breast and women encientes (Da, 183). The Hebus, after dark, make sudden sharp noises like the sounds caused by the breaking of branches: as stated elsewhere (Sect. 19), "You can always distinguish a Spirit's road from any other pathway in the forest, because the Hebus occupying the trees that lie alongside it are always, especially at night, striking the branches and trunks, and so producing sharp crackling noises." Of course, in the case of Bush Spirits that are zoomorphic the sounds they make depend on the nature of the particular animal whose form they have assumed. The Caribs in the Pomeroon plant a certain species of caladium in the neighborhood of their settlement, to give warning of the approach of a Yurokon at night: the plant gives a double signal, a soft yet high-pitched whistling sound, and at the same time somehow contrives to shake the hammock with force sufficient to wake the sleeper and warn him of the coming danger. The following extract is from Bates, with reference to the lower Amazon: "At one time I had a Mameluco youth in my service . . . he always went with me in the forest: in fact I could not get him to go alone, and whenever he heard any of the strange noises mentioned above [due to the Curupira] he used to tremble with fear" (HWB, 36). Dance (262) writes on this same subject of what the duties of a traveler are, and how the influences of evil Bush Spirits may be avoided (Sect. 128).

105.* Bush Spirits may also be recognized through the sense of smell. "When the Island Caribs smell something offensive in a place, they will say 'The Evil Spirit (Maboya) is here: let us therefore go away.' . . . They also give the name of Maboya to certain plants, to toadstools, of a bad odor, and to everything that is capable of imparting dread to them" (RoP, 464). The Pomeroon Arawaks have the same idea.

106.* Bush Spirits are certainly very clever people; nothing comes amiss to them, and they can even bring the dead to life. They may render themselves invisible (Sect. 119).

*THE MUTILATED HUSBAND IS MADE WHOLE (W)

There being nothing to do in the field, a man told his wife one day that he was going to another village to do some work for the headman. She said she would accompany him, but he explained that this was impossible as there were only men there. However, she was so importunate, that although it was quite contrary to his own wishes, he yielded to her entreaties, and took her. But he insisted on her traveling in male attire. She therefore cut her hair short, hid her breasts by means of numerous cotton and hog-tooth neck-chains, and covered her nakedness with a strip of bark. When they reached the settlement, they started work in company with all the other men, and as soon as the day's work was done, they all went down to the riverside to bathe. p. 178The woman was at a loss to know what to do: she was alarmed at the prospect of exposure and yet did not want to draw too much attention to herself. All she could do was to wait until the others had finished and then bathe alone. This went on for some days, until the others remarked upon it, wondering why the new-comer would never go into the water with them, but always waited until they had finished bathing. Two of them accordingly set watch, and as a result discovered that it was a woman who had come among them. They thereupon determined on killing the husband so as to secure possession of the wife. They tried twice, but on each occasion something went wrong with their plans. The third time, they tied him in a corial and let it drift out to sea, but the sea cast it back on shore, where a tiger, scenting him, gnawed through the ropes, and set him free. Tiger did not, however, go to all this trouble for the sake of kindness, but for pure selfishness, telling his captive that he now intended punishing him. "Don't do that," pleaded the man, "haven't I been punished enough in losing my wife?" This was but reasonable, and Tiger let him go. The man then walked along the shore a good distance, until he came to a house, which he was afraid to enter; but the house-master bade him welcome, provided him with a stool to sit on, and with food to eat. Having been asked what he was doing, and whither he was going, the wanderer related how he had been robbed of his wife, what he had suffered on her account, and that he intended seeking her. Now, the house-master was really a Spirit, and knew perfectly that what had been narrated was the truth. He told the man to shut his eyes, and when he opened them again, a third person, another Spirit, was present. "Go with this friend," said the house-master, "and you will find your wife." So they went, and traveled far, and eventually came to a house, where they slung their hammocks and rested. In the meantime, the wife had been taken possession of by a "keeper," and was living in the near neighborhood. The guilty couple used to pass regularly the very house where the husband was resting, and when the wife saw him she exclaimed, "Look! there is my husband," but the keeper said that it could not be, because he had been tied inside a corial and allowed to drift out to sea. However, to make sure, they went in, and when they recognized the husband, they chopped him up with an ax. But the Spirit friend restored him to life, and when the wicked people passed again next day, the wife exclaimed as before, "Look! there is my husband!" So they killed him a second time, but the Spirit again made him whole. And the couple passed the house a third time, and just the same thing happened, except that the keeper burned the body, and scattered the ashes. This, however, made no difference, because the Spirit collected the ashes together in a palm leaf, and made them into a living person again. The resurrected husband, acting under advice, then went and destroyed his faithless wife as well as her paramour: their friends and relatives tried to piece the bits together and "make them alive," but this they could not do. It is only Spirits who can do such things.

107.* Certain of the Forest Spirits have come from the bodies of old-time medicine-men: the present-day celebrant invokes them with his rattle (Sect. 309). Such Spirits may be considered beneficent in the sense of assisting the piai by giving him information concerning the source of the illness from which his patient is suffering, and in other ways. Evidently others have been kindly disposed occasionally in that they have conferred blessings and other gifts upon mankind. Thus, Arawak legends point to the Spirits of the Forest as the introducers among them of the flute made from the femoral bone of animals, and according to Akawai tales, of the sewehekuru, or lace-work of hard nutshells tied on the legs to give proper time to the movements in dancing (Da, 184). Sometimes these Spirits do positive good, as in p. 179 the Jurupari festival, whereby sicknesses can be dispelled, and large wounds healed (KG, I, 320).

108.* Sufficient has already been said to indicate that the Spirits of the Forest may have their good points as well as bad; they may indeed have in their nature more of the imp than the rogue. They have not always borne bad reputations, but the very large majority of them certainly do so now. The Caribs, however, admit that they themselves are responsible for this, and concurrently for the introduction of pain, misery, and death.

*HOW PAIN, MISERY, AND DEATH CAME INTO THE WORLD (C)1

In the olden times, there was no contention, all were happy, and no one became sick or died. It was then that the Yurokons used to come and live among us as our friends and associates; they were short people like ourselves. One Yurokon in particular used to come and drink paiwarri with my people, whom he would visit for the purpose regularly once a month. The last time he came, he appeared as a woman with a baby at the breast. The Caribs gave her of the pepper-pot, into which she dipped the cassava, which she then sucked and ate. The pepper-pot was so hot, however, that it burned the inside of her mouth and "heart," and this made her ask for water, but her hostess told her that she had none. Yurokon therefore asked for a calabash, and leaving her baby up at the house, she went down to the waterside, where she quenched her thirst. On her return, she looked for her little child, but it was nowhere to be seen: she searched high and low, but all in vain, because during her absence some worthless woman among the company had thrown it into the boiling cassiri pot. By and by Yurokon went to stir the cassiri with the usual paddle-spoon, and, while she stirred, the body of her baby rose to the surface. She wept, and then, turning on the people, upbraided them: "Why have you punished me in this way? I have never had a bad mind against any of you, but now I will make you pay me. In future your children shall all die, and this will make you weep as I am weeping. And when children are born to you, you shall suffer pain and trouble at their birth. Furthermore, with regard to you men," continued Yurokon, as she addressed the male members of the company, "I will give you great trouble when you go out to catch fish." And so she did, because in those days we Caribs only had to go to the waterside, bail the water out with our calabashes, and picking up the fish that were left exposed at the bottom of the stream, just put the water back again to breed fish once more. Yurokon altered all this, and made us go to the trouble, annoyance, and inconvenience of poisoning the pools with various roots. What is more, Yurokon killed the worthless Indian who had thrown her boy into the cassiri, and then asked her children what had become of their mother. "She has gone to the field," they said. "No, she has not; she is hunting after genitalia unius personæ tribus meæ," was the insulting rejoinder, a reply which she purposely gave in order to provoke them into a rage. She asked them the same question a second time, and they told her she had gone to bake cassava. "No, she has not," replied Yurokon; "she has bored her way into my ear," an answer supposed to be even more offensive. And she asked them the same question a third time, but on this occasion they told her that she had gone to dig sweet potatoes. As soon as they mentioned the word "potatoes," Yurokon disappeared.2

109.* The general tendency of these Spirits, however, is to do bad, the degree of wickedness of which they can be guilty varying with p. 180 circumstances and locality. Such a Spirit for instance may "be believed in simply as a mischievous imp, who is at the bottom of all those mishaps of their daily life, the causes of which are not very immediate or obvious to their dull understandings" (HWB, 381). When in the manufacture of their native drinks anything goes wrong with the fermentation, the Indians ascribe it to Spirit machinations. The following Warrau story is illustrative of this belief.

*WHY THE DRINK TURNED SOUR

A man went one day to visit some neighbors, but, when he arrived there, found they were all out: as it was already too late in the afternoon to allow of his getting home again before nightfall, he made arrangements to sleep there and return the following morning. He drew himself up on the manicole rafters and turned in. But before I go any further I must tell you that in this house there was a big jar in which drink was being prepared in anticipation of next day's festivities when the

FIG. 1.—Carib String Puzzle, designed to deceive the Bush Spirits.

house-master, his family, and relatives would have returned. Our friend had not been long on the manicole flooring before he saw a lot of Hebus enter the place, and have a look round. He heard them say, "Hullo! here is some drink. Let us bathe first, and then come and taste it. It were a pity to let it spoil." So they all went and washed their skins, and then returned for a good carousal. But when they started drinking, they felt the want of some music, and so they arranged with a labba to play for them. All the tune it could play was its usual grunt, but they were quite satisfied with it, and really enjoyed their dance. Our friend watched them until daybreak, when they took their departure, the little labba tree sneaking away behind a plantain tree. Later on, the household returned, and said, just as the Spirits did: "Let us bathe first and then drink. It were a pity to let it spoil." But the watcher warned them not to touch the liquor because he had kept awake during the night, and had seen the Hebus sipping it. They therefore threw all the drink away. Now, among the household was a widow, who exclaimed: "Yes. I knew that the Hebus were going to spoil our drink." And when asked how she knew, she told them that she had received a sign, or token, because when she was weeping for her late husband, he suddenly appeared before her and told her to cease to cry.

If an Indian loses his way in the forest, the Spirit is the cause. The Caribs, however, know how to circumvent the latter, by making a string puzzle, which is left on the pathway: the object of this puzzle consists in removing, without cutting or breaking, an endless string from off two sticks upon which it has been placed (see fig. 1). The Spirit coming along sees the puzzle, starts examining it, and tries to get the string off: indeed, so engrossed with it does he become, that he forgets all about the wanderer, who is now free to find the p. 181road again. In this connection, it is interesting to note that Bates speaks of his Indian boy, on the lower Amazon, making a charm to protect them from the Curupari: "For this purpose he took a young palm-leaf, plaited it, and formed it into a ring which he hung to a branch on our track" (HWB, 35).1

110.* On the Orinoco, the Mapoyes blamed the Spirits of the Forest for damage to their fields, the Guayquiries held them responsible for all their strifes and disputes, the Guamos ascribed sickness to their occult powers, while the Betoyes regarded them as the cause of the deaths of all their children whose necks they broke so silently as not to be felt (G, II, 23-26). This belief in their being the cause of sickness and death is universal throughout the Guianas. Among the Arawaks it is the Yawahu-shimara, or Spirit's Arrow, which has the property of inflicting pains or ills, the visible causes of which are not discoverable. The Arawaks, however, are not alone in this conception: it is apparently shared by the Caribs, from whom I learned the following:

*WHY CHILDREN BECOME SICK AND CRY (C)

An Indian went into the forest to hunt small deer, and for this purpose built a scaffold upon the trunk of a locust tree (Hymenæa). When completed he sat on top of it, bow and arrow in hand, waiting for the animals to come and eat the seeds that had fallen around. By and by, a Yurokon woman came along with a baby slung over her breasts, and a quake over her forehead. She also was fond of locust seed, and when she saw the fine fruit all scattered about, she put her baby down on the ground right below the spot where the native was seated, and started going round the tree, picking up the seeds, and gathering them into her basket. But while thus engaged, the Indian shot the child, making it cry. The mother rushed back, to find her infant screaming for no apparent cause; she felt it all over, but could discover no arrow. So she took it to the piai of her tribe who soon discovered what was the matter, and extracted the weapon, which he showed her: he sucked it out of the child. "Very well," exclaimed the mother; "Just as that Indian shot my boy, so will my husband shoot his people's children, and make them cry without any one knowing the reason."

111.* In Cayenne, it is Hyorokon, the Bush Spirit, who strangles some, corrupts the blood of others, covers this one with ulcers, and that one inflicts with jaundice. The same Indians believe also in a Spirit called Chinay [thus far not identified by me], who is a real cannibal and sucks their blood, which accounts for their being so thin when sick (PBa, 206). This belief (in the work of the Spirits) explains a peculiar trait of Indian character which would otherwise be inexplicable. Believing that a child who has just fallen into the river or has gotten beyond its depth is being drowned by the will or agency of a Spirit, the Indian who passes by and sees the struggling child is afraid to incur the wrath of that Spirit, by any interference on his part to save the child. He thinks he will have done his utmost duty as a neighbor by informing the parents of the fate of their child p. 182(DA, 290). So again, because sickness is regarded chiefly as due to Spirits, the method of cure is therefore mainly directed to driving them out by means of presents, through the agency of the piai, etc.1

112.* Death, sickness, and other calamities may be inflicted by the Spirits upon mankind, not only out of pure malevolence, but also by way of punishment for transgressions committed against the recognized rules of law and order as understood in Indian society. The other calamities just referred to include, inter alia, transformation into various beasts and birds, and spontaneous disappearance. The following five legends from the Warraus and Arawaks illustrate these points pretty clearly.

*THE WOMAN KILLED BY HER HUSBAND'S SPIRIT (W)

A party of Arawaks, all of them married men, once went to Morawinni, on the way to the Berbice, where they were murdered, Their wives whom they had left behind here [in the Pomeroon] took other men, all except one, who was very sorry at losing her husband, and would not take another one. She found consolation in her two little children. Later on, it happened that the whole settlement went off to a drink-party, but this same woman preferred to remain behind alone. When night came on, she heard the harri-harri (flute) playing in the river, and the sound gradually coming nearer and nearer. Recognizing it as her husband's, she turned to her child and said, "That tune is like what your father used to play. Perhaps he alone was saved when all the others were killed." As a matter of fact, it was indeed the man's Spirit trying to come back home again. On reaching the landing, he tied up his corial and came up to the house, when she recognized him. After saying "How-day?" he asked her if she were well, and then inquired after the two children. He next told her to sling up his hammock, for he was come back sick. When rested in his hammock, he began to relate all that had happened, and how he and his party had all been killed. By and by he said, "Go and fetch a light: there must be a lot of dog-fleas about: they are biting my back terribly." But instead of dog-fleas it was worms that were gnawing into him, and when she brought the fire-stick, his wife could see them all crawling in and out, and said, "No, No! There are no dog-fleas there." Now, from seeing all the worms she knew that it must be her husband's Spirit, and not his Body, that had returned, and it was a token of something that was to happen. Again, and still a third time, he asked her to pick off the dog-fleas, but she persisted in her "No, No! There are no dog-fleas there." At the same time she began to consider how she could best save herself. She began to spit, and continued spitting in the same spot until there was quite a pool of spittle, when she quietly slipped away from the house in the direction of a neighboring settlement. Now, when the Spirit again asked her to come pick off the dog-fleas, it was the Spittle that answered "No, No! There are no dog-fleas there." And so the same question and answer were repeated. But when the Spittle was finally all dried up, it could not speak any more, and as soon as no reply came, the Spirit got out of his hammock and followed his wife's tracks. Now, although the fire that she was carrying had gone out, she still went on in the darkness, the Spirit holloa-ing behind. As he was closing in upon her, she remembered an old armadillo hole, in which she hid herself, while the Spirit, rushing along, passed on. He, however, soon saw that he had been tricked, and returned to the place where she had so suddenly disappeared. Here he stopped and pondered a while, and she heard p. 183him to say to himself: "I am dead. But though dead, I am looking for her, and I shall soon make her dead also," and with this she lost sight of him in the darkness. Emerging from her hiding place, she reached the next settlement, and told her friends exactly what had happened. And what the Spirit had said was quite true: she soon became sick, and died.

112A.* THE RESULT OF STEALING OTHER PEOPLE'S PROPERTY (W)

Twenty men started out to hunt bush-hog, taking with them their hammocks, as they expected to be out some days. They soon picked up tracks and followed them until nightfall, when they camped. Next morning they continued on the tracks until about mid-day, when they noticed plenty of victuals all stacked ready for consumption: there were drink and meat, plenty of everything that an Indian can desire. They asked one another, "Are you going to eat of this?" Some said, "Of course I am. Why not? Isn't it all ready prepared for us?" But others said: "No. It is not ours. We will not eat what does not belong to us." The wishes of the majority prevailed, however, and all except two of the party partook of the fine food. When all was eaten, they resumed the trail until nightfall, and they again camped. The two, however, who had declined to eat, erected their banab at a distance apart from the others. And all, except these two, fell fast asleep. During the night the Hebu came along with a light in his hand, and approached the spot where the eighteen were sleeping. When he got close to the first man, he extinguished the light, and, sucking the air through his half-closed hand, extracted his victim's eyes, just as we suck the flesh out of one end of a crab-claw. He did the same thing in turn to each of the other seventeen, and then withdrew. The two who were camped in the banab apart from the others, kept awake, and watched everything that happened. Next morning early, as each of the eighteen woke, he exclaimed, "Me, eye out! Me, eye out!" The poor fellows who had thus been blinded called out to the other two who had not eaten of the food in question, and asked whether they had also lost their eyes. The latter said "Yes" at first, but being pressed again and again to tell the truth, were finally forced to admit that nothing evil had happened to them. Now, some of these blind people felt their trouble very keenly. Some of them had big women at home, and some had little girls there—little girls to whom they had looked forward to making their wives some day. Indeed, those of them who possessed such little girls grieved sorely, and said: "We have little girls at home, and as yet we have never had anything to do with them. Alas! Alas! If we had only made women of them before this trouble fell on us."1 So as to get home again, the blind ones told their uninjured mates to loosen the strings from all their bows and tie their ends together so as to make one long string of them. The eighteen held on to this string, and the two led the way, and so they proceeded on their journey homeward. But the two uninjured ones led the way, not homeward, as they had been told to do, but toward a big pond that contained a large number of pirai (Serrasalmo) fish. Reaching there, the two made the blind ones surround the sheet of water in the form of a circle, telling them that they were about to cross a river, and that when they heard a splash they must immediately rush in straight ahead. The two leaders then stepping behind, threw over the heads of their blind companions some heavy pieces of timber: as soon as these fell into the water, there was of course a splash, and all the eighteen blind ones rushed ahead only to knock up against one another in the middle of the pond, where the voracious fish mutilated and destroyed them. They were thus punished for taking food which did not belong to them.

113.* THE MAN CHANGED INTO A BEAST (W)

Two brothers set out in their corial to shoot morokot (Myletes) fish, after telling their old father where they were going. The younger, who was steering, started singing. "Don't do that," said his brother; "if you make that noise, we shall get no fish and father will be disappointed." But he would not heed, and went on making a disturbance, so the elder one said: "This won't do. I will leave you on shore." The latter evidently had no objection, and with an "All right; leave me here," stayed on the bank where his brother left him, still continuing his singing, which, if anything, he now raised to an even higher pitch. The elder brother then recognized that it was a token of something that was about to happen, and paddled on by himself to shoot. He shot one morokot, then a second, and then a third, now that there was no noise about. Having shot enough, he went to pick up his brother at the river bank where he had left him, but found him singing even "more high" than ever before: indeed, so deafening was the noise—such a rolling and a roaring—that, becoming frightened, he went home without him. The father asked him where his brother was, and when he was told that he was screaming loud and that there was something wrong with him, he would not believe it, but said he would go to see for himself. So the two returned to the spot where the younger brother had been left; the old man heard the awful noise in the distance and followed the tracks from the waterside. The tracks were very prominent and the leaves on each side were much crushed and damaged, showing that a big carcass must have passed that way. At last the father came upon his son, and said, "Come! Come!" but all the reply he received was a terrible roar, which frightened him so much that he turned back, his son following. The latter had now been changed by the Hebu into an evil beast, which was ready to kill anybody and anything. On reaching the waterside again, the father told his elder boy his experiences with the younger one, that he was on the road behind, and that they must both be prepared to shoot as soon as he put in an appearance. At last the latter came out into the clearing and they shot him. It was lucky they did so, because he was already changed into a beast from the neck downward, with two big teeth on his belly (Sect. 100). Had he kept quiet when his brother warned him, all this trouble would not have happened.

114.* THE MAN WHO DINED AFTER DARK (A)

[Note.—It would appear that in the olden times, it was strictly "taboo" for anyone to take a meal after nightfall, though the true reasons for such a restriction are seemingly not now obtainable. (Sect. 246.) The certain punishment for infringement of this taboo was the transformation of the offender into some bird or beast. The following legend bears on this belief.]

There were once two fishers. I do not know their names, but they were friends. They went out together one day to a neighboring creek, and started building a shed, as they intended setting their hooks in the course of the afternoon, remaining there all night, and visiting their lines next daybreak. The shed built, and the hooks all set, they came back late to the banab, and while resting there, they happened to notice near by a kokerite (Maximiliana) palm with a splendid bunch of ripe nuts. These they cut down and began eating after breaking them on the stones. They were delicious, and they continued eating, until one of them noticed that the Sun was about sinking on the horizon, when he warned his friend to stop, advising him to follow his example and turn into his hammock. But the warning was unheeded: he said they were so sweet that he couldn't stop, and he continued breaking and chewing the nuts until long after dark. Then, all of a sudden, instead of breaking the nuts with a stone, his friend in the hammock heard him breaking them in his teeth, and knowing well that no Indian could do this, the friend felt convinced that something had happened. He lit his wax torch, and instead of a man, he saw a tiger crunching the seeds. He slipped out of his hammock, wandered about till p. 185dawn, picked up his hooks and hurried home. When his mate's mother asked him why her son had not accompanied him, he told her that he had persisted in eating after dark, and that he was now a Yawahu tiger. But the old woman would not believe him; he therefore advised her to come with him so that she could see for herself. He took her to the banab, and told her that her son was in the bush; so she went out and Hallekuba? (i. e., How are you?), and a deep rough voice answered, "That's your son," but again me would not believe. Wanting to see for herself, she went alone into the bush in the direction of the sound, although she was strongly warned not to do so. She went on and on, and at last met the tiger, who sprang upon and killed her. The mother was punished because me would not trust the man when he told her that the tiger really was her son.

115.* HOW THE HAIMARA CAME TO HAVE SUCH FINE BIG EYES (A)

Returning on his way home from the bush one afternoon, a hunter met a Konoko-kuyuha making a basket, but though he did not actually recognize it as the Spirit of the Bush, he certainly recognized the uncanny appearance it presented on account of its having the entire face, body, and limbs covered with thick hair. He asked the Spirit what it was doing, but the only word it deigned to answer was bako, the shortened form of bako-ké.1 At any rate, when he reached home, he related his experiences to his family and friends, and advised them strongly not to go to sleep that night, because It, whatever it was, might pay them a surprise visit after nightfall; all he could tell them was that it was covered with hair, and that it was making an eye-socket basket. But they all laughed at him, and turning into their hammocks as usual, told one another stories, and soon fell off to sleep. The man who had warned them alone kept awake, and, recognizing the low whistle in the distance, tried to arouse his friends by shaking their hammocks; but it was all in vain, and he had only just time enough to clamber up into the roof, when It, which he now recognized to be a Konoko-kuyuha, entered the house. Once in, the hunter was able to watch its movements without being himself seen. He saw the Spirit stealthily approach each hammock and remove both eyes of the snoring occupant without waking him. These eyes it carefully placed in the now completed basket, and then it left the house. Next morning, when all the people awoke, they discovered that they could see nothing, and they wondered what had happened, but he who had previously warned them told them everything. They said they were not now fit to live on the land, and that he must take them to some waterside. He thereupon tied them one to the other, and when they reached the stream he tied the last one to a tree: they could not lose their way now, and they knew where they were. He accordingly left them, as he thought, in perfect safety, promising to visit them shortly. After a time he redeemed his word, but he found that all of them had in the meanwhile been under water, and had changed into fish, the one exception being the individual tied to the tree who, being able to get into the water only up to his middle, had turned but halfway into a fish. So the man went away, promising to come again. He was a long time returning, so long, in fact, that the Spirit took pity on the last man, and completed his transformation, giving him back his own two eyes, which "are all very fine and large," so to speak, especially for a haimara fish (Hoplias malabaricus), which was what the Spirit changed him into. And when their old friend did return at last, he cut the rope from the tree, thus allowing the haimara and other fish to play about with perfect freedom in the water, where they have since remained. They were punished for their unbelief.

116.* Bush Spirits are excellent hunters, and some of them even know how to employ the rattle, just like a medicine-man.

*THE WRONG RATTLE, THE BUSH-HOG, AND THE BABY (W)

A man with his wife and two sons went one day to a neighboring settlement to join a drink-party. In the house they left their two girls, who were busy making cassiri, and this is what happened to them. Going to fetch some more water from the creek, they heard, as they strolled along, a peculiar sort of cry. It was really Siwara, the Hebu (Bush Spirit), intentionally misleading them by imitating the call of the oto, a bird bigger than the Baridi hawk. So they challenged it in the usual way (Sect. 130), shouting, "Don't cry, but show yourself, or kill something for us." They saw nothing, and they heard nothing further. However, after reaching home, and resting awhile, a young man approached the house, and greeting them with "Good-day, Cousins!" he entered.1 "Where are your parents?" was the next inquiry of the stranger, who of course was no other than Siwara, he having put in an appearance in obedience to the challenge to show himself. And the girls, telling him that they were all away at a paiwarri, offered him cassava and drink. When he had partaken of this, Siwara told them to go and fetch in the powis which he had brought for them: this done, he asked them to bring in his hammock, as he proposed staying over night. They fetched the hammock and slung it at that end of the house farthest removed from their sleeping quarters. "Don't be afraid! I am not going to trouble you." And he spoke true, because the girls slept right through the night without being troubled by him. Next morning early Siwara returned to the bush, but before taking his departure warned them not to tell their parents that he had paid them a visit. Not long after, the father and mother came home, and seeing the dried powis, exclaimed, "Hullo! How did you manage to get that?" The girls lied, saying, "We came upon an oto hawk who had caught it, and we took it away from him." By and by, the powis was cooked and eaten, and as the old father was chewing the portion he had just picked out of the pot, he came across a piece of arrow in it, a kokerite one.2 Turning to his daughters, he inquired of them: "If an oto killed the bird, how did this kokerite arrow get in?" and they had to admit that the powis had been brought to them by their "uncle."3 "Then why did you not tell me so at first?" he rejoined. "Why did you not let me know that he had visited you while your mother and I were away? Go straight away now, and call him in!" So they went outside and shouted, Daku! Daku! and who should immediately answer the summons but Siwara himself. As he entered, the house-master welcomed him, and he sat himself down on the chair-bench that was offered him. "Thanks! Thanks!" he exclaimed; "I was here yesterday, and kept the girls company." Now the old father, who had been to the drinking party, was still fairly bemuddled and hardly knew what he was doing; at the same time, although he had not the slightest idea who Siwara was, he certainly offered his elder daughter to him, provided he liked her. It so happened that Siwara liked her very much, and he therefore turned to her mother and asked her whether she would care to have him for son-in-law. She said, "Yes, very much." And thus it came to pass that the Hebu obtained his wife, and arranged to take up his abode with her at her father's place. Siwara, however, proved himself a very good husband and son-in-law, and always returned from his hunting expeditions well loaded with game. He also took the trouble to teach his wife's brothers how to shoot bush-hog. Formerly, whenever these two fellows went out and brought back a bird, they would say they had brought back bush-hog. You see, they did not know what a bush-hog really was. So he took them out one p. 187 day, and when the reached a suitable spot, he shook his maraka (rattle) and bush-hogs came rushing up in obedience to the summons. "This is hog; shoot," said Siwara, but the two brothers, who had never seen one before, were frightened and climbed up a tree, so he had to kill three or four by himself, and these they subsequently took home. Time passed, and, his wife having presented him with a baby, Siwara became a recognized heir of her family's possessions, and removed his own property, which he had hitherto kept in the bush, into his father-in-law's house, which henceforth became his own hearth and home.1 Among the property which he brought with him to his new home were four rattles used for bush-hog only. There are two kinds of hog, the timid (eburi) and the very savage (eburi-oriassi), and there were a pair of marakas for each kind: one rattle to call the beast, the other to drive it away (Sect. 298). So after he had hung them up Siwara warned his wife's people that on no account must they touch these marakas during his absence, because trouble would be certain to ensue. Siwara soon afterward went away to cut a field; during his absence one of the brothers-in-law came home, and, seeing the prettily feathered rattles all in a row, could not resist the temptation of taking one down and scrutinizing it closely. While absorbed in its contemplation, he forgot all about the injunction, and started shaking it. Good Lord! It was the wrong rattle—the one for the wild bush-hog! And now these savage beasts came trooping in from near and far, leaving the poor mother, her two brothers, and the old people barely time to escape with their lives up the nearest trees. In the hurry and excitement, however, the mother had forgotten her baby, which the hogs tore in pieces and devoured. On seeing all this happening below, the fugitives yelled and screamed for Siwara to come quickly and get rid of all these beasts, so that they might descend in safety. Siwara came and, shaking the proper rattle, drove the brutes away. When they had all dispersed, and his relatives had joined him, he looked for his baby, but of course did not find it. He blamed them for disobeying his orders, and was so angered that he left them. It is very hard for them to get food now.

117.* The Spirits of the Forest are blessed, or cursed, with strong patriarchal tendencies, are very fond of women, and of human flesh generally. They have an unconquerable attraction toward suckling babes and pregnant women (Da, 183), a statement which appears to be confirmed in the accompanying legends. I do not know the reason of their supposed relationship to children, but certain it is that among the Pomeroon Arawaks, it was the Yawahus who were asked by the piais to bring babies to those women who wanted them (Sect. 302). On the upper Orinoco it was the Bush Spirit Iolok-iamo who, together with the tikitiki bird, was considered responsible for the deformities of new-born children (AVH, II, 249).

*THE KILLING OF THE BUSH SPIRIT AND HIS WIFE (A)

This is another story about a man who went out hunting one day and took his wife with him. But when he left her as usual one morning at the banab, he did not know anything about a Bush Spirit in the neighborhood and hence could give her no warning as to how she should behave herself. At any rate, it was not long after her husband had taken his departure that a Kokono-kuyuha came to the house and asked her how she fared and where her man had gone. She told him that he had gone out hunting and that she did not expect him until late in the afternoon. The Spirit went away but not before mentioning that she might see him again in the course of the evening: you see, he was greedy and thought it would be less trouble to kill and eat them both at one and the same time. Now, when the husband did return, she told him that a Something had been to see her, and that It intended coming again that very night. "You are not speaking the truth," was all the thanks she got for the warning which she gave him, and after eating his meal, he turned into his hammock where he soon fell asleep and snored heavily. By and by the Konoko-kuyuha came along, giving warning of his approach in the usual way we Indians always signal when we approach a dwelling, that is, by striking a few times on the buttresses of the trees. The wife heard the noise, and recognizing what it was, tried to wake her husband, but was unsuccessful: he slept too soundly. She quickly hid herself. Once in the banab, the Bush Spirit approached the sleeping man's hammock, and tried to wake him: failing in this, he broke his neck, drank his blood, and left him dead. The Spirit then wandered all over the place looking for the wife, but could not find her. She, however, could hear him saying, "If I had known that she intended giving me the slip, I would have finished her off this morning." She saw him leave the banab and go back into the bush, but she remained in her hiding-place until the dawn, when, after burying the body, she ran back home and told her brother all that had taken place, and that she was now a widow. The brother was exceedingly angry, and determined upon killing the Spirit. Next day, he went with his sister to the same banab where the late tragedy had taken place, and the following morning left her by herself there, just as his poor brother-in-law had done, but instructed her to fool the Konoko-kuyuha, should he come, by telling him that her husband was still alive and that he would be glad to see him in the evening. The Spirit did appear again, and was certainly surprised to see her there: he asked her as before, how she fared, and where her man had gone. She told him that he had gone out hunting, that she did not expect him until late in the afternoon, and, if he liked to pay them a visit in the evening, that her husband would be very pleased indeed to see him. The Spirit was only too glad to have the opportunity, and promised to come: in his mind, he said that if he broke the man's neck-bone this time, he would make sure of killing him, and then deal with the wife. As had been previously arranged, the brother returned to the banab soon after midday, and made a special arrow while his sister did the cooking. After partaking of the food, he instructed her how to tempt the Spirit into having a dance with her, and at the same time showed her how to hold his hands, and not to embrace him too closely, so that when he let fly this special arrow it might not, by any chance, strike her. He then went and hid himself. By and by, just as the darkness began to fall, the Konoko-kuyuha walked up, and asked her where her husband was. After telling him that he had not yet returned, she obtruded the glory of all her charms and asked him to dance with her. The Spirit, yielding to her temptations, only too readily agreed. They began to caper, and holding him as she had been warned, she circled him round and round, closer and closer to where her brother lay ambushed. It was not long before the latter was able to take good aim, and, letting fly the special arrow, sent it right through the wicked Spirit who fell mortally wounded. Before dying, however, Konoko-kuyuha looked reproachfully at the woman and said, "I did nothing to you, to make you wish to kill me," but p. 189when her reply came, "No, indeed, but you wanted to," he closed his eyes. How glad the brother and sister were! and the brother said, "We had better tarry awhile, because Konoko-kuyuha's wife will come and look for him." Sure enough, they soon heard the moaning of the Spirit's wife as she came along crying, and saying, "I must get payment for my husband" (i. e., her husband's death must be avenged). So they both hid themselves, and as the Spirit woman passed along, the brother shot her also, and cut up the bodies. When they both got home, they told their friends and relatives about all that had happened, and everybody was delighted.

117A.* THE WOMAN KILLS THE HEBU (W)

When going to a party it is customary among us Indians for the man to start early in the morning, leaving his wife to follow in the course of the afternoon. Well now, on one such occasion, after the house-master had left for the drink-feast, another man came and paid the spouse a visit, telling her that she must come with him to his place. She said: "No! You are not my husband, so I cannot do that." But when he threatened to kill her if she refused, she agreed to accompany him, although her little child told her not to go. This man was really a Hebu, and when he arrived with her and the child at his house, he told her she could have whatever she wanted, pointing at the same time to all the dried meat—game, fish, bird, and human flesh—that was hanging around. Picking what she required, she placed it in the pot and this she put on the fire. All the time she was thinking how she could fool the Hebu, so that when he called her to come into his hammock, her plans were quite prepared. She joined him in his hammock, but refused to lie down in it, and when he told her to kiss and coddle him, she said she couldn't do so because he was covered over so much with hair. He told her where to find a bamboo-knife, and she commenced shaving his face; while holding up his chin, she stuck the knife into his throat and killed him. Rushing off now with her child, the woman joined her husband at the drink-party, telling him exactly what had happened: how the Hebu had made her come to his house, where she had killed him. And when the sport was finished next morning she took her husband to the scene of the tragedy. As soon as he saw the dead Hebu's body lying in the hammock, he was satisfied that she had told him the truth.

118.* THE BUSH SPIRIT AND THE PREGNANT WOMAN (A)

There was a man with his wife living in a house. One afternoon, the husband went to watch for an acouri. By and by she heard a whistling sound, and a man came and paid her a visit: 'tis true he was like a man, but yet different, because there was hair growing all over him. He was really a Konoko-kuyuha, but she did not know this at the time. "Where has your husband gone?" he inquired; and when she told him he was out hunting the acouri, the stranger asked her whether he was very far away, and she replied, "Not very far." To make sure that the husband might not suddenly return and frustrate his wicked designs, the Spirit made the wife shout out three times, and as no answer came, he knew he would be safe. He told her to dance for him, and then came very close to her. This she thought somewhat strange, because she was heavily enciente, but she did what she was told. At last he took his departure, and as he went along he knocked the tree-buttresses with a stick, to make the woman think that it was her husband coming. So the wife was content in her mind. However, it was a long wait for her until her husband did finally come; he had wandered far, and found no acouri. Like a good wife, she made a clean breast of all that happened in his absence, describing minutely how she had been visited by one who was like a man, but yet different, because there was hair growing all over him, and that he had been close to her. The husband laughed, and said: "Nonsense, wife! It must have been some old sweetheart of yours." She replied, "Nothing of the sort;" but p. 190he reiterated, "Yes, it must have been so." It being now already late in the evening, they turned into their respective hammocks, and the husband soon fell into a deep slumber. His spouse, however, could not sleep; she heard the Spirit's warning approach— a low whistling noise—and got up to wake her man, but, tug and push as much as she would, she could not rouse him—he slept too soundly. She drew to one side just in time to see the Spirit enter. She saw him kill her husband and then eat him, and when he had finished, she heard him say: "That was good. But the sweetest morsel has gone—the woman with a baby." She ran away as quickly and as far as her legs would carry her.

119.* THE CONTENTED AND HAPPY SON-IN-LAW (W)

Once upon a time there was a good old man who, possessed of a young wife and a field well planted, lived happily and contented. When off to his field one morning, he met a young man coming in the direction of his house, and noticed that, during the greeting which they gave each other, the stranger kept his eyes fixed hard on his wife in the dim distance. On his return home in the afternoon, he met the stranger again in just about the same place, where his movements seemed very suspicious: he rightly concluded that he was dealing with a Hebu and went on home. Arrived there, he told his wife he was going to hunt a little, and took his bow and arrow with him; but what he really did was to hide in the immediate vicinity. And from his hiding place he saw the Hebu steal into the house and wrestle with his wife, who was just about grating the cassava: he heard her say "No! No! Oh, if only my man were not so far away!" So taking aim, and waiting for a chance not to hurt his wife, he let fly and shot the Spirit. Both Spirit and wife simultaneously disappeared.1 It would seem that the Hebu had dragged his victim to the water's edge and thence thrown her in; fortunately she had caught hold of the bushes alongside the river bank, and came up to the surface. On meeting her husband, she told him she thought she had been dead and never expected to see him more; she told him also how the Hebu had threatened to visit their place again. They therefore went over to her mother's home, and stayed there a long while. At last the old man thought it was time to look over his cassava and plantains, and with his wife and brother-in-law returned to the scene of the outrage. The brother, who was a powerful medicine-man, led the way. As he went along he was accosted by a beautiful girl, who, staring into his eyes, rushed up ready to put her arms around his neck, and then drew back. Now, except at a drinking feast and when she is drunk, no Indian woman would behave in this bold manner, and it was thus that they recognized her to be the Hebu. The medicine-man just looked at her in silence, and she fell dead. The wife also met her death shortly after, and they then remembered having noticed the token; she had omitted to bathe after a meal some days before. But the parents of the deceased girl were very fond of their good old son-in-law, and gave him the younger of their two remaining daughters as a helpmate.2 But the elder one becoming jealous, went over to the husband's place and picked a quarrel with her younger sister; this made the latter go and tell the old man that she was afraid to remain with him any longer. But he said: "No! I don't want your sister. She is much too passionate for an old man like me, whereas you and I get along very well together." The parents then gave a drinking party, at which the old man got so drunk that he fell into his hammock; whereupon the elder sister got in also. He was not so drunk, however, as not to be able to turn her out, which he did. She then said that they would have to kill her before she would let p. 191him alone. And so the brother killed her. On seeing all the trouble that had arisen, and recognizing how he had been the cause of it, the old man offered to go away, but the brother said he would kill him before he would let him go. And so the old man stayed with his wife's parents in the customary way, and continued to live long, happy, and contented.

120.* THE BUSH SPIRIT TRICKED WHILE HUNTING FROGS (A)

A family received an invitation to go to a drink-party, and they all accepted except the daughter, who, in spite of her parents' wishes, refused to go. And so she was left at home, all alone. By and by, late in the afternoon, there came to see her a young-woman friend whom she had not seen for a very long time; at least she thought it was her old friend Dai-adalla (lit., 'My-Knife'), but in reality her visitor was Yawahu, who had taken on the real friend's shape and appearance, the better to carry out his evil designs.1 Being such supposedly good friends, the Yawahu addressed the girl as Dai-adalla, and asked what she was doing at home all by herself.2 When the girl had told her that she had refused to go to the drink-party, the Yawahu said: "Oh, very well. I will stay to-night and keep you company," and so she did. In the evening when darkness was coming on, a lot of frogs were to be heard croaking, which made the girl ask her friend whether she ate those creatures, and finding that she was really very fond of that dish, they agreed to go straightway and catch some. They went out together into the darkness, each in opposite directions, and after a time they began to call out, the one asking the other what she had caught. The Yawahu answered, "Plenty, but I am eating them as fast as I can gather them." Now, this peculiar reply—eating the creatures raw—frightened the girl, who thereupon recognized for the first time the real nature of her fictitious friend. And when the Yawahu called out, "Dai-adalla! how many have you got?" the girl responded, "Plenty, but I am putting them into my calabash." The latter was thinking hard all the time how to escape from her companion to a place of safety; she knew only too well that, notwithstanding the darkness, the Yawahu could tell her whereabouts by the sound of her voice. So when Yawahu called out to her once more, the girl shouted back: "Hush! Don't speak, or make such noise. The frogs are getting frightened, and I shall not be able to catch any more!" When silence reigned again, the girl stealthily retraced her steps to the house, crept gently in, and without the slightest sound turned all the pots upside down. This done, she threw all the frogs away, and climbed up on the roof to await developments. These were not long in coming, nor was the Yawahu, for, waiting a while, and receiving no response to his call, he recognized that he had been tricked and hurried back to the house. Here he groped about in the darkness, and turned up pot after pot, but his prey was nowhere underneath. "Ah!" he exclaimed loud enough for his intended victim to hear, "I would have eaten her at the same time as the frogs if I had thought she was going to get away from me." And so he searched unsuccessfully—there were many many pots—until dawn, when he had to leave. The girl then descended from the roof and waited for her people to return, and on their arrival she told them how the Yawahu had visited her in the disguise of her friend. The father said, "Next time we tell you to come with us, you will obey."

121.* Since Spirits are supposed to have a peculiar fondness for tobacco (Sect. 27), and to be continually inhaling its fumes, the smoke of the fragrant weed is largely used in their invocation (Sect. p. 192 308). Among the Caribs, the first two Spirits that are called on by the medicine-man with his rattle are Mawári (Sect. 309) and Makai-abáni. The latter puts in an appearance with the tobacco smoke, in which he is enveloped: otherwise he remains in the rattle (maraka), coming out only when this is shaken. The former's weakness for tobacco constitutes the subject of the Carib legend here given.

122.* MAWÁRI AND TOBACCO SMOKE (C)

There was once an Indian who was extremely fond of smoking: morning, noon, and night he would bring out his little bit of cotton, strike the stones together, make fire, and then light his tobacco. Even when walking out in the bush he would continue smoking. While thus trudging through the forest one day and puffing out clouds of smoke, Mawári, one of the Yurokons, or Bush Spirits, smelt the tobacco, and, taking such a fancy to it, sent his daughter to fetch the man in. She was a pretty woman and, approaching the Indian, asked him whither he was going. He told her he was searching for game, but she advised him to come with her to her father's place; in fact she warned him that as the old Bush Spirit had really sent for him, it would be wiser on his part not to refuse. And perhaps because she was indeed so pretty, he did not hesitate to accompany her. When he reached her home, Mawári asked him a lot of questions about the tobacco, and begged him to teach him how to smoke. Having learned the art, and taken a violent fancy to it, Mawári next insisted upon the Indian remaining, and preparing the tobacco leaves as they might be required. And so it came to pass that the latter took up his abode with the Bush Spirits as the son-in-law of a Yurokon. When he was given the alligator stool to sit upon, he felt a bit scared, but his wife told him not to be afraid, because the creature would not bite him.1 He remained a long time with these Spirits, so long indeed that a luxuriant growth of hair began to cover his face, body, and limbs. His marital relations prospered, Mawári's daughter in the meanwhile having borne him three children. One day his wife advised him to go visit his mother, so, making ready for the journey, he started off. On reaching his old home, his mother was very glad to see him, but noticing how he was covered all over with hair, remarked, "Where have you been all this while? You have turned into a Yurokon, I think." Although her surmises were not very far from the truth, her son denied all knowledge of those people, and thought it prudent not to remain too long in case he should be asked some more equally awkward questions. And when he took his departure, he carried away with him the cassava which his mother had baked; but neither he nor his wife ate of it, he having become so accustomed now to the various bush friuts and she never touching that kind of food. The Indian never returned home again to his mother, being ever busy preparing the tobacco for his father-in-law.

123.* Whenever my Indian friends wished to impress me with the power and importance of any of their legendary beings, they invariably ascribed to it great size: thus, a black tiger as big as a house meant a very dangerous brute; a bat as big as a tree indicated the "vampire," that sucks people's blood at night with fatal results. I learned that for similar reasons these Forest Spirits are always associated with unusually big things (Sects. 27, 147). Both Arawaks and Warraus have a story of this nature: I attach the former version.

*THE BUSH SPIRIT WITH BIG IDEAS (A)

A Konoko-kuyuka, meeting a man one day far out in the bush, asked him what he was doing there. Learning that he had come to hunt, he told him to go and catch some akara (a species of black land crab). After a while he returned to the banab bringing some with him, but when the Spirit saw them, he said those were not the kind he required. "Come with me. I will show you what I want." With this, he led the huntsman to a big hole in the ground, put his right arm in, and pulled out two armadillos. "This is the sort of akara that I need. What you brought me were only spiders." They returned to the banab, when the Spirit told him to go and fetch some cassava. Proceeding to the nearest house, the man soon returned with a few cassava cakes, but these were not what the Spirit wanted. They went to a neighboring tree, where, pointing to an immense toad-stool, the Konoko-kuyuha changed it into a cassava cake, explaining that this was what he meant.1 The Spirit then sent him for a cooking-pot, telling him that he would find one lying among the roots of a certain tree, which he described to him. The man went as directed, but could see only a bush-master snake. When he came back, and reported what he had seen, the Spirit said: "Didn't you notice that the snake was coiled up like a pot? Why didn't you bring it as you were told?" So the man again went on his way, and when he reached the spot, lo and behold! there was a real cooking-pot painted in all the colors of the snake. When he had brought it to the banab, the Spirit told him to bring firewood next. This he did, but when the Spirit saw it, he said, "That is not what I asked you for." So he took the man with him to a big dead tree, shook it a little, and made it fall, and then carried it to where they were camped. "That is what I call firewood," he said: "What you brought me was only birds' nests!" At any rate, they both soon had the fire lighted, and the armadillos cooked. The Spirit ate all his up in a few mouthfuls, but the man could eat only a portion of his. "Why haven't you finished yours?" remarked the former; "No wonder you Indians are so thin. Look at me. I am big and fat and strong because I have swallowed the whole of my armadillo."2 Having rested in their hammocks, they started hunting again, and by evening time returned with a large quantity of game. When their bellies were satisfied, they stacked and smoked the remainder of the meat on the babracote. After they had retired for the night, the Spirit said that he expected a tiger would come to steal the meat, and therefore instructed the man to keep good watch. By and by, the tiger came, and the man accordingly woke the Konoko-kuyuha. Raising himself from his hammock to get a better look at the creature, the Spirit said: "That is no tiger. That is what I call a yawarri" (opossum, Didelphys sp.), and turned round to resume his slumbers. The man pondered over all this for a long time, and remarked: "Well, if by my kind of tiger he means a yawarri, what sort of a thing does he mean by his kind of tiger?" He thus became much frightened, and cleared out, leaving Ronoko-kuyuha in the hammock.

124.* To conclude this natural history, so to speak, of the Spirits of the Forest, it may be mentioned that, with very rare exceptions, as the Mansinskiri (Sect. 97), they shrink from exposure to sunlight or firelight, from hearing their names called, or particulars of their origin talked about. This idea explains why an Indian will almost invariably refuse to tell these spirit-legends in the daytime, when p. 194 he might be heard by the particular Spirit spoken about and subsequently be mysteriously punished.1 There are certainly many examples in the Indian folk-lore illustrative of the dire results consequent on mentioning either the Spirit's name or his particular origin (Sects. 99, 133, 135, 176).

125.* To mimic the sounds of their voices is of course as bad as laughing at Spirits (Sect. 59) or mentioning their names.

*THE WOMAN WHO MIMICKED THE BUSH SPIRIT (A)

A man went out hunting one day, taking his wife with him.2 Leaving her one morning at the banab, he warned her that a Yawahu would be passing, and that he would be whistling like a bird, but that she must not imitate the sound in any way, because if she did each of her feet immediately would be turned into a sharp piece of stone. She had been by herself some time when she heard a bird whistling, and feeling somewhat lonely without any company, thought she would "call" it. No sooner had she imitated the sound than the Yawahu, which it really was, became extremely angry, and changed her feet into two sharp-pointed stones (cf. Sect. 126): more than this, the Spirit changed her heart into stone also, thus making her "wild" toward her husband. The result was, that when her husband joined her in the afternoon, she tried to kill him, but he, recognizing at a glance what had happened, turned on his heels and ran as fast as possible down to the creek, into which he ducked and dived across; coming up on the oppoaite bank, he rested himself awhile. It was not long before she reached the creek, and failing to see her husband, concluded that he must be in hiding somewhere among the rushes and mud, which she trampled in all directions with her stony spikes. Stamping here and there, she gave vent to her wrath every now and again, saying: "You brute! Wait till I catch you. I know what I'll do with you." She little knew that her husband was listening, and smiling at her all the while. And so she continued stamping and swearing until she at last stuck one of her feet into an alligator that was lying there, and hauled it up on the bank, "sticking" it again and, again, in the full belief that it was her husband. Thoroughly satisfied with her work, she now returned to the banab, her man making tracks for home. But when he got there, his brothers-in-law inquired of their sister, and would not believe what her husband aaid about her having mimicked the Yawahu, and her feet being changed into stone. Finally they tried to kill him. Seeing that they were threatening him, he offered to show them the actual place where it all happened. This being agreed to, they took up their bows and arrows to follow him, and finally reached the banab. No wife was there. So the husband imitated the Yawahu's whistle—now that the Spirit was nowhere in the neighborhood and well out of hearing, no harm could follow—and who should come running up but his stone-footed wife, storming with rage, ready to destroy not only her man but her brothers also. The latter, however, being forewarned, put an arrow into her, and she fell dead; they knew now that the man had spoken the truth.

126.* And so, when all is said and done, it is just as well that we should be circumspect in our conduct and not incur the enmity, with all its attendant consequences, of these denizens of the forest. Indeed, it is far better to keep out of the clutches of these Spirits altogether, and give them a wide berth. Just consider, for instance, what happened to the Warrau who would insist on associating with them.

p. 199
CHAPTER IX
THE SPIRITS OF THE BUSH
ANIMALS AS SENTIENT HUMAN BEINGS

Preliminary (130A). Fables, Tales, and Legends (131-162D).

130A.* It is proposed to devote this chapter to a collection of legends dealing with the many beasts and birds met with in the forest, interesting in that they are all represented as thinking, talking, and acting as do sentient human beings. They are also believed to possess Spirits just like those of human folk. At the same time we must not be surprised to learn that the events and occurrences now about to be recorded are supposed to have taken place a long while ago; but in those days, so the Akawais say, Makunaima made man and animal all of one speech, advising them to live in unity, and judging by the legends here narrated the injunction seems to have been fairly well obeyed. To put the matter shortly, these creatures with human ideas were born so: they "growed." True it is that now and again the fact of the human actor having an animal form, or the animal an anthropomorphic one, is explained as being due to reasons already stated, i. e., by way of punishment or pure devilment at the instigation of the Spirit of some person departed. It is also a firm article of faith that the medicine-man, to whom nothing is impossible, can effect transformation of himself or others, similar to those produced by the Spirits. In addition, there is a widespread Indian belief that at every eclipse of the moon animals are metamorphosed—a tapir may change into a snake, a man into a beast, and vice versa. And so even in the telling of these stories, the Indian expects his hearers to take quite as a matter of course—just in the same way as he is firmly convinced himself—that animals and birds associate with man; that they are all of one and the same breed; that they may equally live, eat, and drink, love, hate, and die. It is small wonder then that the Indian folk-lore is so largely crammed with this same idea of Man and Animal (used in its widest sense) being so intimately interchangeable.

131.* THE HONEY-BEE SON-IN-LAW (W)

A man made up a little family party to accompany him on a hunting expedition, taking with him his two sons and a daughter; he left his wife and the other two girls at home. He took the party far out into the bush, where they constructed a banab and rested themselves. Next day the girl told her father that she was not feeling well, in other words, that it was not permissible for her to build the babracote, to do p. 200 the cooking, or even to touch the utensils [Sect. 274]. "Never mind," replied the father, "just rest yourself. We are not going very far, and we can manage for ourselves." That afternoon they returned from the hunt with nothing, the same result happening on the succeeding afternoon. Was the young woman the unfortunate cause of their bad luck? Next morning, the huntsmen went into the bush as usual, and, not long after they had gone, the girl, who was lying in her hammock, was somewhat startled at seeing a young man approach the banab and stride up to where she was resting; she became very angry when he jumped in. She fought and wrestled with him, informed him of her condition, and tried to get out, threatening what her father would do when he returned. But he held her firmly, assured her that he had not the slightest intention of troubling her, that he had come only to rest himself, and promised to ask the old man for possession of her in the proper manner. So they both lay there quietly in the hammock, discussing their respective prospects and affairs. She learned from him that he had been long in love with her, and that he was a Simo-ahawara [lit. 'bee tribe']; this information calmed her greatly, because it seems that at his first appearance, she took him for a Bush Spirit or Hebu.1 Now, just as Simo had anticipated, when the father returned in the afternoon, he was not at all vexed at seeing the stranger in his daughter's hammock; in fact, he made not the slightest reference to her even having company. And when on the following morning Simo asked the old man for her, the latter told him he could have her if he desired, and the girl consenting, he was received as a son-in-law. Being now one of the family, so to speak, he told all three men to remain in their hammocks, as he would make himself responsible for supplying them with their evening meal. Carrying his bow with two arrows, he accordingly took himself off to the bush, and returning very shortly, instructed the girl to tell her father go fetch in the game which he had killed.2 The father went off to fetch the waiyarri in which Simo had packed the meat, but could not lift it, much less carry it, on account of its great weight, though comparatively small a bundle. He came back for his two sons to help him, but all three together could not raise it from the ground. When they returned to the banab, the old man told his daughter what had occurred and asked her to get Simo to bring up the bundle: the latter accordingly went, but not before telling his father-in-law, through his wife, to get the babracote ready. As soon as Simo brought in the bundle, one of his brothers-in-law loosened the vine rope and, opening the bundle, brought out of it one of every kind of bird and beast imaginable. They had plenty there to last them for months, and it took all three men a long time to clean and cut up the flesh and get it properly smoked. And when all the meat was dried, they started on the homeward journey, Simo arranging for the old man and the brothers-in-law to carry all they could, he following later on with the remainder, which as a matter of fact was five times greater than all their loads put together. You see what a strong man he must have been! And although he gave them a good start he speedily caught up with them on the road, and they all went home together, Simo taking up his residence as is customary, at his father-in-law's place. About a year later Simo found himself the proud father of a beautiful baby boy; in the meantime he had been busy clearing his field. Now it was just about this time that his two sisters-in-law were beginning to give trouble: they had fallen in love with him and were always jumping into his hammock, but as fast as they got in, he would turn them out. He neither liked nor wanted them, and complained to his wife about their conduct. Of course there was p. 201nothing wrong in what her sisters were trying to do, because with us Indians, so long as the women are single, it is no sin for a man to live with his sisters-in-law as well as with his wife.1 But in spite of his objections, the two sisters-in-law persisted in following him about, and while they would be bathing with his wife at the waterside, with him minding the baby on the river-bank, they would try to dash spray over him.2 This was very wicked of them, still more so because Simo had warned them that if water should ever touch him, it would act like fire, that is, first weaken, and then destroy him.3 As a matter of fact, none of the three women had ever seen him bathe: whenever he wanted to perform his ablutions, he would wash himself in honey just as the little bees do. His wife alone was well aware of this, because he had told her that he was Simo-ahawara when they had first met under the shade of the banab. As he was sitting one day on the bank with the baby in his arms, while the three women were washing themselves, the two sisters-in-law succeeded in dashing water over him. The result was that he screamed out, "I burn! I burn!" and flying away, like other bees, into a tree, melted into honey, and his child changed into Wau-uta, the Tree-frog [Sects. 17, 18].

131A.* THE MAN WHO WAS CHANGED INTO A POWIS (W)

A husband, his wife, and her two brothers lived together in a house. One day, when the sky was overclouded, and they all heard the noise of the approaching rain, the husband turned to his wife and told her that the rain always made him sleep soundly. When he turned into his hammock that night, and it happened to rain, the good woman accordingly said to her brothers, "I must tie up my man out in the rain," and they helped her tie him up and carry him outside into the rain where he remained all night. Waking up at early dawn, his first remark was: "I have had a good sleep. You may loose me." And they loosened him. Now although he was in a great passion, he did not show it, but he determined to punish his wife. He bade her get ready to accompany him, as he proposed going a-hunting, and when they reached a suitable spot far out in the bush, he told her to make a babracote and get firewood, because he intended killing the alligator which frequented the neighboring water-hole. But he was only fooling her with the alligator yarn, because as soon as she had completed everything, he killed her, and removing the head, cut up the rest of her body and put it on the babracote to dry. When the flesh was cured, he packed it in a waiyarri, which he had plaited in the meantime, and carried it toward his house, leaving it, as is usual, at some distance from the dwelling. Upon the top of a stick fixed in the ground over the waiyarri he attached his poor wife's head in such a way that her face looked in the direction of her late home. The face carried a silver nose-ornament. He took back with him only her dried liver, and his brothers-in-law welcomed him when they saw the meat. He then gave them to eat of the liver, and they ate it. At last he said, "You must go help your sister; she is weary of carrying such a load of meat." They accordingly proceeded down the path, and it was not long before they saw the head staring at them from above the waiyarri; they recognized it as their sister's and rushed home. In the meantime the husband had left the house in another direction, saying that he was going to bathe at the waterside; but he was again fooling, for on reaching the river-bank, he shoved all the corials p. 202from their moorings, and getting into one, made his way down the stream. The murdered woman's brothers had got home by now, and telling their old mother what they had seen, asked her what had become of the culprit. As soon as they learned that he had gone to bathe, they hastened down to the landing, and finding no corial there, one of them swam across the stream to get one, and both getting in, they gave chase. They pulled hard and soon caught up with their man, but as they drew near, he jumped on shore and climbed a tree, shouting, "Your little sister is there where I left her." They tried to strike him, but he was now changed into a Yakahatata, a sort of powis which thus is always crying out "Sister-little-there" [that is, ija-ko-i sanuka tataha, of which Yakahatata is the nearest approach in bird-language to which he can attain].

132.* THE STOLEN CHILD (W)

A man went out hunting, leaving at home his wife and little baby girl, a child that was just beginning to walk. Night was falling and the mother was preparing food for her husband's return. While thus occupied the child started crying, and just at that moment the old grandmother came from over the way to fetch it. The mother was only too pleased to be temporarily relieved of her responsibilities, and when the old woman asked her to hand the child over, she willingly did so, and was thus enabled to get all the cooking done without further interruption. When this was completed, she went to fetch her baby, and said, "Give me my child." But when the old woman said, "What child? I know nothing about any child," the poor mother knew that she had been tricked. As a matter of fact, it was really a Tiger who had assumed the exact form of the old woman, and so had deceived the mother. When the husband at last returned, the distracted woman told him what had happened, and they both started out to search, but found nothing. Next morning they renewed their search, but were again unsuccessful, and at last gave up their quest. Thus they gradually lost touch with their little daughter, and after a time she was forgotten. A few years passed, and the parents began to lose things about the house. First of all, the beads on their necklaces disappeared one night; on another occasion their cotton garters could not be found; one evening all the ite [Mauritia] starch vanished; one morning the wood-skin [i. e. bark] apron-belt was nowhere to be seen; not long afterward the buck-pots began to disappear one after the other; and so things continued unaccountably to be lost. Though the parents had not the slightest idea that such was the case, it was the Tiger who came every now and then after nightfall to steal all these things for the little girl to use. She was getting of course to be a young maiden now, and Tiger was minding her as his own kith and kin. The young maiden soon became a woman, nourished with all the meat that Tiger provided. [Quandocumque menstruavit sanguinem lambavit.] He was still a tiger and, continuing to do what tigers and dogs do [incepit femmam olfacere]. Moreover, his two brothers, being similarly affected, followed his example. The girl felt very strange at these periods and could not understand the actions toward her of Tiger and his two brothers. So she made up her mind to escape, and asked Tiger one day how far their place was from the spot where her parents lived. He was somewhat suspicious and wanted to know first of all why she asked the question. So she told him something like this: "You are an old man and will die soon. I am young. What will then happen to me? If I knew where they were, I could then go to my parents." Recognizing the force of her argument, he told her that they lived in such and such a direction, that it was not far, and that immediately upon his decease she must hurry to them, lest his two brothers should meet her and tear her up. Contented for the present with this information, the woman bided her time to seize a favorable opportunity of escape—an opportunity which was not long in coming. She planned what to do, she was getting tired of always being alone p. 203in the depths of the forest. So, taking the biggest of the buck-pots, she put all kinds of food into it, and placed it on the fire. When the contents were boiled, she went to take it off, but pretended she could not stand the heat, and turning to Tiger, said, "No! it is too heavy. I want you to help me." So without more ado, Tiger stooped down, put his paws one on each side of the projecting rim of the pot, and so lifted it off the fire. While thus occupied, she smartly tapped the pot from below up, dashing the boiling contents over the creature's face, a procedure which made him fall, yell with pain, and die. His two brothers heard the roaring and said, "Oh! the old man must be sporting with his girl"; but this was not the case, he never having had intimate relations with her. In the meantime, the woman went to the place where she had been told her people lived, and called out: "I am the little girl that was lost many a long day ago. Where are my parents?" The latter showed themselves and said, "You are our daughter," and would have liked a long chat over what had happened during her absence, but the woman warned them that there was no time for this, that they must all escape because Tiger's two brothers would come and kill them for payment [i. e. in revenge]. So they loosened their hammock-ropes and hurried themselves to leave. While they were doing so, a young man, a cousin, said: "Well! I can not leave this grindstone here: I shall want it for sharpening."1 So saying, he placed it in his hammock, folded the latter, and, in the hurry of the moment, not thinking of what he was doing, slung it in the usual manner over his shoulder. The unprepared-for weight, however, broke his back and he fell down dead, and there the others left him.2

133.* THE TIGER CHANGED INTO A WOMAN (A)

There was a man justly noted for his skill in hunting bush-hog. Though his friends might be more than a match for him in hunting other game, with bush-hog he had hardly an equal, certainly no superior. He would always succeed in killing five or six, when the Tiger who invariably followed on the heels of the pack would catch only one or two. The Tiger could not help noticing his success, and on the next occasion that our friend went into the bush changed himself into a woman, and spoke to him. She asked him how he managed to kill so many bush-hog, but all he could tell her was that he had been trained to it ever since the days of his early boyhood. She next expressed her desire to have him for a husband, but he, knowing her origin, was not too anxious to give a decided answer. She overcame his scruples, however, by convincing him that if they lived together, they could kill ever so many more bush-hog than it was possible to do singly. And then he agreed. He lived with her for a long, long time, and she turned out to be an exceedingly good wife, for besides looking after the cooking and the barbecuing, she made an excellent huntress. One day she asked him whether he had father or mother, and learning that his parents and other relatives were still alive, inquired whether he would not like to pay them a visit, because she felt sure that from not having seen him for so long the old people would think him dead. And when he said, "All right! I would like to go home," she offered to show him the road and to accompany him, but only on the condition that he never told his folk from what nation she was sprung. Before they started, she said they must go hunting for a few days, so as to be able to take plenty of bush-hog with them. This they did, finally arriving at the house of his parents, who were indeed glad to welcome him after so many years. The first question his old mother asked him was, "Where did you get that beautiful woman?" He told her that he had p. 204found her when out hunting one day in the bush, at the same time taking care to omit all mention of the fact that she was really a Tiger. While at his old home, the couple went out hunting again and again, invariably returning with an extraordinarily large bag. This, unfortunately, proved to be their undoing. All his friends and family became suspicious of his luck, and made up their minds to discover to what nation his beautiful wife belonged. He was often asked, but always refused to divulge the secret. His mother, however, became so worried and upset that he at last did make a clean breast of it to her, strictly warning her not to tell anyone else, as his wife might leave him altogether. And now trouble soon came. One day the husband's people made plenty of cassiri, to get the old woman drunk, but when asked about her daughter-in-law she wouldn't tell: they gave her more drink and still she held her tongue: a last they gave her so much drink, that out came the secret and all the friends now knew that the beautiful creature whom they had so envied was after all only a Tiger. The woman, however, who had heard her mother-in-law exposing her origin, felt so ashamed that she fled into the bush growling, and that was the last that was ever seen or heard of her. Her husband, of course, upbraided his mother roundly for betraying him but she said she really could not help herself; they had made her so drunk. And the poor husband would often go into the bush and call his wife, but there never never came a reply.

134.* THE WOMAN IN LOVE WITH A SLOTH (A)

A woman had a sloth [Cholopus didactylus] for a sweetheart. Every time that she went into the field or into the bush she used to carry food and drink for him. She would call Hau! Hau! and the Sloth would clamber down the tree: and they caressed each other just like lovers. Other people began to talk, and wondered what she did with the food and drink that she was continually taking out of the house. Among these was a young man who watched her next day, and saw her call her Sloth lover and caress him. But instead of reciprocating her caresses, the Sloth scratched her, and pulled down her hair, conduct which made her remark, "Are you jealous of me, or vexed?" As a matter of fact, the Sloth was very much vexed as well as jealous, because he could see the young man watching all their movements from behind a tree. The woman did not know this, and turned her steps homeward. As soon as she was gone, the man came from where he was hiding, and killed the Sloth. And when the woman returned next day, and saw the animal lying dead, she fell into a great grief and wept bitter tears, saying, "What has killed you, my sweetheart?" But the young man, who had been following her, came up close behind, and consoled her. "Don't be so foolish," he remarked. "A fast fellow is preferable to a slow Sloth. Take me for a sweetheart." And she did.1

135.* WHY HONEY IS SO SCARCE NOW (A)

In the olden times bees' nests and honey were very plentiful in the bush, and there was one man in particular who earned quite a reputation for discovering their whereabouts. He would find a nest where no one else could. One day, while chopping into a hollow tree where he had located some honey, he suddenly heard a voice from the inside calling, "Take care! You are cutting me." On opening the tree very carefully, he discovered a beautiful woman, who told him she was Maba [lit. 'honey'], the Honey-Mother, that is, the Spirit of the Honey. As she was quite nude, he collected some cotton, which she made into a cloth, and he asked her to be his wife. She consented p. 205on condition that he never mention her name, and they lived very happily together for many years. And just in the same way that he became universally acknowledged as the best man for finding bees' nests, so she made a name for herself in the way of brewing excellent cassiri and paiwarri. She had to make only one jugful, and it would prove quite sufficient, no matter the number of visitors; more than this, the one jugful would make them all drunk. She thus proved herself to be a splendid wife. One day, however, when the drink was finished, he went round as house-master, in the usual manner, to his many guests and expressed regret that even the last dregs of the liquor had been now drained. He promised them, however, that the next time they came, there would be provided by Maba—yes, he made a mistake and thus spoke of his wife. And no sooner had he mentioned the name, than she flew away to her bees' nest. He put up his hands to stop her, but she was already flown. And with her, his luck flew, and since that time honey has always been more or less scarce.1

136.* THE MAN WHO CLAIMED THE TIGER'S MEAL (C)

One day an Indian went out hunting and came across a freshly-killed Maipuri. He could see that a Tiger must have slaughtered it only the night before, but as he was greedy he intended claiming the meat for himself. With this object in view, he turned back to fetch his wife in order to lend assistance in smoke-drying it. Now, when his wife saw the carcass, she knew at once by the signs on it that her husband had never killed the beast and had no right to it, but of course did not tell him so: she realized the token that something unusual was about to happen, and took measures accordingly. Hence, when her husband had cut up the meat, she built two babracotes, one close to the ground, and another high up on top.2 The husband, having completed his share of the business, tied his hammock near the fire, turned in, and soon fell fast asleep. The wife, however, went on drying the flesh, and continued doing so until late into the night, when she heard a tiger growling in the distance. She immediately called out, "Tiger! Tiger!" and shook the man's hammock, but he would not wake. She then threw a calabashful of water over him, but this did not rouse him, so she took a blazing fire-stick and placed it close beneath him, but even that did not make him stir. By this time Tiger was close at hand, so climbing up on the top babracote she sat there very quiet. With the light of the fire, she saw the brute jump upon her husband, kill him, and eat one arm. The next night it came again and ate the other arm and a leg: and so for four nights it came, until there was "no more man." The poor woman had to remain all this time up on the babracote, but she knew why her husband had been punished.

136A.* THE WOMAN WHO BATTLED WITH TWO TIGERS (W)3

A man, having tired of his old wife, went off to another settlement to fetch a young one, and brought her home with him. But the two women could not agree, and the new one was always getting worsted, so much so, that the husband, finally obliged to take pity on her, was forced to send her to the home from which he had taken her. In order that she should have protection on the road, he gave her a large sharp knife. Starting in the early morning, the road led her along the bush, and she traveled on until night overtook her, when she selected a young ite palm up which she climbed. But before climbing she cut down a lot of "pimpler" palms [Bactris sp.], which she p. 206 stacked all round the base of the trunk, so as to prevent anyone following her. Well, she got up the tree, which had six bunches of fruit hanging from it, and nicked the stalks of every bunch, so that with the least knock or cut they would break off and fall: this done, she coiled herself up in the young palm-shoot, and fell asleep. She slept until about midnight, when she heard the roaring of a Tiger who, scenting her from a distance, rushed up to the very palm on which she was resting. Jumping on the trunk above the "pimplers," he crawled up it, and thence onto one of the fruit bunches. No sooner had he done so than the young woman above made a cut at the "nick," with the result that down went both Tiger and fruit.1 The Tiger had another chance and jumped on another bunch, but with the same result. He made a third attempt, and on this occasion fell down on the pimplers, upon which he was impaled, what with the weight of the bunch of fruit on top of him. Everything was soon quiet, and early next morning when the young woman looked to see what had happened, she saw the Tiger stretched out below. Now she suspected that Tiger might be only shamming, and so she was afraid to come down at first, but when she saw his tongue hanging out, she knew that everything was all right and that he was really dead. She therefore came down and resumed her journey. After a time she heard the sounds of a tree being cut, and then made to fall; thinking that it was her people felling trees, she hurried on in the direction indicated. But what was her surprise to see another Tiger playing an old trick of his, to make the traveler believe that timber was being cut in the near distance. This trick consisted of his hanging from the branch with his front paws and whipping the trunk with his tail, so as to imitate the sound of the ax chopping. To pretend that the cut trunk was then fallen, he would next pull a big bunch of twigs and leaves and throw them with full force on the ground below. Now, fortunately for the young woman, she came upon this Tiger from behind, just as he was hanging from the branch, and without more ado said to herself: "Well, dead or alive, this is my only chance. I must cut off his tail." Suiting the action to the word, she crept forward very cautiously, and with one swish of the knife cut off the creature's tail. Tiger was so ashamed at his own appearance now, that he went off howling with rage and pain, afraid of anyone seeing him, and thus left the woman free to resume her journey. She again heard the sound of timber being cut, but on this occasion made sure before getting too close that the sound proceeded from people and not from Tigers. To her great joy it was her own people. They were all glad to see her, but asked how she had managed to get through that long stretch of bush in safety. She proceeded to tell them that she had killed one Tiger outright, that she had cut off the tail from another, that—but her brothers stopped her before she could get any further: "No woman can do that," they interrupted. So she took both of them back on the road and showed them the severed tail, and farther back the Tiger's carcass. They would not approach too close to the latter, fearing that it might still be alive, but at any rate they now believed what their sister had told them.

137.* THE MAN WITH A VULTURE WIFE (W)2

There were once three brothers. The middle one was a very good hunter, and this story is all about him and his bird wife. While out in the bush one day he came across a large house wherein people were "sporting". These people were very fair, much like white persons, a thing not to be wondered at, because they were really Vultures [Sarcorhamphus papa] who had taken off their feathers just for the occasion to hang about the place and decorate it. They were dancing and singing the makuari tune [Sect. 75] on all sorts of musical instruments, from the harri-harri flute to the p. 207 rattle. The whole place looked very pretty because it was decorated with their red necklaces, white dresses, and black wing-tips.1 All around, hung up by cords to the beams, were the dau-u hewére; these were long pieces of wood, shaped somewhat like your [i. e. European] "indian-clubs," bigger below than above, all beautifully painted and tasseled.2 Our friend stood there watching and continued watching: so enchanted was he with the sight that, before he was aware, darkness fell, which compelled him to remain there all night. His mother was wondering what had become of him, and was still more surprised to see him return empty-handed next morning. He straightway went into his hammock, without saying a word: his mind was too full of what he had seen. By and by, he took up his harri-harri and began to play on it, but he told no one of his adventures or why he had not brought back home any game. Next day he quietly slipped away before dawn, and wended his way to the beautiful house he had gazed upon two nights before. It was still there and so were all the people, hosts and guests—fair people as I have said—all singing and dancing. The girls looked so pretty that he set his mind on getting one of them. Now there was "lemon-grass" about a yard high growing thick all around the house, and at a little distance from it and under cover of this he gradually crept closer and closer, on all fours, up to just about the spot where the girls during the progress of their mari-mari dance would retreat backward in their steps.3 As they thus made a move a little farther back than usual, he caught hold of the girl he had taken a fancy to, but no sooner had he seized her than all the other people, house, decorations, and music suddenly disappeared, and everything became the same old humdrum trees and bushes again. He had the girl, however, and although she struggled bravely, he never relaxed his hold. Exhausted in her efforts to secure her freedom, at last she panted, "Loose me! Loose me! I want to go home," but this appeal was of no avail, for the only reply she got was: "No! I want you for my wife. If you will only behave and not refuse me, you shall have everything you like." She yielded and she followed him, only insisting on the stipulation that he must not thrash her. He promised her that he never would do that, and thus he brought his bride home. They lived together a long time contentedly, he always giving way to her insistence of never using the meat on the same day that he brought it home from the chase: she would never eat it fresh, preferring to keep it a day or two until it became tainted.4

Now, one day it happened that her husband returned from the hunt extremely hungry, and he told her that she must cook at once the game that he had brought her, and that he would not wait for it until the morrow. She refused point-blank, and forgetting his promise, he gave her a thrashing. Another time the same thing happened, he wanting the meat cooked immediately, but she objecting: he thrashed her again. And he beat her a third time. She bore this brutal treatment meekly and never upbraided him. She merely told him that she proposed taking him to see her father.5 So he went a-hunting, and brought back much meat as a present for her family, and when ready to start she gave him Vulture feathers for a covering; he could not visit her people without this garb. After they had traveled a good p. 208distance into the bush, they came to land that was "like steps," so that the farther they went the higher they got, until at last they reached a very high spot—the very spot indeed where the carrion-crow governors [i. e. the Vultures] lived.1 "You must not be afraid of saying good-day to my father," she was careful enough to admonish him: "although he is a very celebrated man." When therefore the couple reacher her father's place, he went up and shook the old man's hand.2 His father-in-law bade him sit down, and after the usual routine of questions had been asked and answered, told him: "All right. You can stay with me today and return tomorrow. I will come and pay you a visit later on or I will send some of my people to call on you." The old man was well informed as to how badly he had been treating his daughter, and felt too little affection to warrant his asking him to prolong his stay. He knew also that the time would not be far distant when he would have to inflict summary chastisement. Thus it was that the couple returned next day to the mundane home of the husband, who felt sore at the treatment he had received from his father-in-law. Man-like, he vented his spleen on his unfortunate wife, whom he thrashed twice. So badly did he knock her about that even his mother took her part. Addressing her son, the mother said, "You are doing wrong, in beating the girl, especially since she is so far away from all her family.3 I am sure some evil will happen if you continue such conduct." The dame was a wise old woman, because her motherly instincts told her that her daughter-in-law was not "a real person," but had something weird and eerie about her. Did not the girl wear a strange nose-ornament for instance?4 Her son, however, refused "to hear" and commenced beating his wife again.5 On this occasion however, she picked up the feather covering—the very one that she had lent him when they went to visit her father's place—and putting it on, started to fly homeward. He jumped out of his hammock and tried to catch her, but the bird was already flown. As day after day passed, and cheerless night closed in, he became more and more wretched, his misery turning at last into heartfelt sorrow: yes, truth to tell, he wept now because he was so unhappy. But it was too late; the mischief had been done. Every day he went into the bush where the beautiful house once stood, but there was nothing there: he went along the same paths they used to tread together, and cried and called for her, but there never came the voice that he once upon a time loved so well, and now longed so much to hear. And where was she? She too was weeping, but for a very different reason: pain and anguish, not selfishness, were the cause of her tears. Her old father comforted her, saying: "Do not cry. I told your husband that I would come and visit him, or else my people would." And thus it came to pass that he sent the Carrion Crows [Cathartes burrovianus] to visit his late son-in-law. These met him at the very spot where once stood the beautiful house whence he captured his wife, and there, in that very spot, they killed him. They went and told the old man Vulture what they had done, and afterward returned to devour the carcass.6

p. 209

138.* THE MAN WITH A BABOON WIFE (A)

He had been far out into the bush in search of game, and it almost seemed as if he were to find no use for his bow and arrows. I am talking about an Arawak hunter who lived a long while ago. Late in the afternoon, however, he shot a "baboon," as you Creoles call it [Mycetes], which proved to be a female. It was too late to bring it home, so he built himself a banab with a view to making himself comfortable for the night. This done, he cut off the animal's tail, roasted and ate it, putting the remainder of the carcass on the babracote to get smoke-dried during the night. Next morning he was up early, entered the bush again, was very successful, and returned in the evening laden with game. As he approached the banab, you can imagine his surprise on seeing a woman lying in his hammock, and no baboon on the babracote. Not understanding whence she could have come, he asked her what she was doing there, and she told him that, on account of his loneliness, she had come to help look after the meat and keep him company. After further questioning, she assured him that there was no baboon on the babracote when she had arrived. He had his suspicions as to her origin aroused on noticing that her fingers were naturally clenched, and that with the one hand she was continually trying to keep extended the fingers of the other.1 He accordingly asked her straight whether she herself was not the baboon that had so mysteriously disappeared, but she denied it. She was a good-looking wench, however, and he took her as wife, with the result that they lived happily together, so happily that they kept no secrets from each other. One day her husband asked her again about the baboon, and what had become of it. She now admitted that she was the baboon transformed into her present shape, but that he must not speak about it to anyone. A few days later they took their departure from the banab, and made their way to the husband's house, bringing plenty of game with them. And here they lived a very long time—still quite happily together. It is true that he would frequently be asked by his relatives as to what tribe his wife belonged, but he never told them. One morning early, hearing the baboons "calling," she informed her husband that her uncles were drinking cassiri, and suggested that they should both go and join the party. The uncle Baboon was howling on the topmost branches of an immense cashew tree, the trunk of which was so big that it allowed of a proper foot-path being made up it. The couple made their way to the tree, and followed the track. Up and up they went, until they found themselves in the real Baboon country, and arrived at the threshold of a big house. And what a lot of drink there was! And so many Baboons to drink it! Everyone got drunk and then each began to chatter, the one asking all kinds of questions from the other. Our friend was again asked what nation his wife came from and, being now in his cups, let out the secret, and told them she was really a Baboon. But no sooner had he uttered the forbidden word, than everything—his wife, drinks, house, and baboons—all suddenly vanished, and he found himself desolate and alone on the top of the cashew tree. But how to get down was the puzzle: he was at too great a height to jump to the ground, and the trunk was too huge for him to encircle and scale. He knew not what to do, and he felt very miserable. After a time a bunia bird came along, and asked him what he was doing all alone up there. And when the bird learned how the poor fellow had lost his wife just for having said that she belonged to the Baboon nation, he offered to help him out of his difficulties and get him safe to the ground. The man was perplexed, and asked how this was to be managed, but the bird told him to follow the same procedure as he (the bird) did in the making of the aerial roots of the kofa tree [Sect. 168]. Obeying instructions, the hanging vine-roots soon reached the earth, and clinging to these, the man got down in safety. So far, so good; but even yet he did not know exactly where he was, and he had no means of finding in which direction p. 210his house lay. A little hummingbird commenced flying about, and then settled on a neighboring bush: it offered to show the man home, and told him to follow its flight. But it flew far too swiftly, and the man could not keep up with it: so it came back and made a second start, this time following the course of a straight line before it disappeared. The man followed the line, and came to a path, where the bird met him again and said, "Follow the path." The man did so, and got home.

139.* THE DISODEDIENT SON KILLED BY A TIGER (W)

Two boys were playing around the house, Their father became vexed at seeing them idling, and said, "It would be much better if you went hunting and fishing or did something useful for yourselves." The boys got angry at being spoken to in this manner and went to another house far away in the swamps. They were obliged to hunt now, whether they liked it or not: there was no mother to bake cassava, no father to bring them meat. They used to eat the grubs of a certain beetle [the hi-bomo of the Warraus] that grows in the ite palm, after killing them by "nicking" them against the trunk. It happened that, while eating one, the elder brother heard it whistle; he knew this to be the sign or token that he was going to die. When they got back to the house, and were resting on the manicole flooring—a flooring which all our houses built in the swamps used to have—both brothers saw a Hebu enter, pick up his harri-harri, and saying, "This is my plaything," warm himself at the fire, and then go out again. Both brothers knew that this Spirit had come from some grave and that its presence was another sure token of impending doom. After the Hebu had left, a tiger came along, and both boys clambered into the roof. "Poor we tonight," exclaimed the elder; "our father is angered, and this is what he has sent to punish us. We must be content, even if we are killed." Tiger made a few springs, and finally succeeded in pulling down the elder brother; he dragged the dead body into the bush, where it was devoured. Returning to the house, Tiger put out his tongue to lick off all the blood oozing from his mouth, and then sought the other brother. The latter, however, was so well concealed by the roof that he escaped detection, and the more Tiger peered into every chink and cranny, the more disguised was the place of hiding. This alternate seeking and hiding went on all through the night until dawn, when the Tiger slunk off into the bush. The boy finally mustered up courage to come down, and what with the fright, fell in a faint directly he reached the floor. Recovering consciousness, he broke his arrow and beat himself with the two fragments.1 He then ran away to a good distance, and listened: no Tiger. He went farther and listened again: still no tiger. And yet farther did he go, and listened once more: yes, he could just hear the brute growling. Still faster did he run, and what with the extra strength which he had obtained from the broken arrow, just managed to reach his old home in safety. Here he tumbled into his hammock, too upset and excited to talk to his parents. Next morning, however, he told them the whole story, and how the Tiger had devoured his brother. Now, staying in the house there happened to be a champion tiger killer, so the father turned to him and asked him to slay the creature, but he replied, "No. As you are the cause of the two boys being vexed, and one of them being killed, it is your duty to do it." The father thereupon gave him a kind of greenish stone as a present, and said he would accompany him: the champion thereupon agreed to destroy the animal.2 The pair then turned to the men in the company and asked them to join in, but they were all too frightened. The champion thereupon twitted them on their cowardice, saying: p. 211"Now is an opportunity for trying your mettle. I know how well you can thrash your wives. Let me see how well you can thrash a tiger!" This shamed them, and a large number agreed to go, but in direct proportion as they got nearer and nearer to the tiger's lair, the larger and larger became the number of deserters. And, indeed, when they reached the spot, the father and the champion were again alone. The Tiger was lying down, so the champion called out: "Hallo! A small thing like you. Call yourself a tiger? Let us just see if you can hurt me." Of course, all this vexed the animal, which then raised itself up and showed fight; a poor fight, though, because the champion easily slew him. And when dead, they opened the belly, from which they removed the dead boy's flesh and placed it in a grave.1 But they cut up the tiger carcass, "fine, fine, fine." The champion then turned to the father and consoled him thus: "Grieve no more over your son. His death has been paid for [i. e. revenged] by that of Tiger."

140.* DON'T COUNT YOUR CHICKENS BEFORE THEY ARE HATCHED (C)

An Indian went hunting one day far away from his hut, so far indeed that when he thought of returning night overtook him. Losing his path in the darkness, he lay down to sleep under an overhanging wood-ants' nest. These insects asked him by and by if he were asleep, and he told them "Not yet!" After a while they repeated their question and received the same answer, and so the game went on all night until early dawn, when they asked him for about the tenth time whether he were asleep, and as before they were told "not yet!" The ineects, who were really only waiting their opportunity for eating him, could restrain themselves no longer, but let themselves, together with their nest, fall right on top of him. Fortunately, the man had betaken himself to a safe distance before the scattered wood-ants had time to secure him and as they were running hither and thither to learn what road he had taken, a humming-bird kept chirping out, "Give me the head! Give me the head!" This was somewhat annoying to the little insects who had missed their intended victim, and as the bird continued repeating its request, they shouted, "What is the use of asking for the head when we haven't got even the body?"

140A.* THE BITER BIT (C)

Tawaru-wari was a Carib Indian who one day caught a young eagle, which he took home with him. It became quite tame, and Tawaru-wari had to go out regularly and shoot baboons to feed it with. But the baboons did not like this, so they held a meeting among themselves and agreed that if the man were to kill any more of them, they would catch him and tie him up to a tree. Tawaru-wari did kill another baboon however, very shortly afterward. So these animals, having surrounded and caught him, collected vine ropes with which they tied him to a tree trunk, where, after fouling him all over, they left him. Before taking their departure, they said: "That's all right now: the eagles will come and eat him." This was partly true, because soon a big Eagle [Thrasyaëtus harpyia], scenting the man from afar, swooped down close upon him, and asked him why he was tied up in that way. "Only because I shot baboons," was the reply. When the Eagle asked him what he shot them for, he said it was for the purpose of feeding the young eagle that he was minding at home. When the bird heard this, he loosened the vine ropes, giving Tawaru-wari his liberty, and supplied him with two more baboons for the baby eagle to eat.

141.* HOW ALLIGATOR CAME TO HAVE HIS PRESENT SHAPE1

Adaili [Hadalli] is the Sun, but when long ago he came to earth in the shape of a man, he was called Arawidi. Once, after fishing in a favorite stream, he built a dam, with the object of retaining both the water and the fish, for use on subsequent visits. But the otters destroyed it, so he appointed the woodpecker to act as watchman. The latter warned him with a loud tapping of the proximity of an alligator: he hurried along and clubbed the reptile so unmercifully that it offered him a girl for wife if he would only stop, Arawidi accepted these terms, but to this day the alligator shows the marks of the thrashing on its battered head, and in the notches along its tail.2

142.* HOW THE BIRDS OBTAINED THEIR DISTINCTIVE MARKINGS3

An Arawak hunter captures a Vulture, daughter of Anuanima.4 She lays aside her feathers, appears before him as a beautiful girl, becomes his wife, bears him above the clouds, and after much trouble persuades her father and family to receive him. All then goes well until he expresses a wish to visit his aged mother, when they discard him and set him on the top of a very high tree, the trunk of which is covered with formidable prickles. He appeals to all the living creatures around. Then spiders spin cords to help him and fluttering birds ease his descent, so that at last he reaches the ground in safety. Then follow his efforts, extending over several years, to regain his wife. At length the birds espouse his cause, assemble their forces and bear him as their commander above the sky. At last he is slain by a valiant young warrior, resembling him in person and feature: it is his own son. The legend ends with the conflagration of the house of the Royal Vultures. . . . The Kiskedee [Lunius sulphuratus], though a valiant little bird, disliked the war, and bandaged his head with white cotton, pretending to be sick, but being detected, was sentenced to wear it continually. He is noted for his hostility to hawks and other large birds which he attacks incessantly when on the wing.5 . . . The Warracabba, or trumpeter bird [Psophia crepitans],6 and another [the Sakka-sakkali, a kingfisher] quarreled over the spoil and knocked each other over in the ashes. The former arose with patches of gray, while the other became gray all over. The Owl discovered among the spoil a package done up with care, which he found to contain Darkness only; he has never been able since to endure the light of day.

143.* THE DEER AND THE TURTLE (A)

The Deer met the Turtle one day, while cleaning his hoofs—for in those days turtle wore hoofs and the deer had claws,—and said: "My friend, you have nice sandals.7 p. 213 Let me have a trial of them." The Turtle, who was very proud of them, said: "Certainly. Why not?" and handed them over, receiving in exchange the Deer's nails. When the Deer now put on the hoofs, he found that he could walk ever so much quicker than before, and trotted off. The poor Turtle, however, found his progress impeded, and stood still, waiting every minute for the Deer to return, but he never did so.1

144.* BLACK TIGER, WAU-UTA, AND THE BROKEN ARROW (W)

There was once a man who had two brothers-in-law. While he was one of the unluckiest of mortals, they invariably returned home of an afternoon with plenty of game. They said, "As he has no luck, we will lose him away" [i. e. get rid of him]. So one day they took him into the bush: all three went in together, but soon they told him to go in one direction while they went in another, arranging to meet at a certain place. The route which the two wicked brothers instructed him to follow led to the lair of Tobe-horoanna,2 but the intended victim did not know this. He went on and on and came to a big path, which caused him to exclaim, "Where am I going now?" While thus talking to himself, he heard a great rushing noise approaching, and wondered what it was. He had not long to wonder, because he saw the Tobe-horoanna coming. He ran as fast as he could toward an immense tree, with Black Tiger after him. Running round and round the trunk, the one after the other, the man just managed to reach the animal's hind-quarters and cut off both its heels. Tiger then sat down, for it could not walk at all now. Next the man shot it through the neck with his arrow, and after finishing the job with a knife went back home. Now his two brothers-in-law, knowing well how poor a hunter he was and whither they had sent him, never for one moment doubted that they had seen the last of him. Hence, on his arrival at the house, they were greatly surprised, and made excuses to hide their guilty intentions, saying: "We went to the place where we told you, but you were not there. We shouted for you, but we received no answer. So we thought you were dead, and came away. But we were just coming to look for you again," and more of similar tenor. Of course all this was a lie. And when the man told them that he had actually killed the Tobe-horoanna, the two brothers-in-law, as well as their old father, could hardly believe him, but insisted upon his taking them to the place. They all went together, and when at a distance they saw Black Tiger on the ground all except him who had killed it were afraid to go near. He told them again that it was "all dead, dead," but they were still afraid, so, to show them that he spoke true, he boldly went up and trampled on the carcass. It was only now that the old man would approach; his two sons continued to be afraid, and then the whole party returned home. Upon arrival there, the old father-in-law gave him another daughter, so that he had two wives now, the brothers-in-law built him a bigger house, and he was henceforth recognized as Ai-ja′mo [i. e. chief, head-man] of the settlement. But our friend was very anxious to have a reputation for being clever in hunting all other animals, in addition to the glory he had earned in ridding the country of Tobe-horo-anna. Whom could he consult better than Wau-uta, the Tree-frog?3 So he went along until he found the tree wherein she resided, and stepping underneath, he commenced calling upon her to help him; and he continued p. 214calling until the day began to darken. But there came no answer. Yet he went on calling and begging her to show him all the things that he was so anxious to learn, and now that night came on, he started crying. He knew full well that if he cried long enough she would come down, just as a woman does when, after refusing a man once, she finally takes pity when she hears him weeping.1 As he stood wailing underneath the tree, what should come trooping up but a whole string of birds, all arranged in regular order, according to size, from the smallest to the largest? The little Doroquara [Odontophorus] came first, and pecked his feet with its bill, to make him clever in hunting it, and so on in turn with all the other birds, up to the very largest. Wau-uta, you see, was now beginning to take pity on him, but of course he did not know that. When all the birds had finished with him, all the Rats came in the order of their size, to be followed by the Acouri, Labba, Deer, Bush-hog, and so on up to the Naba [tapir]. As they passed, each one put out its tongue, licked his feet, and went on, so as to give him luck in hunting its kind. In a similar manner, next came the Tigers, from the smallest to the largest, all going through the same performance and passing on. Last of all, the snakes put in an appearance, did the same thing, and crept past. Of course, time was required for this performance and it was not until daybreak that it was brought to a completion, when the man finally ceased his weeping. With the daylight he saw a stranger approach. This was Wau-uta, who was carrying a curious looking arrow. "So it was you making all that noise last night and keeping me awake, was it?" "Yes," replied the man, "it was." "Well," said Wau-uta, "look down your arm from your shoulder to your hand." He looked accordingly, and saw it was covered with fungus; he looked at his other arm, which was just the same. It was this same fungus that had always given him bad luck, so he promptly scraped it all off.2 Wau-uta's arrow was very curious looking, as said before. It had been broken into three or four pieces, which had been subsequently spliced. Wau-uta now gave it to the man in exchange for her own, and bidding him put it to his bow, told him to shoot at a thin vine rope3 hanging a long way off: the arrow hit the mark. Replacing the arrow on the bowstring, Wau-uta instructed him to shoot into the air, and in whatever direction he sent his arrow, so soon as it came to earth it stuck into something—first of all a doroquara, and so on in the same rotation of birds that had pecked his feet, right up to the powis; every time a different bird, and yet he himself could see nothing when he started the arrow on its flight. As he went on shooting into the air in all directions, he found that he had hit a rat, an acouri, etc., until there fell to his arrow a beautiful tapir. Continuing to shoot as directed, he knocked over the tigers and snakes according to their proper order. When all this was finished, Wau-uta told him he might keep this broken arrow, for which she would accept his in exchange, but on condition that he must never divulge to anyone that it was she who had taught him to be so good a marksman. They then said good-by and parted company. Our friend returned home to his two wives, and soon gained as great a reputation for stocking his babracote as he already bore for his bravery in killing the Tobe-horoanna. All did their level best to discover the secret of his success: they asked him repeatedly, but he refused to tell. So they bided their time, and induced him to attend a big paiwarri feast. The same old story: Drink proved his undoing; he let loose his tongue, and divulged what had happened. Next morning, after regaining consciousness he went to fetch his arrow, the one that Wau-uta had given him, but he found it replaced by his own that he had given in exchange. From that time he lost all his luck.

145.* THE STORY OF ADABA (A)

There were once three brothers who went out to hunt, taking their sister with them. Far out in the bush they built a banab, where the sister was left all alone, while they wandered about in search of game. Every day the three brothers went hunting in all directions, but never brought back any meat except a powis. This happened for many days. Now there was an Adaba [tree-frog] living in a hollow tree [Sect. 144] which contained a little water, close to the banab, and one afternoon he was singing his song, Wang! Wang! Wang! when the girl heard him. "What are you holloing for?" she said; "it would be much better if you stopped that noise and brought me some game to eat" [Sect. 130]. So the Adaba stopped holloing, changed himself into a man, went away into the bush, and returned in about two hours with some meat for her. "Cook this," he told her, "before your brothers come back: as usual they will return with nothing." Adaba spoke truly, for soon after the three brothers came back empty-handed. You can imagine their surprise when they saw their sister barbecuing plenty of meat and a strange man lying in one of their hammocks. Yes, he was a strange man indeed: he had stripes all the way down his thin legs, and he wore a lapcloth; otherwise he was quite naked. They spoke to him, and they said, "How day" to one another. After Adaba had asked them whether they had been hunting, and was informed that they had shot nothing, he told them he would like to see the arrows they were using. When they showed him these, he burst into a hearty laugh, and pointing to the fungus that was growing everywhere on them, said that so long as they did not remove this stuff their arrows would never shoot straight [Sect. 144]. He also cleaned their arrows for them. Adaba then told their sister to spin a fishing-line which, when completed, he tied between two trees. He next told the brothers to take aim at the fishing-line, with the cleaned arrows, and shoot. They did so, and each brother's arrow stuck into the very center of the fishing line. Adaba also had a curious trick in shooting with his arrow, because instead of taking aim at an animal direct, he would point the arrow up into the sky, so that in its descent it would stick into the creature's back. The brothers began to learn this method, and soon became such adepts at it that they never missed anything. Indeed the brothers became so proud of themselves and of Adaba that they took him home with them, and made him their brother-in-law. And Adaba lived a long, long time very happily with their sister. But one day, the woman said to him, "Husband, let us go and have a bath in the pond." They went away together, and when they reached there, the wife got in first and called upon Adaba to come in also. But he said: "No, I never bathe in places like this, in ponds. My bathing-place is in the water-holes inside the hollow trees." So she dashed some of the water over him, and after doing so three times, she jumped out of the pond and rushed to seize him, but directly she put her hands on him, he turned himself into a frog again, and hopped away into the hollow tree, where he still is. When the sister came back home again, her brothers asked her where their brother-in-law was and all she would tell them was that he had gone away. But they happened to know how and why he had gone away, and so they beat their sister unmercifully. This, however, did not mend matters, because Adaba never came out of the hollow tree again to bring them luck. The three brothers often went out hunting after that, but they never brought back of an evening anything like the quantity of game that they used to get when Adaba was present.

146.* WHY THE INDIANS KILLED BLACK TIGER (W)

A man went to fish. He went far into the bush to the upper creeks, and while fishing heard a noise like thunder, but did not pay much attention to it. By and by he heard the noise again; this made him exclaim "Well! What can that be?" When he came to think over the matter, he recognized that the sound came, not from p. 216the clouds, but from some spot on the earth. The horrible sound approached closer, and he now knew it was the voice of Tobe-horoanna, the Black-skin Tiger. "I must get away from here," he said, and with this he fell into the water and hid under tree-root alongside the creek bank. Tiger now reached the spot, sniffed away, and felt right round the root. As he crept along one side the man shifted his position to the other. It was time now for the man to say, "I shall die if I stay here; I must get away." Suiting his actions to the words, he dived from under the tree-root deep into the water. After a while he put just his nose above the surface to catch his breath and then went down again. He repeated this performance a second time, and again a third time, when he landed on shore. Here he started running as hard as he could go. By and by he stopped to listen whether anything was coming up behind, but he heard nothing. Nevertheless he rushed on again, and after a while stopped to listen as before, when he distinctly heard the Tiger following him. Running as fast now as possible, he managed to reach home in safety, and told his wife and the other people in the settlement to clear out at once, as Tobe-horoanna was coming along. He and his family accordingly got into their corial and paddled away down the creek, but all the other occupants of the settlement paid no heed to the warning—they said the man was lying. The corial went gaily along the stream and after two days' paddling the man said, "I wonder what has happened to my friends at the settlement," and thereupon returned to find out. When he got back, there was not a single person to be seen: he saw only blood all over the place as well as scattered beads from necklaces, bracelets, and garters, but no bodies anywhere. He then said, "I must see where this Tobe-horoanna has gone. I will collect the remnants of my people and kill him in payment for my friends." So he traveled far and wide and gathered together the remnants of his people. Having made plenty of arrows and lances, they all proceeded to where Tobe-horoanna had his lair, and at last reached a large open space in front of which was an immense tree. Up this they clambered and then one of them blew his shell. Tiger heard the noise and, replying with a terrible roar, advanced toward the tree, where he was met with a volley of lances and arrows, but these had no effect on him. Tiger drew nearer, and, as he reached the spot exactly below the hiding-place of the people, they all jumped upon the immense brute's back. This contained a large cavity, so they were able to work with their axes from the inside, and soon Tobe-horoanna fell dead. After they had thus killed and cut him up, they blew their shell again, but getting no answer, knew that there were no more tigers about. They then said, "Let us go see where Tobe-horoanna lived," and after a while they discovered the spot: it was a rocky cavern as big as this house. Looking carefully around, they found a number of human heads at the cave-mouth, and searching further they came across Tiger's baby. Although this creature was as big as a Maipuri, it could not walk yet; nevertheless all helped to kill it, and when they had beaten the carcass out of shape, they returned home.

147.* BRAVERY REWARDED WITH A WIFE (W)1

Some men were out hunting, when they came across a dead mora tree that had a daiha creeper2 growing over it. So soon as they reached home they told their wives, who were very glad to hear of the find, and arranged among themselves to go next day to gather the bark. They took a little boy with them for company, and, having reached the spot indicated, started removing the bark. Each pounded a piece to make it pliable, and while they were thus engaged, the child amused himself by climbing into a manicole tree. The noise made by their wooden staves drowned the roar of an immense Tiger, which, before they were aware of its presence, suddenly appeared p. 217among them, and without giving them a chance of escape killed every one—all except the little boy, who, like a watchman, could see everything that took place. He saw the Tiger eat a piece out of this body and a bit out of that, finally dragging the bodies into the bush. As soon as the coast was clear, the child slid down the tree, ran fast down to the landing, jumped into the corial, and loosening it from its moorings shoved off. He was only just in time, because Tiger was after him, but unable to catch up with him, on account of being gorged with human flesh. The boy reached home all in a tremble, and could not speak, but next morning told the men about everything that had taken place, and how all their women had been killed. The men then went off to kill the Tiger, but when they reached the spot they saw only blood: they went farther, and one of them, Tobe-akuba, recognized the body of his wife, whose breasts had been eaten away: still farther on they found another body, also mutilated, and so on, one after the other. At last they came across the Tiger, but what with the ghastly scenes that they had just witnessed, all except two of the search party turned cowards, and climbed for safety up the neighboring trees. The two exceptions were Tobe-akuba and Sika-waka [lit. jigger-plenty], the latter being half-lame owing to the number of jiggers that infested his feet. These two men alone fought that tiger and ultimately managed to destroy it. When he was stone dead, Tobe-akuba called on the remainder of the search party to come down from under cover of the trees which they had climbed during the progress of the fight. He then taunted them, "You have no jiggers in your feet as this man has, and yet none of you dared come help me as he did." After leaving all their dogs behind to eat Tiger's carcass, they returned home, where Tobe-akuba picked out the jiggers from Sika-waka's feet, and then gave him his daughter to wife. When ten days were finished, they went to fetch their dogs, but the latter had not yet devoured all the flesh, and did not want to return; so they went for them again after another ten days had passed, by which time all Tiger's flesh had been consumed. You can easily learn from this what a big brute he must have been.

148.* WHY BLACK TIGER KILLED THE INDIANS (W)

One day Tobe-horoanna caught a young man out in the bush and, dragging him home, put him inside the pot, saying: "You must not be frightened. I do not intend killing, cooking, and eating you. You are going to live." When Black Tiger's brother and sister came home they said: "We have heard that you caught a young man. Where is he?" "In the pot," replied Tobe-horoanna. "Have you fed him?" was their next inquiry, and upon receiving a negative reply, they said, "Well, give him a bush-hog, and if he does not finish the whole of it, we shall have to finish him." The man was indeed frightened to hear his captors talking like this, and when they gave him the hog, did his best to eat it, but by the time he had stowed away the two hind legs his belly could hold no more. Tobe-horoanna then handed him a calabashful of cassiri, telling him to drink it all, but the poor fellow insisted that his belly was full, and that he could not possibly do so. However, as they all three insisted on his drinking, he swallowed the cassiri, but he was forced almost immediately to vomit it all. "Eh? What are you doing?" said Black Tiger who, thinking there must be something wrong in the man's mouth, got his brother to help hold him, and keep his jaws open while he should pour more cassiri down. But their sister told them to let the man alone, as she had taken a liking to him, and wanted to live with him. Therefore they loosened him, but told him to go into the bush and hunt, so as to show them that he could support a wife. When he returned next time from the forest, he brought back with him ten dried bush-hogs, which made Tobe-horoanna say: "All right! I am satisfied. You can have my sister." Thus the man came to live a long time there with his Tiger wife, who ultimately bore him twin sons. As the children became older, and could manage to crawl and creep, the father was minding them p. 218while his wife went out to the field: all of a sudden they howled and made a noise just like Naharani [thunder]. This frightened him somewhat, but when their mother returned she told him that such a noise really meant nothing, that it was but the same row which the Black Tiger nation always made when they traveled in the bush. Soon after this he began to feel homesick, and told his wife that he proposed visiting his mother and sister; and he went. How happy indeed was the welcome he met at his old home, where they had long given him up for lost. His mother asked him whether he had a wife, and when she learned that he had not only a wife, but also two boys, who could make peculiar noises, she begged him to bring the family with him when next he paid her a visit. This he did very shortly, but when they reached his mother's place all there were drinking and the old woman's tongue was well stimulated. She upbraided him for bringing home to her such a daughter-in-law; could he not see that she was not "a proper people" but a tigess, who would fall upon and destroy him some day? Was he not ashamed to bring such an one home to her? and so on. And in her drunken fury she and her daughter killed him: his wife did her best to defend him, but they slew her also. His two boys would have shared the same fate had they remained, but they managed to make good their escape, and reached home in safety. Uncle Tobe-horoanna asked them, "Where is your father?" "Dead," they replied. "Where is your mother?" "Dead also," they answered. When he learned from them what had happened, he became very angry, changed himself into a Black Tiger again, trotted off to the place where they were all drinking, and killed everyone—mother, daughter, and all the guests.

149.* BÁ-MU [BAHMOO] AND THE FROG

To account for the division of mankind into races, the following little story is given by Brett (BrB, 167):1 it is not Arawak.

Bamu came to visit some friends who were about to go frog-hunting—hunting for none of your small-sized frogs but for frogs as large as bush-hogs. They told Bamu to take a cudgel and come with them, but he, being a braggart, said that he did not want any weapons, but would jump on the back of the first frog he met and twist its neck around. The Chief of the Frogs heard him boast, and purposely squatted close to the river just in front of the path along which Bamu was coming. Bamu made a jump and so did the Frog, right into the water, the latter taking him over to the opposite bank, where he jerked him off. When his friends first saw Bamu on the Frog's back in the water, they started laughing, and when they saw him on the other side, they continued chaffing, telling him to twist the Frog's neck and bring the dead animal over to them. Having finished their frog-hunt, his friends again called on him to come over and join them, but he was too much ashamed to swim back and be laughed at again. So it came to pass that Bamu remained on that side, begat children, and became separated from us.

150.* HOW THE MAN FOOLED THE TIGER (C)

An Indian went to a somewhat distant settlement to drink paiwarri, and on arriving there in the early afternoon, commenced imbibing. By midnight, the drinks being finished, he started on the return journey, although the house-master warned him not to leave then but to wait for daybreak, because an immense Tiger was known to be prowling about. Our friend would not be persuaded, however, to postpone his departure, but only said: "Oh! never mind. I am not afraid, and if I meet him I p. 219 will kill him." So saying, he hung his poto [stone-club]1 over his arm, and went out into the darkness. Being more or less drunk, he staggered along, and soon fell dead asleep on the road just about the very spot where the Tiger, of which he had been warned, used to cross. Tiger found him lying there motionless in the early morning, felt and sniffed him all over to see whether he was dead or alive, and finally sat down on him. This sobered the Indian, and Tiger, seeing that he was alive, started pulling down the bushes so as to clear a pathway along which he could drag the body to his lair. Having thus cleared a few yards, the animal returned and slung the man over his back so that the head and arms hung over one flank and the legs over the other. This gave the man his opportunity, for as the animal carried him along he caught hold of the bushes with his teeth and hands and so impeded Tiger's progress. The Tiger thought that the pathway which he had cleared was still too narrow, and accordingly replaced the burden on the ground and pulled down more bushes. The Indian thus fooled his captor some three or four times and, having now collected his wits, watched for the tiger to sling him once more on his back. No sooner had Tiger done so, than he struck the animal's head just above the ear with his stone-tipped club, and thus killed him. Making sure that Tiger was quite dead, he returned to the place where he had been drinking the night before, and told the house-master what had happened. The latter would not believe that any drunken Indian could have killed so big a tiger, but when he went and saw with his own eyes, he had to admit that his late guest had spoken truly.

151.* Among the Arawaks tradition has it that the old stone axes, or wakili-na-baro (lit. ancients-their-ax), came from a far distant country, from a place so far away that it took years for those who went in search of them to get back home again. Many a bizarre exploit is told in connection with the search for these stone implements, in the same way that many a superstition is attached to the weapon itself among several nations, both civilized and savage, elsewhere. The very length of the supposititious journey to be accomplished has given opportunity for fictions to be introduced with regard to the rivers and seas that had to be crossed, and the animal and plant life met with on the way. But beyond all the exaggeration consequent on the well-known desire of the foreign-traveled narrator to tell his stay-at-home friends so much more than his real experiences, and after making allowances for all the personal additions and embellishments that, in the absence of any written records, must necessarily and pardonably have crept into the telling of the story from one to another—there still flows through most of these extraordinary adventures a sort of ethical undercurrent conveying the lesson that disobedience to one's elders never remains unpunished. At the same time, I am not prepared to say whether the introduction of this ethical element is purposeful or accidental on the part of the old people, who usually relate these legends. The following exploits and occurrences, as well as others which I can not detail here, are all comprised in a story which I propose naming—

*THE SEARCH FOR THE STONE AX (A)

There was a corial full of people, with a very old man, a medicine-man, in charge. They were about to search for some stone axes, but as they had a long, long way to go, their wives whom they were leaving at home had made a plentiful supply of cassava for them. In the boat they took also cassava-sticks, so that when they reached the spot where the axes were found, they might plant them, and after reaping obtain cassava for their home journey. It might be years before they would be able to see their wives and children again. Down the river they paddled, out into a sea which had blue water in it, and with so many submerged rocks that there was a great risk of the vessel being smashed to pieces if they went farther. The old man told the crew to shoot arrows into this blue water; where an arrow sank, there did danger lurk; where one floated, there the corial was enabled to pass. The sea was ultimately crossed in safety by this means. (Cf. Sect. 330.)

*THE HURI FISH NATION

152.* They visited many nations. One day, as they were traveling along, the old man told them that they were approaching the Huri [Macrodon sp.] Fish Nation [Sect. 178] and that, when they reached the landing place, they would see large numbers fish lying in the sand, but they were neither to shoot them with their arrows nor chop them with their knives, because they were really men and women. What the old man said actually happened when they landed that night. But when all the others slept, one of the crew stealthily arose, and went down to the water-side to have another look at these fish. He drew his bow, shot one of the fish, roasted it without making any noise, ate it all by himself, and returned to his hammock without anyone else apparently being the wiser. Next morning at early dawn a large body of Indians came trooping down to the encampment, and asked for the head the boat's crew. The old man arose, and said he was the head of the crew. The Indians said, "One of our men is lost: we suppose some of your party have killed him." Turning to his crew, the old man made inquiry as to whether anyone had been killed while he had been sleeping, but of course received a negative reply. So the Indians took the old man with his whole party away out back to their own camp. Arrived there, they put water into a large pot over the fire. When boiled, they gave to each of the visitors, beginning with the old man, a calabashful of the hot water to drink, so as to make each one vomit. The individual who had killed and roasted the fish remained to the last: when he was called, he did not want go, so the Indians took him by force and compelled him to have a drink. And as soon as he had drunk, he vomited all the bits of the forbidden fish. They said, "You are the one that killed our brother." Whereupon they threw him into the boiling pot, in the presence of all his comrades. The old man and his crew were now free to resume their journey.

*HOW THE ANT-EATER FOOLED THE MAN

153.* They went on again and, reaching another country, woke up one morning very hungry. The old man sent all his crew out a-hunting, and told them that no matter what animal they saw, they were to shoot with their arrows, or club it, as the circumstances warranted. With one exception, they all did as they were told and brought back late in the afternoon plenty of game. The disobedient one was tired, and went to sleep in his hammock the greater part of the day; he went out into the bush only as the sun was already in the west. He took only his knife with him. He had not walked very far when he came on a large ant-eater lying fast asleep in the shade. So soundly was it sleeping that it allowed the man to come quite close. Then he touched it with his big toe, and said: "Hullo! I wonder what has killed p. 221you; but as you are yet quite fresh, I will take you home." He accordingly went in search of a piece of strong bark-strip wherewith to tie up the animal and carry it. He was very slow, and sauntered about carelessly, and when he had secured the strip, he even then dallied in returning where the carcass lay. But when he did get back to the spot, lo and behold, the ant-eater was gone! He looked up, and he looked down, and he looked all about. "This is the very spot," he said, "where I saw it lying dead. Some one must have taken it away." When finally he returned empty-handed to the camping-place, he told the rest of the crew what had happened. The old man said; "You are a fool. The ant-eater was not dead, but only sleeping. Didn't you see it blowing?" (i. e., breathing). They all laughed heartily at him, and he recognized only too late that if he had obeyed orders, he would have had something good to eat.

*HOW THE INDIANS LEARNED TO PADDLE

154.* Another country which they visited in the course of their peregrinations was peculiar in that its inhabitants could travel in their corials only with the tide. As a matter of fact, they had paddles, but did not know how to use them in the proper way: they held the paddle edgeways instead of broadside to the water. Furthermore, this method of progression entailed always having to travel with a very long pole. When the tide turned against them, they would drive this pole into the bottom of the stream, and make fast their corial in it until the tide turned again. The old leader, who, as has already been stated, was a medicine-man, changed himself into a bunia, and yelled out its note Tarbaran! Tarbaran!1 Now, when some of the people who were paddling in this curious fashion heard what the bird said, they were annoyed, and remarked: "Nonsense! If we were to take the broadsides of our paddles and hit you on the head with them, how would you like it?" But the bird still continued shrieking, Tarbaran! Tarbaran! and would not stop. So each paddler at last turned his paddle round, and pulled it broadside with the water, and found he could travel three times as fast as before. And then all the others and their friends tried the new method that the bunia had shown them, and found that by this means they could go up and down the stream quite independent of the current. They never used their paddles edgewise again.2

*THE BIG BATS

155.* The search party continued their journey, and at nightfall reached a landing. Now this was in the country of the Bat Tribe, and the old man warned his crew that it was very dangerous for them in sling their hammocks on the trees (as Indians usually do in the dry season) because the Bats here were as large as cranes. He therefore called on them to build an inclosed camp, that is, a banab with covered sides. One young man, however, was slothful, and very backward in assisting the others in build the shelter. He said he did not believe that the Bats, however big they were, would hurt him before the morning. In spite of the old man's entreaties, he refused in come into the inclosure, but, fixing his hammock between two trees, rested outside. The others did as they were told, slinging their hammocks inside the banab. Late in the night, when it was quite dark, they heard the man outside entreating in be allowed to come in. But they said: "No. We cannot open the door now. You must bear what comes on you [i. e. you must take the consequences]." And when they opened the door in the morning, all that was left of the individual was some bones. The Bats had sucked him dry indeed.

CHAPTER X
THE SPIRITS OF THE BUSH
ASSOCIATED WITH PARTICULAR PLANTS

Derivation of Man from Plants, and vice versa (163-163A); Association of Bush Spirits with Silk-cotton Tree (164), Cassava (165-166), Maize (167), Kofa (168), Snake-bush (168A), the Whistling Caladium (Kanaima), Blow-tube Grass and Dakini Tree (168B), Ite and Mora (168C), and possibly with the "Tree of Life," the "Devil-doer," Silverballi, Darina, Hiari, and Bamboo (169). The belief in Binas may be but a development of this association of Bush Spirits with plant-life (170).

163.* So far as mankind is concerned, their original derivation from trees, trunks, and fruits is accepted by many of the tribes (Sect. 57). As to the converse idea—the transformation of human beings, or their Spirits, into plants (Sect. 59), I can find only two traces of it: one, in an Arawak legend relative to the discovery of the whip used in the makuari dance (Sect. 75), and the other, in the Yahuna story of the Jurupari ceremony (Sect. 163A).

*THE FIRST "MAKUARI" WHIPS (A)

There was a family of two sisters and two brothers. Going out one day to cut firewood, the former proceeded to the forest and cut the timber; on splitting a log, they found inside a pretty little whip. After closely examining it, each girl proceeded to make another exactly like it. Then they proceeded to their provision field, put up a little banab, and hung inside it the three whips. When they reached home they made some drink, two jugsful altogether, one for their two brothers, and one for themselves: they took their portion to the banab, where they left it. On three occasions they did this [i. e. they made drinks and took their own share to the field]. The brothers, suspecting that something was wrong, and being unable as brothers to talk with their sisters on so delicate a matter, sent the little hummingbird to make inquiries. While the girls were working in the field, the bird flew into the banab, saw the jug of drink there, and the three whips hanging up, and reported accordingly. The brothers thereupon asked the sisters to explain what they had been doing in the banab, and when the latter said "Nothing," they reproached them for not having mentioned anything about the whips, the possession of which they were then forced to admit. The brothers then asked to have a trial of the whips, but this the sisters refused: they would not deliver their charge over to anyone. So the brothers said, "Well, if you won't let us touch them, you can at all events let us look at you when you are sporting with them." No exception was taken to this, and the girls, making some drink, enlarged the banab and widened the pathway leading up to it. At the entrance to the pathway they placed the jug of drink. The brothers came, stopped to refresh themselves with its contents, began to sing, and then proceeded to the banab, where, addressing their sisters, they asked them to take down the whips and show their manner of play. This the women did, but it was soon evident that they knew neither how to sing, to dance, nor to whip properly with them. Admitting this, they were finally constrained, after repeated entreaties, to hand the whips over to p. 229their brothers, who now showed them how the real thing ought to be done. Furthermore, they "called" their sisters Kussaro-banna [= Kuraua plait] and Koro-botoro [= Ite fiber], the elder and younger, respectively, that is, they transformed them into Kuraua [Bromelia] thread and Ite fiber, the two materials out of which the Arawak have ever since made their Makuari whips.

163A.* In the origin of the Jurupari festival according to the Yahuna Indians of the River Apaporis there is also a conversioa of a human being into a plant. This is their story (KG, II, 293):

A long time ago, from out of the great Water-house, the house of the Sun, came a little boy Milómaki, who sang so beautifully that everyone came from far and near to hear him; but when they reached their settlements again, all died. Their relatives thereupon came and burned him on a large pyre, but he continued singing until he died. Thus was his body destroyed, but his spirit went up to heaven. From the ashes grew a long green leaf, which visibly became greater and greater and turned into the first Paxiuba palm [Iriartea exorrhiza], a timber used for all kinds of weapons and articles. The people made big flutes of this tree, which produced the same melodies that Milómaki had sung. To honor Milómaki the men dance and blow on these flutes nowadays when the various fruits, as Inga, Pupunha [Guilielma speciosa], Castanha, Umari, are ripe, because it was he who created them all. The women and children must not see these flutes: the former would die, and the latter would eat earth, become sick, and die.

164.* Several examples are to be met with of Bush Spirits being associated with particular plants or trees. Perhaps the most interesting is that of the silk-cotton tree (Bombax sp.), the superstitions concerning which have been incorrectly surmised (Br. 369) as communicated from the negroes to the Indians. The earliest reference in this connection that I have been able thus far to find for it, in the Guianas, is by Stedman (St, II, 261), in Surinam: "Perceiving that it was their [negroes'] custom to bring their offerings to the wild cotton-tree . . . under this tree our gadoman or priest delivers his lectures: and for this reason our common people have so much veneration for it, that they will not cut it down on any account whatever." It would be interesting to learn whether the so-called fromager of the French Ivory Coast is identical with our tree. Certain it is that the records are abundant as to both Indians and negroes (AR, 45) refusing to cut one down. As a matter of fact, however, the superstitions of the Bombax were cherished in middle America long before the arrival of the negroes: the Mayas of Yucatan spoke of it as the Tree of Creation, etc., under whose shade the spirits of mortals reposed. I know Arawaks who firmly believe that this tree moves within a circuit at midnight and returns to its proper place again. Dance (57) states that its guardian spirit "walks round the tree at mid-day, and at mid-night." Brett (377, 398) informs us of an Arawak tradition that men and other living creatures were originally made out of its bark and timber (Sect. 57). Women have told me that the Adda-kuyuha, in the form of a large bird, lives on the buds (i. e. picks out the cotton to build its nest with); p. 230that the shedding of the leaves is a sign that the Spirit has taken its departure; and that when the foliage is resumed, the Spirit has returned. Considering that there are some four or five other deciduous trees known to the Arawaks, it would not appear that their superstitious regard for it can be due to the periodic shedding of the leaves. From the fact of the silk-cotton tree being credited with the power of moving within a circuit (Sect. 8), a separate sentient existence may have been claimed for it; but such a property might equally be due to the particular medicine-man or Bush Spirit (Sect. 167) happening to occupy its trunk or branches.

165.* The cassava plant affords a very good illustration where the associated Spirit remains distinct, and is given a separate existence, so much so that it may be attacked by evil Spirits to prevent it distributing its favors, or may be thanked and honored for the benefits bestowed by it upon mankind. The Arawaks, even at the present time in the Pomeroon District, with the building of a house, or rather at its completion, give a party: when all the guests are arrived, some of the cassiri, before its distribution among the guests, is thrown by the house-mistress on the uprights; she also places pieces of cassava at the four corners under the eaves. This is supposed to feed the Yawahus, or Spirits of the Bush, who, unless thus treated, would not permit the Spirit of the Cassava to furnish the next crop. The Warrau Indians of the Moruca River had also a special festival, or thank-offering to the Cassava Spirit for the bountiful harvest which it had supplied them with, such festival taking the usual form of a drinking bout and a dance: they called it the Aru-hoho (lit. cassava festival).

166.* So also, the first baking of cassava bread from a new field formerly was attended by unusual ceremony. "The cassava, which on ordinary occasions is scraped and washed, at the preparation for the first baking, was scraped but not washed. . . . The juice extracted from the grated cassava by means of the matapi (and which otherwise would be boiled into cassirip) is, on this occasion . . . poured out on the ground as a libation for this, its first fruits" (Da, 102—at Berbice). This is still done on the Moruca River, the Arawaks here making the juice from the first cassava collected off the new field, sprinkling it a few days later here and there over the center of the field. The Indians say that this is a gift, a sort of thanks, to the Spirit of the Cassava. On the upper Amazon a purely Indian festival is celebrated the first week of February, which is called the Feast of Fruits, several kinds of wild fruit becoming ripe at that time (HWB, 280): this may have a meaning similar to that ascribed to the ceremony in connection with the cassava.

167.* Another curious sort of Spirit, that of "the Rot," is associated with buck-corn (maize). Here is an account of it:

*THE SPIRIT OF THE ROT SAVES THE YOUNG WOMAN (C)

Two girls were left in charge while the remainder of the household went to a drink-party. The former had been told by their parents to accept the invitation, but had preferred staying at home. About sunset a Yurokon emerged from a neighboring silk-cotton tree: he had an arrow and with it he shot a parrot. He brought the bird to the young women and asked them to cook it, and they, not knowing that he was a Bush Spirit, were only too ready to oblige him. After they had eaten the bird and he had slung his hammock, into which he threw himself, Yurokon called on the younger sister to join him, but she, not feeling so inclined, sent her sister instead. Later, when all was still and dark, the younger sister heard extraordinary noises and growling proceeding from their visitor's hammock, [Credens eos copulare], she paid no further attention to them. After a while, however, the clamor was even worse than before, so, blowing up the fire, she went over to Yurokon's hammock, whence she saw blood trickling to the ground. Looking inside, there was her sister lying dead. [Yurokon intravit eam.] She now recognized the tribe to which the man belonged, and hastened to save herself from a similar fate. She had a stack of buck-corn, which had all become mildewed and rotten, and in this corn she hid herself. To make assurance doubly sure, she further warned the Spirit of the Rot that if he allowed the Yurokon to come and catch her, she would never supply him with any more corn. By very early dawn, Yurokon had completed his work of destruction with the elder sister, and now asked the Spirit of the Rot whether he had not seen another woman about, but this Spirit refused to answer the question, being so busily engaged in eating the corn. Yurokon therefore walked all about, looking everywhere for the younger sister, but could not find her, and now that the day was just breaking, he had to hurry back to his home in the silk-cotton tree. All this time the poor woman was crouching in her hiding-place, and it was not until midday when the sun was shining brightly, that she dared emerge. Directly she did so, she rushed down the pathway to meet her people, who were returning from the drinking-party, and, as soon as she saw them, she fell exhausted, and commenced halloa'ing and crying. "What's wrong?" asked the mother. "The komaka [silk-cotton tree] Yurokon has killed my poor sister," was the reply. This made the mother say, "You ought to have come with us to the party, as you were told, instead of staying behind by yourselves." When at last they reached home, the parents picked all the peppers around, gathering twenty basketsful of them. They then made a ring of fire right round the komaka tree, which the surviving daughter had no difficulty in pointing out to them, and as soon as the flames began to blaze, threw peppers into them. There must have been a big family of Yurokons in that silk-cotton tree, because as the irritating, pestiferous smoke arose, down came a lot of small baboons of which the fire made short shrift. They threw on more peppers, and down fell a number of bigger baboons, and they soon shared the same fate [Sect. 242]. The parents now threw in the last of the peppers, and down scrambled the very Yurokon who had killed their elder daughter: they clubbed him to death, and the father said, "I am killing you in payment for my daughter." They then opened the corpse's belly, in which they found woman's flesh. The younger sister obeyed her parents from that time onward.

168.* Another tree which, according to Arawak beliefs, has intimate association with the Spirit world, is the Clusia grandiflora, an epiphyte, which throws down straight aerial roots that finally fix themselves in the ground below. Indian belief explains this peculiarity by the statement that the bunia bird roosts on the host, whence it drops its castings (Sect. 350), which are nothing more p. 232 than the aerial roots in question. The Arawaks speak of this epiphyte as the kófa.

168A.* Space must be found here also for mention of the Pomeroon Arawak belief in some intimate relationship between certain plants (known as "snake-bush" to the creoles) and venomous serpents, the poisonous effects of which they can avert. A similar idea prevailed among the same tribe on the Demerara River:

The Indians advised that when the snakes (a bush-master and a labaria that had been killed and buried) were supposed to be decomposed, they should be dug up the bones burned, and carefully replaced, and the spot of ground fenced in. From the ground manured with the burned bones of the snakes, would grow up, they said, snake-bushes that could be used as antidotes to the virulence of snake-bites. Some plants called "snake-bush" resemble a group of small snakes flattened laterally, standing upright, from twelve to twenty inches, with their tails planted in the ground. [Da, 324.]

168B.* Among the Caribs, the masiemo (i. e. kanaima), Caladium, would seem at first sight to possess qualities almost distinctive: it is a large-leaf species which I have seen cultivated at Carib settlement on Manawarin Creek. Its peculiarity lies in its supposed power of uttering a long low whistle, and shaking the sleeper's hammock with the object of rousing him from slumber to a sense of his danger on the near approach of the human and animal kanaima, or blood-avenger (Sect. 320). The plant from which the blow-tube is derived commonly grows in wet places, as wide stagnant marshes, and superstition has stationed an Evil Spirit to defend it, whence the Indians have the apprehension that some ill must befall him who ventures in to procure the reed (Pnk, I, 488). In especially bad cases of sickness among the Surinam Caribs the chief remedy is the sap of the Dakini tree: to obtain this, the piai has to get the permission of the Spirit of the Tree, and only after many a parleying will he cut an opening to obtain it (AK, 193).

168C.* THE ITE PALM AND THE MORA TREE (W)

In the days of long ago there was always to be found growing a Mora near an Ite: wherever one was to be seen, there sure enough, close by, would be found the other. The Baboon would forage on the Ite and eat of her fruit, and this is just what made the Mora jealous. In those times the trees, like the animals, would converse with one another just as people do; and these two trees must have been women, for did they not each bear seed? At any rate the Ite said she would leave the Mora and travel eastward, but the Mora followed her: she wanted the Baboon to come and stay with her. She was very jealous. As they both traveled on and on toward the east, they left some of their seeds behind: on and on they went, farther and farther east. As the ground of course gradually changed from dry bush to swamp, the Baboon more and more preferred to feed on the Mora, whose branches were always well above the water surface, and so finally left the Ite altogether. The Mora now at last satisfied, and was no further cause for jealousy, remained where she was, while the Ite traveled still farther eastward, stopping only when she came to the heavy swamps of the Orinoco. And here was too much water for the Baboon to follow her. Hence it happens that the p. 233Baboon is never met with nowadays on the Ite palms, but always on the topmost branches of the Mora. All the Ite palms that you see here and there more or less isolated in this district are stragglers from the original palm which traveled to the Orinoco. It is only on that mighty stream where you see the real Ite palms. There they yield starch and fruit and drink in plenty: the stragglers left behind here are so miserable and poor that it is not worth our while to cut them down.

169.* Among remaining plants which may, perhaps, be regarded as associated more or less intimately with Spirits and the like, are the "Tree of Life," the Devil-doer, the Silverballi, the Darina, the Hiari, the Kanaima (Sect. 168B), and perhaps the Bamboo. A leaf of the plant of the "Tree of Life" (Bryophyllum calycinum), the Kakuhu-adda of the Arawaks, is sometimes suspended in the house, both on the Demerara and the Pomeroon, when one of the inmates is ill. Should the leaf germinate, as is its nature to do under ordinary circumstances, it is accepted as a sign that the sick man will recover. But if it wither, that is an indication he will die. The Devil-doer, the uses of which have apparently been taught by the Indians to the blacks, is a bush-rope, called by the latter, the Fighting Stick, or Debbil-dooha, Debra dwar, or Zebra dwar. It is said to have the effect when dried, pulverized, and smoked with tobacco, of rendering all within the influence of the smoke pugnacious—and a row is certain: it is used to stimulate virility, and excite venery (Da, 286). So again, the Indians are of opinion that the scent of the burning chips of the Silverballi (Nectandra pisi) makes people quarrelsome (ibid.). At a certain season, the Darina has every appearance of being dead. But having shed its bark it begins to revive; the new bark becomes red like the bloodwood and thickens; new leaves spring forth, and the tree resumes its beauty. At midnight the Arawak Indians hear the chants of the medicine-man emanating from the tree (ibid.). The Hiari [Hearih], a large tree with thick leaves, which bears a small seed, is probably the Aiuke of the Akawais. The gum, or the inner bark, scraped, mixed with water, and given to the sick will cause the Spirit of the tree to appear to him, and point out the person who inflicted his illness upon him: thrown into the fire, it stupefies all who inhale its fumes (Da, 285). The smoke of the wood when burning is fatal to all kinds of animals (Bol, 258). The Pomeroon Arawaks believe that if the leaves fall into the river from an overhanging tree, sickness will fall upon the people farther down the stream. The same folk believe that the Bamboo flowers and seeds only during the night, which certainly accounts for the fructification not being seen, if for nothing else: any alleged Indian superstition concerning this palm must be counteracted of course by the fact that it is an introduced plant. The ability of the house-posts to talk (Sect. 16) may be traces of a Spirit originally associated with the timber.

170.* I am very strongly inclined to regard all the (vegetal) attraction-charms, or binas, used in hunting (Sect. 233) or love-making p. 234 (Sect. 237), and otherwise, as survivals of an original belief in plants possessing associated Spirits; while the presence of the originally associated Spirit has been lost sight of, and more or less forgotten, its attributes, properties, and powers have been retained. It will be remembered that all such binas have an exceptional source of origin—the calcined bones of a snake (Sect. 235), and in this connection it is no less interesting to note that the Haiari root (Lonchocarpus sp.), fish-poison, which can equally be regarded as an attraction-charm, should also possess animal (with its contained spirit) relationships, in that it has been quickened in human blood. I here paraphrase the Legend of the Haiari Root, given by Brett (BrB, 172):

An old fisherman noticed that when his boy accompanied him, and swam about in the river, there the fishes would die, and yet were quite good to eat. So he made a point of making the lad bathe every day. But the fish were determined upon putting an end to this. Accordingly one day when the lad, after a swim, was lying basking in the sun, those fish which were possessed of spines, and especially the sting-ray, sprang quickly up at him and pricked him. The lad died of his wounds, but before dying told his father to watch for the strange plants that would spring up from the ground in those spots where his blood had fallen. The father did so, and found the haiari.

CHAPTER XI
THE SPIRITS OF THE MOUNTAIN

Their presence due mainly to: Peculiarities in geological conformation, markings, etc. (171), for example, in legend of Kaieteur Fall (172), Rock-engravings (173); Actual Transformation of Sentient Beings into rocks and stones (174); Site of some long-past remarkable occurrence (175-176).

171.* The belief on the part of the Indians in the presence of Mountain Spirits in certain localities would seem to have been due in large measure to one or another of three sets of causes: peculiarities in conformation, marking, position, and other features of the rocks (on the principle of suiting a picture to the frame); the supposed transformation of the person or animal into stone; or the association of the locality with some remarkable event that took place in the long-ago.

There are an endless number and variety of Spirits connected with mountains, precipices, rocks, cataracts, etc. (cf. Sect. 58). South of the Takutu River is a mountain chain taking its name from a hill resembling a crescent in the distance, whence the Wapisianas have compared it to the moon (Kaira in their language), and designating it in consequence Kai-irite, or Mountains of the Moon (ScT, 48). Now all this country in Schomburgk's time was terra incognita to both Brazilians and Indians, and hence, as might have been expected, and as he tells us, "the Indian banishes all evil spirits to this region, while the Brazilian considers it the abode of wild Indians who massacre any person foolhardy enough to come within their precincts." So extraordinarily has nature molded her mountain forms in different parts of the Guianas, that there are seldom wanting resemblances, comparatively striking, to common everyday objects. I can quite sympathize with Schomburgk when he so much regretted that the little knowledge which he possessed of the Makusi language did not permit him to understand some of the many wonderful stories the Indians had to tell him of every stone they met on the road that was of more than ordinary size or fantastically shaped by nature (ScF, 199). Along the valley of the Unamara, a very good example is Mara-etshiba, the highest mountain, where the bulging out in the middle of this mass of rock has been identified with the maraka. Another is Mount Canu-yeh-piapa (lit. "guava-tree stump"), while a third is Mount Puré-piapa ("headless tree") (ScF, 197). Elsewhere, there is Mount Pakaraima, a singular isolated mountain which from its figure "has been called the Pakara or Pakal, meaning p. 236a basket" (ScF, 221). Mount Sororieng, the "swallows' nest," an object of much dread to the superstitious, is another good instance (BW, 177). The Takwiari offset of the Twasinkie Mountains, Essequibo, derives its Carib name from a remarkable pile of large granite bowlders so placed as to resemble a water-jar, called Comuti by the Arawak Indians, and by this name they are more commonly known (ScR, I, 328). Ayangcanna Mountain can be seen in the distance from the upper Mazaruni, forming a most singular picture. The word means "lice-searchers," this disagreeable name being bestowed on account of a row of huge pointed rocks on the crest, which are sharply defined against the sky, and to the Indian eye resemble a row of women seated one behind the other, searching each other's head for vermin, a custom very prevalent among all Guiana tribes (Bro, 390). It must be admitted that such fancied resemblances are not always too clear to European eyes. Clear or not, however, once the resemblance admitted, then follow the explanation and the "padding," the pointing of the so-called moral to adorn the tale. Wayaca-piapa Mountain, northwest of Roraima, is the "felled tree" which, as the Indians say, the Spirit Makonaima cut down during his journey through these parts. On the Mazaruni, near Masanassa village, relates Boddam-Whetham: "We passed a peculiar rock in the middle of the river somewhat resembling a human figure: the Indians thought it was a river-god watching for pacu" (BW, 179). On some granite blocks, above the Waraputa Rapids, Essequibo River, "I found," says Schomburgk, "two impressions of a man's foot, as if he had sprung from one rock to the other. The imprint of each foot, even to that of the five toes, was really striking. The Indians told us that these were the tracks which the Great Spirit had left behind when he took his departure along this route from among their forefathers with whom he used to live" (ScR, I, 326).

In passing the Carowuring [branch of the upper Mazaruni] the guide informed us that when high it is navigable for canoes for half a day's journey up, to the foot of a high fall, at which there is a large sand-beach, marked with mysterious footprints resembling those made by the human foot. The sand also is thrown up as if children had been playing there. If the Indians who visit the spot trample down these heaps, and go away for a short time, on their return they find them there again as before. The Indians believe that wild men live near the spot, but have never succeeded seeing them. [Bro, 385.]

The torrential streams which so suddenly gush down from the heights of Roraima are but the sorrowful tears of the Mother of Pia and Makonaima—she who had been left behind on top of this mountain by the former (Da, 342). At least that is what the Makusis affirm. Some people say that over the tops of Roraima and Kukenam are spread seas filled with all kinds of fish, especially dolphins, and continually circled by gigantic white eagles, which act as perpetual watchmen (ScR, II, 265).

172.* Another example of this series of cases is the legend relative to the calebrated Kaieteur Fall (pl. 4), which I give here in the words of Barrington Brown (Bro, 214), the discoverer of this wonder-spot:

Once upon a time there was a large village above the fall, situated on the little savanna, amongst the inhabitants of which was an old Indian, who had arrived at that period of human existence, when his life had become a burden to himself and a trouble to his relatives. Amongst other duties, there devolved upon his near relations the tedious one of extracting the jiggers from his toes which there accumulated day by day. These duties becoming irksome at last, it was arranged that the old man should be assisted on his way to his long home, that spirit land lying two-days' journey beyond the setting sun. He was accordingly transferred, with his pegall of worldly goods, from his house to a woodskin on the river above the head of the great fall, and launched forth upon the stream. The silent flood bore him to its brink, where the rushing waters received him in their deadly grasp, bearing his enfeebled body down to its watery grave in the basin below. Not long after, strange to relate, his woodskin appeared in the form of a pointed rock, which to this day is seen not far from our lower barometer station; while on the sloping mass of talus to the west of the basin, a huge square rock is said to be his petrified pegall or canister. Thus has the fall been named Kaieteur in memory of the victim of this tragic event.

173.* The remarkable petroglyphs, scattered through tha Guianas, to which so many travelers have drawn attention, are in the same way credited with a supernatural origin. Thus Schomburgk relates, when at the Waraputa Rapids: "I was most anxious to carry away part of one of the rocks . . . and neither threats nor promises could induce any of our Indians to strike a blow against these monuments of their ancestors' skill and superiority. They ascribe them to the Great Spirit, and their existence was known to all the tribes met with. The greatest uneasiness was depicted upon the faces of our poor crew; in the very abode of the Spirits, they momentarily expected to see fire descend to punish our temerity" (ScG, 275). The Piapocos of the lower Guaviar River ascribe such rockgravings to their Mami-naïmis, or Water Spirits (Cr, 525, 529). The amount of intelligence displayed by the expression of such a belief was however, within comparatively recent times, paralleled by that of a European Power, for on the Montagne d'Argent on the coast between Cayenne and the River Oyapock, the rock-carvings were claimed by the Portuguese to represent the coat-of-arms of Charles V when they had a dispute with the French over their boundary line (Cr, 145).

174.* The existence has been shown (Sect. 58) of a belief in the origin of human and animal life from rocks or stones and in the transformation of such sentient beings into the inorganic material similar to that from which they have sprung. This transformation is regarded not only as a natural departure from the normal course of events; but also in the light of a punishment (Sect. 67). At Aramayka, a settlement on the Mazaruni, close to Karamang River, the cliffs of Mara-biacru become visible to the height of about one thousand feet, with perpendicular faces on the north. A remarkable detached peaked p. 238rock on the western face of the cliffs is called the Caribisce. The legend says it is a man of that nation turned into stone for attempting to scale the cliff (HiA, 32). The Nation of Stone-adzes, where all the people are really stones, has been mentioned (Sect. 158). But however produced, these inorganic objects with human instincts, powers, and ideas, so to speak, all play a more or less important part on the world's stage. Thus, a rugged rock, a real good friend, comes and quells the fountain which threatens to overwhelm the nation (BrB, 106). In those cases in which the transformation is the result of punishment it might only be expected that the propensities of such rocks and stones would be directed into channels other than good. Perhaps it was some idea similar to this which led to the loss of Schomburgk's geological specimens: "One of the Indian carriers said he had lost my geological specimens: my brother had previously warned me of this—the Indian thinks it something evil, and will secretly throw it away" (ScR, I, 433). The same may possibly be said of the following: Above the cataracts of the River Demerary are abundance of red and white agates, which remain untouched by the natives, who avoid them from a principle of superstitious veneration, as they are dedicated to the service of their magical invocations (Ba, 21). Probably some idea of this nature may form the basis of the practice noted by Brown, in the Cotinga District, in connection with certain small artificial stone-heaps on the sides of the paths over the Savannah Mountains. These were 3 or 4 feet in height. The Indians with him, in passing, had added to the heaps by dropping on them stones picked up near by; he could never learn their object in so doing, for when questioned about it, they only laughed (Bro, 276). (In the Gran Chaco, the Indians, on going over a pass, will place a stone on the ground, so that they will not get tired on the way (Nor, 12).)

175.* Again, just as in the Old World, the scene of some tragedy, apparition, or of any untoward event—real or imaginary—may ultimately assume by the addition of tale and fable a halo of reputed sanctity, so may many a local feature of natural scenery in the Guianas constitute the landmark as it were of some notable occurrence—a death, a bloody feud, the appearance perhaps of some extraordinary animal—with the result that such a spot becomes weird and eerie, and all kinds of fanciful stories are told in connection with its immediate neighborhood. The Indians have a tradition that the cliffs, hillocks, and other places, about a mile from Kayiwa on the Corentyne are inhabited by a large snake, which from time to time goes to drink the water of the river, and that its passage thither has deprived the cliffs of vegetation (ScC, 289). On a low hill above the Waiquah River, a branch of the Cotinga, Barrington Brown "observed p. 239a huge artificial mound of earth and small stones, which the guide said was the grave of Makunaima's brother. It would seem that the Great Spirit is a dweller in this region, for an isolated rocky mountain, seen from the Cotinga lower down, at the head of the Mauitzie River, is called Makunaima-outa, which me ans the 'Great Spirit's House'" (Bro, 276). In the Pakaraima Mountains there is a singular rock called by the Makusis Toupanaghœ, from its resemblance to a hand. The Indians make it the seat of a demon and pass it under fear and trembling (ScG, 256). At the Merume escarpment, upper Mazaruni, says Brown, "the Indians begged my men not to roast salt fish on the embers, fearing thereby to rouse the ire of a large eagle and camoodie snake, which they said lived on the mountain side, and would show their displeasure by causing more rain to fall" (Bro, 399). According to the tale told by a medicine-man, Mount Roraima was guarded by an enormous camudi, which could entwine a hundred people in its folds. He himself had once approached its den and had seen demons running about as numerous as quails (BW, 225). Another Indian in the same neighborhood objected to camping near what he believed to be the cave of a celebrated "water-mama," near which it was dangerous to sleep (BW, 210).

176.* Sometimes the facts of the original occurrence have been lost sight of and only a memory remains, but this memory is grafted on the minds of the Indians apparently in the form of a Spirit, if we are to judge by the procedures adopted on their visiting such localities—these must neither be approached too closely, nor pointed to and sometimes not even looked at, or spoken of. Although it is permissible to single out a person by a nod with the head, to point the finger at a fellow-creature is to offer him as serious an affront as it would be to step over him when he is lying on the ground (Sect. 72); in the latter case he would tell you that he is not dead yet, and that you must wait until he is. To point the finger at a Spirit must necessarily be a much more serious matter. We have the Old Man's Rock in the Essequibo, which a murdered buckeen continually haunts, and at which it is dangerous to point the finger (A, I, 93). So also, there is a large bare rock (the Negro Cap) standing with its head about six feet above the water, close to the Three Brothers Islands, in the same river, concerning which the natives entertain a most curious superstition. They believe that if any individual points at this rock a heavy storm will immediately overtake him for his audacity (StC, II, 37). The dangers consequent upon talking about Spirits have already been dealt with (Sect. 124), hence the following allusion from im Thurn is of interest: "In very dry seasons, when the water in the rivers is low, the rocks in their beds are seen to have a curious glazed, vitrified and black appearance, due probably p. 240to deposits of iron and manganese. Whenever I questioned the Indians about these rocks, I was at once silenced by the assertion that any allusion to their appearance would vex these rocks and cause them to send misfortune" (IT, 354). The most curious, however, of all the procedures indicative of a Spirit's presence somewhere in the immediate neighborhood is that which concerns the sense of sight; several examples of this temporary occlusion of vision are recorded elsewhere (Sect. 252).

CHAPTER XII
THE SPIRITS OF THE WATER

Names and general appearance: Anthropomorphic (177); partly human, partly animal (178); Zoomorphic, as porpoise, manati, macaw (179), snake (180), big fish, Omar (181-182); derived from men or animals (183); kindly disposed on the whole—they gave man his water-jug and potato (184), the rattle and tobacco (185); of an amorous disposition (186-187), with strong likings for menstruating women (188-189); share, with Bush Spirits, the responsibility for sickness, accident, and death (190); responsible also for the Tidal Wave (191); they object to mention of their names and antecedents (192); to a pot-spoon being washed outside the traveling boat (193); and woe betide the yoyager if he dares to utter certain forbidden words (194).

177.* The Water Spirits, whether anthropomorphic or zoomorphic, are known as Ori-yu or Orehu (Arawak), Ho-aránni (Warrau), Oko-yumo (Carib), etc. The Warraus, especially a swamp-inhabiting tribe, seem to have made several distinctions in their Spirits: they had their Ahúba, Ho-inarau or Ho-aránni, and Naba-rau or Naba-ranni. The Ahúba is the "Fish-mamma," the chief of all the fish—one male and one female. The two live in underground water; their heads are like those of people, but their bodies resemble those of fish though they are provided with all the different kinds of feet belonging to land animals. They work evil on mankind; when shipwreck takes place they eat the bodies. The Ho-inarau and Naba-rau represent the Water Spirits of the sea and the rivers, respectively; they are sometimes like people, sometimes like fish, and were once good and kind, but the Warraus have made them bad. Indeed, there was a time when these Water People used to live in amity and friendship with the Land People. There are two reasons for the termination of this ideal state of existence. The Warraus used to exchange wives with them in those days, that is, a wife would be taken as required alternately from the one and the other tribe (see Sect. 190). The Warrau supply ran short, however, and the Water Spirits accordingly became vexed and angered with them. The second alleged reason is that the Warraus insisted on the isolation of the women at their menstrual periods, a practice to which the Water Spirits were unaccustomed and strongly objected (Sect. 190).

Though some of the Water Spirits have been repeatedly described by certain authors as the Water-mamma, they have nothing whatever to do with the African-Creole superstition represented under that designation. Still less have they necessarily any connection with the water-cow or manati (the Kuyu-moro of the Arawaks), or with the water-camudi (the madre del agua of the old Spanish authors), p. 242 except of course in the possibility that the physical attributes and peculiarities of these and other huge creatures have had to be accounted for in the Indian cosmogony. The natives of the Amazons country have their mai d'agoa—Mother or Spirit of the Water—the shape of a water serpent said to be many score fathoms in length, a monster doubtless suggested by the occasional appearance of the anaconda (Eunectes murinus), which assumes a great variety forms (HWB, 236). One of the many mysterious tales told of the Bouto, as the large dolphin of the Amazons is called, "was to the effect that a Bouto once had the habit of assuming the shape of a beautiful woman, with hair hanging loose to her heels, and walking ashore at night in the streets of Ega to entice the young men down to the water. If anyone was so much smitten as to follow her to the water-side, she grasped her victim round the waist and plunged beneath the waves with a triumphant cry" (HWB, 309).

The accounts of these Water Folk vary a great deal, but I believe the following represents the consensus of Arawak opinion. The Oriyus always live in the water and one at least accompanies every corial. If an accident takes place the Spirit is blamed for it. These Spirits may appear in human shape, impersonating both sexes. The female sometimes can be seen bathing on the banks of a stream, or combing her long hair with a silver comb, which she occasionally forgets and leaves behind in her hurry to return to the water when suddenly surprised.

178.* Oriyu sometimes splashes and tramples the water like a horse where horses are known not to exist; Brett even goes so far as to tell us that "she sometimes presents herself above the water with the head of a horse or other animal as it may suit her fancy, or the object she has in view" (Br, 367). On the other hand, I have often heard her or him described by Warraus as having a fish's head. Brett as a matter of fact always speaks of Oriyu as a female. Of remaining Water People those mentioned by im Thurn as the Huroni (cf. the Warrau term Ho-aránni, Water Spirits in general), "a tribe of Indians living beyond the Pakaraima [mountains], who are men by night, but fish by day," etc. (IT, 384), will doubtless remind the reader strongly of the Huri Fish story (Sect. 152). People may actually be transformed into fish (Sect. 115). The Piapocos of the lower Guaviar, a branch of the Orinoco, have a belief in Evil Spirits who live by day at the bottom of the water, but emerge at night, when they walk about, screaming like little children: they call these Spirits Mami-naïmis, and consider that the various rock-carvings are their handiwork (Cr, 525, 529). Endowed with somewhat similar habits there must be included here the Water People mentioned by Brown (Bro, 247), who apparently received his information from the Tarumas of the upper Essequibo, and by Crévaux (274) who derived p. 243his from the Indians of the upper Parou, in the far eastern Guianas. The former tells us that the Toonahyannas, or Water People, are said to live more to the south, near the headwaters of the Trombetas River (in Brazil). These have ponds encircled by stockades, to which they retire for the night, sleeping with their bodies submerged. The latter authority states that "on a march of four days to the westward, we would meet some very bad Indians whom it would be impossible to take by surprise because they plunged in a stream called by the same name (Parou) as that which we were now on. . . . Let us note in passing that toona signifies 'water' not only amongst the Taruma, but also in the language of the Trios, Roucouyennes, Apaläi, Carijonas: the Caribs of the Antilles call water toné." Perhaps these Water People were undergoing a gradual transformation before reaching the final change with advancing European civilization, after the style of the Partamonas at Waipah village on the Ireng, who stated that it was currently reported among the surrounding inhabitants that now that a white man had come among them, their country would sink under water (Bro, 283).

179.* When zoomorphic the Water Spirit may take on the form of a porpoise, manati (Sect. 183), macaw, snake, or fish. Thus, the Pomeroon Arawaks believe in the kassikuyuha, a white or a black variety of porpoise: the latter will hunt and injure a person who happens to fall into the water, whereas the white species will save one from drowning and carry him to shore. All that one has to do is to jump on the Spirit's back—it will do the rest and will always help anyone who is not afraid of it. Caroquia, on the Demerara River, is a place avoided by the Indians: Water-mámmas in this place take the form of huge scarlet macaws, which rise out of the river and drag them beneath the water, woodskins and all (Ki, 179). On the Moruca River an old Warrau piai friend of mine told me that it is the macaw who tells the Ho-aránni to come and upset the canoe, as well as to destroy the occupants: the bird itself may also assist directly in the work of destruction.

180.* The Caribs talk of their Okoyumo being like a camudi snake, but much bigger; it lives in underground water: in habitat, it corresponds closely to the variety of Water Spirit which the Warraus call Ahúba. In cases of snake-bite among certain tribes, in addition to any other treatment the bitten person must neither drink water, bathe, nor come into the neighborhood of water, during the period immediately following the accident [cf. Sect. 317]: the same prohibition, for a similar period, is incumbent on his children, his parents, and his brothers and sisters so long as they reside in the same settlement. His wife alone is free from the taboo (ScR, II, 130). The freedom of the woman from such an inconvenience is interesting when regarded in conjunction with the belief in human milk as an efficacious antidote for snake-poison.

181.* Of Water Spirits in the form of fish I must note the Omars, of which, so far as the name is concerned, the only record I can find is given by im Thurn. These are beings—

With bodies variously described as like those of exaggerated crabs and fish, who live under water in the rapids, and often drag down the boats of the Indians as they shoot these places. . . . A story was told me at Ouropocari fall on the Essequibo. . . . This Omar used to feed on rotten wood, and he dragged down many boats merely in mistake for floating logs, but all the same the Indians were drowned. So one day an Ackawoi peaiman carefully wrapped up two pieces of the wood with which fire is rubbed, so that no water could make them damp. Then he dived down into the middle of the falls, and got into the belly of the Omar. There he found whole stores of rotten wood. So he set fire to this. Then the Omar, in great pain, rose to the surface, belched out the peaiman and died. [IT, 385.]

I do not know whether this author was aware that omar is the Arawak term for that terrible little fish, the pirai, whose peculiarly destructive powers would constitute a capital groundwork on which to weave fabulous embellishment, though there is a suspicion that the word is but a play on the word Jonah, the exploits of these extraordinary individuals being so closely parallel.

182.* I obtained a somewhat similar story from the Warraus of the Moruca River.

*THE PIAI IN THE WATER SPIRIT'S BELLY (W)

Plenty of men would go fishing down the river, but every now and again one of their number would disappear: a Ho-aránni, one of the Water Spirits, caught him. It caused the son of the local piai to exclaim: "What ever can be the matter with the stream? Friends of mine go regularly to fish, and just as regularly does one of them disappear." Traveling to the particular spot where the alleged "accident" always took place, he himself was caught and taken away by Ho-aránni. It was now the turn of the piai to say, "I will go to the place where my son disappeared," and wise in his generation he carried with him, in his corial, banab posts, firewood, and fire. Before taking his departure he warned his wife that perhaps Ho-aránni would swallow him also, but that if not, she might expect him to return within a month. He traveled down the stream, and turning a point, his boat was suddenly engulfed within the open jaws of the Water Spirit there lying in wait: boat, posts, firewood, and fire were all swallowed with him. When at last the piai "caught himself" [i. e. came to his senses], he was in complete darkness; so after lighting his fire, he began to make himself comfortable and set up his banab, by sticking the half-dozen rods in regular sequence deep into the Water Spirit's belly; Ho-aránni naturally experienced acute pain and went to consult a piai friend of his who, however, could give him no relief, but advised him to go elsewhere. The sufferer therefore visited another medicine-man, who told him practically the same thing: "I cannot help you. It is just what you can expect for treating people of my profession in the way you do." As a last resource he went to a third doctor, of even greater renown than the others, but by this time the piai within was making the pains ten times worse, with the heaping up of the firewood on the lighted fire, and the sticking in of the posts around. All the consolation he got was, "There's nothing to cure you. It is all your own fault and you must die." Ho-aránni accordingly considered it time to retrace his journey and make haste homeward. The pains becoming so strong, he raised himself out of the water just as a fish does when he becomes poisoned with the haiari root and, rising to the surface, gasps for breath. The piai inside kept a sharp lookout, and when Ho-aránni p. 245gasped, he recognized an immense sheet of water which showed that they were still far away out at sea. In a little while the Water Spirit gasped again, and the piai could just see a small bush in the far, far distance. On the third occasion he recognized clearly the trees, and taking the next opportunity of Ho-aránni rising to the surface, he shoved himself and his corial out of the creature's jaws and hastened home. When he saw his wife, all he could say was: "I am come only to show myself, for what with all the heat, my hair is dropping off and I must die." And he did die soon. Several of the Water Spirits used to be bad, like the one we have just been talking about, but fortunately for us present Warraus, our ancestors killed most of them, and this is the reason they are so scarce now.

183.* Some of these Water Spirits have been derived from human mortals as well as from animals.

(In connection with the following story see Sect. 162D.)

*SISTERS PORPOISE AND SEA-COW (Manatus) (? A)

Once there were two sisters who had a Bush-cow [tapir] for a sweetheart: he used to live with both of them. They had a habit of regularly going to their field, collecting the plums (hobu), of which their lover was so fond, and making drink from them; when it was ready they whistled for him to come. They whistled by putting their fingers into their mouths and blowing. They did this every day. Their brother in the meantime had his suspicions as to what was going on, so one day he followed them, and without being himself seen watched everything that took place. He said nothing, but returned home. Soon afterward the two girls went to a field other than that which they hitherto had been in the habit of visiting, in order to dig cassava. The brother seized the opportunity of visiting the place where the Maipuri lived and where the plums were. Having arrived there, he whistled as the girls used to do, and as soon as the creature put in an appearance, he shot him with his arrow: he then cut the body into pieces, which he scattered. Next morning the girls went as before to the old place to make the plum-drink, and when it was ready, they whistled. But no Maipuri came. They whistled again, and still their lover came not. Tired of whistling, they commenced to search in order to discover what had happened to him. It was not long before they found the place where the slaughter had taken place, and soon they came upon the mangled remains. They both began to cry and determined upon throwing themselves into the water. This they did. One sister turned into a manati, and the other into a porpoise.

Others again may claim genealogical relations with a totally different beast. On the left bank of the Pomeroon, just above the mouth of Wakapoa Creek, is a place where the water used to be generally "on the bubble": this is believed to be the spot where some gigantic Salapentas (lizards) after being vanquished by the Indians threw themselves into the river and became Oriyus.

184.* Certain of the Water Spirits are of a kindly nature, in the sense of having conferred gifts and blessings on mankind (Sect. 185), in saving men from drowning (Sect. 179), and in other ways.

*THE FISHERMAN'S WATER-JUG AND POTATO (A)

There was once a fisherman who went fishing daily, and whose catch was invariably large. One day, when out in his corial something pulled at his line but he missed it: three or four bites followed, yet he caught nothing. Once more he tried. Something tugged at the hook; he hauled in the line, and what should he drag up to the p. 246surface but Oriyu herself! There she was, the real spirit of the Water, with all her beautiful hair entangled in the line. It was but the work of a minute to get her into his boat, and she was indeed beautiful to look upon. So beautiful was she that he carried her home to his mother, and made her his wife, the only condition that Oriyu stipulated being that neither her prospective husband nor her mother-in-law should ever divulge her origin. Being so accustomed to the water, Oriyu proved an excellent helpmate: out she would go with her husband, in his boat, and look into the depths for fish. These she could see when no one else could, and she would advise him not to throw his line in here, but over there, and so on. And thus day after day they returned home, always bringing the old mother-in-law plenty of fish. As you can well imagine, this happiness did not last very long; it came to an end through the old woman, when in liquor, loosening her tongue and letting out the secret of Oriyu's origin. Oriyu said nothing at this time, so grieved she was, but she waited her opportunity to take her husband with her to her former home under the waters. So on the next occasion that the crabs began to "march" from out the ocean to the shore, the family made up a large party, and all took their places, with their quakes, in a big corial. As they were coming down the river, Oriyu all of a sudden told her companions that she and her husband were about to pay a visit to her people below, but that they would not be gone long, and that in the meantime she would send up something for them to eat and drink, but they must share everything fairly. Without more ado she and her man dived into the water. After awhile up came a large jar of cassiri, and a lot of potatoes, a very welcome addition to the few provisions they had on board. When they had each had their fill of the cassiri, and had eaten the potatoes, they threw the jug and the useless skins back into the water, where the Oriyu turned the former into the giant low-low [Silurus] and the latter into the squatty little imiri [Sciadeicthys]. This is why we old Arawaks always speak of the low-low as the fisherman's water-jug, and of the imiri as his potatoes.

185.* Brett mentions certain other good qualities of the Oriyus. Out on one of the islands all the men, women, and children were struck down with sickness. Arawánili [cf. Hariwali, Sect. 3], the island chieftain, begged Oriyu for some charm to withstand the Evil Spirit's power which had made his people sick. She gave him the branch of an Ida tree, which she told him to go and plant, and to bring back to her the first fruit that should fall from it. This turned out to be a calabash (Crescentia), with which he did what he was told. Having emptied the rind through certain holes cut in in it, she provided him with the feathered handle, and dived into the sea whence she brought the shining white stones to put into it; with these she thereupon showed him how to invoke the Spirits. Thus was the first maraka (rattle) formed. Besides this, she taught Arawánili the use of tobacco, till then unknown to man (BrB, 18).

186.* Like the Spirits of the Forest, the Oriyus have strong sexual predilections. Every night, in their anthropomorphic form, both males and females may come after Indians of the opposite sex respectively, and no disastrous result follows the intimacy.1 But the Indians who happen to have such dealings must keep the fact absolutely secret: if divulged, either they will not live long, or they p. 247will never be visited again by their Spirit friends. Furthermore, those Indians who foster such friendships must on no account have similar dealing with their own people.1 Perhaps it is as a result of these sexual weaknesses of the Spirits that some of the Arawaks believe in the possibility of an Oriyu introducing into the womb a full-term fetus, provided the woman really wants to be pregnant (Sect. 284A.)—a real water-baby.

187.* HOW THE WATER SPIRIT GOT THE MAN'S WIFE FROM HIM (W)

A man took his wife with him on a fishing expedition. He built a banab on an island in midstream and as night came on told his wife to remain there, while he went to fish. She was very anxious to accompany him in the corial, but he insisted on her remaining and of course she had to obey. Being very tired, she soon afterward fell asleep, and about midnight the Water Spirit paid her a visit. . . . Half-dazed, she woke up, and asked him whether he had done anything to her, and when he told her that he had, recognizing a stranger's voice in place of her husband's, she felt very much ashamed. However, the Water Spirit told her who he was, of his great love for her, and that he would now take her to wife: all she had to do was to tell her previous husband that it was entirely his fault that she had been left alone and taken advantage of, and that henceforth she declined to share his hearth and home. So when the latter returned next morning from his fishing, the wife made a clean breast of everything, for which she blamed him, as he had refused to let her accompany him in the corial, and she told him further that she intended living with him no more. They started now on their way home, and getting into the boat, they paddled a short distance, when the wife said: "After today you will not see me. You must tell all my family to meet me tomorrow at a spot that I will show you." As they traveled along, she showed him the very spot and at the same moment the boat stopped, just as if some one were holding it. She got out, the water coming up to her knees, and the corial continued on its journey. After a while the husband turned around to have a look, and saw his wife with another man, the Water Spirit, just stepping ashore: as he turned the point, the couple were walking together along the river-bank. Now, when he reached home without his wife, all her people wanted to know what had become of her; the mother especially was angry, but became somewhat mollified when he assured her that next day he would take her to the very place where her daughter had left him. He also gave her a message from his late wife that she was to bring the silver nose-ornament and the bead bracelets and necklets which the latter had left behind. So on the following morning he took the mother down to the river-bank, and there sure enough they saw the guilty couple, the daughter and the Water Spirit, behaving in a very friendly manner. As they got quite close, the Spirit suddenly disappeared, leaving the woman by herself. The mother then handed over the beads and ornaments, while her daughter murmured: "Your son-in-law caused this trouble: he would not let me come into the corial with him; and so when I was fast asleep the Water Spirit took advantage of me." Mother and daughter sobbed, and the latter said: "You will see me sometimes, but never distinctly: directly you think you see me clearly, I will disappear." No one knew at the time that the Water Spirit had taken advantage of the man also: but it was this Spirit who had made the husband refuse to let his wife keep him company in the corial, so as the better to carry out his wicked design.

187A.* HOW THE WATER WOMAN SECURED A LANDSMAN FOR HUSBAND (W)

A corialful of men were paddling down the river to catch crabs. They reached the sea, and while hunting in and among the bushes one of the party heard a noise behind him, and turning around was much surprised to see a young woman there, and still more so when he heard her say: "Brother! I am come.1 My father sent me to you to give me a quake of crabs." Having handed them over to her, she paid him with the loan of her body. Before taking her departure she told him that, while the boat containing him and his friends would be passing up the creek on the way home, it would suddenly stop of itself in a certain spot: he was then to jump into the water and join her, and she would bring him to his own home later on. This is exactly what did occur. When the man and his friends had filled their quakes and boarded the corial, he told them that he had acted in an evil way to a girl among the crab bushes, and that when the boat suddenly stopped of its own accord, he would have to jump out, but that he would join them later on. After a while the corial suddenly came to a standstill, our friend jumped out, and his friends left him standing in the water where the girl was holding him up. They reached home at last, and on arrival at the landing-place their women were waiting to carry the crabs up to the house. The one who was disappointed at not seeing her husband asked what had become of him. They told her that he had acted wrongly with a girl, and that they had left him behind. In the meantime the erring spouse was taken by the Ho-aránni girl [Sect. 177] to her people below, and her father told him that he had been sent for because his daughter wanted him. But he added: "You can go home to your own people this very day, and enjoy the feast of crabs that you and your friends have been gathering. I make only this one condition. If there is any disturbance or fighting at the sport, you must come back here at once: otherwise, you may remain with your own people, and we will not trouble you further. I am sending both my daughters with you." And so it came to pass that the two girls took him to his own landing-place, and when they got near, they told him to shut his eyes. As soon as he opened them again he found himself on land, close to his house. He entered, and telling everyone "how day?" sat down: his wife brought him food and drink. But as the evening progressed, the people all began to be quarrelsome in their cups, with the result that his brothers-in-law, sisters-in-law, and wife all threatened to beat him for sporting with the strange girl. This was quite enough for him. He rushed out of the place right back to the landing, where the two Water Women were awaiting him, and who asked why he was not enjoying himself at the party. But when he told them how his people had commenced to interfere, and had threatened to beat him, they took him back into the water, where the old Ho-aránni father said, "Take my two daughters to wife."

188.* These Water People have great liking for women at the menstrual period, so much so that, at such a time, no Carib, Akawai, Warrau, or Arawak woman will travel by boat or even cross water.

*THE MOON-SICK GIRL AND THE WATER SPIRIT (C)

A young girl had reached the age when she was developing certain signs indicative of approaching womanhood. Her mother went as usual to work in the field, but on her return was much surprised to see neither daughter nor house, and in place of the latter a large sheet of water. She said that Okoyumo must have carried her girl away, and began to weep. When her husband later on came back from the chase, she told him p. 249that Okoyumo had swallowed her daughter, and this news upset him much. "I do not want to live without my girl," he cried; "Okoyumo must swallow me also," and so saying, he jumped into the flood. The Spirit of the Water, however, did not want to punish him, and so would not let him drown, but just made him float level with the surface; he of course could not be sick in the same way as the girl. It is the scent of a woman's sickness when in that condition that makes her so attractive to Okoyumo.

189.* THE MOON-SICK GIRL AND THE WATER SPIRIT (W)

There was once a little girl by the river-side catching fish with a cassava-sifter. She caught one little fish entirely different from anything she had ever seen; it was so pretty, with beautiful eyes, and a slim body, covered with red spots. "What a pretty fish you are!" she exclaimed; "I must really keep you all for myself." So she put it alive in water in her calabash and took it home, where she dug a little hole near the house. Into this hole she poured water, and there she placed the fish. Then she tended it, and strange to say the water never dried up. The fish gradually grew bigger and bigger, and when it had arrived at a good size, its guardian, who had already entered womanhood, took it down to the water-side just where she used to bathe. There she set it free. As soon as she got into the water, it would approach and nestle quite close to her. The mother often saw it swimming about there, and would often warn her daughter that it was not a real fish, but something else, and when it got very big, she recognized it as the Ho-aránni, or the Water Spirit. Then she warned her girl especially to keep out of the stream when she was moon-sick. "Don't go anywhere near the water until so many days are passed," the mother repeated; but her advice was not heeded, and the young woman, although sick, insisted next day on bathing. As soon as she touched the fish, as had hitherto been her wont, it became much excited, and instead of coddling up to her, swam zigzag around her. This was repeated three times: the fish meant to tell her that she must return at once to shore, but she evidently did not understand, because she touched it a fourth time. But on this occasion the Water Spirit swallowed her. The father was sorely grieved at this, and came and asked the Ho-aránni why he had treated his daughter in that shameful manner, but the latter defended himself by saying that she had insisted on bathing herself too soon after she had been moon-sick, and that he had already warned her three times. So saying, the Water Spirit withdrew. When he was gone, the father exclaimed, "As Ho-aránni has eaten my daughter, he must eat me too: I cannot rest until he does." Being a piai, he knew where to find the Water Spirit, so collecting his relatives around him, he told them what he proposed doing, and that when they heard him blow his shell they must dig at the very spot indicated. With this, he dived into the water, right down below the river bank under an overhanging hill, straight into the underground cavern of the Water Spirit. And there Ho-aránni killed him, but before he died, he blew his shell; his friends heard him, and digging quickly, soon unearthed the pair. They killed the Water Spirit, and left his bones to rot. Some fifteen years ago, when I was so high [indicating his size], I saw the bones rotting on Wakapoa Creek, above where the Mission now stands. Why was the piai killed? Because he ought not to have gone alone; when people start on such expeditions they should always have company.

190.* Like the Bush Spirits, the denizens of the deep are in large measure responsible for the disease and sickness existent in the world: the Carib medicine-man still invokes them (Sect. 309).

*HOW SICKNESS AND DEATH CAME INTO THE WORLD (W)1

A man went fishing, and wished for a wife from among the Water People, the Ho-aránnis. Every time he went to the water his heart yearned to see a Water Spirit, and one day, while fishing, one put in an appearance waist-high above the surface, and came quite close. "Would you like to take me home with you?" was the first question she asked him, and when he told her "Yes," she clambered into his corial, and he took her home. When they reached there she told him not to roast the morokot fish [Myletes] which he had caught, but to boil it, and impressed him that for the future he must never bring fish for her to eat, but only animals and birds. The next day she went with him in the corial while he fished, and after a time got into the water and went deep down. After a while she came up to the surface again, with a message from her father, who said he would be very glad to welcome him below. The man was afraid to go, but the woman told him to have no fear as nothing would happen to him. Just to show that there was no danger she stood straight up in the water, which came to the level of her hips. "Come along! Don't be frightened," she repeated, and so he jumped in close by her side. Saying that she was going to tie the boat up with a rope, she bent down and seizing the head of a big water-camudi, clamped its jaws on the gunwale. She now took the man's hand, and led the way below: as he sank below the surface he shut his eyes and opening them almost immediately afterward, found himself in the house of his father-in-law. The latter gave him a bench to sit on, which was really a large live alligator. This is how it has come to pass that we Warraus always use a bench carved in the likeness of that creature. When he had sat on it some time the old man said, "I sent you my daughter for your wife: you must live a good life, and must now send down your sister for my son." This was all agreed to, and the man's Ho-aránni wife brought him dry boiled meat and cassava: the eating done, she gave him to drink. When all was finished, she led him up to the surface again, They got into the corial and reached his home once more. She then said to him: "Remember, when I am moon-sick you must not send me away to the naibo-manoko,2 but you must let me remain in the hut with you. In fact, if you insist on my going there I shall die, and if I die, my father will have a spite against you, and send you sickness and death." Now the Warrau people were strongly averse to such a defiance of their long-established custom, and when the man's wife did at last become moon-sick, the women insisted on her going into the naibo-manoko, but they found her lying dead there the following morning. Placing her body in a hollowed-out piece of the palm, they put it on a sort of babracote under a banab [as the Warraus of the Orinoco treat the bodies of their dead]. After a few days the widower went back to his usual fishing-place, wishing he could see his wife again, but being unable to see her anywhere, he became exasperated and flung himself into the water, sinking down in just the same spot as on the previous occasion. He reached the house, and there on the farther side lay his poor wife. She looked ill; indeed, she was quite dead. Her old father turned to him and said: "Why didn't you listen to my daughter? Why didn't you do what she told you? You see how you have killed her. From now on sickness, accident, and death will come among your people from mine, and what is more, if any of your women-folk travel on water while they are moon-sick [Sects. 188, 189], my people will 'draw their shadows'." [Sect. 253.]3 The man was much grieved to p. 251 hear all this, and returned to his own home by the way that he had come. By and by he arranged with his friends and relatives to go to sea, never thinking of the warning which the Water People had given him. They started in two big canoes and got out into deep water; so deep that to the Ho-aránnis at the bottom the corials looked like two parrots flying in the skies. Nevertheless, these Water People shot at them with their round-knobbed arrows, hit them, and both boats sank. When they got to the bottom, the Water People put one of the canoes on each side of the old man's home, and unchained their sharks—for these people keep sharks as we keep dogs—which tore to pieces the bodies of the already dead occupants of the two canoes. Before that time Warraus never had accidents or death; they had only moon-sickness. It was in this manner that the Water People punished the Warraus.

191.* Not only are many of the troubles afflicting mankind, as just recorded in the legend, ascribable to the machinations of Oriyu, but he (or she) is held responsible for more than one natural phenomenon. The tidal wave, or bore, known as appapuru [an Arawak term] on the Berbice and other streams, in certain of this colony's rivers is a case in point. Among the natives the popular explanation is that when this River becomes inconveniently low for the bad things of the deep, they show their uneasiness by moving furiously about, and thus agitate the river (Da, 21). The several tribes on the coast, we learn from Doctor Hancock, usually give it some name, signifying "head of waters" or "mother of waters," and in connection with this have many strange stories to tell of the Loku-kuyuha (people's spirit) mermaid, or "watery mamma" as they translate it (ScC, 288). Again, Wailak-paru, a creek on the right bank of the Potaro, is so called from a part of the human body, and is believed to be the home of Oriyu: the turbulence of the water as it runs into the Potaro is caused by water issuing from the body of that Spirit.

192.* The Water Spirits must not be talked about, nor may their names be mentioned.

*AMANNA AND HER TALKATIVE HUSBAND (C)

Heated with the fumes and liquor of a big paiwarri feast, an Indian succeeded in making his way to the pond where he intended bathing his skin and getting cool. On arrival there, he was met by Amanna, one of the Okoyumo Nation, a very pleasant-spoken woman, who asked him to join her in the water. He demurred at first, but what with her repeated requests coupled with the attractiveness of her physical charms, he ultimately consented. Even at the last moment, he said he felt sure that he would be drowned; but she promised to look after him and see that no harm befell. When they got below the surface, he saw a number of houses, plenty of people, and many young women:

he felt quite content now, especially when the latter offered him drink. But Amanna would have none of this, and took him straight away to her old father, who gave him welcome and instructed his daughter to look after him properly. And this she did. In the meantime the man's mother had missed him from the convivial gathering, and following his tracks, traced them to the water's edge; and there the tracks disappeared. "My poor son, must have been drowned," she murmured, and proceeded to look for his floating body; but of course it was nowhere to be seen, and she mourned him a long time as dead. Thus, time slipped on, and the desire came on him to see his mother; so he visited her. After she had asked him where he had p. 252been in the meanwhile, he told her that he had been for a "walk-about." This made the old woman say: "Well, you must not go away again, because I am aged now and starving. I cannot depend on your little brother to support me, and you know I have no other children." But the man had a bad mind, and went back that very afternoon to his Water Spirit wife, and on this occasion remained with her even longer than he had done before. When at last he returned after his second absence, he found his mother and little brother drinking paiwarri. The latter questioned him point blank as to whether he was living with the Okoyumo People. This naturally made him extremely angry and, with a "How dare you ask me such a question?" he hurried back to the water, where he remained a still longer period than that of his second absence. In the meantime Amanna had borne him three children, and leaving the latter behind, he told his wife to accompany him on a visit to his mother. The couple on arrival found the old mother and her younger son again at a drinking party, but this time the son was absolutely drunk, and nothing would do but he must ask his elder brother as before whether he was living with the Okoyumo People. "Yes, I am!" replied the exasperated man, "and this is my wife, Amanna, one of that nation." Directly the woman heard this, she made all haste to the waterside, and jumped into the water, her husband in close pursuit. As soon as he got below her friends and relatives set on him and killed him for having mentioned her name and telling people who she was.

193.* Besides their dislike to hearing mention of their names and antecedents, as well as their passion for menstruating women, it is interesting to note the strong objection of the Water Spirits to a pot-spoon being washed outside of the traveling boat in either river or sea (Sects. 214, 219).

194.* The surest way of offending the Water Spirits, however, and thereby getting caught in a storm, and being capsized, wrecked, or drowned by way of punishment, is to utter certain words strictry forbidden under the circumstances. Thus, among the Arawaks of the Pomeroon and Moruca Rivers, there are certain terms which must never be employed when on a boat: they have to be paraphrased. The majority of these tabooed words are evidently of foreign (mostly Spanish) origin: a few are certainly indigenous. Thus, the occupants of a corial will never be heard to use the term arcabuza (gun), but they will speak of a gun as kataroro (foot, referring to the stock); they talk of kariro (the one with the teeth) instead of perro (Span., dog); of kanakara-shiro (load on the head, the cock's comb) instead of gai-ina (Span., gallina, fowl); of akwadoa-kotiro (round foot) instead of kawai-yo (Span., caballo, horse); of kakwaro (horn) instead of bakka (Span., vaca, cow); of tataro (something hard) instead of sereri (grindstone, or saw, probably from Span. sierra); of majeriki (the untrimmed one, referring to the hair) instead of hó-a (monkey); of ehedoa (frothing, brimming over, in reference to its snarling or growling) instead of aroa (tiger); of katau-chi (the one with wisdom) instead of semi-chichi (meclicine-man), etc. The Warraus, it seems, had also various words strictly taboo when traveling by boat. The same holds good for Cayenne, where the superstitious Indians take care not to speak of several things by their right names: p. 253thus, if one has to speak of a rock, it must be described as "that which is hard;" if it is a lizard, they must similarly paraphrase by saying "that which has a long tail." It is dangerous also to name the streams and little islands that they pass en route. Even the medicine-men may not be mentioned as such: infringement of this rule will cause at least rain to fall, without reckoning that one is exposed to shipwreck, together with the likelihood of some frightful monster rising from out the deep, and swallowing the whole lot (PBa, 184). Records have been left to us of similar practices by the Carib islanders. When they have to cross the sea . . . upon approaching land, this must not be named or pointed out, but it can be noticed by shouting Lyca! "It is there!" (BBR, 245).

Footnotes

p. 246

1 Among some of the old Warraus the product of an abortion is described as the Water Spirit's child, being 2 or 3 inches long, with the head like that of a horse and the feet like those of a lizard.

p. 247

1 This explains a curious phase of Indian character: Celibacy in either sex is regarded as something uncanny or unnatural. It is on this account that two very respected residents in my district, leading presumably irreproachable celibate lives, were believed by many of the Indians to have enjoyed intimate relations with the Oriyu.

p. 248

1 For this mode of address, see Sect. 116.

p. 250

1 See Sect. 108.

2 The Naibo-manoko is the little out-house for the special use of women at their periods, and sometimes for the use of a female during confinement. It can always be distinguished by the tassels of "skinned" Mauritia leaves (those from which the cortex has been removed for twine manufacture), hanging from the posts and other parts. This building is of course taboo to the males, though I am afraid that advantage is often taken by bachelor friends of this isolation of the females from their husbands.—W. E. R.

3 What is intended is, that just as a person draws the entrails out of a fowl, so will the Water People, or Ho-aránnis, draw the Shadow, or Life-essence, out of a person, that is, kill him.

CHAPTER XIII
THE SPIRITS OF THE SKY

The Sun, male: Greeted of a morning (195); eclipsed (196); origin of his warmth and heat (197). The Moon, also male: Cause of the "spots" (198); beliefs concerning the "new" moon (199); when eclipsed, a transformation of animals occurs (200); causes of eclipse (201-202). Comets (203). Stars: Morning and Evening, etc. (204); the Milky Way (205); Southern Cross (206); Babracote and Camudi (207); Pleiades—their story told by Arawaks (208), Akawais (209), Warraus (210), Caribs (211); Orion's Belt (211A). Other Sky Spirits derived from man (212). The Woman of the Dawn (212A). Rain: Can be made as required (213); punishment for infringement of taboo (214); can be stopped (215); Rainbow (216). Weather-forecasting (217). Thunder and Thunderbolts (218). Storms generally (219).

195.* The Sun seems to have been regarded invariably as a male (Sect. 29): The Salibas of the Orinoco—certainly a section of the tribe—claimed to be his children (G, I, 113). At Enamouta Village, on a branch of the Ireng, it would appear to be the usual practice for the Indians to issue simultaneously from their houses at daylight and greet the morn with cries and loud shouts (Bro, 129). It was customary for the Otomacs to bewail the dead as a matter of daily routine. "Thus, as soon as the cocks crow, about 3 o'clock in the morning, the air is rent with a sad and confused sound of cries and lamentations, mixed with tears and other appearances of grief. They mourn not by way of ceremony, but in very truth. When day breaks, the wailing ceases and joy reigns" (G, I, 167). So also on the Vichada, a branch of the Orinoco, the Guahibos at sunrise come out with a pan-pipe and make the round of the village while playing on this instrument, but their purpose in doing so is not made clear (Cr, 554). Among the Wapisianas of the upper Rio Branco, the first to awake strikes a drum until all jump out of their hammocks, and, in the meantime, with a quick step, he will promenade around the maloka with his barbarous music (Cou, II, 268). With the Island Caribs the flute is ordinarily played in the morning when they rise (RoP, 509).

196.* It is said by im Thurn that on one occasion, during an eclipse of the sun, the Arawak men among whom he happened to be rushed from their houses with loud shouts and yells: they explained that a fight was going on between the Sun and the Moon, and they shouted to frighten and so part the combatants (IT, 364). Brett speaks of Oroan,1 the great Demon of Darkness, who causes eclipses; he seizes p. 255 the Sun and strives to quench the fire, till scorched and blackened, he retires, only to return another time (BrB, 189). In Cayenne, eclipses of the Sun and Moon upset the Indians a good deal: they think some frightful monster has come to "devour these heavenly bodies. If the eclipse is total or of short duration, they consider it a fatal thing for them: they make a terrible noise, and shoot a volley of arrows into the air to chase away the monster (PBa, 232). Island Caribs attribute the eclipses to Maboia, the devil, who tries to kill Sun and Moon: "they say that this wicked seducer cuts their hair by surprise, and makes them drink the blood of a child, and that, when they are totally eclipsed, it is because the Stars, being no longer warmed by the Sun's rays and light, are very ill" (Ti, 1886, p. 227).

197.* THE STORY OF OKOÓ-HI (W)1

Waiamari was the name of a young fellow staying at the house of his uncle. One day he went down to the water-side to bathe. When in the water, he heard some one running down the pathway and then a splash. This made him look around, and, recognizing his uncle's young wife, he commenced swimming to a distance. But she chased him. The girl wanted him very much, and as she got close to the spot where he was, whispered, "Don't you want me?" Instead of replying quietly, however, Waiamari loudly upbraided her by shouting Bila! Kwahoro! ["Incest! Shame!"], and the girl drew back. The uncle, hearing the noise up at the house, called out to his wife, "What's the matter? Don't trouble the boy," because he thought that she must be at fault, and not his nephew. At any rate the couple got out of the water, and came up to the house, which the aunt entered, the boy passing on to go to stay with his elder uncle, Okohi, at whose place he slept that night. Now, the very fact of not going home as usual with his aunt made Waiamari guilty in the eyes of her husband, who followed his nephew next morning to Okohi's place. When he reached there, he reproached his nephew for having attempted improper conduct with his wife, a charge which was indignantly denied. At any rate, they started fighting and the uncle was thrown down. They fought again and the uncle was thrown a second time. Okohi now interfered, and said, "Boy! That will do," and so stopped the contention between his brother and nephew. Indeed, to save further strife, Okohi thought it best to take Waiamari away with him on his journey, and told the youngster to prepare the waija [canoe], as he proposed leaving next morning. So Waiamari went down to the water-side and painted the sign of the Sun on the bows of the boat, while at the stern he painted a man and a moon.2 Next morning the two got away, the nephew paddling in the bow and the uncle steering: it was a big sea that they were crossing, and as the paddle-blades swept along one could hear the water singing Wau-u! Wau-u! Wau-u!3 At last they crossed this big sea and reached the opposite shore, where they landed, and then they went up to a house near by, where they met a pretty woman, Assawako.4 After greeting Okohi, and telling him to be seated, she asked him to let his nephew accompany her to the field, and, this permission being granted, the young couple started off. When they reached there Assawako told Waiamari to rest himself while she gathered something for him to eat. She brought him yellow plantains and pines, a whole bundle of sugar-cane, p. 256some watermelons and peppers; he ate the lot and spent a very happy time with her. On the way back, she asked him whether he was a good hunter: he said never a word but stepped aside into the bush, and soon rejoined her with a quakeful of armadillo flesh. She was indeed proud of him, and resumed her place behind.1 Just before reaching home, she said: "We are going to have drink when we get in. Can you play the kahabassa?"2 "Yes, I can play it a little," was the reply. When they got back to her place Assawako gave him a whole jugful of drink all for himself, and this primed him for playing the music; and he played beautifully, making the kahabassa sing Waru-huru-téa.3 They sported all night, and next morning Okohi made ready to leave. Of course poor Assawako wanted Waiamari to remain with her, but he said: "No! I can not leave my uncle. He has been good to me, and he is an old man now." So she began crying, and between her sobs told him how sad she felt at his going away. This made him feel very sorry also, and he consoled her by saying, "Let us weep together with the kahabassa." And there and then he sang Heru-heru, etc., on the instrument, and thus comforted her before he left.

Now when at last uncle and nephew got back to their own country, old Okohi bathed his skin, and after seating himself in his hammock, gathered all his family around and spoke to them as follows: "When I was young, I could stand traveling day after day, as I have just done, but I am old now, and this is my last journey." So saying, his head "burst," and out of it there came the Sun's warmth and heat.

198.* The Moon also is clothed with male attributes, and among the tribes here dealt with, as is the case with many another savage race, is held responsible for certain conditions met with during the child-bearing period of woman's life. I have heard the following tradition among both Arawaks and Warraus:

*HOW THE MOON GOT HIS DIRTY FACE

Long ago a brother and his sister were living by themselves. Every night after dark some one used to come and fondle and caress the sister, attentions which she was very far from being averse to, but she was very curious to discover who her unseen visitor was. She could never find out. She therefore blackened her hands one day with the soot from the bottom of the pepper-pot, and when her lover came that evening, she smeared her hands over his face.4 When day dawned she thus came learn that it was her own brother who had taken advantage of her. She was extremly angry, abused him roundly, and told the neighbors, who in turn spread the story of his conduct far and wide. The result was that everybody shunned him and he became at last so thoroughly ashamed of himself that he declared he would keep away from everyone, and live by himself. He is now the Moon, and the marks which can still be recognized on his face are those which his sister imprinted with the soot (or blue paint) years ago. Even to this day women do not trust him, and no matter whether he is new, full, or on the wane, there will always be found somewhere a female who is in such a physiological condition as will preclude all possibility of the moon wishing to pay her a visit.5

p. 257

199.* A peculiar custom among the Makusis, practised as soon as the new moon is visible (Sect. 227), is that of all the men standing before the doors of their huts, and drawing their arms backward and forward in its direction at short intervals: by this means they are strengthened for the chase (ScR, II, 328). "As soon as the new moon appears, they all run out of their huts and cry Look at the moon! . . . They take certain leaves, and after rolling them in the shape of a small funnel, they pass some drops of water through it into the eye, while looking at the moon. This is very good for the sight" (BBR, 228). The first night of the incoming moon was considered the proper occasion for obtaining clay for the manufacture of pots and other utensils which, it was believed, would not speedily be broken (Sect. 258).

200.* With regard to the explanations given as to the nature of the eclipse of the moon, I have obtained the following at first-hand from the Pomeroon Arawaks. The phenomenon is due to its traveling along the Sun's path, falling asleep, and so not being able to get out of the way quickly enough. With the object of awakening the Moon members of this tribe strike drums, blow shells, and make a big noise generally, whenever the eclipse takes place. They must also keep themselves lively and active, and during the whole night must eat absolutely nothing; were they to break the fast, they would change into whatever animal or plant they might be eating (Sect. 248). Indeed, it is a common belief among these people that, at the time of an eclipse, there is a constant change or transformation-scene taking place on Nature's stage, in both animal and vegetable kingdoms, owing to this cause. The transformation is not necessarily sudden but may take time. I can call to mind an old Arawak story of a hunter who had gone to visit one of the streams away back from the Moruca River: On the first occasion he sees a huge land-camudi; on the second, at the time of an eclipse, he finds the snake changed into a tapir; and on the third he sees it swimming in the water as a manati.

201.* As to the Orinoco Indian tribes, Gumilla has left us some very interesting records concerning the eclipse of the moon. Some of these nations believed that it was about to die: others that it was angry with them, and that it would give them no more light. The Loláca and Atabáca Indians held to the death theory (G, II, 274) and were under the conviction that if the Moon were indeed to die, all exposed fires would be extinguished. Their women, crying and yelling—an outburst in which the men joined—accordingly would each seize a glowing ember and hide it, either in the sand or underground. Moved by their tears and entreaties, the Moon however recovers, and the hidden fires are extinguished: but were he indeed to die, the concealed embers would remain alight. The Salivas had different views (G, II, 277). All the warriors stand up in rows facing the Moon, offering him their prowess and strength and entreating p. 258 him not to leave them. The young men, of 15 to 20 years of age, stand in two rows apart while certain old men roughly thrash them in turn with whips. Finally, the women, in a sea of tears bewail the Moon's projected departure and fatal absence. The idea would seem to be that the Moon has enemies whom, through fear, he is anxious to avoid, and he is therefore desirous of giving the benefit of his light to other nations. It is only the promises of these Indian warriors to fight in his favor which allay his fears, and hence there is no necessity for him really to take himself off. As soon as the Guayánas (G, II, 278) recognize an eclipse of the moon, they take up the implements used in cultivating their fields. With much talk and gesticulation, some cut the undergrowth, others clear it, and others again dig up the ground, all of them loudly proclaiming that the Moon has cause for being annoyed, and particularly good reason for forsaking them, considering that they had never made a field for him. They accordingly beg him not to go, because they are now providing him with a field, in which they propose planting maize, cassava, and plantains. With these promises and entreaties they continue at their task, working on it with vigor so long as the eclipse lasts; and as soon as it is over, they return to their houses overjoyed. But there is no more working on the field in the Moon's behalf until the next eclipse takes place! Among the Otomacs (G, II, 279), when the event occurs, the husbands aimlessly take up their weapons, skip about, and yell beyond measure, stretch the arrow on the bow in sign of anger, and ask, beg, and implore the Moon not to die. While they continue in their grief, the Moon goes on diminishing and languishing. Recognizing from this that their actions are not understood, they run back to their houses, where they bitterly reproach their wives for not grieving over and bewailing the Moon's sickness. The latter make not the slightest sign that they understand what is expected of them, and answer never a word. The men then change their tactics and start begging and beseeching their wives to cry and weep, so that the Moon may revive and not die. Still the women act as if they do not understand what is besought of them. So the men give them presents—glass-beads, monkey-tooth necklaces, jewelry, and the like. The women now understand in truth, and saying many prayers soon make the Moon shine as bright and clear as before— for doing which they earn their husbands' gratitude. According to their idea it is the female voices that move the Moon to take compassion on them, and save them from extinction.

202.* The Uaupes River (Rio Negro) Indians believe that at an eclipse, Jurupari (Sect. 101) is killing the Moon; they make all the noise they can to frighten him away (ARW, 348). So again, the Island Caribs say that Maboya (Sect. 84) is eating the Moon on such an occasion: they dance all night, and rattle their calabashes with p. 259 little pebbles inside (RoP, 461). Schomburgk points out the curious fact that the Taruma word for a moon eclipse is piwa-toto, the literal translation of which is 'Moon-Earth' (ScR, II, 469).

203.* Any reference to comets in the Indian literature is extremely scarce. With regard to the one that was seen by Schomburgk in the early forties, the Arekunas and Makusis regarded it as a sign of pestilence, famine, and disaster. One night they all emerged from their huts . . . men, women, and children extended their arms expressive of supplication and beseeched it to leave the heavens, so that they should not come to grief under its influence . . . the Makusis called it Ca-po-eseima, "Fire-Cloud," or Wae-inopsa, "Sun that throws its rays behind"; the Arekunas gave it the name of Wa-taima, and the Wapisianas Capische, both terms signifying "Spirit of the Stars" (ScR, II, 308). The Pomeroon Arawaks speak of the present year's (1910), Halley's, comet, simply as Wiwa-kihi-koro (lit. "Star-tail-with"), but have no information to furnish concerning it. Among the Island Caribs, Limacani is a comet sent by Coualina, the "boss" of the Chemeens [i. e., Familiar Spirits] to cause evil when he is vexed (BBR, 231).

203A.* In the Makusi legend of Murapa-yeng (lit. Bat Mountain, one of the Pakaraima Range) the phenomenon is ascribed to an old woman carrying a fire-stick under somewhat pathetic circumstances: Schomburgk tells the story.

*THE LEGEND OF BAT MOUNTAIN

A long, long while ago, an immense Bat lived on the mountain and spread fear and terror among the Makusis. As soon as the Sun had sunk in the west, the huge creature left its unknown dwelling, swept down upon the happy homes, and, swift as an arrow, pounced upon and carried off anyone whom it found out of doors: it carried the individual in its powerful claws up to its unknown nest and there devoured him. Fear reigned of an evening throughout the settlements and in the huts, and lamentation filled the air of a morning when often two, sometimes three, persons would be missing; not a night passed without an abduction, the tribe daily numbered less, and its entire annihilation seemed at hand. The medicine-man exorcised the Spirit; it returned again: the men went to discover the residence of the cursed murderer, but they did not find it— Makunaima was not with them. To prevent the total destruction of her tribe an old woman arose and declared herself ready to sacrifice herself for the good of her nation. When night fell, she stationed herself, with a covered fire-stick, in the middle of the village while the remainder of the people crouched in terror within their houses. The fluttering of the wings is heard, and the heroine, seized in the creature's frightful claws, is carried aloft to the charnel house. She now uncovers the fire-stick, which like the Sun throwing its rays backward (the Comet), shows by the streak of light thus produced the direction that the people must follow to find the mortuary house of their brethren. The high flames of fire from the burning nest upon this very mountain showed the folk next morning where to go: they succeeded in killing the creature. History does not say whether the old woman lost her life in this heroic deed; but even now immense heaps of bleached bones are to be found there. (ScR, II, 189.)

204.* Arawaks, Warraus, in fact all the Indian tribes of whom we have reliable accounts, possess myths and legends indicative of more or less animistic conception of the stars and constellations.

Dance (270) says that Eweiwah, or Huewah (Arawak), and Koiunuk (Akawai) are the names of the Morning and Evening stars interchangeably, these tribes supposing that they are one and the same. Brett (Br, 107), on the other hand, gives the Arawak name for Venus as Warakoma [Warukóma], and that generally used for Jupiter as Wiwa Kalimero (i. e. the star of brightness). The Warraus here on the Pomeroon call the Morning Star Okona-kura. She it was who stuck in the hole when her people first came down from above the skies to populate the earth (Sect. 51). The Makusis speak of the Evening Star as Kai-wono, wife of the Moon, because she is to be seen in his near neighborhood, and also on account of her shining more brightly than all the other stars (ScR, II, 328). According to Father Gili, the Indians of the Casiquiare believed that the dew which falls by night was the spittle of the stars (AR, 207), a belief similar to that reported of the Makusis. The Caribs ascribed it to the urination of the stars (ScR, I, 429). The Makusis speak of shooting stars as Wai-taima (ScR, II, 328). The Island Caribs regarded all the heavenly bodies as Carib. Father de la Borde mentions some five or six stars in their cosmogony, but unfortunately has apparently not identified them. Racumon was one of the first Caribs made by Louquo; he was transformed into a large snake with the head of a man; he was always seated on a cabatas (a hard and high tree); he lived on its fruit, which resembles a large plum or small apple, and which he gave sometimes to those who passed; he is now changed into a star. "Savacou was also a Carib. He was changed into a large bird; he is the captain of the Storms and Thunders; he has caused the heavy rains, and is also a star now. Achinaon, a Carib, at present a star, causes light rain and strong winds. Couroumon (a Carib), also a star, causes the heavy sea waves, and upsets canoes; he is also the cause of flood and ebb." (BBR, 229.)

205.* Arawaks speak of the Milky Way under two names, one of which signifies the Path of the Maipuri (Tapir), and the other is the Path of the Bearers of Wai-é, a species of white clay of which their vessels are made. The nebulous spots are supposed to be the tracks of Spirits whose feet were smeared with that material (Br, 107). On equally reliable authority we are told that the three nebulæ within the Milky Way represent a tapir being chased by a dog, followed by a jaguar, who is not particular in choice, so that he take either the dog or the tapir. Another legend is that the nebulæ were formed by celestial wild hogs rooting up the white clay (Da, 296). The Makusis call the Milky Way Parana, a term which they apply also to the sea.

206.* With regard to the Southern Cross, Dance talks of it as being the great White Crane, and gives a legend relative to it (Da, 296). Arawaks and Warraus, however, have told me that this represents the powis (Crax sp.), the nearer "pointer" to it being the Indian just about to let fly his arrow, the farther one indicating his companion with a fire-stick running up behind. This constellation serves also as an indication for the hunting of the bird, Schomburgk recording (ScT, 23) how, when the Cross stands erect, the powis commences its low moan (Sect. 98). The Makusis apparently regard the Southern Cross as the home of the Spirit of this bird.

207.* There are two groups of stars described by the Arawaks and certain of the Warraus, as the Babracote and the Camudi: four bright stars (Pegasus) with four imaginary connecting lines constitute the square frame of the former, another thick cluster (Scorpio) representing the Snake. This is the Arawak story:

*THE BABRACOTE AND CAMUDI (A)

There was a man living with his wife and mother-in-law in the same house: the wife's father had been dead a long time. The man was always going out hunting, but, although he started early, and returned late, luck never seemed to attend his efforts. This made the mother-in-law very angry, and one day she said to him: "You are a worthless son-in-law. Day after day, you go out hunting, and you bring back nothing. Day after day, you go out fishing, and bring back nothing." The man made no reply to all this, but just laid himself quietly down in his hammock where he remained until next morning. Next morning he called his wife and told her to pack the hammocks with sufficient cassava for two or three days, as he intended taking her out hunting with him. After they had traveled a long way, he killed her, cut her into pieces, and dried the flesh on a babracote. Next day he returned home with his victim's liver, and handing it to his mother-in-law said, "Here's the liver of a tapir for you. The wife is laden with the flesh and is slowly coming on behind." The old woman, who was so hungry, spared no time in eating it, and when finished got into her hammock quite satisfied, anxiously looking down the pathway for her daughter. After watching for some hours in vain, she began to think that the alleged tapir's liver must really have been her daughter's. Turning to her son-in-law, she charged him with having killed her daughter, because it was then very late and still she had not returned. He denied it and swore that she would soon be coming, but the woman would not believe him. She continued watching until late in the night, and then she knew that the liver she had eaten was indeed her own daughter's. Of course she slept but little, and early next morning crept quietly out of the house, and made her way to her brother, the large camudi, that lived at the head of the neighboring creek. She told him how her son-in-law had killed her child, and given her the liver to eat. She told him also that she would send the culprit along that very creek, and that as soon as he got within reach he was to catch and swallow him. When she reached home again the old woman said nothing, but next day told her son-in-law that she was feeling very hungry, that he must go out hunting, and that if he went up to the head of the creek, he would find plenty of game to shoot. The son-in-law suspected something, so he went to a younger brother of his and told him to put in a day's hunting at the head of that very same creek, while he took good care to take his bow and arrows in exactly the opposite direction. That same evening, instead of returning to his own place, he came back to his younger brother's house. No brother returned p. 262that night, nor the next day. Indeed, he never came back, because he had been killed and swallowed by the camudi, who had mistaken his man. The son-in-law, after waiting there a few days, then knew what had happened, and made his way to another settlement, far, far from the nagging old woman. On a clear night you can still see the babracote where he barbecued his wife, and close to its side you can just make out the camudi with its swollen belly, due to the younger brother being inside.

208.* The Pleiades, the Seven Stars, bore a very important rôle in the daily life of the Guiana Indians in that, among several other reasons, their rising from the east marked the commencement of their new year: this measurement of time was adopted from the Orinoco to Cayenne. All the legends relating to the constellations Taurus and Orion have something in common in the detail of an amputated arm or leg. Dance speaks of the Stars forming the belt and sword-sheath of the constellation Orion (Da, 343) as Mabukuli (Arawak) or Ibbeh-pughn (Akawai). Now the word Mabukuli signifies "without leg," and the corresponding little story which he relates (Da, 296) will not prove out of place here: "A huntsman being unsuccessful in the chase one day, and being loth to return without flesh for his stepmother, whom he loved, cut off one of his own legs, and wrapping it up in leaves, presented it to her as veritable game; and then ascended into the heavens as Mabukuli (Ibbeh-pughn) or one-legged."

209.* The Legend of the Tumong, or Seven Stars, as told by Dance (296), apparently from Akawai sources, is this:

*THE LEGEND OF THE SEVEN STARS

A man having lustful inclination toward his brother's wife killed his brother while hunting in his company, and cutting off an arm of the murdered man, presented it to the widow as a proof of her husband's death. He then took her as his own wife. But the spirit of the murdered man haunted a tree near by his brother's house, and filled the air at nights with his laments, so that the widow, discovering the treachery of her new husband, became disconsolate. The fratricide, from vexation, decided to rid himself of her, and of her little child. For this purpose he took her ostensibly to hunt with him, and observing a hole at the root of a large tree, he desired her to stoop and search therein for a suspected acouri. While she looked in, he pushed her in completely, and also her child after her, and then stopped up the hole. On that night the spirit of the murdered man appeared to his brother and informed him that he knew of his deed of violence, and was not angry; for his wife had been transformed into an acouri, and his child to an adourie, so that his unnatural malice, save by the infliction of death, could not any more affect them. For himself, he would not cease to render the murderer's life miserable so long as his own mangled body remained unburied. But if the wicked brother would disembowel the body and scatter the entrails, after interring the other remains, not only would the dead cease to be a terror, but at that season every year an abundance of fish would gather in the river. The wretched brother then went to the place of the bloody deed, and did what he was told, when the scattered entrails of the murdered man floated upward to the skies, and assumed the appearance of the Seven Stars. And truly, as was predicted, on the annual appearance of those stars, the yarumak [Pimelodus maculatus], tibicurie [Prochilodus rubro-teniatus], caburessi [Chalceus tæniatus] and several other excellent fishes are abundant in the rivers.

210.* THE STORY OF NOHI-ABASSI (W)1

There were once two brothers: the elder, a celebrated hunter, was called Nohi-abassi; I do not know the name of the younger one. Every day Nohi-abassi went farther and farther afield in the pursuit of game, and at length he reached a creek, where he climbed a tree, watching for the animals to come and quench their thirst. While waiting among the branches, he saw a woman wading up the creek toward the tree and noticed that every time she put her hand into the water she drew out two fish: one of these fish she put into her mouth; the other she put into her basket. She was a very big woman, Nahakoboni by name.2 She was carrying a calabash upside down, like a cap, upon her head, and would every now and again toss it into the water; as she jerked it in, she made it swirl round and round like a top, and there she would stand a few minutes watching it spinning on the surface. Then she would proceed on her way, put her hand into the water, draw out two fish again, devour one, and place the other in her quake. And so she proceeded on her way, passed the tree where Nohi-abassi was in hiding, and still catching two fish at a time, went on her way to the creek-head. Night caught the hunter, and so he had to sleep up the tree. Next morning he reached home, and told his brother what he had seen. The latter said, "I should like to see such a woman, who can catch so many fish, and can eat them as well." But Nohi-abassi answered him: "No! I don't care to take you with me to show her to you: you are always laughing at everything, and you might laugh at her."

And it was only when his brother faithfully promised not to laugh at anything that he might show him, that Nohi-abassi agreed to take him. So they started on their journey and reached the creek where the adventure with the big woman had taken place the day before. Nohi-abassi climbed the identical tree whence he had originally seen Nahakoboni, this tree being situated a few yards away from the creek bank. His brother, however, who wanted to get a good look at the wonderful woman, insisted upon climbing a tree close to the water's edge, and made his way up and along a branch which overhung the stream. Both brothers sat quiet, and by and by Nahakoboni came along as before, doing just the same thing, spinning her calabash, putting her hand into the water, drawing out two fish at a time, one of which she put into her mouth, the other into her basket. At length she came along right underneath where the younger brother was in hiding, and recognized his shadow in the water. This shadow she tried again and again to catch; she put her hand in quickly, first this side and then that, but of course she did not succeed, and what with all her queer gesticulations and funny capers made so ridiculous an appearance that the brother up above could not resist laughing at her vain attempts to seize the substance for the shadow. He laughed again and again and could not stop laughing. Unfortunately for him, Nahakoboni, hearing the sound and looking up, recognized not only him who was just over her head, but also Nohi-abassi, who was on the other tree some few yards distant. Furious at being ridiculed [see Sects. 59, 125], she ordered the former to come down, but he would not. So she sent the "yackman" ants [Eciton sp.] up the tree; and when they reached him, they bit him, and stung him so hard that he had to pitch himself into the water, where she caught and ate him. She then ordered Nohi-abassi to come down, but he would not either, and so she played him the same trick by sending the yackman ants again in pursuit. These forced him to come down, and so soon as he reached the ground Nahakoboni caught him, put him into her basket, which she tied up tight, and carried him home. Arrived there, she placed the quake in a corner of her house, covering it with leaves and bushes, at the same time giving her two p. 264daughters strict injunctions that they were under no pretext whatever to touch it during her absence. Directly her back was turned however—and it was not very long before she remembered that she had to go to her field to pull cassava—the two girls wanted to see what their mother had been at such pains to hide from them. They said, "Why did mother tell us not to trouble the basket?" and, promptly removing the bushes and leaves, cut open the quake and found a real live man inside. They took him out to have a good look, and the younger sister could not help exclaiming, "Oh! what a fine fellow he is, isn't he?" They then asked him if he was a good hunter, and he answered them that he was and would always bring them plenty of game. Both girls therefore fell in love with him, and the younger made him hide in her hammock. Now, when old Nahakoboni returned with her cassava, she busied herself grating it, and it was not until everything else was prepared for the feast that she went to the quake to kill Nohi-abasi with a view to eating him. Judge of her surprise when she found it empty! When asked about it, the girls admitted that they had been to the basket and let the captive free, the younger one adding, "and as he said he was a good hunter, I took him for my husband." The old mother was quite satisfied with this arrangement, and said: "All right! You can have him for your man, so long as he regularly brings me something to eat, but remember, on the very first occasion that he returns home with nothing, I shall eat him." From next day on, Nohi-abassi started going down to the sea regularly to catch querriman [Mugil brasiliensis] for her. No matter the size of the load of fish he procured, old Nahakoboni would eat the whole lot, except two. Fishing like this day after day soon had its effect upon poor Nohi-abassi, who got heartily sick of the task of having to procure so much food for his mother-in-law. His girl fell in with these views and consented to release him from so thankless a task by running away with him. So on the last trip he intended making in the way of bringing home fish, he left his corial, with the catch in it, a little farther out from the bank than had hitherto been customary with him; indeed, he anchored it in deep water and told a shark to lurk underneath. When Nohi-abassi reached home he told his wife as usual to inform her mother that he had brought home a load of fish in the corial, and that she must go down to the water-side for it.1 So old Nahakoboni went down the pathway, reached the creek, and went into the water to haul in the corial with the load of fish, but as soon as she reached the deep part of the stream, the shark seized and devoured her.2 In the meantime, our hero and the younger daughter made preparation for their journey, but the elder one, beginning to feel anxious about her mother staying away so long, went down to the water-side to seek the cause, which she was not long in discovering. She returned in haste, and could hardly speak for passion. She sharpened her cutlass and slashed a tree with it; the cut reached only half through. She sharpened it again, and slashed another tree-trunk; the blade cut it clear through. When Nohi-abassi saw what she was doing, he recognized that his sin had been discovered, and without further loss of time made all speed with his wife to run away. Now, although they had a good start, Nohi-abassi soon recognized that his sister-in-law was quickly gaining on them. He therefore made for the nearest tree and, telling his wife to climb quickly, helped her up with an occasional push behind, he following closely at her heels. He had just made his third step up when his sister-in-law reached him with the cutlass, and making a slash, managed to cut off a portion of his leg, which stuck upon one of the branches. This leg makes a noise like the "maam"—it is in fact the mother or spirit of the maam [Tinamus sp.] [Sect. 98] and when people are out shooting this bird, it is this same leg which occasionlly falls down and kills the hunters. We can still see Nohi-abassi's wife climbing the p. 265tree: she is what we call Kura Moku-moku [lit. stars little, i. e. the Pleiades]. Behind her is Nohi-abassi himself [the Hyades], and farther back is his cut-off leg [Orion's Belt].

211.* Brett's account (BrB, 191) is of interest in comparison with the Warrau story, and I accordingly adapt it here from the metrical version. Before doing so, however, I can but express the probability that the idea of making Aldebaran (the Bull's-eye in our constellation Taurus) the organ of vision for the Tapir—making, in fact, the Tapir correspond with the Bull—is the result of contact with African or European influences. Brett calls the myth the Legend of Sirikoai, and from internal evidence (cf. Sect. 38) I am inclined to think that he must have received it from Carib sources. Sirikio is the Carib name for a star, Wailya for a watchman, and Wawa (cf. Wawaiya) for a sister or a wife: on the other hand, Sahtai is the Akawai name for an ax.

*THE LEGEND OF SERIKOAI

Wawaiya, the lately-made bride of Serikoai, was one day off to her cassava field, when she met a Tapir. He said his name was Wailya, that he liked her, and for the same reason had assumed that form so as to have the chance of coming near her. He came the next day, and the next, and every day while Wawaiya was on her way to the field, and she became fonder and fonder of him. He finally tempted her, and promised her that if she followed him to the eastward, until earth and sky met, he would resume his human shape and take her to wife. But she refused. So he charmed her ax, and assured her that if she did what he told her to do, she would be safe with him. Soon after, Serikoai asked Wawaiya to come with him and gather avocado pears [Persea gratissima], which were now ripe, so that while he climbed the trees, she might collect firewood. She did so, and while her husband was up a tree, she went to grind her ax, but every time it touched the stone it called out, "I must cut. I must wound!" [Sahtai!]. She asked her husband whether he could hear it talking, and he said, "Yes;" that it always spoke like that when being sharpened there, but she must not worry over it. However, while Serikoai was descending the tree she cut his leg clear through and took to flight. Though exhausted by loss of blood, Serikoai plucked an eyelash, and blew it into the air, where it became a beautiful little bird, which he told to fly away to his mother's place and call his name. When the latter heard her son's name, she did not know what the bird meant, and so sent the bird back again to find out. On its return, she immediately rushed off and nursed her son so tenderly that he recovered of his wound. Serikoai now managed to walk about with a crutch, and took up the search to find his wife, but all traces of Wawaiya had then disappeared, what with the lapse of time and the heavy rains. Nothing daunted, however, he traveled on and on, until at last he discovered a sprout of avocado pear. A little farther on he saw another, which revived his hope of finding her, because he now knew that she who had taken the pears must have eaten them on the road, and cast the seeds by the wayside. Traveling on and on, always to the eastward, he saw at last Wawaiya's and Wailya's footprints, and a little farther on saw them conversing right ahead of him. He thereupon shot the Tapir and, cutting off its head, implored his wife to return, saying that if she refused he would follow her forever. She did refuse, nowever, and hurried on with her lover's spirit still after her, and her husband behind them both. Still rushing headlong, the husband reached the earth's steep edge, where Wawaiya threw herself into the deep blue sky. If you watch on a clear night, you can still see Wawaiya p. 266[the Pleiades] with the Tapir's head [the Hyades: the red eye is Aldebaran] close behind, and Serikoai [Orion, with Rigel indicating the upper part of the sound limb] farther back—all three in pursuit.

211A.* Orion's Belt is part of the leg of a woman (Sect. 98)—of Mabukuli (Sect. 208), of Nohi-abassi (Sect. 210), of Makunaima (Sect. 38)—and the arm of the murdered husband (Sect. 209).

212.* As has been already mentioned, the Spirits of people departed may wander upward to join other Spirits in Sky-land (Sect. 81). Some of these may pass their existence happily, and harm no one, or in the course of their transformation (Sect. 69) they may become changed into birds—perhaps into birds of ill omen sometimes—and so have their place in the heavens. Again, the Spirits of good medicine-men travel upward to Cloud-land, and may be invoked by their surviving professional brethren with the aid of the rattle and tobacco (Sect. 309). There are a few other Spirits of the Sky who are essentially bad-minded in the sense of bringing sickness into the world: these also are referred to elsewhere (Sect. 309).

212A.* THE WOMAN OF THE DAWN (W)

Plenty of people went out to hunt, but on the way back, four of them were caugt by nightfall when far away from home. These four comprised a man, his wife, and two daughters; and a long, long way behind them was yet another man. This last man shouted out to the four others, "Hi! Stop! wait for me! wait for me!" to which they replied, "Come along quick, and follow us." But as he could never reach them, he kept on singing Mawa-kakotú [lit. "for me—wait"]. He is the little night owl, who still sings like this. The darkness was now so thick that the four could get no farther. They had to remain where they were, and though they waited and waited, no daylight came. In the meantime they made a fire from ite-palm leaves, but it burned away too quickly; it was no good. They then rolled some wax in a leaf, but this also burned away too quickly: it too was no good. The parents, seeing a little dawn a long distance away in the bush, sent the elder daughter to go and bring it. She went on and on, but zigzag and crossways just like a drunken man, a token that she would never obtain the daylight. She walked in a crooked way because she had already had dealings with a man. Finally she reached the spot where the daylight was, and there she came across an old man and his wife. She asked for his son, but as he was out at work, the old man bade her to wait. When at last the old man's son did reach home, the mother said: "A friend has come to see you. She has waited long. You had better ask her what she wants," And when he asked her what she wanted, She told him how her father had sent her to fetch some daylight. [Extrahens suum clavem, incepit arcam intrare], but the key1 would not fit, the lock1 having been tampered with, and he therefore sent her home again. When she got back, empty handed the younger sister said, "I will try to get some daylight," and although her father told her she was too young to go, she insisted, and went. She did not stumble on the road from one side to the other because as yet she had never had anything to do with a man, and she reached the spot without trouble. Like her sister, she had to await the young man's return, and when he did arrive, his old mother said: "I don't know what is the p. 267matter with your friends. They have never come to visit you like this before. There is another young woman come to see you." On learning that she had come to fetch daylight [inseruit clavem in arcam eius et demonstravit quoquo modo opportuisse uti]. He gave her the Daylight, which she brought back to her parents and sister.

[Among the Paressi (Peru) there is a vaginal origin ascribed to both organic and inorganic nature (PE, 33).].

213.* Rain can be produced as well as stopped by human, animal, or spirit agency, but at the same time would appear to have an independent existence. To make rain on the Pomeroon, one of the authorized methods consists in plunging into water a length of cassava stalk held at one extremity. Next the stalk must be tied up in the center of a bundle of other cassava stalks, and the whole left to soak in water: rain is sure to fall within twenty-four hours. Another method practised here is to wash in water the scrapings from one of an alligator's largest teeth. Arawaks as well as Warraus believe also in the piai or any layman burning the carcass of a camudi as an inducement for the rain to fall. The Oyambis of Cayenne have the same belief in the efficacy of the killing of a snake (Cr, 174). On the Kamwatta Creek, in the Moruca River district, there is a half-submerged tree stump, known as Ibúma (lit. "young woman," in the Warrau language), believed to be the site where either an Indian murdered his wife or where she killed herself. In dry weather the tree is exposed, and as the Indians pass it in their corials, they call out, "Ibúma!" and slash their cutlasses into it, with the avowed purpose of making the woman vexed, and so causing the rain to fall. Rain can also be made to fall in this district by cursing the black kurri-kurri bird as mentioned in the story of the Medicine-man and the Carrion Crows (Sect. 303). On the upper Mazaruni it is a large eagle and a camudi that can cause the rain to fall (Bro, 399); frogs are reputed to be able to do the same thing (Sect. 46).

CHAPTER XIV
OMENS, CHARMS, TALISMANS

Omens, tokens, auguries, etc., dependent on—human beings (220-221); quadrupeds (222); birds (223); insects (224-225); plants (226). Ordeals, Preparatory Charms, for the Chase, with: Incisions, mutilations, nose-stringing (227); frogs, toads (228-229); caterpillars and ants (230); perhaps have a physiological basis (231). Hunting-dogs have to undergo similar ordeals (232). Attraction charms, Binas (1) for hunting: Plants, used on hunter (233), or on his dog (234), originally obtained from a snake (235). Animals used on the hunter and on his dog (236); (2) for sexual purposes: Plants (237); animals (238). Talismans, Repellent (and so Protective or Defensive) Charms: Plant (239), animal, tooth (240), blood and red paint (240A), stone (241).

220.* Omens, tokens, auguries, etc., are known to the Arawaks as adibuahu, to the Warraus as asijatai-ahá. Lucky indeed are those children who are born with a caul (shibo-addahu), because they are going to see spirits (Yawahu) and so become more clever. If the husband is away fishing or hunting, and any little child of his, boy or girl, takes up a pot, and puts it on the fire pretending to cook something (leaves, etc.), the mother can rest assured that their father is bringing something home with him. If a healthy person is suddenly overcome by a sleepy feeling, or if during sleep he happens to spit, this means that he is about to be visited by some one (Arawaks). During sneezing and yawning, the spirit temporarily leaves the body through nose and mouth (KG, II, 152). To point the finger at a fellow creature (Sect. 263) is to offer him as serious an affront as it would be to step over him when lying on the ground; in the latter case, the recumbent person would rightly say, "You can cross me when I am dead. I am not dead yet!" (Arawaks). Our old chieftain, says Schomburgk, had during the morning sprained his foot, while jumping from rock to rock, an accident to which he paid little attention, but which showed he was unable to proceed on the journey to Nappi: this accident was taken as a bad omen by both the Makusis and Arekunas who, with the exception of those who were bound to us by agreement, all turned back to their settlement on the following morning (ScR, II, 291). If the occupants of a settlement [Pomeroon Caribs] wish to assure the victory for their warriors on the march, and want to assure themselves at the same time of the issue of the battle, perhaps already fought, they place two boys on a bench and whip them without mercy, especially over the shoulders. If the boys bear the pain without shedding a tear or uttering a groan, victory is certain. One of the boys is then placed in a hammock, from which he has to shoot at a target fixed to one of the roofs: as many arrows p. 272 as hit the target, so many of the enemy will be killed by the warriors (ScR, II, 431). If after their descent upon the Arawaks, they are discovered before striking the first blow, or a dog yelps at them, the Island Caribs take the incident for a bad augury, and return to their boats; they believe that hostilities, begun openly, will not succeed (RoP, 529).

221.* As a matter of fact, anything that occurs out of the ordinary is accepted in the light of a token of something evil about to happen. For examples of this, I am taking at random the following extracts from the legends already given:

He brought them a turtle, which they put on the hot ashes without killing it, so it promptly crawled out; they pushed it on again, but with the same result. It was the omen betokening their death [Sect. 4].

And when asked how she knew [that the Bush Spirits were coming to spoil the drink], she told them that she had received a sign, or token, because when she was weeping for her late husband, he suddenly appeared before her and told her to cease to cry [Sect. 109].

The elder brother then recognized that it [the fact of the younger persistently making a noise while fishing] was a token of something that was about to happen [Sect. 113].

The wife also met her death shortly after, and they then remembered having noticed the token: she had omitted to bathe after a meal, some days before (Sect. 119).

Her visitor eating the frogs raw was a sign of something wrong somewhere, causing the girl to become suspicious (Sect. 120).

It was not long before the brother again put his feet into the fire, a fact which, considering that he was not drunk, led his brother to believe that it was a token of some evil about to befall (Sect. 126).

When the husband claimed the beast which he had not killed, as his own, the wife realized the token that something unusual was about to happen (Sect. 136).

While eating the beetle grub out of the Mauritia palm, the elder brother heard it whistle: he knew this to be the sign or token that he was about to die (Sect. 139).

221A.* The token or augury may be in the nature of an indescribable sort of feeling.

*THE OBSTINATE GIRL WHO REFUSED THE OLD MAN (W)

An old man asked a woman to come and live with him. She, however, was young and wanted a younger husband, so she declined him. This made the old man much vexed, and he threatened to punish her badly. By and by the woman took as husband a young man. He was a splendid hunter, and always killed anything and everything; even at night, if he heard a tiger growling anywhere in the neighborhood, he would never hesitate to go out into the darkness and slay it. One day he went into the bush to cut out honey, his wife accompanying him. "That will do," she said when she thought he had cut enough, but he wanted to cut one more tree. "No, don't cut another," she repeated, "I feel frightened. I feel strange, as if something were about to happen."1 But he insisted upon cutting one tree more, and no sooner had he done so than two creatures like tigers rushed out of a neighboring thicket and killed him. They were not exactly Hebus, and they were not exactly tigers: they were Spirits of some sort whom the old man had sent to revenge himself with. Now the deceased husband had left two brothers behind him, and when they heard of his death, they made inquiry and examined the place in the forest where he had p. 273been attacked, but could find no trace of the body. The young widow then wanted to take unto herself one of these brothers-in-law, but he was afraid after what had happened to her first husband. Nevertheless, she loosened her hammock, and slung it next to his; she even brought him food, water, and other things, but he refused to handle anything that she offered. Had he done so, she would have said to herself, "He loves me" [Sect. 275]. Nevertheless, she persisted in her attentions, and followed him everywhere; where he went, she went. He told her he was going to cut out honey and that she must go back; she refused, so he threw her into the river. She did not mind, but clung to the edge of the corial, and though he bashed her fingers with the paddle, she refused to let go her hold—well, at last he gave way and let her join him. So they went together to the place where the honey was to be procured, and filled all their goblets,. The woman said, "Don't cut any more. I feel strange. Something is about to happen." He stopped cutting, and helped to pack the corial ready for the return journey. While doing so, the two Tiger creatures came from out of their hiding-place and killed him. And the woman was for the second time a widow. The remaining brother and other members of the family came and visited the spot as before, but there was no trace of the body to be found. It was this remaining brother that the woman next wanted, but after what had happened, he was too much afraid to have anything whatever to do with her. However, she persisted so much, that he was finally forced to consent. They went for the honey as before, the strange feeling came over her, she warned him to stop, they started packing, and the two Tiger creatures appeared. On this occasion, the man killed one of his assailants before being himself dispatched by the other. At any rate, the woman was for the third time a widow. Did she then marry the old man who wanted her originally? No; she would not even look at him.

221B.* HOW THE LITTLE BOY ESCAPED FROM THE CARIBS (W)

A party of women and girls went to gather wild pineapple. They traveled in a large corial, and at last landed. Having roamed the bush and gathered a number of pines, they all sat down in a circle to eat them, and commenced laughing and chattering, as women do. Now there was a little boy among the party, who climbed up all overhanging tree, where the corial had been tied up at the water-side, in order to keep watch; he was afraid that something was going to happen.1 After a while he called out that some men were swimming across the stream, but all that the women jokingly said was: "All right. Let them come. We will have some sport and fun with them." But the men were really Carib cannibals, and as soon as they reached land, they rushed upon the women, slaughtered every one of them, and began cooking the flesh. The boy up the tree was much frightened at seeing all this, but did not dare descend just yet. The Caribs were watching the corial lest anyone should come and fetch it away, and at irregular intervals would wander backward and forward from the scene of the outrage to the landing-place. It was during one of these intervals that the youngster slipped down the tree, and, breaking his arrow, rubbed the pieces over his body to make him brave [Sect. 331]. He then slipped off into the corial, and as quickly as possible reached midstream. By this time the Caribs had recognized him and shouted for him to return. "Come back! Come back!" they screamed: "Your sister is alive and calls you," but the lad knew better and, paddling strongly, got home safe. He told his father and other relatives all that had happened. These hurried back, only to find that the Caribs had made their escape, and so they "received no payment" [i. e. they did not get their revenge on them].2

222.* With regard to animals, let us see what they or their actions can presage.

Serious sickness or death is indicated by either small or large species of armadillo (yeshi and monoraima, respectively), of the jaguar, burrowing or digging up, for the purpose of covering its excreta, any portion of the road leading up to the house. Similarly it is a bad omen for any droppings of the buhürri (a bat) to be found on the pathway (Arawaks). There is a frog with a spotted back which jumps well, and is known to the Pomeroon Arawaks as sorukara. A pregnant woman will tickle it to make it jump, and according as it lands on its back or its belly, so will her child prove to be girl or boy. The Island Caribs regarded bats as their guardian Chemeens or Familiar Spirits, and believed that whoever killed them would become ill (BBR, 235). When the warritimakáro (Bradypus tridactylus), the smallest kind of sloth, which has a curious habit of always covering its face with its crossed hands, uncovers its face, it is a sure token that some one is going to die (Arawaks).

223.* Birds of ill omen are present in plenty. Chief among these is the goat-sucker (Caprimulgus). Writing from the Takutu, Schomburgk says that—

The Indians have the greatest superstition with regard to this bird, and would not kill it for any price. They say it keeps communication with the dead, and brings messages to their conjurers. Even the common people on the coast retain in a great measure this superstition, and hold the bird in great awe. Its nocturnal habits, the swiftness and peculiarity of its flight, and its note, which breaks the silence of the night, have no doubt contributed to the fear which Indians and Creoles entertain for the Wacarai or Sumpy Bird [ScT, 67].

As is the case with even far more civilized nations, owls are of equally evil portent and may indicate sickness, death, the presence of an as-yet-unborn babe, or a birth. Thus, among the Pomeroon and Moruca Arawaks, the boku-boku, and the waro-baiya or maletitoro (both of them species of night-owl), and among the Demerara River Arawaks, the hututu (night-owl) and makudi (small owl) are said always to be heard when a person is sick or about to die. In the Pomeroon the morokodyi (night-owl) cries when a female in the house is enciente. On the Demerara, when the night-owl calls cuta! cuta! cuta! quickly, it is to notify that one in the family is about to give birth to a child; and when that bird mews like a cat, it is the notification of death (Da, 269). In French Guiana, on the upper Parou River, at an Apaläi vinage, Crévaux had a curious experience: "Arrived in the forest where we proposed camping, we heard the notes of a bird which I have reason to believe is a kind of screech-owl. A panic seized my escort, the torches were put out, and men and women saved themselves in the obscurity of the night. We were obliged to return to the village for our night's rest" (Cr, 300). On the Pomeroon p. 275and elsewhere, probably from their custom, when in large numbers, of flying in pairs, one behind the other, the baridi hawks are taken as an omen of a funeral. On the lower Amazon, a black eagle (Milvago nudicollis) locally known as the caracára-i, is considered a bird of ill-omen by the Indians; it often perches on the tops of trees in the neighborhood of their huts and is then said to bring a warning of death to some member of the household. Some say that its whining cry is intended to attract defenceless birds within its reach (HWB, 146). With regard to remaining species of birds, the Pomeroon Arawaks believe that if the koko-bero flies over the house, some one in it will shortly prove pregnant, that or a little baby is about to be taken sick. The voice of the kwa-kwarra brings an evil message, similar to that of the boku-boku. The karéo-obannahu is a small night-bird, so named after its note, karau! karau! and obannahu (the liver, the color of which it resembles). If its note is heard but faintly, some individual must be exceedingly ill: if distinctly, the patient is getting better and stronger. When the beletika cries, some one is about to be married; hence this token may be both of good and bad omen. Another set of bird-tokens may indicate approaching rainfall as well as accident (Sect. 217). There is still another class of omens, indicative of either prospective good luck or bad luck. Thus, when on a hunting expedition, one hears the karrasuri, a small bird, uttering a kind of laugh, he is sure to kill something, but if it should cry shirai, he will get nothing. According as the bukulaura, another bird, turns its back or its breast toward a person, so will fortune or misfortune attend that person's wishes in obtaining whatever food he wants. [Furthermore, when walking along the pathway one must not mind if a munirikuti (species of black ant) bites his foot, because this means that he will obtain something very good and satisfying.] Some Indians will never turn their back on a trogon: "He [the Indian] attributed his safety (from drowning) to the strictness with which the Indians had observed the proper respect due to a trogon that had flown over our heads in the morning: they have a superstition that if, on setting out on a journey, they should turn their backs to this species of bird, ill luck will surely follow." (BW, 146: on the Mazaruni, with an Arawak and Akawai crew.) The following are some miscellaneous examples of bird-omens: On the Pomeroon one must not gaze too long on the great red macaw, unless the individual wishes to become bald, presumably in view of the bird having its cheeks so markedly devoid of feathers. The advent of strangers is notified by the warracabba (trumpeter-bird) when it is seen playing about near the house, having in its mouth a leaf with which it is believed to be building a banab. On the Orinoco, in token of the Father coming to visit them, the Cacique said that on the previous day he had seen a bird with peculiar feathers and colors passing over his house: it gave p. 276 them notice of his approach (G, I, 311). Children are discouraged from picking up certain feathers, as these tend to weaken memory, and the handling of the feathers of a scissor-tail hawk, called by the Atorais chaouneh, conduces to insanity (Da, 250).

223A.* THE NIGHT-OWL AND HIS BAT BROTHERS-IN-LAW (W)

Boku-boku, the Night-owl, married the bats' sister, and often took his brothers with him at night to rob peoples' houses. One night they came across a house where the people were drying fish on a babracote: just to frighten them, they all sang out, boku! boku! boku!—this made the occupants run out into the bush, and so gave the bats their opportunity for stealing the fish. The trio played the same trick at many a settlement, until one day the owl told them he had to travel about for a while, and that during his absence they must behave themselves, and stay indoors at night, as otherwise trouble would be sure to happen. But no sooner had Boku-boku turned his back, than the bats, unable to resist temptation, continued their evil courses, They got to a place one night where the fish were being dried, but having no owl with them on this occasion, they could not shout boku! boku! boku! as loudly as they did before; hence, the people not being so frightened now, ran away only a little distance, just far enough to be able to watch everything and to see that it was only the bats who were stealing their food. But the bats, remaining undisturbed, thought they could now do what they liked with impunity, and hence returned again upon the following evening, when the people remained just as they were, some seated, some lying in their hammocks. The bats still thought of course that nothing bad could happen them, and were laughing chi! chi! chi! for very joy. But the house master took out his bow and arrow, the latter tipped with a knob of wax, with which he shot one of them on the rump, stunning it.[1] The other bat, escaping into the forest, met Boku-boku, who had just returned from his travels, and to whom he narrated the circumstances of his brother's untimely death. Nothing daunted, the two returned to hunt that night, and on this occasion the noise of their voices, now that it included the owl's, created such a stir that the folk ran as before into the bush, while Boku-boku and his brother-in-law stole the fish. But lying on the babracote was the dead bat, which they took home with them, and there they soundly smacked him on the spot where he had been struck with the arrow: this brought him round, the fire not having withered him up beyond recovery, and he laughed chi! chi! chi! on awakening. And although Boku-boku was prevented accompanying them the following evening, the two bats insisted on repeating their nocturnal excursion: as before, the folk were not frightened, and again one of the bats got shot in his posterior. Next night, the surviving bat returned with Boku-boku, and they found as before upon the babracote, the body of their relative: this they took away with them, but on this occasion, when they smacked the corpse, it never woke—it had been dried too much over the fire. The surviving bat however continues to take his revenge upon people and sucks them and their fowls, as well as doing other damage, while the presence of Boku-boku, his brother-in-law, invariably means mischief: when heard at night, some one is surely about to sicken and die.

224.* There are two bees which indicate the arrival of a stranger. One of these insects (honorari) comes in the morning early, and in the afternoon late, while the other (wariro) lives in the ground; when either of these buzzes Arawaks are convinced that people are about to visit them. The modudu is another bee that flies round p. 277somewhere between 4 and 5 a. m.: should a young person hear it buzzing he (or she) must immediately get out of the hammock, on penalty of having pains all over the body. The Arawaks of the Pomeroon believe that if a candle fly, Pyrophorus noctilucus (koko-i) is seen coming into the house, it may mean three things: supposing it falls to the ground, this indicates the near death of one of the inmates; if it falls into the fire, this shows that a deer has sent it along to fetch a light for him; but if it settles down under the roof, the arrival of a stranger is to be expected. The bite of a certain ant is lucky (Sect. 223).

225.* THE CANDLE-FLY SAVED THE LOST HUNTER (C)

Five men formed themselves into a hunting party, and went out into the forest. At nightfall they built themselves a banab, and next morning they all started in different directions to scour the neighborhood. Late in the afternoon they had returned to the resting place, all except one. Three of the four said, "Our friend is either lost or a tiger has eaten him," but when they discussed the matter further, they remembered that they had seen no tracks of a tiger throughout the district. The head-man was therefore right when he said, "No. He must be lost." This was really what had happened to the fifth man, who, penetrating deep into the forest, was overtaken by the darkness, which made him miss the track. He wandered on and on, and laid himself down under a tree. By and by, a Pu-yu [candle-fly] came along and asked him what he was doing all alone there: when it learned that he had lost himself, it offered to show him the way. But the man doubted how such a little thing could help him, and it was only when the Candle-fly told him that it intended warming itself at the very fire which his four friends had made at the banab, that he agreed to follow it. And as the two approached the camping-ground, they heard the voices of people talking. "Listen!" said the little Fly: "That's where your people are. We are going there." When they at last reached the shed, the Candle-fly flew in ahead, and told the four men that it was bringing them their lost companion; the latter then came in, and his four friends were right glad to see him.

226.* The only example of plant-life in connection with omens and auguries so far met with is that recorded by Bernau: "Marriage is frequently contracted by parents for their children when infants; and trees are planted by the respective parties in witness thereof: it is considered a bad omen if either tree should happen to wither as in that case the party is sure to die" (Be, 59).

227.* The Guiana Indian voluntarily submits to various painful ordeals or preparatory charms, previous to setting out on, and with the object of winning success in, the chase. He believes in priming himself whenever his hunting powers appear to be impaired, and may spend some two or three months or more in the process; during this period he abstains from salt and peppers, also perhaps from sugar. The ordeals apparently consist in the "mortification of the flesh" by scarification, etc., and its irritation with various frogs, toads, caterpillars, ants, or by special nose-stringing apparatus. I purposely use the term "apparently" because their real signification p. 278 (see Sect. 231) is evidently not even known to the Indians who practise them. In Surinam, among both the Ojanas (Caribs) and Trios (Caribs) it is customary (Go, 21) to slash arms and legs with a knife, and the scars may be rubbed perhaps with turalla (Caladium bulb). An Ojana told de Goeje that he cut his arm in order to be able to shoot the quatta monkey well. A Trio slashed his arm and forearm and rubbed earth into it, to become a good hunter; another cut his thigh in order to become a strong mountain climber; some women also had on the outer side of the thigh scars from wounds inflicted to make themselves strong. With the Island Caribs, the forehead and nose were flattened artificially (RoP, 437). This was done as soon as the infants were born by exerting pressure in such a way as to cause a slight backward slope of this part of the head. Besides being considered a sign of beauty, this shape was said to be advantageous in shooting arrows from a tree-top, in securing a foot-hold, etc. (RoP, 552). Among the Yaruro Indians of the Orinoco, in order to become skillful with the bow and arrow the men submit to a sexual mutilation with a sting-ray "barb", which is made to pierce the prepuce (Cr, 570). The Cayenne Caribs never go on a big hunting expedition without drawing a little blood from their arms to prevent them shaking when pulling the bow: to give them greater strength for paddling, the young men scarified themselves on both arms. Similarly, before undertaking a journey on land they never fail to make incisions at the level of the calves (Cr, 280). Schomburgk reports seeing Indians bleeding each other as a remedy for over fatigue (ScF, 235). There is still a nose-stringing procedure to be mentioned: "In most Indian houses pieces of thick roughly-plated fiber or cord, as thick as codline, and a yard in length, are seen hanging up in the roof. These have all been used once . . . that is, passed up through the nose of the owner of the house, and drawn out by the mouth, for the purpose of giving him good luck in hunting" (Bro, 302). The string tapers "from a very small point at one end to a considerable thickness at the other end, where the fibers hang loosely in a bunch . . . the thin end [is passed] up his nostril . . . employed by Makusis, Arecunas, and Ackawoi" (IT, 228). The "exercising" of the limbs at each new moon may perhaps be regarded in the light of a preparatory ordeal (Sect. 199).

228.* In British Guiana, on the Kaieteur savannah, a frog is rubbed on the transverse cuts made adown either side of the hunter's chest, a different frog being used for different game. In the same district a small live toad is said to be swallowed for the promotion of general success in hunting.1 "Having scratched his wrist with the telson or sting of a scorpion to insure precision in darting the arrow from the bow, and cut his arms and legs with the flakes of a broken bottle, he p. 279rubs the back of the kunaua toad over the wounds; the virus of the reptile burns like fire" (Da, 253). In the Pomeroon District, in addition to abstention from salt and peppers, cuts are made on the arms, and the spawn of the akura frog (Sect. 229) is rubbed not only into the incisions, but also into the mouth, nose, eyes, and ears, where it is said to cause acute irritation. It is difficult to understand the relationship, if any, between the frog or toad, and success in the chase (Sect. 144), except on a basis of some original belief in the divinity (Sect. 46) of these batrachians, as we know to have existed in other parts of the Guianas (Sect. 349). The following is an Arawak story:

229.* THE WIFE TEACHES HER HUSBAND TO HUNT (A)

There was a man who though he went off regularly to the forest; never managed to bring home anything, while his brothers-in-law, who seldom went out, always returned with plenty of game; but they gave none of it, either to him or to their sister. She, however, determined on asking other people how she could teach her husband to be as lucky as her brothers, and after a long long time she found out what to do. She then took him one day into the bush to hunt for the akura frog, and when they had found the nest she introduced some of the spawn into his ears, eyes, nose, and mouth. This burned him terribly, and made him vomit, so much so that he was obliged to roll about in the sand to ease the pain. After this, she made him bathe, and then brought him home. She next asked her brothers to make a small bow and some arrows for her, and with these she sent her husband out to shoot small birds only, and not to shoot more than four. While he was away she made pepper-pot, using very few peppers and no salt whatsoever. He returned with the four little birds, which she cooked, giving him two, and retaining two for herself. The same procedure was repeated daily for a week. The wife then destroyed the small bow and arrows, and asked her brothers to make bigger ones, and instructed her husband to shoot bigger birds with them; this also continued for a week. She next sent him out with this big bow and arrows to hunt game of all and any description, but with a certain proviso: as each animal or bird would approach him in answer to the "call" which he would imitate, he was not to shoot, but merely to point his arrow at it; only when it was time to return home in the afternoon was he to kill one animal, and fetch it to her. At the beginning of the fourth week, she sent him out hunting again with fresh instructions: he was now to shoot and kill everything that he could. He killed and brought home plenty. From that time he and his wife were never in want of food, and they took care to treat her brothers as they had treated them. What they could not eat, they would barbecue, and then hide. The selfish brothers accordingly wondered how their sister's husband now always managed to kill more game thnn they did. They asked their sister, but she refused to tell them.

230.* In the Pomeroon District a hairy caterpillar may be rubbed into incisions made on the wrists and thighs. This creature, obtained on the Rupununi and brought down here in barter, is said to be soaked in water the whole of the night previous to the solution being applied, by means of cotton-wool, to the cuts. I have also seen a Pomeroon Arawak wear one on his neck. Im Thurn (230) speaks of caterpillars "the hairs of which break off very readily, and have a great power of irritating flesh. These caterpillars he rubs on his p. 280chest or thighs, and thus produces a considerable and very painful-looking rash." This method employed by Makusis, Arekunas, and Akawais. Or the hunter may mortify his flesh with ants, a practice indulged in by a member of any of these three tribes who—

Takes a small mat, about six or eight inches square, made of narrow parallel strips of the skin of a reed-like plant [Ischnosiphon] tied together somewhat as are the laths of a Venetian blind. Between each two of these strips he inserts a row of living ants, their heads all one way. The strips are exactly at such distance apart that the ants when once inserted can not extricate themselves. The huntsman then presses the whole mat, on the side on which are the heads of the ants, against his own chest; and the ants, which are of a large and venomous kind, bite most painfully." [IT, 229.]

231.* While recovering from the effects of his self-inflicted cuts and other injuries, the Carib and Akawai nimrod may be waited upon and nursed by some woman, but she must be past the climacteric; he is strictly forbidden to take liberties with any female. Though, at first sight, the inconvenience and suffering entailed by certain of the above procedures might seem to constitute a sort of sacrifice or free gift for favors to come, or at all events expected, I am afraid all the evidence is in the negative. On the other hand these practices may have a physiological basis of fact, and so of reason. The passing of the nose-string would certainly tend to clean the nasal mucus membrane, and so render the olfactory organ more keen; the prohibition of women combined with an enforced diet would certainly tend to make the individual more fit and thus get him into better training; the stimulation of all his sense organs with the particular frog slime may possibly hypersensitize them: while the infliction of physical pain within certain limits can reasonably be expected to irritate the nervous system to such an extent as to render it responsive to but the slightest external stimulus—qualities, all of them, advantageous for the hunter to insure success in the chase. It is perhaps on somewhat similar lines that, with a view to stimulating the child quickly to learn to walk, the Arawak mother will get a tibi-tibi lizard and encourage it to "bite the infant's feet and knees; the child is also incited to activity by putting a small stinging ant on him (Da, 250). But it is certainly difficult to understand how the artificial flattening of the children's foreheads by the Carib Island mothers can be vindicated in the belief that it helps the victims in years to come the better to fly their arrows from the tree-tops by securing firm foot-hold for them (RoP, 552).

232.* Hunting dogs are also made to undergo similar ordeals, but whether as part and parcel, or independent, of their general training (Sect. 234) it is difficult to say. On the Pomeroon in addition to, or in lieu of, the rubbing of a leaf (Sect. 233) the animal's snout may be rubbed with a certain tree-bark peculiar in that, when squeezed in the hands, a sort of frothiness exudes [? a species of Inga]. Or p. 281 again, the Pomeroon Indian will gash the snout with a sting-ray barb and pour on the raw surface a few drops of a solution made as follows: Some of the hot test kind of peppers are squeezed into a swab of cotton already moistened with a little water; a sugar-loaf funnel is then made of a suitable leaf, the cotton swab expressed into it, and a few drops allowed to trickle down through the funnel on the incisions. It is said that in two or three days' time the animal is ready to hunt, and when on the chase will keep his nose close to the ground, this action allowing of all grass and undergrowth being well turned over and scoured. Ants are also sometimes made to bite the creature's snout; or the same hairy caterpillar previously mentioned (Sect. 230) is rubbed into it. There is reported, however, an equally painful method as practised by the Makusi, Arekunas, and Akawaios.

Two holes are dug in the ground, and by pushing a stick from one to the other of these, and then withdrawing this, a tunnel or covered passage is made between the two holes. A fire in which parings of the hoofs of tapirs and other animal substances are burned, is then kindled in one hole; ants and wasps are also put into this hole, and it is then covered over with sticks and earth. The smoke . . . passes through the tunnel into the second hole. The poor dog is then caught, and its head is held down in the second hole, until the animal sometimes drops senseless from pain. [IT, 228.]

233.* Bínas are charms, plant or animal, which effect their purpose by enticing or attracting the particular object or desire yearned for, whatever it may be—from the capture of an animal to the gratification of a wish. The real source of the term bín-a is from the Arawak bia-bina, meaning "to entice, attract," etc., and so comes to be applied to all those things, plant or animal, which act on those lines. I have found nothing of this nature in the inorganic world, unless the quartz-pebbles within the piai's rattle are to be considered such. As against this view, it might be urged that the medicine-man's tobacco-smoke constitutes the real or at least co-equal attraction for the Spirits (Sect. 170). Im Thurn is certainly incorrect in speaking of the word being of Carib origin. As a matter of fact, the Carib term is turallári; for example, the Caribs speak of the bush-hog bina as ponjo-turallari. The Warrau word is aibihi; for instance, toma-aibihi means the bina for meat, in general. As a rule there is but one bina for each special object or thing, but not necessarily. I know of one that is employed for small hog, deer, and acouri; and with very few exceptions, the plants employed as binas are the different varieties of caladium. Indian huntsmen place great value on the use of the caladia, each variety being a bina or charm to assist in the taking of a particular kind of game. Not only do these plants grow spontaneously in old fields, but the Indians carefully remove and plant in the immediate neighborhood of their dwellings the most valued kinds, as the binas for tapir, wild hogs, deer, labbas, turtle, and those for the various p. 282kinds of fish (Da, 253). As a rule, women are supposed neither to see nor to handle such plants thus cultivated. Even in so comparatively civilized a district as the Pomeroon and Moruca, I have collected more than a score of such plants, the respective leaves of which in the majority of cases bear some real or fancied resemblance to the animal for which they are reputed to have so peculiar an affinity. Thus the bush-hog bina has a leaf easily recognizable by the small secondary leaf on its under surface, representing the animal's scent-gland, though some Indians say that it indicates the tip of the nostril; the deer bina shows the horns, in its general contour, and the coloration of the fur in its venation; the armadilio bina typifies the shape of the small projecting ears; the lukunanni bina bears a variety of colors resembling those around the fish's gills; the gillbacker bina develops the same yellowish color as the fish which it attracts; the labba bina has the typical white markings; the powis bina bears the identical shape of that bird's wing-feather—and so on for turtle, huri, etc. Some of these binas seemingly must be of comparatively widespread use; thus, that for the bush-hog is known in the Makusi country, those for the turtle, and armadilio, in Surinam (J. Rodway), etc.

The hunter puts the particular plant to use by taking off a young as-yet-unopened shoot, and placing it, in the rough, in his powder-flask, or rubbing it up into the paint, with which he smears his face and body, but especially all the main joints; or, on the other hand, he may employ only the leaf, which he rubs on his arrow, his fish-hook, his gun-barrel; or on his dog. In Cayenne, these binas (des herbes enchanteresses) are said to have been hung up on the trees (LAP, II, 221).

234.* In Cayenne, the dog was also rubbed with "simples," for which procedure Pitou gives the negative reason, "so that the game should not take itself off on its approach" (LAP, II, 220). The Roucouyennes, a Carib nation of the same colony, cuitivate in their clearings the Hibiscus abelmoschus, from which they make a musk-scented infusion for washing their dogs before taking them to hunt jaguar (Cr, 330): this, however, has nothing to do with the binas, the object of its application being to prevent the tiger biting the dog, owing to the pungency of the smell. Hunting dogs are also rubbed over with ruku (Bixa orellana) both by Indians (Trios, Ojanas, and others) and Bush Negroes (Go, 3): in British Guiana the practice said to keep off certain ticks (Ki, 184). The methods adopted by the Corentyn Arawaks for "training" (Sect. 232) their dogs to hunt may be included here. While the procedure may be correctly given, the statements relative to the naming of the particular leaf after the animal which feeds on it and the alleged odor are of course imaginative. These Arawaks first choose the dogs for hunting various animals, according to strength, having p. 283each one broken for hunting a different species of game; taking the largest for the wild hog, and the smaller ones for the smaller animals. When about six months old they are taken to the hunt with their sires, having previously gone through the process of being washed and rubbed over with a particular leaf named after the animal which feeds on it, and which the dog is intended to hunt; and it is curious that these leaves should partake of the odor of the animal. The game being discovered, the young dog is taken forward, and set on him; but he generally turns tail for the few first times, as this breed is naturally without spirit. He is then taken up, and again goes through the same process of washing and rubbing with the leaf; and at length he is treated to a piece of the animal's flesh, which

FIG. 2. Carib drinking-cup, Pomeroon River, bearing design showing
the two trees (a) in the tops of which lives the wonderful Aramári
Snake (b), while the roots (d) are surrounded by scorpions (c).
makes him more keen and ravenous. In this manner, exerting patience, of which these Indians have a most abundant stock, and seldom correcting the animal, it becomes in time a reliable and valuable dog (StC, I, 315). The method sometimes used by the Záparo Indians of the Napo River (upper Amazon) in training their celebrated hunting-dogs consists in putting a dose of tobacco down the animal's throat, his nose and mouth being then also stuffed full of it, until he nearly chokes; this is to clear his scent and sharpen his perceptions (AS, 169).

235.* Old Caribs, Warraus, and Arawaks of the Pomeroon and Moruca Rivers agree in telling me that they originally obtained their hunting binas—they are not so sure about the binas employed for other purposes—from certain very large snakes, which are invariably to be met with only in localities so far distant from the source of information as to preclude the possibility of my ever obtaining specimens. The Caribs refer me to two snakes, the Orupéri (Sect. 3) and the Aramári (fig. 2). The former lives on the ground, beyond the Waini and the Barima. The latter, which is much the bigger, lives in the tops of trees and catches its prey by pouncing upon it from above: it p. 284is also the more dangerous because from it can be obtained binas which, in addition to attracting all kinds of game, can attract thunder, lightning, and rain. The Warraus admit that almost all they know about the binas has been taught them by the Akawais and Caribs. The Arawak serpent is known as Oroli (Sect. 363), or, on account of its rate of progression, Kolekonáro (the slow walker). The traditions of all three tribes agree in that, after having been killed, the snake was carefully burnt, and that from the ashes there subsequently arose all the different plants, mostly, but not all of them, caladiums, which are now employed as binas (Sect. 168A). The Arawaks say that—

A long time ago people noticed how every now and again one of their friends would leave his house, go into the forest, and never be seen more, They accordingly made up a big party, and tracked the latest victim to two immense silk-cotton trees, and there was the huge serpent stretched across, somewhat like a bridge, from the summit of one tree to the other. They found out that from this serpentine bridge, pieces of the flesh would fall to the ground where they took on the form of dry firewood, which the innocent folk passing by, would gather up in mistake: that immediately upon just touching this dead timber the awful snake pounced down and seized its human prey. It was accordingly agreed that Oroli must be killed, a deed which they succeeded in effecting by means of blow-pipes and poisoned arrows. The carcass was then covered with bushes and saplings, and set fire to; as already mentioned the binas all grew out of the ashes.

How the special efficacy of each bina was originally discovered has been explained to me somewhat on the following lines: Trial would daily be made of one plant after the other. Taking, for instance, Plant No. 1: On the first day, the hunter might come across a tiger. A plant that enticed or attracted such an animal would certainly be of no use to him, and would accordingly be discarded. Another day, he might try Plant No. 2, and run across a snake; that plant also could be cast aside. If on the other hand, with Plant No. 3 he were to fall in with some scrub-turkey or similar game, he would reserve that plant for future use—and so on with each animal or bird of economic value. But of course nowadays since they know of and cultivate these different plants around their houses, such trials are not necessary; they are quite aware what particular plant will specially attract some particular animal.

236.* Corresponding animal binas for attracting game must be somewhat scarce: I have succeeded in obtaining only the following examples. When Arawaks on the Pomeroon kill a bush-hog which happens to contain young, they bury the latter under the house in a spot below the place where the cassava is usually grated, the idea being that other bush-hogs may come near the house to the spot whither the young are calling them. So among the Uaupes River Indians, when they kill a bush-hog they bury the head at the spot where they first met the band, so that the latter may not stray away but return p. 285 there (Cou, II, 171). If a fisherman [Pomeroon Arawaks] has been unlucky, and finally catches any little fish, he will take it off the hook and, blowing into its mouth, say: "I will let you go again, if you tell your friends, the bigger fish, to come." Of course it tells them, and the fisherman's luck is rewarded. But the little fish is not given its liberty again as promised, for the Indians say that if they returned it to the water, it would tell its friends not to bite at the hook. There are three such fish that are thus supposed to act as binas: the wé-shi (Crenicichla saxatilis), "sun-frsh," the shiballi (Acara); "patwa,"—and the hura-diro (? Eigenmannia lineatus), a fish 12 to 14 inches long, but of which the long thin tall constitutes a good third. Similar ideas underlie a procedure reported from Caracas: "When an Indian slays a wild beast, he opens its mouth, and pours down its throat some intoxicating liquor, in order that its soul [Spirit] may inform others of a similar species of the kind reception it received, and that they may be encouraged to come and share the same favor" (FD, 52).

Game, however, can be attracted to the hunting-dog. There is a certain ant (kudu-kudu-barilya of the Arawaks) which, after being roasted, is put inside a piece of cassava, and given to a dog to make it a good hunter of any animal; the dog is simultaneously trained to go into wood-holes and earth-holes by having its food placed inside a cassava-squeezer.

237.* The next class of binas deals with phases of the sexual question: conjugal rights, mutual love and affection, and babies. Where plants take the title rôles, these are again mostly caladia. Arawak, Warrau, Akawai, and Carib women all have their own binas for managing the opposite sex. The Arawak young woman plants her hiaro (girl)-bina usually in some secluded spot known only to herself; she will bathe with a leaf of it, or carry it about with her, and, provided the opportunity offers, without her being seen, may rub it over her lover's hammock, or she may rub her own hands with it, and then touch his. In any case, the man must be ignorant of what is going on, and, provided the procedure is strictly carried out as described, he will never have any desire to transfer his affections elsewhere. Again, the same woman may employ another plant, not a caladium, called the kurua-bina, apparently a Rajania of the Yam family; she will similarly bathe with the leaf, but retaining the water in which she has thus made her ablutions, will strew it on the path along which her sweetheart is about to travel, tening it to make him return soon. The male Arawak has a corresponding belief as to the wajíli (man)-bina, the leaf of which he generally carries about with the object of brushing over his girl's face or shoulders: he is very intent on going through this performance when he notices that she has a weakness for other men. Other peoples (as the Caribs) have p. 286similar practices, I know of three plants that are used by these people on the Pomeroon. Wai-áru: squeeze and pinch up a leaf or two in water, rub one's self now with the leaf, and throw the water just used in the direction of the person desired, at the same time calling his (or her) name. Wamba: used by the father for an absent elder son, or by the mother for an absent elder daughter; take a leaf with you in your hammock and call the boy's or girl's name. Akámi: when a person has come with the object of picking a quarrel, rub the leaf over one's head and face: it will make him quite amicable and friendly. So also among the Surinam Kaliñas (Caribs) de Goeje tells us that to evoke affection, one rubs the hands and face with turalla (Go, 14, 15): a woman, for instance, can do this when her man is away traveling, so that he may not forget her. When an Arawak or Warrau woman is desirous of having a baby, and none happens to appear in the natural course of things, she pounds up in water a certain fungus, and drinks the infusion. As I have shown elsewhere, the absence of a boy is a slur on the Indian's womanhood and entails many opprobrious epithets. The fungus in question, a species of Nidularia, is known to the Arewak as Kassato-lokono-biabina (lit., "baby-plenty charm"), or, in its shortened form, as Kassa-lo-bina, These women here never eat of a "double-fruit" which would mean twins for them (Sect. 284A).

237A.* The following is one of the few legends met with that contains reference to the application of Binas:

*THE BINA, THE RESURRECTED FATHER, AND THE BAD GIRL (W)

There was once a man with wife, two children, and his brother staying together in the one house. They were all Warraus. Going one morning to their field, husband and wife left the brother-in-law with instructions to go fishing so there might be something to eat on their return; but when they came back, they found he had been lazy, had never even been outside the house, and had eaten even the little that was in it. This made the man angry, and he upbraided his brother-in-law thus: "I have to go and cut the field. I have to go into the bush to get game, and down to the water to catch fish. I have all the work to do, while you do nothing but lie idle in your hammock all day. Although I am now tired, I must go and catch fish." Saying this, he took his harpoon1 and went down to the creek. The brother-in-law thereupon took up his cutlass, and after sharpening it followed him and got into his corial. They met just as the husband was returning with his boat, bringing a large fish that he had speared with his lance. "Hallo! finished already?" said the one. "Yes," replied the other, "I caught a fine fish, and have it here." "Well, lend me your lance," said the brother-in-law, "and I will go and shoot a fine fish also." The two corials thus drew near, and raising his lance, the man put it into his brother-in-law's boat. Just as he did so, the latter struck him with the cutlass and he fell dead after giving his assailant two cuts. The brother-in-law then tried to get rid of the corpse by throwing it into the water. Now it seems that when the sister saw her brother, after sharpening his cutlass, leave the house in a passion, she knew that some evil was about to happen, and said to the children: "Your uncle is vexed: he has sharpened his cutlass and followed p. 287your father. Let us see what he intends doing." So with her children she followed the two men, and came upon them just as her brother was trying to throw over the body. "No! don't do that, brother," she said: "Since you have killed him, you must take the body back to his house and bury it there." He did what he was told: took the body home, and started felling a tree in which to bury it. In the meantime the woman sent her children to fetch the deceased's brother and his old mother, at the same time sending them a message that they must not be vexed. The mother and brother came, and as they drew near they saw the murderer finish scooping out the trunk and take it to the house, where he commenced digging the grave. The brother was vexed, but his mother said: "Don't trouble the man: we will see first of all what the widow intends to do. The latter, holding a cutlass in her hand, was watching the murderer dig; she told him to hurry and finish his task quickly.

When the grave was finished, he put the coffin in, and then the corpse, which was properly dressed with paint and ornaments, and with which were placed knife, fish-hooks, and other things.1 As he was filling up the grave with earth, his hands all bleeding from the wounds the deceased had given him, his sister struck him from behind on his neck with her cutlass. After standing awhile, he dropped dead and a new grave was dug for him, alongside of the other. They put him into this bare as he was, without dress or ornaments, or any of his belongings; this was because they had no pity or sorrow for him. The mother and brother of the dead man returned to the old woman's home that very same day. They prevailed on the widow much against her will to come with them and bring the children. When they reached home the brother took charge of the widow, placed her in his hammock, and turning to his first wife said, "I am going to take this woman: she can make children: you cannot make them." But the two children that she had already did not like staying in their new home, and regularly every morning, after they had had something to eat, they would hurry off to their father's grave and would not return until late. On the third day of their visit to the grave they met a Hebu, but the children did not recognize him. He said to them: "If you want your father you must pick a leaf of a certain tree [which he mentioned] and rub it over the grave, when he will appear to you." "But we don't know the leaf," they replied: so the little man gathered some of the leaves for them. He told them to rub the leaves over the ground where the body was buried, directly they reached there on the following morning, and then to come again at mid-day, when their father would be present. They did exactly as they had been told next morning, and when they returned at mid-day they saw their father seated on a bench. They approached. He said, "Fetch me water to drink." After he had drunk, he said, "Where is your mother?" and when he learned that she was at their grandmother's he told them to go and fetch her. Now as soon as they reached their mother and told her all these things, she exclaimed, "How can this be? How can your father send for me when he is dead?" Thus it was, she would not believe all this at first, but when the boys pleaded, "Come, Mother! It is all true!" she went. The boys wished her to bring her hammock along, but she refused. "What is the use of it?" she said; for she did not believe as yet what they told her. However, she did go, and sure enough when she reached the place, she recognized the very man, her husband, seated there on the bench right in front of her. The first thing he asked her was, "Where is your brother?" to which she replied, "Why! I killed him, and buried him beside you." "Well," came the husband's answer, "you will never see him again." Now although her husband was very weak with all that he had suffered and passed through, she nursed him carefully and brought him back to health, so that within a week he was quite himself again.

238.* There are certain animal binas corresponding in their action with the plant binas just mentioned in connection with sexual matters. Among the Pomeroon Arawaks, when the husband is very jealous and ill-tempered, his wife will cut off the head of a small lizard (yamorro), burn it, and put the ashes into the water which she gives him to drink; any man or woman can then make the husband do whatever he or she likes. When one woman wants another's husband she will manage to put marabunta (wasp) eggs into his drink, which will make him leave his own wife and go off with her (the eggs are pounded up and roasted before mixing). On the upper Amazons, the native women, even the white and half-caste inhabitants of the towns, attach superstitious value to the skin and feathers of the papá-uira, believing that the relics will have the effect of attracting for the happy possessors a train of lovers and followers [The Indians have noticed these miscellaneous hunting parties of birds, but appeared not to have observed that they are occupied in searching for insects. They have supplied their want of knowledge . . . by a theory which has degenerated into a myth to the effect that the onward moving bands are led by a little gray bird called the papá-uirá, which fascinates all the rest and leads them a weary dance through the thickets. There is certainly some appearance of truth in this explanation; for sometimes stray birds encountered in the line of march are seen to be drawn into the throng, and purely frugiverous birds are now and then found mixed up with the rest, as though led away by some will-of-the-wisp (HWB, 346).] When it is known to her intimate friends and relatives that an Arawak woman wants an infant, they will give her to drink of a mixture, in which, unknown to her, they have placed the roasted and pulverized remains of either a cockroach (matero), the eggs of a certain spider, or the paw of an opossum (yawarri).

239.* Talismans, the last group of charms to be dealt with, include those which repel evil, bad luck, and the like, and so have a protective or defensive character—those which endow the Indian with such superior advantages of body and estate as enable him to get the better of his fellow-creatures, human and animal. Matters of courage, health and strength, power to withstand sickness and his enemies, craft to excel in the chase, trade and barter, all find a place here. With regard to the chase, the provisions mentioned in Sect 243 might very reasonably be regarded as talismanic. Among the Trios (Caribs) of Surinam, says de Goeje—

We saw afresh how one of our party rubbed the palms of his hands with turalla [caladiuim bulb] on arrival at a village of which they had much dread. A young man on the journey through the forest carried siinti [turalla] in a little palm-leaf box attached to the neck, in order to strengthen his head and shoulders. A child with fever was one afternoon washed by its mother with water into which finely ground siinti had been placed. As after two days, the fever again appeared, it was streaked with ruku paint, with which the same stuff had been mixed. [Go, 14-15.]

De Goeje states also that when making a purchase, the buyer will take a little turalla between his lips to prevent the seller overreaching him. According to Schomburgk (ScF, 215), the Maiongkongs used for necklaces a bunch of the slender stems of a cryptogamous plant, a fern called Zinapipo by them, to which they ascribed talismanic property.

240.* On the Pomeroon one can string the tail-rings and claws of a scorpion, and tie it round his little girl's wrist. By and by, when she becomes a woman and makes paiwarri, the liquor will be "strong and biting."1 Tiger teeth, threaded and tied on the child, will also insure its gaining strength [Arawaks]; bush-hog teeth will make a good huntsman of him [Atorais and Wapisianas] (Cou, II, 315); tiger

FIG. 3. Carib goblet, Pomeroon River, decorated

with pot-hook (scorpion) pattern.
teeth or bush-hog teeth will preserve him, when he grows up, from being attacked by wild beasts [Uaupes River] (Cou, II, 171). Makusi women and children wear round their necks tigers' teeth, to which they ascribe talismanic power (ScT, 61; ScR, II, 83). On the Berbice the sticks cut down by the sawyer beetle are given by the Indians to children cutting teeth, to rub their gums with, under the impression that as a result the teeth will grow strong and sharp (Da, 15). With the Indians of the upper Napo River (Amazons) bracelets and armlets of iguana skin are much affected, as in some parts of Central America, with the same association of their imparting bravery and pugnacity to the wearer (AS, 154). To obtain sharp vision, a Kobeua Indian will rub his eyes with those of a certain falcon (KG, II, 153). The Caribs and almost all other Indians ascribe talismanic powers to the large teeth of an alligator (ScA, 336). West of the Orinoco alligator teeth are employed by the Indians as an ornament for the neck and arms; they are also regarded as an antidote for certain poisons, and as an alexipharmic in general (FD, 151). As an antidote for poison, within the Orinoco area, Gumilla speaks of alligator teeth mounted in gold or silver and tied by a small chain on one of the arms or p. 290 made up into rings worn on the fingers; but this would appear to be a discovery learned from the negro slaves (G, II, 225).

240A.* The application of red paint was sometimes considered a talisman against sickness and disease. Thus, among the Makusis of the Rupunini the mothers ceremonially rub red (aromatic) paint on the heads of their children, who are then supposed to be protected from illness and the power of Evil Spirits (ScR, I, 366). The men [Guahibos of the Vichada River, Orinoco] then squatted on the little benches, and the women painted them from top to toe with a red paste; this, the women said, would protect them from sicknesses (Cr, 548). On the branches of the upper Rio Negro also red paint was considered a prophylactic against disease (KG, I, 158; II, 85, 150). The application of blood would almost seem to have had an antecedent origin, from which that of the red paint was but a development, and yet, strange to say, the positive evidence now available points rather to the reputed curative than the protective power of the vital fluid. Thus in some cases the father, when the child is weakly, has his own flesh cut in close parallel lines: the blood flowing from the wounds is mixed with water for washing and strengthening the child (Da, 250). Among the Island Caribs, after the couvade the child's face is smeared with the father's blood to impart courage (RP, 550). On the Orinoco, when the Guama women recognize that any of their children—nurslings or somewhat older ones—are sick, they transfix their own tongues with finely-ground bone lancets; the blood gushes forth in torrents and with it they bespatter their youngsters by mouthfuls, while, with their hands, they smear it all over them from head to foot (G, I, 164). In the same area, for older people it is one of the duties of the captains of the Guama nation to slash his flesh daily and drain off his blood in order to besmear the breasts of all those under his command who are sick (G, I, 164). Dance (250) speaks of an old man being washed in turtle's blood.

241.* The widespread belief in Spirits connected with mountains, rocks, stones, etc., will probably help to explain the talismanic virtues ascribed to the green Amazon-stones (Lapis nephriticus), the piedra hijada of the Spaniards. Out on the islands "they also wear necklaces made out of large crystals and green stones which come from the mainland toward the Amazon River, and have a healing virtue; it is their precious ornament and is only worn at feasts" (BBR, 248). Humboldt found them among the Indians of the Rio Negro, where they are carried on the neck as amulets for protection against fever, and the bites of poisonous snakes (AVH, II, 395, 462); Martius found them on the Rio Negro among the inhabitants of Sylves, and Schomburgk in Demerara. The last-named authority says:

Through the Caribs along the Guiana coast these stones were brought into Demerara where they are known as Macuaba or Calicot stones. On the Orinoco they are called p. 291 Macagua. They were formerly brought in considerable quantities by the Caribs to Demerara, but now very rarely . . . As I was told by people, these stones were also formerly brought to Demerara in the form of fishes and other animals, as well as with figures cut into the surfaces. . . . According to Barrere, they were treasured more than gold by the Caribs: such a stone was the price of a slave. Raleigh saw them on the Orinoko, and noticed that every Cacique had such a stone which was usually carried by his women: they treasured them more than gold. Lawrence Keymis says of the Carib and other tribes who dwell on the Arawari, below the Oyapoke: "Their money is white and green stones." He found the same thing on the Corentyn . . . According to Clavigero they are identical with the green stones of the Mexican Anahuacs: these people could cut all manners of figures out of this stone, and knew also how to cut diamonds. [ScR, II, 330-2.]

These Amazon stones, as just mentioned, were highly valued by the Galibis of Cayenne, who called them takourave, about which Pierre Barrere has left us this account:

This stone is of olive color, of a slightly paler green, and close to a pearl gray (presque d'un gris de perles). I have brought all colors from Guiana. The most common shape one gives to this stone is cylindrical, length of 2, 3, up to 4 inches, by six or seven lines in diameter, and drilled their whole length. I have seen some of them that were squared, oval, to which one had given the shape of a crescent and imprinted upon it the figure of a toad, or some other animals. This stone is known by lapidaries under the name of jade. It is highly polished, and so hard, that one can hardly work with it except with diamond powder. One has assured me that it is artificial: that a nation called Tapouye who live 150 leagues, or thereabout from Para, busy themselves in making them. [PBa, 175.]

There is another interesting reference to these green and gray jade stones in Surinam. They are stones harder than jasper, susceptible of a fine polish and making fire with a steel, although oily to the sight and touch; they are extremely hard to work. The Indians also set such great store on them that they regard these stones as very precious jewels, with which they decorate themselves when disposed to, show themselves with an their fine attire (Fe, II, 351). I have come across a possible reference to them in a Warrau legend (Sect. 139). A comparison between these Amazon stones and the drilled stones of quartz imperfectly crystalized, used as neck ornaments and as symbols of authority by the chiefs among the Uaupes River Indians (ARW, 191), is well worth consideration.

Next

p. 272

1 This was really the token.

p. 273

1 When I asked the narrator how the little boy knew that something exceptional was about to take place, she told me that when young people and children travel far afield, they often get frightened and nervous.—W. E. R.

2 For another Warrau version of this story, see Sect. 147.

p. 276

1 On the upper Airy the children's toy arrows are tipped with a button of black wax (KG, I, 106-7).

p. 278

1 H. W. B. Moore, in Daily Argosy, Aug. 12, 1910.

p. 286

1 Fish-lance with detachable head.

p. 287

1 It is usual among the Warraus, some six days or so after a death, to prepare a small quantity of drink, to cut the wife's hair, and make a bundle of the deceased's remaining belongings, which are then buried separately.

p. 289

1 This comparison between scorpions and strong liquor is very characteristic with the Pomeroon Caribs. A typical decoration on their drinking vessels is the pot-hook (i. e. the scorpion, fig. 3). See also around the central ring in fig. 2.

CHAPTER XV
RESTRICTIONS ON GAME AND FOOD, VISION, ARTS AND CRAFTS, NOMENCLATURE (TABOOS)

Restrictions on Game and Food: Must not hunt too many of one kind (242); spirit of slain animal must be prevented injuring slayer (243); hunter must not himself bring his "bag" into the house (244); when animal is killed by arrow or gun-trap, meat has to be cooked in special manner (245); food not eaten after nightfall (246); Food restrictions on age, sex, and nation (247): at moon-eclipse, puberty, pregnacy, and other periods, in mourning, sickness, traveling (248); of totem-animals (249); Attributes of animals eaten may be transferred by ingestion to the consumer (250). Dogs also restricted as to food (251).

Restrictions on Vision: Protective or defensive measure to prevent Spirit being attracted toward visitor (252); same principle applied to taking of a photograph, etc. (253); practice may be accompanied with flagellation (254); a sign of envy, hatred, and malice (255); concurrent expression of a wish (256); at place of entertainment (257).

Restrictions on Arts and Crafts: Manufacture of pottery (258-259); hammocks, canoes, huts, and field-work (260); the uses of the fan, and dress (261); preparation of curare (wurali) poison (262).

Restrictions in Nomenclature—Personal Names: Association between individual and name, which must not be mentioned in his presence (263); naming of child (264); change of name (265). Reasons for giving certain names to dogs (266). Special words have to suit special circumstances (266A).

242.* If Indians hunt too many of one kind of game, the Bush Spirit of that particular animal may come and do them harm (Sect. 98).

*THE BABOON COUGH (W)

There was a party of Indians hunting baboons. They would take their hammocks out into the forest, kill a baboon, dry it, smoke it, catch another, rest themselves there, and start a similar procedure on the morrow. They made a continuous business of baboon-hunting, and did nothing else. One day they went away as usual, leaving but one woman behind. After a time she heard a roaring in the distance, just like thunder, and waiting a while she heard a whistling, just like that of a man when he is tired.1 It was indeed some one coming along, and at last she saw an old man with bent back supporting himself with a stick. He approached the woman and said, "How do you do, grandchild!" Now, as she was quite an old woman you can imagine how old he must have been. He was really the Hebu grandfather of all the baboons. She got up, fetched a stool, bade him be seated, and offered him dried meat and cassava. The old man had a good look at the dried meat and started crying: "Oh, my poor grandchildren! So that is how I am losing every one of you." He told the woman to take the food away, that he wanted none of it, and he then asked her where all the rest of the people were gone. She told him that they were all out hunting the very same game that he had refused. "Very well," said he, "let them all remain at home tomorrow, and I will meet them." He then went away. At evening time, the hunting p. 293party returned, and the old woman told her husband what had happened, and all about the queer old man, but he would not believe her, saying that she must have been visited by some old sweetheart. So she went and told the rest of the people, and when the head-man had listened to her story, he said, "Yes, what she says must be true. We will remain with her tomorrow." They therefore stayed with her next day. At the appointed time they heard the roaring followed by a whistle. Now when the old woman, who was still angry with her husband for not having believed her, heard the whistle, she said mockingly, "There you are! That's my sweetheart!" and a few minutes later the old man put in an appearance. He was given a seat, and having learned that everybody was at home, he told them all to stand up in a line, side by side. One woman, who was in advanced pregnancy, was half ashamed to take so prominent a position, and recognizing that the queer old man's hand was big and sharp like a claw, she became frightened; she felt sure she must be dealing with a Hebu of some sort, and made her escape. Having thus got all the people into line, the Hebu quickly passed down the ranks, and "clawing" in the air, so to speak, at each person's head, killed every one of them. This done, he called out twice for his wife to come, and she answered him; she was a very old granny carrying an immense quake, so big that she could cram four or five people into it. And this is just what the old woman did; she carried the dead bodies, quakeful by quakeful, over to her own place. In the meantime, the old man Hebu examined the roof and under the flooring; he even opened the troolie covering of the banab to see if anyone was in hiding. But both he and his wife were being watched by the pregnant woman, who had made her escape; she saw everything, and then reported to her friends at the next settlement. The head-man and the others accompanied her to the spot where the Hebu's wife had carried all the dead bodies. They came to an immense silk-cotton tree, so huge that the cavities of its entire trunk and branches were occupied by members of the baboon-Hebu family. The party made a large fire around the tree, and threw peppers into it;1 this smoked out and killed all the Hebu baboons, from the youngest to the oldest, the queer old grandfather Hebu being killed last [Sect. 167]. Of course before giving up the ghost they did a lot of choking and coughing, and in his dying rage the old Hebu swore that this choking and coughing would remain with us forever. Indeed, it is this pepper sickness which is causing so much mischief now and killing so many of our children. We Warrau Indians have known the sickness for a long time as the "baboon cough," but you white people are ignorant of this, and persist in calling it whooping-cough.

243.* Special precautions have to be taken when any large animal has been slain, to protect the hunter from any harm that might be expected from the Spirit of the animal he has just destroyed (Sect. 129). Thus, when a big snake or other large animal is killed, arrows are stuck into the ground in the middle of the pathway leading from the place of destruction toward the house, with a view to preventing the Spirit of the beast coming to do the slayer or his family any hurt. The peculiar arrangement of the pointed sticks which Barrington Brown described from the Emoy River between Enaco and Taiepong villages toward the upper Potaro, probably served a similar purpose: "In many places on the path we had to step over arrangements of little sharpened sticks, placed loosely together in a p. 294variety of ways. These, the guide said, were put by the Indians using this path for the purpose of keeping the pumas and jaguars from traversing it. These sticks were not meant to injure the animals, in fact they were too loosely stuck up for that, but were merely intended by their artificial appearance to scare off the tigers" (Bro, 198). The pointed hardwood sticks, stuck into the ground, guarding the pathways leading to the houses of the Akawaios (Ba, 268-9), of the Oyapock River Indians (Cr, 169), and others, may have been employed for corresponding reasons, although other reasons have been given. The same may be said of the following: "Before leaving a temporary camp in the forest, where they have killed a tapir and dried the meat on a babracot, Indians invariably destroy this babracot, saying that should a tapir, passing that way, find traces of the slaughter of one of his kind, he would come by night on the next occasion, when Indians slept at that place, and, taking a man, would babracote him in revenge" (IT, 352). In Cayenne, between the upper Yary and Parou Rivers, Crévaux (252) makes this interesting note: "I see ten boucans disposed in a line along the pathway. What puzzles me is that there is no fire beneath. Another thing, instead of being charged with smoked meat, they are covered with several billets of dry wood alternating with stones. I learn that these altars . . . have been made by ten hunters of a neighboring village who started some days ago on a big expedition. Every time the Roucouyennes go hunting (shooting with arrows) the quatta monkey, they stop to trim these boucans."1

244.* An Indian must never himself bring into the house any game that he has caught, but leave it for his wife to carry in if she has been accompanying him; otherwise he will place it on the pathway, some four roods or so from the house, whence the women-folk will fetch it. Pitou gives a very interesting example of this from Cayenne (LAP, II, 220, et seq.). Similarly, with fish—unless very small, or unless there is only a single one that he can carry on the stick with which he has skewered its gills—he never brings them into the house, but makes his wife go fetch them from the waterside. The reason given for this custom is that, were the food to be brought home direct by the man he would have bad luck in fishing or hunting on the next occasion. A similar practice is recorded from Cayenne and from the islands. When the men (Roucouyennes) return from the chase, they bring the game as far as the edge of the forest, whither the women go to fetch it (Cr, 283). Carib Island women go and fetch the venison from the spot where it has fallen, and the fish on the p. 295banks of the stream (RoP, 493). When they have caught anything, they leave it on the spot, and the women were formerly obliged to go and fetch it to the house.

245.* Among the Pomeroon Arawaks, when an animal is killed with an arrow-trap or a gun-trap, its flesh has to be cooked in a pot without a cover, over a fire which is not too large, so as to avoid any water boiling over. Were either of these matters not attended to, there would be no further use either for the arrow or for the gun, as all the game of the same kind as that recently trapped would take its departure to another region.

246.* Among the Arawaks it would seem that food in general was not allowed to be eaten after nightfall, any person guilty of this offence being invariably changed into an animal. The story of the man who dined after dark (Sect. 114) has reference to this belief. The origin of such a custom it is somewhat difficult to trace. That it can not be due to any desire to prevent exposure to the enemy through the lights of the fires required for cooking is evident from the fact that fires for purposes of warmth, protection from jaguars, and other beasts of prey may be kept burning all night. It may be due to some such superstition as is met with among the Jivaros of the Pintuc, the Piojés of the Putumayo (upper Amazon), and others, who argue that all food which remains in the stomach overnight is unwholesome and undigested, and should therefore be removed;

accordingly they have the habit of inducing vomiting every morning by the use of a feather (AS, 93).

247.* On the Amazons, "the children, more particularly the females, are restricted to a particular food: they are not allowed to eat the meat of any kind of game, nor of fish, except the very small bony kinds; their food principally consisting of mandiocca-cake and fruits" (ARW, 345). We must accept with caution the opinion implied or expressed by various authorities that each nation as such differs from the others with respect to the indigenous foods from the use of which the people abstain. A certain food may be taboo to any one or more individuals, independently of membership in a certain tribe, at the instigation of a medicine-man as a part of the treatment for illness, on account of his wife's condition, or for other reasons. While we have the definite assurance of Schomburgk that the Caribs never eat monkeys (ScR, II, 434), Gumilla says that each nation is fond of one kind of monkey but loathes the others. The Achaguas are very fond of the yellow ones, which they call arabata, the Tunevos like the black ones, while the Jiraras, Ayricos, Betoyes, and other nations prefer the white ones (G, I, 260). The present-day Pomeroon Caribs will eat neither armadillo, alligator, camudi, nor monkey, but no reasons for such restrictions are obtainable. Kappler speaks of the Surinam Indians refusing p. 296to eat snakes and large sea-turtles (AK, 188). "All tribes . . . agree in refusing to eat the flesh of such animals as are not indigenous to their country but were introduced from abroad, such as oxen, sheep [pigs], goats, and fowls; . . . It must, however, be added that, under great pressure of circumstances, such as utter want of other food, these meats are occasionally rendered eatable by the simple ceremony of getting a piaiman, or even occasionally an old woman [who may play the rôle of piai], to blow a certain number of times on them; apparently on the principle that the spirit of the animal about to be eaten is thus expelled" (IT, 368). Schomburgk tells us how the aversion to European pork was never so strongly met with as among the Wapisianas; at Watu-ticaba Village the indisposition of a little girl was considered due to the circumstance that his cook, who had helped the child carry wood and water, had given her some to eat (ScR, II, 389). In Cayenne, they do not eat fowls (poules) and other birds though they be delicious; they imagine that out of spite these animals would cut their stomachs to pieces, gnaw their intestines, and cause frightful colic with the beak and spurs, although only the meat portion should be eaten (PBa, 231). The bush-negroes at Apikollos Village (Surinam) said that all the Trios Indians would die because the Europeans had partaken of the same food as they had (Go, 22). All the old piais that I have met still persist in their refusal to partake of European food (Sect. 286).

248.* Food may be restricted or taboo only under special circumstances, as at an eclipse of the moon (Sect. 200). In Cayenne, apparently men and women religiously abstain during the period of mourning from eating certain meats, or from cutting large timber, and several other practices of this nature (PBa, 229). The whole family may be restricted in the way of food, when a member of it happens to be ill (Sect. 317). The taboos of various foods at the physiological periods of a man's or a woman's life are noted elsewhere (Sects. 267-284). Among the Makusis, during the time that the natural colors of the feathers are being artificially altered the owner of the bird eats very sparingly and chiefly of certain kinds of food (Ti, 1882, p. 28). The Island Caribs eat flesh only when there are strangers at table; otherwise, they hunt but for lizards and fish: it is only on those special occasions when they want to entertain their European friends or for purposes of trade and barter, that they hunt anything else (RoP, 506). "When they have to cross over sea to go to another island like St. Alousi, or St. Vincent, they eat no crabs or lizards, because these animals live in holes: consequently this would prevent them getting to another land" (BBR, 245). An Indian does not eat an animal that he may have domesticated and tamed.

p. 297

249.* Unlike what might have been expected from a consideration of other savage races, even so near as those of North America, there seems to be no record of the taboo of the so-called totem-animal, but I can not assume for this reason that such taboo is, or was, non-existent. As a matter of fact, during the whole course of my annotation of all available literature relative to the Guiana Indians, I can find but one statement bearing on the question and that in the negative. This is from Crévaux (523). On the Guaviar, a branch of the Orinoco, he found an Indian who, although a Piapoco (i. e. Toucan), had no qualms about killing the bird after which his tribe was named. All the other references are of doubtful totemic significance.

250.* Certain indigenous animals are not to be eaten, apparently for no assignable cause. On the Moruca, the Arawaks do not use the flesh of the Palamedea cornuta Linn., although they employ the tail feathers for arrow-barbs (ScR, II, 457). While the Makusis touch the flesh of the ant-bear only when forced by want, the Caribs regard it as the greatest delicacy (ScR, II, 434). So also the Uaupes Indians do not eat the large wild pig (Dicotyles labiatus), the anta (Tapirus americanus), or the white-rumped mutun (Crax globicera ?) (ARW, 337). In the Pomeroon when men kill a bush-hog or any other animal that happens to contain young, there are always to be found Indians who will not touch the flesh. Other animals will be avoided for more or less defined reasons. Thus, the savannah pewit (Vanellas cayennensis) is never eaten by Indians, as they say that partaking of its flesh produces deafness (Bro, 104). At Carichana, near River Meta, Orinoco, the Piaroas said that the people of their tribe infallibly die when they eat of the manati (AVH, II, 492). In Surinam, an old Trio informed de Goeje that he would never eat the head of a quatta monkey, because his mother had told him that he would get gray hair like it, and women consider gray hair hateful (Go, 22). Though hog and turtle were abundant on the islands, the Caribs there eat neither, for the assigned reasons that their eyes might become small like the former animal, that they might participate in the clumsiness and stupidity of the latter (RoP, 465). The attributes of the animal eaten could be transferred by ingestion not only to the person eating [compare ingestion of human flesh to obtain attributes of the deceased, in Sect. 77], but even to the child of such person (Sect. 279). The Zaparo Indians of the Napo River (upper Amazon) are "very particular in their diet: unless from necessity, they will, in most cases, not eat any heavy meats such as tapir and peccary, but confine themselves to birds, monkeys, deer, fish, etc., principally because they argue that the heavier meats make them also unwieldy, like the animals who supply the flesh, impeding their agility and unfitting them for the chase" (AS, 168). On the upper Amazon the p. 298flesh of the male turtle (much less numerous than the female) is considered unwholesome, especially to sick people having external signs of inflammation (HWB, 309).

251.* Dogs also are precluded from eating certain foods. In Cayenne Crévaux noticed that his Roucouyenne cooks threw the beaks of the kinoros birds (Ara canga) into the river, in the belief that were their dogs to eat them, they (the dogs) would be poisoned (Cr, 284). Here, on the Pomeroon, in many an Indian house you will often find stuck under the eaves of the overhanging troolie roof or slung up in a basket, the wings and breast-bones of certain birds and often the bones of a labba or an acouri. It was a long time before I learned that they were placed there for a purpose other than ornament or decoration. If a dog were to eat either of those particular bird bones or any bones whatever of a labba or an acouri that it had not itself hunted, such dog would never catch any of these animals again.1

252.* The temporary occlusion of vision, as with tobacco and peppers, on the occasion of visiting, for the first time any strikingly peculiar landmark of natural scenery, especially in the way of mountains, or even on entering a new region, would seem to have been a custom very prevalent among the Indians. From the examples which I propose here submitting it will be seen that the procedure specially concerns the particular Spirit with which such landmark or region is connected. Its object, partly perhaps to placate this Spirit, and so turn aside the sickness or any other evil it might otherwise choose to send, is mainly to prevent the visiting individual attracting it toward himself. The procedure is protective or defensive in the sense of thwarting evil. On first gaining sight of the Arissaro Hills, Essequibo River, the Caribee Indians, who had never ascended the river so far, had to undergo an initiatory sight, which consisted in squeezing tobacco juice into their eyes (ScG, 229). So again, at the Twasinkie or Coomootie Mountains, much superstition, as usual, was attached to them, and those who had never seen them before were obliged to drink lime juice, and to have tobacco water squeezed into their eyes to avert the Evil Spirit (ScG, 231). Im Thurn (368) speaks of peppers (Capsicum) being employed for a similar purpose, and says: "Once, when neither peppers nor limes were at hand, a piece of blue indigo-dyed cloth was carefully soaked and the dye was then rubbed into the eyes." While on the Cuywini, writes Barrington Brown: "We passed a place one afternoon where the river was studded with high granite rocks two of which rose ten feet or so above the level of the highest floods. . . . Our guide, Edward . . . turned his head away and would not look at them: Eruma, one of p. 299our Caribs, took some tobacco, and dipping it into the water, leaned back and squeezed the juice into his eyes, and as soon as the tears thus produced had subsided, he calmly gazed upon the rocks" (Bro, 30). Near the mouth of the Cuywini River, upper Essequibo, to quote the same author, "were some large granite rocks in passing which our Carib . . . turned away his face in an opposite direction. Upon questioning him as to his reason for so doing, I learned that if he looked at them, he would get fever" (Bro, 244). Another interesting extract is from Jenman (23):

We met on the Savannah about a hundred Indians of all ages and both sexes, resting on their way down to the hill to the landing at Tukeit, going down to the Mission. It was the first time they had passed the "Kaietuk" (Kaieteur) as they called it, though they were careful to keep almost beyond the sound of its roar and far out of sight of it. Each one, from the newly-born baby in arms, to the oldest man and woman, had pepper-juice applied to the balls of the eyes, carefully inserted within the lids, with a small loop made of a finely twisted piece of Tibesiri [Mauritia fiber] to avert any evil which might otherwise befall them from having come near the Fall and into a new part of the country. Its application appeared to give acute pain for a short time, and brought a copious flow of tears. Some courageously just kept the eyelids open without touching them; others, with less nerve, had to hold theirs open. . . . The pepper-juice . . . was applied by one man, a middle-aged person.

The present-day Arawaks when visiting any new place for the first time, whether now connected with Spirits or not, put creek water or river water into their eyes: they tell me here that it is with the object of placating any spirits that may be lurking in the vicinity, for should they neglect the custom, the Yawahus might not only send them sore eyes, but many other sicknesses. One woman maintained that, independently of any evil spirits, the very novelty of the scene might give her sore eyes, in the absence of the usual precaution.

253.* Warraus assure me that on looking at a mountain for the first time the eyes are shut to prevent the person attracting or drawing the Shadow of the Spirit toward him (Sect. 190). When one person looks at another, the former draws or drags the latter's shadow (Sect. 68) toward him, a principle on which these Indians explain the taking of a photograph. The Island Carib corpse is laid out with two weights on the eyes, that he may not see his parents thus making them ill (Sect. 80). Catlin gives an amusing instance among the Conibos of the Amazon, of the local medicine-man preventing him painting any more portraits by exhorting the tribesmen as follows: "These things are a great mystery, but there you are, my friends, with your eyes open all night—they never shut: this is all wrong and you are very foolish to allow it. You never will be happy afterwards if you allow these things to be always awake in the night. My friends, this is only a cunning way this man has to get your skins; and the next thing they will have glass eyes, and be placed among the skins of the wild beasts and birds and snakes." (The medicine-man p. 300had been to Para or some other place where he had seen the stuffed skins in a museum.) (GC, 321-323). For a pregnant woman to look at the face of a corpse will draw trouble on her unborn child (Sect. 279). It is possible that, perhaps on principles analogous to some of the preceding, most European races have adopted the practice of closing the eyes when in the attitude of prayer; it is therefore not so very remarkable that I found the aboriginal communicants of a certain Mission speaking of prayer generally by a term which, literally translated, means "to shut the eyes."

254.* But this temporary occlusion of the eyes may be accompanied with another procedure, that of whipping. Thus, at the Cara-utta Rocks, head of Wenamu River, a branch of the Cuyuni, "the Indians who had never been here before, gave themselves up to the wildest orgies. Several calabashes were placed on the rocks, before which two old Arekunas, with faces turned toward the north, squatted, and murmured unintelligible words, while an equally old piai rubbed powdered capsicum into the eyes of each of the novices. When the first pains were over, they broke twigs off from the nearest bushes, and whipped one another on the legs and feet, until blood was drawn" (ScR, II, 346). In the last group of cases, it is not the body, but the rock or other natural feature that is whipped. And so it happens that while Boddam-Whetham admits that they will never point at certain rocks with a finger, although one's attention may be drawn to them by an inclination of the head, other rocks "they beat with green boughs" (BW, 182); that along the slopes of the Seroun Mountains, Mazaruni River, under some of the enormous masses of conglomerate rock, were flowers and green branches that had been offered to the Rock Spirits by the superstitious natives (BW, 190). But as this author may have obtained his information concerning the very same place (Seroun River valley) from Brown's work, published a couple of years before, I quote from the latter as well: "On the way we passed a very large isolated rock of diorite which had formed part of one of the great layers of this rock, horizontally bedded in the sandstone, upon which were lying the bruised remains of a small tree branch with many more around its base. These were offerings left by Indian travelers at the shrine of the spirit of this rock, who believe that if they did not perform the rite of breaking off a green bough and beating it on the rock, evil would assuredly befall them" (Br, 78).

255.* In a sense analogous to the idea of thwarting or avoiding evil may probably be regarded the closing of the eyes as a sign of "envy, hatred, and malice." Thus, among Warraus and Arawaks, as between man with man or woman with woman, the angered one will look at the other, suddenly shut the eyes, keep them closed a few seconds, and then turn away. The person thus treated will know that he or she must be prepared for the coming storm. So also the following p. 301occurrence reported frem the Parou River in Cayenne may find place here: "In a retired spot, I surprise a little girl who, like the ostrich, hides her face in a hole, leaving her body entirely exposed" (Cr, 273). It is possible that the peppering of the witch's eyes before clubbing her was intended to prevent the poor wretch attracting toward herself the Spirits of those people she might otherwise have looked at (Sect. 319). Compare also the binding of the girl's eyes in the puberty ceremony (Sect. 271).

256.* The closing of the eyes and the concurrent expression of a wish I am unable to obtain explanations for, except on the hypothesis of some Spirit being supplicated, and deal with the practice here only as a matter of convenience. Mention is made of the custom in the Carib story of—

*"SHUT YOUR EYES AND WISH!" (C)

There were two brothers, and each had set a spring trap to catch Maipuri [tapir] but it had proved too smart for them. One day the younger came home and said, "I have caught a bush-cow." This made the elder one jealous, and hence his remark, "If you have fooled me, I will kill you." So they went together into the bush, and sure enough there was the tapir caught by the leg in the trap. The elder brother thereupon killed the beast, cut up the meat, and took it all for himself, leaving only the entrails for the younger. The latter returned home, and telling his mother how greedy her first-born had been, prevailed upon her to leave the place with him. When they had traveled a great distance, they reached a hill, and the son said: "Mother! Shut your eyes, and say, 'I want a field here, with plantains and potatoes, together with a house right in its very center.'" The old woman did what she had been told, and lo, and behold! there she had exactly what she had asked for. The two of them remained there for a long period, quite happy and content, but the mother was getting old now. So the son said, "Mother! Shut your eyes, and say, 'I want to be a young girl again.'" This she did, and her wish was immediately granted, she becoming so very sweet and attractive that her son became quite proud of her and wanted other people to see her also. Indeed, this made him say, "Mother! Shut your eyes, and say, 'I wish my big son would come see me.'" No sooner said than done, and the elder brother put in his appearance. Now that they had a visitor, they must of course have paiwarri, so the younger brother told his mother as before to shut her eyes and wish for drinks—and accordingly they had a big jar of paiwarri. All three of them drank, and the big brother became beastly intoxicated, so much so that he commenced trying to take liberties with the pretty young woman. "How dare you!" expostulated the younger one. "Don't you know that she is your mother?" "No! I don't," replied the elder, "and what is more, I don't believe it," and as he insisted upon attempting to carry out his wicked designs, the two men fought. When the elder brother finally awoke from his drunken brawl, he found himself all alone in a strange broken-down old hut, and so he returned home disconsolate.

The Makusis also would seem to have had similar ideas about wishing, for in their legend of Pia and Makunaima the former tells his mother that whatever of good she desired she would obtain if she would bow her head and cover her face with her hands while she expressed her wish (Sect. 41).

257.* It was a superstition of the Indians in Cayenne that the first person to see the dancers arrive at the actual place of entertainment p. 302would die during the course of the year or meet with other misfortune. Hence, directly the dancers left the public meeting-house (karbet) to go to a retired spot for the purpose of decorating themselves, the audience took good care to go into hiding, and to return in a body, shouting and screaming like madmen, when the performers put in their appearance (PBa, 201; LAP, II, 242).

258.* The following are examples of what might be called restrictions in arts, crafts, and manufactures.

On the left bank of the mouth of the Cuyuni is a small hill whither Indians come from long distances to obtain clay, which is believed to be especially desirable. Schomburgk tells of a certain superstition which accounts for such large numbers of people congregating there. The Indians believe, for instance, that only during the first night of the incoming full moon (Sect. 199) dare they carry on their business. Hence, numbers of people congregate at these times, as Bernau vouches for, and at break of day start for home laden with a large quantity. The Indians cling fast to the superstition that if the clay is obtained at any other times, the vessels acquire an evil peculiarity not only for becoming speedily broken, but also for bringing numerous diseases to him who eats out of them.

259.* Such vessels could be even more intimately associated with Spirit life, as witness the following story of—

*THE LUCKY POT (W)

On his way home from the bush one day a man came across a banab, with no human occupants but with a Pot simmering on the fire. The Pot addressed him, asking if he were hungry, and having received an affirmative reply, said, "All right! I will cook bird for you," and began to boil. When ready, the man ate of the contents, and went home. His wife put fish before him, but he said, "I do not want it. I am satisfied." By and by her husband made an excuse to leave the house, and having arrived at the banab, said to the Pot, "I am hungry. You must cook meat now." So the Pot boiled away and supplied him with pure bush-hog. When he got home his wife put some cassava before him, but he said, "I do not want it; my belly is full." After remaining at home two days and refusing the food which his wife regularly brought him, he paid another visit to the lucky Pot, gorged himself with both bird and meat, and returned home again, where, as before, he assured his wife that he was satisfied and wanted for nothing. Now the two sons looked at him and at one another and then whispered to themselves: "What does this mean? Our father stays at home two whole days, and is not hungry. He goes into the bush and even when he returns will not eat. Whence does he procure his food?" So they watched his movements, and next day, following him at a distance, saw him talk to the Pot and help himself. On his return home, he still refused to eat what his wife continued to offer him. As they were getting short of food for the household, he went away to shoot morokot [Myletes], the sons in the meanwhile going to the banab, asking Pot to cook bird and meat for them. After eating they washed the vessel "clean, clean," so as not to leave even the trace of a smell in it. By and by the father came home from his fishing excursion, handed over to his wife the morokot which he had caught, but refused as usual to eat any himself. "I do not want it. I am satisfied," was all he said. He then slipped away to his lucky Pot, and told it to cook for him, but it would not boil any more for him or for p. 303 any one else, so perfectly had it been cleaned out.1 He then commenced to cry, but the Pot reminded him: "You were greedy. You gave the bird and meat neither to your wife nor to your children. You ate it all yourself."

260.* Among the Island Caribs, when the women make hammocks they place at each end a small parcel of ashes. Unless this ceremony were observed the hammock would not last. Should they eat figs when in possession of a new hammock, they think it would become rotten. They take great care also not to eat of certain fish with sharp teeth; for this would cause the hammock to be soon torn. The men erect the houses, except the roofs, which are made by the women, and canoes (BBR, 242). With the same people, during the course of manufacture of a canoe, while being burnt out, sticks are placed across, so as to enlarge it. If a woman did but touch it with her fingers, they believe it would split (BBR, 243). Father Gumilla, the missionary of the Orinoco, evidently commiserating the unhappy lot of the weaker sex, and recognizing the hardships to which they were exposed in carrying on their field work, made the attempt to get the men to lend assistance. His exhortation with its fruitless results is given here in his own words: "Brethren," said I to them, "why don't you help your poor women to plant? They are tired with the heat, working with their babies at the breast. Don't you see that it is making both them and your children sick?" "Father," they replied, "you don't understand these things, which accordingly worry you. You have yet to learn that women know how to bring forth, and we don't: if they plant, the maize stalk gives two or three ears of corn, the cassava bush yields two or three basketsful of roots, and similarly everything is multiplied" (G, II, 237).

261.* A woman must preserve her fan for the uses for which it is intended, namely, for blowing up the fire; should she use it on herself, she would become thin—at least this is what the Pomeroon Arawaks tell me.

Among the nations bordering on the Amazon the Indians are entirely nude. They regard it as an almost certain sign that he who would cover what shame obliges civilized man to hide would soon be unfortunate, or would die in the course of the year (PBa, 121-2). It might be pardonable perhaps to mention here the reproof which the Island Caribs gave their European visitors when the latter, regarding them too closely, laughed at their nudity: "Friends! You should look only at our faces!" (RoP, 461.)

262.* Waterton has recorded the following beliefs in connection with the manufacture of curare (wurali) poison:

The women and young girls are not allowed to be present. The shed under which it has been boiled is pronounced polluted and abandoned ever after. He who makes the poison must eat nothing that morning and must continue fasting as long as the p. 304operation lasts. The pot in which it is boiled must be a new one, and must never have held anything before, otherwise the poison would be deficient in strength; add to this that the operator must take particular care not to expose himself to the vapor which arises from it while on the fire. . . . Still the Indians think that it affects the health; and the operator either is, or what is more probable, supposes himself to be sick, for some days later . . . and it would seem that they imagine it affects others as well as him who boils it; for an Indian agreed one evening to make some for me, but the next morning he declined having anything to do with it, alleging that his wife was with child! [W, 93-4.]

Schomburgk more or less confirms these restrictions when he says that before and during the making of the poison the operator must submit to a strict fast, and that during the cooking, no woman, especially a pregnant woman, or maid may come near the house; furthermore his own wife must not be pregnant. In the particular instance cited the distinguished traveler was asked not to eat sugar-cane or sugar during the manufacture of the poison (Sc, RI, 455-7). "Thus the greater the abstention from food on the part of the peai men, the greater the virulence of the urali, its action being supposed to be deadly in correspondence with the degree of hunger of the maker" (J. J. Quelch, Ti, 1895, p. 262). Im Thurn supplies the following "Water was fetched especially for the poison-making from a stream nearly a quarter of a mile distant; and care was taken in carrying this to the house, to rest it on the ground every few yards. For, say the Indians, a bird wounded by a poisoned dart will fly only as far as the water, with which the poison was made, was carried without rest" (IT, 311).

263.* There would appear to be some intimate relationship between an individual and his personal name (cf. Sects. 124, 125), of such nature that the very mention of it in his presence would be fraught with serious consequences; neither, as in the case of spirits (Sect. 172), may he be pointed at, or trodden over (Sect. 220). The name is deemed to be part and parcel of the individual, and the mention of it under those circumstances would put him in the power, as it were, of the person speaking. This rule held good for both Mainland (KG, I, 184; II, 147) and Island Indians. According to age and sex, one will address another as brother, sister, father, mother, son or daughter, etc., or will speak of him or her as the father or mother, etc., of such an one; or, to specialize, "they will speak half the name, e. g. Mala instead of saying Mala-kaali, and Hiba for Hiba-lomon" (RoP, 451; KG, II, 147). This fact will thus render the following statements of de Goeje and Kirke more intelligible: "Some Trios have two names, one reserved for friends, the other for strangers: Crévaux says that the Ojanas might have two names, one for addressing the person and the other for referring to him when absent" (Go, 26). "It is a curious thing that you can never discover an Indian's real name . . . he never divulges it, nor is he ever called p. 305by it. He is always known by some nickname or name of distinction for his prowess in war, hunting, or fishing" (Ki, 120). So also when dead, the name of the deceased must not be mentioned.

263A.* HONEY-BEE AND THE SWEET DRINKS (W)

There were two sisters looking after their brother, for whom they were always making cassiri, but try their best, the drink had no taste; it was never good and palatable, so the brother did not enjoy it. He was forever complaining, saying he wished he could find some one who would make him a real sweet drink, something like honey. His sisters sympathized, and said they would be only too glad if he could find the right woman, who would make good liquor. One day while wandering through the bush he expressed aloud his wishes as to finding some woman who could manufacture a drink as sweet as the honey-bee makes it. No sooner had he expressed his wish than he heard footsteps behind, and, turning round, saw a female approach. "What is it? Where are you going? You called Kohóra, my name [lit., Honey-bee], and here I am!" He told her about his own and his sisters' wishes, and when she asked him whether he thought his people would like her, he said he was quite sure they would. Kohora accorqingly went home with him, and when his parents asked her how he had met her, she said that she had come because their son had called her. She then made the drink. And the way she made it! All she had to do was to put her little finger into the water, stir it up, and the drink was ready! It tasted sweet! sweet!! sweet!!! and never before had it tasted so good. From that time onward they always had sweet drinks; on every occasion that Kohora brought her husband water she would dip her little finger in and so make it sweet. But at last the man got tired of all this sweet drink, and began to quarrel with Kohora. "Well, that is funny," she said. "You wanted sweet drinks, you called me to get them for you. I came and made them, and yet you are not satisfied. You can get them for yourself now!" With this, she flew away and ever since then, people have been punished by being put to all the trouble of climbing up, and cutting the honey out of, the tree, and having to clean it before they can use it for sweetening purposes.

264.* Among the Pomeroon Arawaks the mother always gives the name first to her child, independently of the piai, who bestows one subsequently. It is said that friends, brothers, and sisters may call them by these names, which stick to them throughout life, but it should be borne in mind that these Arawaks have been in closer contact with Europeans than any of the other tribes. The following are some of the names given by the mother at birth:

Girls' names			Boys' names		
Satu	=	darling			
Kakushika	=	big eyes			
Korelyaro	=	baby girl	Korelyali	=	baby boy
Kai-inasaro	=	big buttocks	=	Kai-inasali	
Sato-bara	=	pretty hair	=	Sachibara	
Kuroshiro	=	brown hair	=	Kurashili	
Kabararo	=	plenty of-hair	=	Kabarali	
Kakarishiri	=	curly hair	=	Kakarishili	
Irihibaro	=	dark hair	=	Irihibali	
Ilihiro =		dark girl	Ilihili	=	dark boy
Natukoro	=	sp. of pretty flower	Deringko	=	sp. of parrot
Kuyari =		toucan	Wé-shi=		sp. of little fish
Durakuaro	=	bird (Odontophorus)			

The name bestowed subsequently in this tribe by the piai takes place about the period when the child begins to creep; he asks the Spirit in the maraka (rattle) to give the name. "An offering of considerable value is necessary on this occasion, as, according to the fee given to propitiate the pe-i-man, is the virtue of the incantations pronounced: an unnamed Indian is thought to be the certain victim of the first sickness or misfortune that he may encounter: accordingly, only the very poorest of them are without names" (HiC, 229). At the present time, it would seem that the piai gives a name only if he has been called in to attend a child when sick; under such circumstances he will say that he has dreamed that the child requires a name, and the parents accordingly ask him to give one. Such names are given with regard to the personal appearance, to birds or other animals, to tobacco (e. g. Yuri-niro, Yuri-tukoro = tobacco flower), after the piai's kickshaws, etc. (e. g. Shibari, "stone," Kalliko-yang, "crystal," Wara-maraka, a name derived from his rattle), or "after some quality or title." With the Makusis it was either the grandmother or grandfather, who, on the conclusion of the couvade, gave the infant one of the names customary in the family (ScR, II, 315). Among the Tukanos it is the father, under similar circumstances, who gives the name, generally that of an animal (KG, I, 313). So also on the Islands the Caribs do not bestow names immediately after birth, but wait for twelve or fifteen days when they call in a man and woman who take the place of sponsors, and pierce the child's under-lip and nostril. The majority of the names which the Caribs impose on their children are taken from their ancestors or from various trees which grow on the islands, or from something that has happened to the father at the time of his wife's pregnancy, or during her lying-in (RoP, 552-3). A convalescent patient may start life afresh with a new name (Sect. 305).

265.* The circumstances vary under which the name already given may be changed. As already mentioned (Sect. 264), this was the case with the Arawaks on recovery from prolonged sickness. On the Carib Islands the names given to the male children shortly after birth were not retained throughout life; they changed them when old enough to be received into the rank of warriors, or if they had borne themselves bravely in battle and had killed an Arawak chief, they took his name as a mark of honor (RoP, 552-3). Both on the Islands and on the Mainland names were exchanged in testimony of great affection and inviolable friendship (RoP, 513): "When they want to make friends, they ask for our names and give us theirs. To show affection and friendship they want us to exchange names" (BBR, 237-8). In Porto Rico "Juan Ponce de Leon, in fact, was received into the bosom of the family, and the Cacique exchanged names with him, which is the Indian pledge of perpetual amity" p. 307(WI, 778). With the present-day Arawaks and Warraus, among members of the same sex it is of common occurrence as proof of friendship and affection not to exchange names, but for the younger to adopt the name of the older one (Sect. 120). The Island Caribs have also in their drinking bouts or on occasions of public rejoicing, some one appointed to give them a new name, whom they address after having drunk well. "I wish to be named. Name me!" one will say, whereupon the other immediately satisfies him and is rewarded with a present—a quartz-crystal, or other article (RoP, 552-3).

266.* With a view to their becoming good hunting dogs, the Warraus name their canine friends after those animals which are known to hunt well, as certain ants and bees which catch plenty of other prey; after warribisi (Sect. 88), a big wasp that lays its eggs in the ground and brings various worms from the bush for its young, when hatched, to feed on; after sakaro and buruma, two crabs which run quickly and hunt well; after the giant anteater, the shark, and the small wild dog (karisiri), all of these possessing undoubtedly good hunting qualities.

266A.* Special words, or paraphrases, have to be used under particular circumstances; thus, in traveling over water—river or sea—the use of certain names otherwise employed in ordinary every-day conversation, is absolutely forbidden (Sect. 194). On the Aiary River (Rio Negro) the villages have secret names which are not mentioned except under pressure (KG, I, 184). There are some few words which may be employed only according to the sex speaking, or spoken to. Thus, among the Arawaks, to express the word "surely" or "certainly" a man will say tashi to a woman, but tade to a man, whereas a woman will use the term tara when conversing with one of her own sex, but tashi when talking to one of the opposite. "Oh, yes!" "So you say," is similarly expressed by three words: babui between woman and woman, or woman and man, but dadai when a man addresses a woman, and daido when he is talking to another man. The signification of this distinction I have not been able to discover; it is not connected, of course, with the use of different languages by the opposite sexes, as was the case in the Lesser Antilles with the Carib warriors and their Arawak wives. And, finally, with the mainland Arawaks a particular plaintive intonation is used in inquiries after the health or welfare of those who are ill or unfortunate; and the tone is always suited to the circumstances and situation of the party addressed (HiC, 248).

Next

Footnotes

p. 292

1 When a Warrau is very very tired he gives a whistle, something like ho-ho´-wi! ho-ho´-wi! to catch his breath. The Indians say the old people do it still.

p. 293

1 This idea of throwing peppers into a fire appears to have been an old trick. It is stated by Captain Jean-Pierre that, when the old Oyampis, of the upper Yary, Cayenne, wished to stop an enemy, they surrounded their village with a circle of fire into which they threw handfuls of dry capsicums. It is impossible to fight when one is seized with an unconquerable sneezing (Cr, 271).

p. 294

1 It is only proper to state that Crévaux gives it as his opinion that the object of these boucans is to placate (calmer) Yolock, the Bush Spirit, who can prevent them killing game. With this opinion, however, I am unable to agree, but can only regard these structures as having something to do in the way of protection from the injuries which one might reasonably expect the slaughtered monkeys would do their best to inflict.—W. E. R.

p. 298

1 The alligator skull stuck up in the Carib houses serves a different purpose; it keeps away the Bush Spirit, the Yurokon.

p. 303

1 The vessel in which the staple Indian dish known as "pepper-pot" is daily warmed, cooked, and added to from time to time is never cleaned.

CHAPTER XVI
SEXUAL LIFE1

Puberty Ordeals (267): fasting (268); exposure to ant bites (269); scarification (270); flogging (271); other inconveniences in connection with isolation, water, fire, cooking, and the hair (272); conclusion of ceremony (273). Similar ordeals at subsequent menstruations (274).

Courtship: Tokens of accepted proposals (275).

Marriage Ordeals: Similar to those at puberty (276), but additional trials of skill, etc., for males (277-278). Family Restrictions on Marriage (278A).

Childbirth Ordeals: Pre-natal, for one or both parents (279); Post-natal—fasting, scarification, flogging (280), isolation and couvade (281); Male as parturient parent (281A); Miscellaneous restrictions (282, 283); Destruction of new-born child, Twins (284). Asexual genesis of children (284A). Birth marks (284B).

267.* In many of the tribes, as the Warraus and the Caribs, the young people of both sexes can not enter into permanent sexual partnership until they have successfully undergone the puberty ordeals (Cr, 612); in others, the betrothal or perhaps even the consummation of the marriage follows as a direct consequence of such ordeals. The result has been that some authors have referred certain marriage customs to puberty ceremonies, while occasionally the reverse has happened. As a matter of fact they would seem to be more or less identical. The puberty ordeals include (a) more or less rigid fasting, combined with (b) exposure to the bites of ants, etc., (c) severe scarification, or (d) sound flogging—all to be borne without visible signs of suffering. A careful study of these leads one to the conviction that with both sexes the effect is to ensure the young people being healthy and strong, willing to work, skilful, and industrious. In the case of the female, the general tenor of the facts points to a belief in her being possessed by some Spirit prone to evil, whose influence so far as practicable, has to be counteracted and destroyed. Hence the piai blows on (Sect. 85) and mutters over the [Makusi] girl and her more valuable belongings so as to disenchant her and everything she has come into contact with (ScR, II, 316) Some of the ordeals may be repeated, though in a less degree, at the second, perhaps at the third menstrual period.

268.* To account for this enforced abstinence from sufficient food on the part of the women at times of menstruation, a cacique on the Orinoco told Gumilla: "Our ancestors observed that wherever the women, during their monthly periods, happened to tread, there p. 309everything dried up, and that if any man trod where they had placed their feet, his legs would swell: having studied the remedy, they ordered us to starve them, so that their bodies should be free from the poison" (G, I, 159). So with the Pomeroon Caribs, it was essential that when the girl was carried from her hammock to the place where the scarification had been effected, and back again, her feet must not touch the ground (ScR, II, 431). Among the Pomeroon Arawaks, at the puberty ceremony of first menstruation the girl is allowed no meat, but a little fish (and these must be only of small size), together with small cassava cakes, of which she must eat only the center, and a modicum of water in a very small calabash. For the next six months or so, according to circumstances, the young woman does not eat any meat of large animals, or fish which has much blood in it, as flesh of the tapir, yarau, turtle, etc. With the Warraus the girl must not speak or laugh or eat during the two or three days of the period. Were she to do so, she would lose all her teeth when she grew into a big woman. The first thing she is allowed to eat is a little cassava flour wrapped in a leaf. The Pomeroon Carib girl who, for the space of three days had to do without food or water, was not allowed to utter a word. She was subsequently starved for a month on a diet of roots, cassava bread, and water (ScR, II, 431). Girls may die under this treatment.

269.* In order that the Arawak girl, now become a woman, may henceforth have strength and willingness to work, some old stranger whose character is known to be strong and good, and a willing worker, is chosen to place an ant-frame on the young woman's forehead, hands, and feet. The ants are attached at their middles in the interstices of the plaited strands forrning the framework, the frame itself being applied on the side from which all the little heads are projecting. In Cayenne, Pitou (II, 267) describes the ant-frame as being applied by the girl's mother. Among the Warraus, as with the Caribs, the young people of both sexes cannot marry until they have gone through the ordeal of the ants. Among the Warraus [mouth of Orinoco], the sufferer is put in his hammock; they apply the tari-tari ants to him; if he cries out he is condemned to celibacy (Cr, 612), My Warrau friends on the Moruca recognize the above-mentioned insects as their natatari. They tell me that long ago the same practices were carried on here. If the girl cried it meant that she could not work, and was therefore not deserving of a husband. The Roucouyenne (Cayenne Carib) would-be bridegroom has to submit to a corresponding ordeal at the hands of the piai: the latter applies ants to the chest and wasps on the forehead, the whole of the body being subsequently stung with ants and wasps (Cr, 245-50). According to Coudreau, the Ojanas believe that the wasp ordeal undergone by the men renders them p. 310skilful, clever, and industrious; and certainly the obligation of publicly braving severe bodily suffering has an assured intrinsic value (Go, 21). If the parents had not previously submitted themselves to these ant and wasp tests and other ordeals the Cayenne Apaläis and Roucouyennes believe that "only emaciated and sickly children would be born to them" (Cr, 307). It is noteworthy that in both Surinam and Cayenne the insects above referred to "are held in frames of bizarre shapes fringed with feathers, representing quadrupeds and birds (Cr, 245-50). In such cases it certainly seems a very fair question to inquire whether it is the properties and qualities of the particular quadruped or bird represented in the shape of the frame, or those of the old stranger, piai, or other individual applying it, that are supposed to be impressed on the young person's character; unfortunately the evidence thus far collected is insufficient to furnish a satisfactory answer. But in the following example the object of applying the ants at all would seem to be—though the suggestion after all may be wrong—to obtain the personal characteristics and qualities of the European traveler: "On entering the Apaläi village—a custom we did not find among the Ouayanas—they brought me a framework of palm leaves to which were attached at their centers, some big black ants. All the people of the tribe, irrespective of age or sex, presented themselves for me to apply it to their bodies, loins, thighs, etc." (Cr, 300).

270.* The Warrau boys had to undergo at initiation greater ordeals than the girls, to demonstrate their strength and manly prowess. These ordeals consisted principally in the infliction of painful wounds upon the breast and arms with the tusk of the wild boar or the beak of the toucan. If the boy endures all this without showing signs of pain, he can rank thenceforth with the men; if not, he has to submit to the ordeal on another occasion

(ScR, I, 168). The Carib girl of the Pomeroon is operated on by the piai, who with the incisors of the Dasyprocta [acouri] makes deep incisions down her back, and from shoulder to shoulder; he then rubs pepper into these wounds, without the poor tortured creature daring to utter one cry of pain (ScR, II, 431). So also in Cayenne, a number of bloody incisions are made in her body, and it is only subsequent to this that she is allowed to wear the apron-belt (kewé-yo): the young man is allowed to wear the lap-cloth only after having passed the necessary ordeals (PBa, 225). In Cayenne again, the girl is said to have her teeth filed down by the piai at her puberty initiation (LAP, II, 267).

271.* On returning from her first bath [after the first menstrul period] the Makusi girl must during the night sit upon a stool or stone, to be whipped by her mother with thin rods without raising the slightest cry to wake the sleeping occupants of the hut, an occurrence which would prove daugerous for her future welfare. The p. 311 whipping takes place also at the second menstrual period, but not subsequently (ScR, II, 316). Among the Puinavis Indians of the Ynirida [upper Orinoco], the "Devil" who three days before has been making terrible music in the forest at last enters the house of the poor young girl, who tries to take to flight. A piai at this moment runs up and, binding her eyes (Sect. 255), leads her through the village while the Devil all by himself is making a frightful hubbub. Now is the time for the festival of the beating with the sticks, when the men strike the unfortunate girl, who dares not complain. At last a young man, admiring her courage, takes her place, and exposes himself to the blows of the company; if he bears the pain without murmuring she chooses him for her husband (Cr, 532). [Compare Sect. 276.] With the Uaupes River Indians, "all relatives and friends of the parents are assembled, bringing, each of them, pieces of sipó (an elastic climber); the girl is then brought out, perfectly naked, into the midst of them, when each person present gives her five or six severe blows with the sipó across the back and breast till she falls senseless, and it sometimes happens, dead. If she recovers it is repeated four times at intervals of six hours, and it is considered an offence to the parents not to strike hard. During this time numerous pots of all kinds of meat and fish have been prepared, when the sipós are dipped in them and given to her to lick1 and she is then considered a woman and allowed to eat anything, and is marriageable. The boys undergo a somewhat similar ordeal [at puberty, as the girls] but not so severe, which initiates them into manhood, and allows them to see the Jurupari music" (ARW, 345).

272.* What may be regarded as remaining puberty ordeals to which the young girl has to submit at her first menstruation, and to a minor degree at all her subsequent ones, are certain procedures connected with her isolation, with water, fire, cooking, and cooking apparatus, and with the hair. In the "old days" of the Pomeroon Arawaks, the girl would remain with her mother in a separate logie, or in a specially constructed compartment of the house. The former would be distinguished by hanging from the posts waste shreds of the ite (Mauritia) palm, that is, the leaves from which the outer fibrous layer, for making twine, has already been removed. The specially constructed room was called the aibona-léhi. The Warraus are said to have used a separate closed house. With the Makusis, at the first signs, the girl is separated from all intercourse with the occupants of the hut; her hammock is taken from its usual place and slung in the highest part of the hut, where the poor creature is exposed to all the smoke which, if that be possible, is now increased. For the first few days she must not leave her hammock at all during the daytime. When the most active p. 312and striking of the symptoms have passed she can come down from her height, and occupy a small place partitioned off in the darkest corner of the hut (ScR, II, 315). So also in Cayenne, the girl's hammock was slung high up to the ridge of the karbet (PBa, 225). On the upper Amazon, she is similarly banished to the girao [an overhead staging inside the oblong hut] under the smoky and filthy roof (HWB, 383). She must not go near water until when the period is past; her mother bathes her in the closed room. If, during the day, the Arawak girl wishes to micturate she must do so into a goblet, which she empties after dark in the bush. When she thus similarly goes to ease herself, she must be accompanied by her mother, and must take with her a lighted fire-stick, which otherwise would not be used. The Makusi girl uses a fire which she herself has to light, and alone gets the benefit of. For ten days she cooks her cassava meal in her own pot at her own fire. Pots and drinking vessels that she has used are broken, and the chips buried (ScR, II, 316). The Arawak girl must not comb her hair but must let it hang loose until such time as her mother combs it after bathing her when the event is over. The Warrau matron (or the father sometimes) crops her (or his) daughter's hair; the Carib girl has hers burned off (ScR, II, 431). On the Aiary River (Rio Negro), the hair cut from a girl at menstruation is used for head and dance ornaments by the men (KG, I, 181; II, 253).

273.* As a rule the puberty ordeal is brought to a conclusion with drink-and-dance party, in which the girl herself neither drinks nor dances, though she constitutes of course the central object of attraction. If an Arawak, she is brought out of the closed room by a middle-aged man, and shown in her decorations to the assembled guests; she then takes her seat on a stool especially made for her, shaped like a crocodile or a "tiger." Previous to these festivities her brother or father has killed a hummingbird, dried it, and cut it up into very small pieces. Every visitor, male or female, now gets a bit of this on a small piece of cassava, the idea being that when the girl grows older she will obtain her share of any of the good things that the other people may possess. The Warrau young woman is decked with beads and the white feather-down of various birds, as Crax and Ardea, apparently stuck with some gummy substance to the smooth head [the hair having been cut], and the arms and legs (ScR, I, 168). The Caribs paint her red all over. In place of the stool they would seem to have employed a stone or (?) plate (ScR, II, 431).

274.* The following are the ordeals regularly undergone by Arawak women at subsequent menstruations, and which I understand are undergone, to a greater or less extent, by women of other tribes also, for example, the Warraus. The girl takes up her quarters in a separate logie or banab, distinguishable from all other structures by the suspended bunches of waste ite shreds. She lies in a smaller hammock p. 313than usual. She must not eat meat from any big animal (as tapir and turtle), or fish which contains much blood. The flesh of any game hunted by dogs is strictly forbidden her; otherwise the dogs would be permanently spoiled for hunting. On no account may she cook, bake, or prepare drink, for other men or women. She must not cross water, travel in a corial, or bathe in a river or a pond; if she wishes to wash she may pour water out of a calabash over herself. Using a separate fire for herself, it is imperative that she never blows one out. She has to cook in a smaller pot, and employ a smaller fan, goblet, etc., all especially made for the purpose. In this connection I would suggest that many of the "toy vessels," described by im Thurn as being "seen in and about almost every Indian house" (IT, 278), are in reality the pottery-ware used specially during the periods of menstruation. Finally, the girl must not comb her hair but must let it hang loose.

In addition to the bathing prohibition, the Makusi women during these times must not go into the forest, where they would be exposed to the embraces of snakes (ScR, II, 316). On the lower Guaviar the Piapoco husband is said to bring the wife her food during the few days that she remains isolated in the special hut (Cr, 526).

275.* In matters of courtship the would-be benedict knows that the acceptance of an offering of food or of other objects is the token of a favorable, the rejection, that of an unfavorable issue. The Arawak lover, after making sure beforehand through the girl's relatives that he will not meet with a refusal, pays a visit to her parents, tells them how poor he is, that he has no wife, etc. At the conclusion of these preliminaries the young woman puts before him something to eat (SR, II, 459). He knows that the path of true love is going to run smooth. So again in the same tribe if a father wants some well-known person for son-in-law, he lets his daughter place food before the latter during the course of a visit; if he partakes of it, the union is assured; if not, the old man knows that their wishes do not agree (ScR, II, 459). At the present day, on the Pomeroon, when the Arawak young man returns on the appointed day to receive an answer from the father, he takes care to leave his hammock at the waterside, or on the pathway. If the girl brings this in, he knows that his prospects are favorable, any doubt being clinched by the father telling his daughter to give the young man cassava, pepper-pot, beltiri, or anything else that may be on hand. In Surinam, it is sufficient for the man anxious to marry, to take to the girl all the game and fish that he has caught during the day; if she accepts this present it is a sign that she is willing to have him (Fe, 38). In Cayenne, with the Galibis, as soon as a girl has taken a fancy to an Indian she will offer him drink, together with firewood to light near p. 314 his hammock; if he refuses the offer it means that he does not want her (PBa, 220).

276.* In none of the tribes is any sexual union publicly recognized as permanent—the closest correspondence I can find to our idea of marriage—prior to the advent of womanhood. Certain of the ordeals of puberty are closely paralleled: indeed, as at puberty, the candidates for matrimony have to submit to a rigid fast with or without exposure to ants, wasps, etc., a sound flogging (KG, II, 144), or a severe scarification. It is only the males on whom something additional is imposed in the way of trials of skill and the like. Among the Makusis the man, for some time before marriage, abstains from meat (IT, 221-3), which was apparently the case with the Guiyquirie and Mapoye females of the Orinoco. Concerning the latter tribes Gumilla says: For forty days before marrying, their girls are locked up to a continuous and rigid fast: three seeds of the Murichi, three ounces of cassava with a pitcher of water is their daily ration; and so, on the day of the nuptials, they are more like corpses than brides (G, I, 159). No reasons for this abstention are given, though it was asserted for the Carib girls on the Islands, who were treated similarly, that the idea of the fasting was to prevent them becoming sluggards, not likely to work when married (BBR, 250). The young Apaläi males on the Parou River, Cayenne, have to undergo the maraké (the ant and wasp ordeal) prior to attempting the trials of skill. Among the Guahibos of the Vichada River (Orinoco) on the occasion of the marriage of a widow, after having covered her husband's remains with earth, they put her on the grave, and remove the rag which, for the time being covers her chest: she then holds her hands above her head: a man comes forward and strikes her breasts with a switch—this is her future husband: the other men hit her on the shoulders, and she receives the flagellation without a groan: her fiancé in his turn is struck with the switch, his hands joined above his head and without a murmur (Cr, 548). [Compare Sect. 271.] After the above ceremony, they place another woman on the grave and pierce the extremity of her tongue with a bone: the blood runs down her chest, and a sorcerer besmears her breasts with it (Cr, 548).

277.* In most of the tribes there were certain trials of skill (Sect. 30), certain marriage ordeals, which the would-be suitor had successfully to surmount before gaining permanent possession of his wife, in addition to the puberty ordeals that had previously to be passed. These marriage ordeals at the same time may be admittedly regarded as omens or tokens of what the father-in-law or his daughter might reasonably expect from the husband in the future. The Uacarras Indians, a tribe on the River Apaporis, a branch of the Uaupes, of the Rio Negro, have a trial of skill at shooting with the bow and arrow, and if the young man does not show himself a p. 315good marksman, the girl refuses him on the ground that he will not be able to shoot fish and game enough for the family (ARW, 346). On the Orinoco, he had to kill a bush-hog all by himself and bring it to his future father-in-law's house to show that he was indeed a man (G, II, 285). The young Apaläi Indians on the Parou River, Cayenne, after submitting to the maraké (ant and wasp ordeal) must now "go through the target test: with their backs turned, they have to throw cassava pellets (boulettes) at a piece of wood upon which a circle has been traced, and must hit it three times running, etc." (Cr, 307). In its most complete form, however, the shooting ordeal seems to have been carried out by the Arawaks, and it is from the very old people of this people that I have been able to gather the following facts concerning what used to take place in bygone days. When the youth went to his future father-in-law and asked for the girl, the old man would consult his wife and daughter, as a rule, and if everything were satisfactory would say "yes," but would not give him actual possession of her until he had performed certain deeds, the first and foremost of which was to shoot into a certain woodpecker's nest. He would accordingly ask the suitor whether he were ready or whether he wished to wait a few days. The latter would of course say he was quite ready, so impetuous is youth, and would give a minute description of the situation of the particular tree, usually one close to the water-side, into which he proposed shooting the arrow. The girl's father, however, would invariably plead some excuse to put him off, say to the next day, and in the meantime would get ready a big corial—big enough to carry 10 or 12 men—and engage his crew. When next morning the young man turned up again, the old man had everything ready and would get them all into the boat, he himself steering. The girl herself had to sit on the left of her would-be husband in the bows. When within a comparatively short distance from the tree wherein the woodpecker's nest lay concealed, the old man would call upon the crew to pull with all their strength—and the young man to draw his bow. Before, however, the arrow had sped, and while yet the bow was fully stretched, the woman had to touch his left side with her hand signifying that if his arrow reached its mark she agreed to be his. If he missed, the performance had to be postponed to another occasion, he having the right to try as many times as he liked until he succeeded and in the meantime he might continue practising on his own account. Luck might assist him on the first occasion, sometimes on the second, third, or fourth, or he might have to make the trial so many times that he would give up the attempt as well as all thoughts for the girl, and proceed to some other settlement where the woodpecker's nests were situated to better advantage. Without shooting his arrow into the nest the wooer would certainly never get possession of the girl—neither father nor mother p. 316 would give way on that particular point. On the other hand, supposing his aim to have been finally successful, the girl would be as wife to him, and he would take up residence in his father-in-law's house. The next thing was for the old Arawak paterfamilias to mark out a piece of ground, which within so many days the young man to whom he presented an ax for the purpose, had to cut and clear for a provision field. The time specified was usually short, the young man having to work with might and main, starting early and returning late, but finally completing the task. A similar ordeal was exacted among the Makusis and other tribes (ScR, II, 316). But there was still something else for the Arawak would-be bridegroom to do. For during the time occupied in cutting the field, the old man had busied himself in collecting a large number of crab quakes (baskets), and subsequently he would accompany the lad out to sea, and would himself watch to see that within the one day the youngster really filled all the baskets through his own exertions, and did not obtain the assistance of friends. This completed, the youth became henceforth one of the legal heirs of the house. Should, however, the lad not have cut the field nor filled the requisite number of quakes within the allotted period he would have been laughed and jeered at when attending subsequent paiwarris. The two ordeals, just described, however, were never so essential as that of the shooting of the arrow into the woodpecker's nest.

278.* A WARNING TO WIVES (A)

You must remeinber that in the days of long ago we Arawaks would never accept a suitor for our daughter unless he gave us some proof that he was skilful in the chase, and able to support a wife. Among such tests were those of shooting into a woodpecker's nest from off the bows of a swiftly paddled corial, the filling of so many baskets with crabs during the course of a single tide, and the clearing of a field within a certain specified period. The first of these was a severe test, it is true, and gradually fell into disuse, though the others were long retained. It was just about the time when the first-mentioned ordeal had been done away with, that a young man, courting a girl, thought he would have no difficulty in gaining permanent possession of her now that all he had to do for his father-in-law was to catch some crabs (Sect. 365) and cut a field. So when he went and asked the old man for his daughter and obtained his consent, he had no compunction in settling down at his new quarters, for with us a husband always lives with his bride before he completes the tests: on their fulfilment, however, will depend his fate—whether he retains permanent possession of her. Two or three weeks having been spent on the honeymoon, the old man talked to the lad about going to sea, after the usual manner, to catch crabs, and advised him to get his quakes (baskets) ready for a certain day. The youth went into the bush with his companions to cut the necessary mukru [the Creole term applied to the material used in weaving baskets], and, on his return, sat down to prepare it (that is, to split it into strands, and to tie them into bundles). As a matter of fact, he did not know what else to do with them! And when his comrades, who were already weaving baskets for themselves, saw that he had stopped operations, they inquired the cause, and were told that he intended making his when he p. 317got out to sea. (He was ashamed to expose his ignorance of their manufacture.) "You must be very quick at it," they said. "Not at all!" he replied, "there is no difficulty whatever in the matter. Indeed, I bet that I will make my quakes and catch crabs while you are catching yours, and that I will even then beat you." They then all made a start: in the corial were the would-be husband, his new wife, the old father-in-law, and some five or six other young men. When they reached the sea, they anchored their boat at a little distance from the shore, all except the honeymoon couple getting out, each with a basket, to hunt for crabs. After they had gone, the young man told his bride to jump out also, and drive all the little "four-eye" fish [Tetrophthalmus sp.] toward the boat. And while he was there squatting on the bench, with the mukru strands in his hands trying to make his basket, the fish all passed by.1 As might have been expected, he realized that he was making no progress, so he made the woman surround the shoal a second time, and drive the fish back again, thus allowing him to have another look. She thus continued driving the fish backward and forward, and still he made no progress. She finally became very angry, and picking up one of the quakes out of the corial, waded on to shore: he called out to her to come back, but she took no heed of him. Now the particular quake which she had taken belonged, as she well knew, to one of the other men who had accompanied them on the expedition and who was an old lover of hers; it was this same man whom she proceeded to join when she reached shore. She came close to him, and saying that she wanted to help him, lent her assistance in the usual manner: as he dragged the crabs out of their holes, he would every now and then jerk one near her, and she would gather it up into her basket. Her husband now came over and joined them, and though he would drag out a crab, and throw it toward her, she took not the slightest notice. Although he repeatedly shouted, "Look out! It is escaping. Put it into your basket," she would not even recognize him. With her old lover, on the other hand, it was quite different: they soon filled their quakes, and went back to the boat for two more baskets; and these were soon filled. Back to the boat for two more, and so on, backward and forward, until all the quakes were full. When the husband realized that the others had gathered almost all the crabs that they could possibly carry home with them, he became desperate, and taking his hammock, wrapped within its folds as many of the crustaceans as he could gather. It was now time for them to start on their return journey, but getting into the boat the bride squatted, not on her husband's bench as was the proper thing for a recently married young woman to do, but on that of her old lover. The would-be husband said, "Come here: you are sitting in the wrong place;" but she and the old man took no notice of the remark, and simply snubbed him. Furthermore, when they reached home, all the men turned into their hammocks, while the wife busied herself over the cooking. This did not take very long, as she was only roasting the crabs, so she was soon able to announce, "Father! It is quite ready now." Getting out of his hammock, the old man called the young men up one after another, giving each one his name, and then called Satchi! Now, on hearing this term of endearment, the husband thought he was intended, and accordingly replied, Wangj [i. e.

Yes, thanks, etc:]. "No, no!" said the old father, "I mean the son-in-law whom I brought in the boat back with me today. He knows how to make quakes. You don't." Naturally, the erstwhile husband was put to shame, and immediately wended his steps over to his mother's place, carrying with him his hammock and the few crabs it contained. His mother was indeed a dear old soul, and after cooking the crabs, and giving him a real square meal, consoled him as only a mother p. 318can, advising him at the same time that he must wait a while, and be patient, because she was sure the girl would make up to him again. A few days later she took her son away to visit an old friend of hers, a man who was very wise in his way. She told this man all her son's troubles, and begged that he would teach him not only how to hunt, but also how to make quakes, pegalls, matapis, sifters, and fans, because it was due only to her boy's ignorance of these matters that he had lost his wife. The old man agreed, for friendship's sake, and mother and son remained with him for more than a year, the latter finally becoming quite as proficient in all the manly arts as his teacher. The result of all this instruction was that when the two of them, after leaving the old man's place, returned to their own little house, they never experienced those pangs of hunger that they did in the old times. Each day her son brought home something, and the babracote was almost groaning under the load of dried meat that it now carried. It happened that a woman passing that way called in one afternoon, noticed all the smoked game, and accepted a choice piece which the old woman offered her when she was leaving. Of course, woman-like, she must needs straightway go and show this very piece of meat to all the inmates of the house where the faithless wife of a year ago was residing, telling her and all her people that her late husband was not such a fool as they had thought: did she not with her own eyes see all the game that he has killed, and all the quakes and matapis that he had made? Of course, conversation of this nature, and lots more of it, only made the late wife more and more anxious to visit the spouse whom she and her father had spurned. And there was good reason for it too. The past year's experience had been a sad one for her: she had discovered too late that her second husband was not only worthless, but in addition lazy, and that all he was now bent on doing was to lie in his hammock all day, and make her work for him. So next morning, she and her mother, telling their people that they were going for a walk, set out in the direction that led to the house where lived the master of whose prowess and skill they had heard so much about the day before. They arrived there. The man was lying in his hammock, but his mother received them, placed stools, asked them to be seated, and put cassava with peppers before them. She also took pains to apologize that there was nothing else to offer them, notwithstanding that the babracote with its load of meat was, as it were, staring at them. The visitors gave a significant look at one another, at the babracote, and at the pepper-pot with the cassava and peppers: they now felt so ashamed of themselves at having treated the young man so badly a little more than a year ago that they could not even eat the cassava, and without even touching it, told their hostess to "take the pot away."1 The elder of the two visitors rose to leave, and expected her daughter to do the same, but the latter said, "No! I intend staying here, with my first husband; whether he beats me or not, I don't care. He has turned out far better than my second one!" So when her mother had got out of sight, she went up to the hammock where the man was resting, and climbed in, saying, "I have come back to you, my sweetheart." He, however, immediately pushed her out, saying, "I don't want you. I am the lazy, ignorant, and worthless man whom you scorned a year ago." She tried again to climb into his hammock, but he would not have her: she spoke "sweet-mouth" to him; but he would not listen: crestfallen, she left him, to return to her own people and her second husband, but the first one remained alone in his hammock and was glad to hear her go.

278A.* I have been un able to confirm Brett's statement as to the members of the Demarena, a particular family group, being restricted to connubium only with those of the Korobohana family group (BrB, 179); otherwise, all the Guiana Indian tribes are exogamous p. 319 and trace descent exclusively through the mother. Certainly among the Arawaks and Warraus, sexual union between persons of certain degrees of cousinship is regarded in the same light as is incest by Europeans. (See Sect. 131.)

279.* An analysis of the pre-natal and post-natal ordeals undergone by father and mother bring into prominence the fact that they bear remarkably strong resemblance to those submitted to at puberty (by both sexes) and at menstruation (Sect. 267 et seq.). In the main, these ordeals consist of food restrictions; the tolerance of severe physical pain without visible signs of suffering; and procedures connected with isolation, with water, fire, and cooking. The proper performance of the childbirth ordeals insures that nothing will go amiss with the baby. With regard to the food restrictions, before the child's birth, these may be imposed on both parents.

Some of the men of the Akawai and Carib nations, when they have reason to expect an increase of their families, consider themselves bound to abstain from certain kinds of meat, lest the expected child should, in some very mysterious way, be injured by their partaking of it. The acouri (or agouti) is thus tabooed lest, like that little animal, the child should be meager; the Haimara also, lest it should be blind, the outer coating of the eye of that fish suggesting film or cataract; the labba, lest the infant's mouth should protrude like the labba's, or lest it be spotted like the labba, which spots would ultimately become ulcers. The marudi is also forbidden, lest the infant be still-born, the screeching of that bird being considered ominous of death. [Br, 355.]

Among the Pomeroon Arawaks, though the killing and eating of a snake during the woman's pregnancy is forbidden to both father and mother the husband is allowed to kill and eat any other animal. The cause assigned for the taboo of the snake is that the little infant might be similar, that is, able neither to talk nor to walk. Neither parent, however, when carrying a piece of cassava cake, may either turn it over in the hand, or curl it up at the sides; otherwise, the ears of the child, when born, will be found curled over. Any game hunted by dogs is strictly forbidden the pregnant woman of this tribe, just as it is at her menstruation; otherwise the dog would be spoiled for hunting purposes, permanently in the latter circumstances, temporarily in the former, the dog recovering its powers only when the baby was born. Hence, when a man brings home any animal that has been hunted by a dog, it is his wife's business to see that it is not partaken of by any woman in either of the states named. An interesting reference to this belief will be found in Timehri (vol. II, 1883, p. 355), in which report is made of a woman's wages being stopped because, while weeding, she partook of the game caught by a hunting dog and so rendered the dog useless. She is forbidden to eat when pregnant any "big meat," as turtle or tapir, or fish that has much blood in it, as at menstruation; she can now eat only the tail portion of a fish. Infringement of any of these rules will result p. 320in something being amiss with the child when born. The Indians of the Uaupes River, Rio Negro, "believe that if a woman, during her pregnancy, eats of any meat, any other animal partaking of it will suffer; if a domestic animal or tame bird, it will die; if a dog, it will be for the future incapable of hunting; and even a man will ever after be unable to shoot that particular kind of game" (ARW, 349); hence, meat has to be avoided by her. A Pomeroon Arawak female will beget twins through eating any double fruit during the period of her pregnancy. The Saliva husband, however (G, I, 189), regarding such a result as a sure sign of his wife's disloyalty, believing that only one of the twins could possibly be his. Another pregnancy restriction on the Pomeroon is that the Arawak woman must not laugh, and must not grieve; neither may she look at the face of a dead person though it is permissible for her to gaze on the body.

280.* And even when the baby does put in an appearance, the mother's troubles, like the father's, are far from over; for until her youngster is able to walk well, the Arawak mother on the Pomeroon must eat neither deer, turtle, nor iguana, animals which, for some days after birth, creep or crawl very slowly, in contradistinction, for instance, from the bush-hog, that will start to run directly it has littered. The idea is that by eating such flesh the mother will cause her infant to walk too slowly. On the islands, the Carib mother abstained from female crabs, which would give the child stomachache, while the father had to avoid certain animals for fear of the youngster participating in their natural faults. If a father ate turtle, the child would be heavy, and have no brains; if he ate a parrot, the child would have a parrot nose; if a crab, the consequence would be long legs (BBR, 248-9). The mainland Caribs of Cayenne (Galibis) avoided deer, hog, and other large game (PBa, 223-4). Brett, in a quotation apparently from McClintock, says that the Akawai, Carib, and Warrau husband abstains from venison after his wife's delivery for the same reason that the Arawak mother shuns it (Br, 356). The Roucouyenne father must eat no fish or game that has been caught with an arrow, but must content himself with cassava and with small fish that have been poisoned with the "nicou" plant; should he disregard this taboo the child will either soon die or develop vicious propensities. For the Carib Islander, paternity must undoubtedly have proved somewhat trying; for ten or twelve days he had "to take to his bed," and subsist on a little cassava and water; he ate only of the insides of the cassava cakes, leaving the outsides for the subsequent feasting; for from 6 to 10 or 12 months later he had to abstain from several meats, as manati, turtle, hog, fowl, and fish, for fear of hurting his infant, but such extreme fasting was carried out only at the birth of the first male child. p. 321When the fasting period was approaching its conclusion, he had to submit to a scarification, by means of agouti teeth, upon his shoulders without a murmur, and the better he bore this infliction the more valiant would his son prove; the blood thus made to flow was not allowed to fall onto the ground, but was smeared on the child's face to make it courageous (généreux) (RoP, 550). The actual termination of the fast must here have been celebrated more or less ceremoniously: "Placed on a red-painted seat, the women bring him food, which the old men put in his mouth, as they would do to a child, the cassava and the fish being in small pieces; he eats the cassava, but ejects the fish after chewing it. He would become sick if he began to eat too well at once; he is made to drink by being held by the neck" (BBR, 249). The scarification and flogging ordeals of puberty are repeated on the Carib father, both island and mainland, after his wife's delivery of either boy or girl: the reputed idea is "to transfer his courage (muth) to the children" (ScR, II, 431). In the former case, after a course of very limited diet he is "brought to a public place, looking like a skeleton, and standing upright on two large flat cakes of cassavas. The sponsors then begin to scratch and cut his skin with very sharp agouti teeth. They first begin on the sides, then the shoulders, from the arm to the elbow, from elbow to wrist, and from the thighs to the ankles. . . . He is then painted and rubbed with roucou leaves, pepper seeds and tobacco juice, and placed on a red-painted seat" (BBR, 248-9), and fed, as already mentioned. The Mainland Carib, the Galibi of Cayenne, after some weeks' subsistence on a stinted diet, is "scarified on various parts of the body with fish-bones or agouti teeth: very often even he is given several lashes with a whip" (PBa, 223-4).

281.* After the birth of the baby come the various procedures connected with the isolation of one or both parents; in the case of the father, his so-called "lying-in" is spoken of as the couvade, and is met with in many tribes, for example, Arawaks, Warraus, Caribs (who call the practice kenonimáno), Makusis, and Wapisianas. In the case of the mainland Caribs (Cayenne) "when their wives are confined for the first time, the newly married husband has to sling his hammock high up to the ridge of the house" (PBa, 223-4). With the Island Caribs, if the child is a firstborn male, the husband, as soon as the woman is delivered, goes to bed, complains and acts as though he had been delivered (BBR, 248), and submits to a restricted diet, etc. As with the Caribs, so with the Arawaks and Warraus, it is practically the husband who is isolated, and does the "lying-in." Indeed, in these three tribes, the woman is isolated only during actual delivery, which takes place either out in the bush, in a separate shelter, or in a compartment specially partitioned off from p. 322the rest of the house. With the bath that she takes within a comparatively few hours after the interesting event has occurred, her isolation, and with it any dangerous influence of her recent condition ceases. The woman is her own accoucheuse; even during the night and in wet season she will leave the house and retire to a secluded spot near by. She occupies herself with her daily affairs until the last moment: she may come home with a quake containing the baby instead of the usual cassava; and "on the morrow she is prepared to undertake all the indoor work of the household" (Da, 248). Confinement takes place either in the forest or in some little hut; she is always alone unless some difficulty presents itself, when an old woman will attend (PBa, 226). With the Makusis and Wapisianas, both parents engage in a "lying-in" for a shorter or longer period after the appearance of baby. The Makusi father takes to his hammock placed near that of his wife, until the navel-string falls off; but before doing this, if he has no separate building, he will prepare a palm-leaf partition in the hut (ScR, II, 314). When the partition was finished the [Wapisiana] husband hung up in it both his own and his wife's hammock, and therein they lay to "take to bed" (die Wochen zu halten) like the Makusis (ScR, II, 389). During the lying-in of the mother, or couvade of the father, they are considered equally unclean, such uncleanness being occasionally regarded as persisting for long afterward. Thus, the Mainland Carib (in Cayenne) is obliged to devote himself to the service of an old Indian and to leave his wife for some months; during this period he has to be submissive and regard himself as a real slave (PBa, 223-4). When in couvade a visitor enters his house, that visitor's dogs will soon die

(Cr, 241). The Arawaks and Warraus say that if a man during the period he ought to remain in couvade indulges in sexual relations with any woman other than his wife, the infant will die through inability to exert its emunctory powers. After lighting her fire and supplying her with drinking cups it is the duty of the female Wapisiana population to keep as far away from the lying-in woman as possible for the few days that she is deemed unclean (ScR, II, 389). With the completion of the couvade, on the upper Tiquie River, among the Tuyuka and other Indians, the grandmother "smokes" the pathway leading from the maloka to the water as well as the water itself, before the parents have their first bath (KG, I, 312). With the Uaupes River (Rio Negro) Indians, when a birth takes place in the house, everything is taken out of it, even the pans and pots, and bows and arrows, till the next day (ARW, 345).

281A.* In connection with this question of couvade, it is of interest to note that from among the Caribs I obtained a trace of an idea of the male acting as the parturient parent.

*THE BROKEN EGG (C)

Uraima once had in his possession a bird's egg, which he kept in a calabash; he took great care of it until it should hatch out. He met two girls on the road: they saw the egg and asked him to let them have it. "No!" he said, "I can not." They worried and even followed him, but he still refused. So they seized the egg, and in the course of the scuffle broke it. Uraima then spoke to the women as follows: "Since you have done this, trouble will follow you from now onward. Up to the present, the egg has belonged to man. For the future it will belong to woman and she will have to hatch it." It is only the female that lays eggs nowadays.

282.* There seem to be some curious restrictions concerning water, so far as the father is concerned, both previous and subsequent to birth. R. L. Kingston gives the following interesting pre-natal example: "While some (True) Caribs were poisoning the upper Pomeroon with haiari for fish, I saw one of them rub his shins with the beaten and washed-out haiari. Asking why he did this, he told me his wife was with child, and that he could not therefore go into the water without first rubbing his legs with haiari, lest all the fish should sink to the bottom" [instead of floating narcotized on the surface] (Ti, II, 1883, p. 355). It was said to be a custom of the Island Caribs that "they often deliver near the fire, and the child is bathed at once; but a funny precaution is, that if it is born at night, the men who are sleeping in the house go and bathe so that the child may not catch cold" (BBR, 248-9). It is curious that the Pomeroon Arawak women will not bathe their infants until such time as the navel-string heals, for fear of the same contingency happening. On the other hand, his usual bath is forbidden the Makusi father (ScR, II, 314) during his time of couvade. Strange to say, it is the bath which in most tribes constitutes the final purification of the mother, at the end of her lying-in period, whether such period be of a few hours' or several days' duration. Beyond what has already been mentioned concerning fire—how some women (Island Caribs) will often deliver near a fire and how others will apparently have one lighted for them—I have found no further references to childbirth in connection with fire, except one in connection with the navel-string. Bancroft is the only author who speaks of the division of "the umbilic vessels, which they do with a brand of fire, which cauterizes their orifices, and renders a ligature unnecessary" (Ba, 330). Two old Arawak women are my authority for saying that in the old days the cord was burned off with a heated nail. Cooking for a man is strictly prohibited to a pregnant woman: she may however "clean" the meat, but in cleaning any animal or fish she must not cut off the ears, nails, or fins. In this latter connection there is a curious prohibition concerning fingernails in force among the Makusis: neither men nor women at times of couvade or lying-in must scratch their bodies or heads p. 324 with their nails. A piece of the midrib of the kokerite palm is specially employed for the purpose (ScR, II, 314).

283.* In many of the tribes during the couvade, and often for long afterward, the husband is prohibited from engaging in certain of his ordinary occupations. The Pomeroon Arawak must neither smoke, lift any heavy weight, use a fish-hook, nor have intimate relations with any woman. The Mainland Carib of Cayenne was not allowed to cut any big timber with an ax (PBa, 223-4). The Makusi must not touch his weapons (ScR, II, 313). Should these and similar prohibitions be not observed, some evil would be sure to befall the child. There is another interesting example recorded of a man (? Arawak) during couvade lying in his hammock and twisting a new bowstring; baby began to scream, with the result that the father had to undo the whole line (Ti, II, 1883, p. 355).

When one realizes what the Indian conception of child-life is, the explanation of the above otherwise extraordinary customs becomes comparatively simple. In its material as well as in its spirit nature the baby is believed to be part and parcel of both parents, and even at birth is not considered to have an independent existence. Its material dependence on the father ceases only when the navel-string is finally detached, the signal for the male parent to conclude his "hatching" or couvade. The baby's spirit nature does not, however, usually free itself from the mother until the lapse of many months, when it begins to crawl or walk (an occasion which in some tribes seems to have been celebrated by a festival, with hair cutting and other features); hence, all this time, whatever can affect the mother in the way of food, or otherwise, exerts a corresponding influence on the child. On the other hand, its spirit nature may occasionally tend to wander all on its own account. Thus, when a Moruca River woman is carrying her very young infant along a pathway and happens to meet a cross path, she will break off a leaf or two from an adjoining bush, and throw it on the latter; baby's Spirit must follow her and not go off in another direction. On the conclusion of the couvade the baby's spirit nature, though physically freed from the Spirit of the father, and in that sense independent of it, nevertheless accompanies the father for a similar period, that is, until it can crawl, and can be influenced by it so long as the companionship, so to speak, is retained. When the infant begins to crawl, its hair is cut for the first time. Rev. Mr. Dance was, I believe, among the first to appreciate fully the true signification of these facts in connection with, presumably, the Arawaks. I myself have had opportunities for studying them among Arawaks as well as Warraus.

The infant Spirit clings to the father, gazes upon him, follows him wherever he goes, and for the time being is as intimate and familiar with the father, as he is with his own infant body with which the infant Spirit is only recently associated. How p. 325then can the father . . . go out to the forest or field to use an ax or cutlass, when the Spirit of the child which follows him as a second shadow might be between the ax and the wood? How climb a tree, if the infant spirit is also to essay the climbing, and fall, perhaps to the injury of the infant lying in the hammock? How hunt when the arrow might pierce the accompanying spirit of the child, which would be death to the little mortal at home? If, traveling through the woods you happen to meet a tairu leaf, which is formed very much in shape of a corial, floating on a stream or pond of water, and furnished with a tiny wooden seat and paddle, cut out and placed therein: or should you, in stepping over a fallen tree discover two sticks each placed from the ground to the trunk of the tree, disturb them not. . . . When the father wades through the water, the toddling spirit . . . must paddle over in the tairu-leaf boat: and when his sire crosses over the stump, the little temporary bridge enables the infantile Spirit to climb over. . . . But notwithstanding the greatest vigilance, the little Spirit is sometimes lost, and then the body pines and dies if the Piai doctor is not fortunate enough to recover it. [Da, 249.]

For my own part, I am very much inclined to believe that this little Baby Spirit is identical with the Familiar Spirit (Sect. 93A).

284.* In view of the facts mentioned throughout this chapter it is as well to note that, on the Orinoco, when an infant (male or female) was born with any defect or monstrosity it was put to death (G, II, 60). Similar procedure was in vogue in Cayenne (PBa, 227), while Schomburgk states that "the shocking practice of destroying deformed children is not so general among the savages of Guayana as has been supposed" (ScF, 219). On the Amazon there was the curious custom of killing all the first-born children among the Ximánas and Cauxanas, tribes met with between the Içá and Japura Rivers (ARW, 355). Among the Zaparos of the Napo River (upper Amazon), when a mother having a very young child dies, the child is sometimes buried alive (Sect. 76) with her (AS, 175). On the Orinoco, among the Salivas, twins were considered a sign of dishonor.

They call the mother nicknames; some say that she is of the rodent family, which bear little rats four at a time, etc. Directly a Saliva savage gives birth to a baby and feels that still another remains, she will bury the first rather than put up with the jokes and chaffing of her neighbors, or merit the frown with which her husband regards it. The husband's view is that only one of those twins can possibly be his; the presence of the other is a sure sign of his wife's disloyalty. One of the Indian captains gives his wife a whipping in public for having dared to bring forth twins; and warns the other women as to the serious beating he will give them if they do the same. [G, I, 189.]

The same thing takes place on the River Cuduiary, among the Kobéwas, at the present day, the second-born of the twins being killed, but if of different sexes, the girl is sacrificed (KG, II, 146).

284A.* There are certainly traces of a belief in sexual relationships having no necessary connection with the production of children. Even at the present day women can cohabit with Water Spirits without disastrous consequences resulting (Sect. 186). On the other hand women can get babies if they want them, by eating certain binas, plant or animal (Sects. 237, 238); in a case of this kind the p. 326 child is already in existence, its body being attached to, and by some mysterious means passing into, the body of the mother. As to the origin of such babies, all I can gather is that they arrive in the water of in the bush, and hence may make their appearance in our mundane world either as a gift from the Water Spirits (Sect. 186), or at the instigation of the Spirits of the Forest (Sects. 117, 302), with or without the agency of the piai. The following is a Warrau story bearing on this subject:

*THE LITTLE BUSH CHILD (W)

A long time ago it was customary for a woman, when she yearned for a child, to wander about in the forest until she found one. It so happened that a certain woman, Yaburawáko, in going to her field found a little child on the road—a pretty boy he was—and she brought him home. She minded him, and he had sense enough to call her "Mama." By and by, however, the child got mischievous, and made her vexed. She said, "You have really nothing to do with me; so why should you annoy me?" The husband remonstrated with her, expressing himself to her somewhat as follows: "You must not be angry with the child, but must mind him carefully." She continued, however, to be cross with the boy, and finally ill-treated him. "I am not going to be bothered with you any more," she exclaimed. "You have nothing to do with me. You are not mine. You don't belong to me." With this, the child disappeared, whereupon the husband said: "Well, he's gone now, but he will come back again, and this time enter your body, and you will have trouble enough to get rid of him." Sure enough, after a time the child did enter her womb, and, oh! the trouble and the pains she suffered before she was delivered of him. Women ever since have borne children in this manner just because Yaburawáko was so unkind to the little bush child.

284B.* Arawaks believe that birth-marks and moles (namarakan) are due to the failure of the mother, during pregnancy, to get what she wanted. She may have said, "Oh! how I should like to have just a bit of marudi!" thoughtlessly placing her hand on her face, breast, body, or thigh; her baby, will be born with a corresponding mark on the particular part touched. The "Mongolian spot" is regarded by the women as due to the position of the afterbirth being near the surface in the corresponding part of the mother's body. The Moruca River Arawaks call this spot tu-tebe, but as it begins to fade it is known as anakwarro.

Next

Footnotes

p. 308

1 For the various charms connected with sexual matters, love and affection, see Sects. 237-238.

p. 311

1 Compare the licking of the stick by the Kanaima devotee to obtain purification (Sect. 329).

p. 317

1 The pattern of the weft of these crab-quakes is known to the Arawaks as the kassaroa, or "four-eye fish," from the manner in which the starting strads are arranged, like so many "eyes." The idea intended to be conveyed here is that as the man in question did not really know how to make these baskets, he was anxious to get a full view of the fish, so as to serve him for a model which he could copy.

p. 218

1 Whenever a visitor comes to a house, he is offered something to eat or drink; to express his satisfaction at having had enough, he informs his hostess accordingly in this terse manner.

Sacred-Texts Native American South American Index Previous Next

p. 327
CHAPTER XVII
THE MEDICINE-MAN

from patients (316); dieting of patient's relatives and family (317); medical fees (318); Quack doctors (319).

285.* There is abundant evidence that the medicine-men practised what they preached, and had every confidence in the powers with which they had been intrusted. "They practise those incantations over their own sick children, and cause them to be practised over themselves when sick" (BrA, 117). "They act the farce on themselves when they are disordered: a practice which has not a little contributed to overthrow all doubts of the sincerity of their pretensions" (Ba, 314). "The piai himself believes in it: one will put himself in the hands of another when sick" (Go, 13). Schomburgk was "convinced that the piai believes in the efficacy of his witchcraft as firmly as his protéges" (ScR, II, 146). The real causes of the existing prejudice against the medicine-men are not far to seek, and have often been clearly expressed. "As doctors, angurs, rain-makers, spell-binders, leaders of secret societies, and depositaries of the tribal traditions and wisdom, their influence was generally powerful. Of course it was adverse to the Europeans, especially the missionaries, and also of course it was generally directed to their own interest or that of their class; but this is equally true of priestly power wherever it gains the ascendency, and the injurious effect of the Indian shamans on their nations was not greater than has been in many instances that of the Christian priesthood on European communities" p. 328(Bri, 55). On the other hand, there is not a single recorded instance of the Guianese Indian priesthood ever having submitted those of their people holding religious views different from their own to either torture or the block. The Creole term for the priest-doctor is piai-man, a hybrid that seems to have been first recorded by Waterton in the form of pee-ay-man, who is an enchanter; he finds out things lost (W, 223). In its simple form, the word of course came into use much earlier, and is seemingly derived from the Carib piache, which Gumilla employs, and is still met with among the Pomeroon group of these Indians as piésan. Brett (Br, 363) derives it from the Carib word puiai, which denotes their profession. The Akawais call it piatsan. Dance seems to derive the name from that of the tribal hero, Pia (Sect. 41). Crévaux in Cayenne speaks of piay, de Goeje in Surinam of piai, and Bates, throughout the extent of the Amazons visited by him, of pajé. The Warrau word for the priest-doctor is wishidatu (wisidaā, according to Brett), similarly applied to the kickshaws. In some of the Orinoco nations, they call these men Mojàn: in others Piache: in others Alabuqŭi, etc. (G, II, 25) The Piapocos Indians of the lower Guaviar River speak of them a Kamarikeri (Cr, 526); the Caribs of the lower Caroni River as Marirri (AVH, III, 89), and the Island Caribs as Bové (RoP, 473). The Arawak designation is of equal interest and also of extended range: it is Semi-tchichi or Semi-cihi, the same term applied generally to the kickshaws and various apparatus employed in the pursuit of the craft (Sect. 93).

286.* Both alive and dead, the medicine-men had the respect and fear of the community. They were the teachers, preachers, counsellors, and guides, of the Indians; "regarded as the arbiters of life and death, everything was permitted, and nothing refused them; the people would suffer anything at their hands without being able to obtain redress, and with never a thought of complaining" (PBa, 210). They thus lived "in clover," (G, II, 24), better than all the rest of the people (St, I, 399). And yet in a sense they were restricted: they must not partake of the flesh of the larger animals, but limit themselves to those only which are indigenous to their country (ScR, I, 173); they had religiously to abstain from certain fish and game (PBa, 211); no animal food was publicly tasted by these priests, while they abstained, even more strictly than the laity from the flesh of oxen, sheep, and all other animals that had been transported from Europe (Sect. 247) and were "unnatural" to their country (St, I, 399). They were said to renew their piai power from time to time by drinking tobacco juice, but in doses not so strong as at the time of installation (PBa, 211). As stated above, even dead the medicine-men were still respected.

They also keep the dead bones of these sorcerers with as much veneration as if they were the Reliques of Saints. When they have put their bones together, they hang them in the Air in the same cotton beds those Wizards use to live in when alive. [Da, 98.]

Bates gives a curious example of such veneration and sanctity, met with at a spot on the Jaburu channel, Marajo Island, at the mouth of the Amazon, "which is the object of a strange superstitious observance on the part of the canoe-men. It is said to be haunted by a Pajé, or Indian wizard, whom it is necessary to propitiate, by depositing some article on the spot, if the voyager wishes to secure a safe return from the sertaô, as the interior of the country is called. The trees were all hung with rags, shirts, straw hats, bunches of fruits, and so forth. Although the superstition doubtless originated with the aborigines, yet I observed, in both my voyages, that it was only the Portuguese and uneducated Brazilians who deposited anything. The pure Indians gave nothing; but they were all civilized Tapuyos" (HWB, 115). Koch-Grünberg gives a similar example on the River Caiary-Uaupes (Upper Rio Negro), where the practice is undoubtedly observed by the Indians (KG, I, 237), while Coudreau (II, 404) has observed it on the Rio Branco. (Compare the protective charm against the Curupira, etc., in Sect. 109.).

287.* It sometimes happened that the captain and the piai were one and the same person, as in Cayenne (PBa, 208). But on the other hand, however great his abilities, the medicine-man did not obtain any distinctive position, as head of the farnily, through his proficiency (Go, 14). Bancroft (310) says that in almost every family, there is a person consecrated to the craft. There was apparently nothing characteristic about the piai in the way of ornament or decoration. I can find no confirmation of Bernau's statement that the novitiate's "right ear is pierced, and he is required to wear a ring all his lifetime" (Be, 31).

288.* The insignia and "stock-in-trade" of the medicine-man, in his highest stage of development, comprise a particular kind of bench, a rattle, a doll or manikin, certain crystals, and other kickshaws, generally something out of the common, all except the first mentioned being packed away when not in use, in a basket, or pegall, which is usually of a shape different from that employed by the lay fraternity. The peculiarity of the basket among Arawaks and Warraus lies in both top and bottom being concave. St. Clair (I, 330) reports that on the Corentyn, among Arawaks, he came across the "magical shell" (rattle) supported by three pieces of stick, the ends of which were stuck into the ground, in the middle of the floor; it is not clear, however, whether in this situation the implement was being used or not. At any rate, all the insignia were taboo to the common folk and were kept out of harm's way in a special shed, the piai's consulting-room, p. 330so to speak. Were they to be profaned, they would lose their intrinsic virtues, while the delinquents would suffer misfortunes of various descriptions. The bench (the ha-la of the Arawaks), plate 5, differed from the ordinary article of furniture usually met with in Indian houses, in being larger, often painted, and carved in fanciful designs of various animals, but little is known concerning the why and wherefore of the selection of the particular beast; thus, I have seen the turtle, alligator, tiger, and macaw more or less faithfully represented on such Warrau and Arawak divining-stools.

FIG. 4. Piai's rattle (Arawak), Pomeroon.

289.* The rattle, maráka (an Arawak word), the shakshak of the Creoles, differs somewhat in shape, size, and ornamentation throughout the various tribes. It consists essentiany of a large cleaned-out "calabash," containing stones and other objects, through which a closely fitting tapering stick is run from end to end by means of two apertures cut for the purpose (fig. 4). This gourd shell (Crescentia cujete Linn.), which may or may not be painted in various colors, is provided with certain small circular holes as well as with a few long narrow slits, both kinds of openings being too small to allow of the contents (either quartz-crystals or a species of agate) dropping out. Seeds may be employed with or without the stones—small pea-like seeds variegated with black and yellow spots which, it is commonly believed, will occasion the teeth to fall out if they are chewed (Ba, 311), or hard red ones (StC, I, 320). But whether seeds or stones, they usually have some out-of-the-way origin; the former, for instance, may have been extracted from the piai teacher's stomach (PBa, 208); the latter may be the gift of the Water Spirits (Sect. 185). According to a Kaliña, the power of the maráka lies in the stone contained therein (Go, 14). The thicker, projecting part of the stick constitutes the handle, to prevent its slipping; it may be wrapped with cotton thread. The exposed thinner end is ornamented with feathers, as those of the parrot, inserted in a cotton band, which is then wound spirally on it. An Arawak medicine-man assured me that the feathers must not only be those of a special kind of parrot (Psittacus œstivus), but that they must be plucked from the p. 331 bird while alive. A string of beetles' wings may be superadded. Gumilla (I, 155) states his belief that the Aruacas [Arawaks], the cleverest of the Indians, were the inventors of the maráka, which even in his day, some two centuries ago, had "also been introduced into other nations." From the fact that, according to Indian tradition (Sect. 185), the original rattle was a gift from the Spirits, Dance (290) accounts for the great veneration in which it is held even by Christian converts who have ceased to use it. Brett (Br, 364) confirms this, saying that there are Indians who fear to touch it or even to approach the place where it is kept. I have had personal experience that the same holds true today in the Pomeroon. So again, on account of the agates being put to use in the construction of the apparatus, Bancroft (21) records how these white and red stones remain untouched where they are found in abundance above the cataracts of the Demerara. In speaking of the Warrau rattle, Schomburgk says: "If the sick man dies, the piai buries his rattle also, since it has lost its power now, and with the sick person its healing properties die" (ScR, I, 172). I can not, however, find this statement anywhere confirmed.

290.* Gumilla (I, 155) says that the medico makes the Indians believe that the maráka speaks with the Spirit (demonio), and that by its means he knows whether the sick person will live or not. This statement does not exactly agree with the evidence handed down to us by other reliable authors, nor does it quite agree with what I have been taught and have seen put into practice. The object of the rattle is to invoke the Spirits only; it is rather the business of the manikin, or doll, to give the prognosis, to lend assistance, etc. Mention is made of such an object in Timehri (June, 1892, p. 183): "Some few months ago, a gold expert and prospector while traveling along the Barima River, came upon the burial-place of an Indian Peaiman or Medicine-man. The house under wliich the burial had been made was hung round with five of the typical peaiman's rattle or shak-shak, and over the grave itself was placed the box of the dead man, containing the various objects which had been the instruments, or credentials, of his calling. The contents of this box . . . were a carved wooden doll or baby." The doll, or manikin (fig. 5), which I saw used for the purpose on the Moruca River, was a little black one about 2½ inches long, balanced "gingerly" on its feet, which bore traces of having been touched with some gummy substance: if during the course of the special incantation it remained in the erect position, the patient would recover, but if it fell over, this would be a sure sign of his approaching death. In parts of Cayenne the doll is replaced by the Anaan-tanha, or Devil-figure (Sect. 311), which is unmercifully thrashed with a view to compelling the Evil Spirit to p. 332 leave the invalid. The identity of this mainland doll, or manikin, with the idol, or cemi, of the Antilleans has already been indicated (Sect. 93).

291.* The crystals are employed for charming, bewitching, or cursing others, though the references in the literature to their application in this manner are exceedingly scarce. Indeed, I can call to mind only the following from Crévaux (554): "I notice on the neck of one of them [Guahibos of the Orinoco] a bit of crystal set in the cavity of an alligator's tooth. The whole has the name of guanare. . . . It is with this guanare that the Guahibos throw spells (jettent des sortilèges) on their hated neighbors, the Piaroas. . . . Every mineral that presents in its lines and shape a certain regularity is to

FIG. 5. The piai's manikin, or doll
(Arawak), Moruca River. (Note
the chest-ornament; see fig. 6.)
them the work of a devil or a sorcerer." Cursing and similar procedure are not, however, the sole prerogative of the medicine-man, at least not in the Pomeroon District of the present day; the procedure is known as hó-a to both Warraus and Arawaks, and is practised, I am told, by very old people. As a remedy for over-fatigue, Schomburgk describes "Macusis and Wapisianas cutting each other's legs with a piece of rock crystal, an instrument to which they ascribed particular virtue, refusing instead of it my offer of a lancet" (ScF, 235).

292.* With respect to remaining kickshaws, Pinckard (I, p. 505) says: "And having faith in spells, they make little decorated instruments, of tender rushes about a foot long, which their physicians or priests called Pyeis employ together with other magical implements, as wands to drive out these demons of Ill." These instruments I have been unable to identify thus far. Finally, on the authority of the old medicine-man who taught me the greater part of what I know concerning the practice of the art, a "charm" of some description was worn on the chest suspended by a cord hung round the neck (Sect. 93). The one that my late teacher (Bariki) employed is flat and oval, made of some resinous material, and ornamented on one side with the incised figure of a female frog (fig. 6). It had been given Bariki by his grandfather when the latter taught him his profession, and when the old man died, he left it to me. In the extract from Timehri (1892, p. 184) above quoted, where is to be found a list of the kickshaws appertaining to the piai-man's stock-in-trade, is mentioned: "a neatly carved representation, in reddish quartz, of a dog sitting on its haunches p. 333and holding its front well up. In this figure the base of the fore legs is occupied by two clearly-bored holes, into which, evidently, it had been the custom to fit strings by which to pull the little object along on the ground, just as toys are usually drawn along by small children." It seems to me far more reasonable, under the circumstances, to suppose that this object was the doctor's chest-ornament just referred to. There is absolutely no evidence of any Guiana Indian toy being used in this manner, and it is ridiculous to believe that the vast amount of labor necessarily involved in carving

FIG. 6. The piai's chest-ornament (Arawak), Moruca River.
quartz and boring holes through it, would be expended on a child's play-thing.

293.* The office of the medicine-man appears to have been hereditary and to have passed to the eldest son (Ba, 316). If he has no son the piai picks a friend as his successor (ScR, I, 172), although the same authority (Schomburgk) elsewhere states that, under these circumstances, he chooses the craftiest among the boys (ScR, I, 423-4). It is likely that the secrets and mysteries of the profession may also have been imparted to outsiders for a consideration. I happen to have known one of the fraternity who taught another his profession for the sum down of eleven dollars together with the gift of his daughter. Im Thurn (334) says: "If there was no son to succeed the father, the latter chose and trained some boy from the tribe—one with an epileptic tendency being preferred. . . . It has been said that epileptic subjects are by preference chosen as piaimen, and are trained to throw themselves at will into convulsions." Perhaps this idea had its origin in the fact that through the use of a narcotic powder, the piais can throw themselves into a condition of wild ecstasy (ScR, I, 423-4): several such powders were known to some of the Guiana Indians, as the Yupa (G, I, 181), etc. On the other hand I can find no references in the literature to the choice of epileptic subjects; furthermore, the unlikelihood is turned into impossibility, when it is borne in mind that the victim of such a convulsion would be unconscious during its progress.

294.* Occasionally the piai may be a woman. Thus, I knew an old Warrau dame who used to practise her profession in the neighborhood of Santa Rosa Mission, Moruca River, under almost the very nose of the unsuspecting Father. On the authority of Joseph Stoll, Arawak, catechist at St. Bede's Mission, Barama River, young women, certainly among his own tribe, used to be trained in the same manner as the boys for the profession of piai: his own grandmother (on the father's side), and his father's cousin were both trained piai-women. On the other hand, I can find no references whatever to woman "doctors" throughout the early literature of the subject.

295.* The medicine-man usually possesses a little outhouse (Pomeroon and Moruca Rivers), plate 6, in which he keeps his various insignia: the Warraus call it hebu-hanoku (Spirit-house). This building is of course taboo, as indicated by a bundle of kokerite leaves hung over the entrance. As a matter of fact, I have never seen the doctor's "consulting-room" in the Pomeroom District built of any leaves other than kokerite. At Savonette, Berbice, the "consulting-room," so to speak, must have been a somewhat more complicated structure, for the use of medicine-men in common. "Near to the cabins that were inhabited, we observed a detached building inclosed on all sides, forming a single room, into which light and air were only admitted at the doorway. Upon inquiry we learned that this was devoted to the use of the sick—not as a hospital, but as a temple of incantation, for the purpose of expelling disease" (Pnk, I, 505). On the Amazons, Father Acuña (98) also leads us to believe that there was in each settlement one special building for the use of all these doctors: "There is a certain house devoted to the use of these sorcerers, in which they perform their superstitious exercises, and converse with the Devil."

296.* The original piai forms the subject-matter of legends with which Arawaks, Warraus, and Caribs are all more or less conversant; members of all these tribes assure me that tobacco was brought here from the islands, but I will let a Warrau give two of the versions:

*THE HUMMINGBIRD WITH TOBACCO FOR THE FIRST PIAI (W)

A man had been living with a woman for a long, long time: she was very good at making hammocks, but could not bear a child. So he took unto himself a second partner: by her he had a baby and was now happy. The infant, Kurusiwari, grew apace, and while the step-mother would be weaving her hammock, it would often come and hang on the suspending cord and slacken it. The old woman stood all this little annoyance for some time, but one day when the child was even more mischievous than usual, she said, "Go away, and play over there." It obeyed, went to a distance, but soon toddled back and once more interfered with the string. The woman now pushed the youngster aside, and in so doing it fell and cried. No one took notice of the incident and no one saw it toddle out of the house. All this time its father and mother were lying together in their hammock, and it was late in the p. 335day when its presence was missed by them. The child was nowhere to be found, so they went over to a neighbor's and there they saw their little one playing with some other children. They explained their errand to the house-people, how they had come to seek their little one, and so, one thing leading on to another, they entered into an animated conversation, and forgot all about their real business, with the result that when they did finish talking, not only was their own child, Kurusiwari, but also one of the house-children, Matura-wari, nowhere to be seen. So the four parents started in search of the two little ones, and went to a neighbor's house, where they saw them playing with a third child, Káwai-wari. But the same thing happened at this house as at the previous one—the parents all got into conversation, and forgot their real business until finally they found all three children missing. It was a case now of six parents searching for three infants; but at the end of the first day the third couple abandoned the search, and at the end of the second day the second couple did likewise. In the meantime the three children had wandered on and on, making friends with the marabuntas [wasps], which in those days talked but did not sting. It was these children that told the black ones to sting people, and the red ones to give them fever in addition. And it was when the children arrived at the seashore that the first pair of parents met them. However, by this time they were children no more, but big boys. When the parents expressed their pleasure at having found them at last and of course expected them to return home, the leader of the three— Kurusiwari, the boy who had been lost from the first house—said: "I can not go back. When my stepmother pushed me, I fell down and cried, while you would not even look at me. I will not go back." But when both father and mother implored him with tears to return, he relented, and promised them that if they built a proper hebu-hanoku [lit. Spirit-house], and "called" him with tobacco, they should see him. He and the two other boys crossed the seas, and the parents returned home. No sooner had the latter arrived there than the father started building the Spirit-house, and when completed he burnt pappaia leaves, and cotton leaves, and coffee leaves, but all were of no use—there was no "strength" in any of them, and this strength could be supplied only by tobacco. But in those days we had none of this plant here: it grew far away out in an island over the sea. I do not know whether this island was Trinidad, or not, but we Warraus call it Nibo-yuni [lit. Man-without] because it was peopled entirely by women [cf. Sect. 333], according to what the old people tell us. Well, the sorrowing father sent a gaulding bird [Pilerodius] over to fetch some of the tobacco seed: but as it never returned, he despatched various kinds of sea-birds one after another, and they all met with the same fate. They were killed by the watch-woman as soon as they alighted on the tobacco-field.

Giving up all hope of ever seeing any of his messengers again, he went to consult a brother, who brought him a crane. This bird went to roost down near the seashore so as to have a good start on the following morning. While resting there, his little friend the hummingbird came along and asked him what he was doing. "Getting ready for the morning," he replied; "I have to fly over to Nibo-yuni and fetch tobacco seed." The hummingbird suggested his going instead, but the other regarded the proposal as absurd, and reminded him that his boat was too small, and that it would sink. Nothing daunted, however, the little chap rose before daylight, as is his custom, and saying, "I'm off!" took to flight. At daybreak the crane spread his wings, and, sailing majestically along, got about halfway across, when he met the hummingbird struggling in the water. The latter had made a gallant attempt, but could not of course make headway against the wind. The crane picked him up and placed him on the back of his own thighs, which stuck out behind. Now, this position was all very well for the little hummingbird so long as no accident occurred, but when the crane commenced to relieve himself, the hummingbird's face got dirtied, and he thus found himself forced to take to the wing again, with the result that, reaching Nibo-yuni first, he waited for his big friend, who arrived shortly. He now told the p. 336crane to remain where he was, while he would visit the tobacco field; he was small, could fly swiftly, and no one would see him stealing the tobacco seed.

While carrying out his design, the watch-woman tried to shoot him, but he was too smart for her, and darting quickly from flower to flower, soon collected as much seed as he required, and returned to the crane. "Friend," said he, "let us get home now," and suiting the action to the word the little creature started ahead, and now with the wind behind him, reached home first without mishap. Here he delivered the seed to the crane's master, and the latter handed it to his brother, telling him to plant it. When planted it grew very quickly, and when the leaves were fully grown, the brother showed him how to cure the tobacco. The brother also sent him to search for bark to suit the leaf [i. e. to make the cigarette], and he brought the winnamóru, which was just what was required. He next sent him for the hebu-mataro [rattle] and he brought gourds of all sizes, but at last he returned with a calabash that he had picked from off the east side of the tree; this was the very thing. The bereaved father thereupon started "singing" with the rattle, and his son and the other two lads came in answer; they were three Spirits now, and all three addressing him as father, asked for tobacco, with which he supplied them. It is these same three Tobacco Spirits, Kurusiwari, Matura-wari, and Káwai-wari, who always answer when called by the piai's rattle, and as a matter of fact it was the poor bereaved father who came to be the first piai, all through his great grief at losing his child, and longing so much to see him once more.1

296A.* KOMATARI, THE FIRST MEDICINE-MAN (W)

Komatari wanted some tobacco, but as there was none about, he searched for it. He had heard of its growing on an island out at sea, so he went down to the shore, where he came across a house with a man inside. Approaching him, Komatari said: "I am poor, and want tobacco. I hear you have it growing on an island. Could you get me some plants?" While thus engaged in conversation, the hummingbird came along, and said, "Hullo! What are you two talking about?" "Tobacco: we want tobacco," they replied. "Oh, is that all?" the little bird said; "why, I'll go and fetch some for you. I shall be making a start before the morning, and you can expect me back just as the sun begins to turn that way" [pointing in a direction which would indicate about an hour after midday]. The hummingbird kept his word, and returned as promised, but when the house-master saw what he had brought back, he said, "Why, that is no tobacco leaf: it is only the tobacco flower," and, turning to Komatari, he said, "I will go myself." The house-master started next morning for the same island, telling Komatari to expect him back as soon as the hummingbird, that is, shortly after midday. But as a matter of fact, he never returned until the following morning. The cause of the delay was that so many people were watching the tobacco that he had to wait for nightfall before he could steal the leaves. However, giving Komatari some of the seed, he told him to go down to the waterside, where he would find his corial, and if he looked inside he would see two or three tobacco leaves, which he might take. Komatari did as directed, but instead of two or three leaves he found the whole corial full of them. He helped himself to as many as would fill a quake and went home. Before taking his departure, however, the house-master said: "I have a name, but will not mention it: when you know all about Piai [i. e. 'Medicine'] you will be able to find it out for yourself." At last Komatari reached home, and naturally all his friends came to pay him a visit, to get some of the tobacco; but he was shrewd, kept the tobacco under the roof [i. e. hanging up to dry in the ordinary manner] in charge of the marabuntas [wasps], left home very early of a morning, and only returned late, so as not to be at home when anybody called. But at last a visitor p. 337came and made a very long stay purposely. They thus met, Komatari gave him three leaves, and sent him away. Next day, another man paid him a visit, but Komatari had already left, and only marabuntas were there—many marabuntas, all of different kinds. The visitor went home, and, taking some fish with him, returned to Komatari's place and asked the marabuntas to let him have some tobacco, at the same time showing them his fish and saying, "Look! this is the payment." And so, while the marabuntas all swarmed down upon the fish, the man climbed up, got what tobacco he wanted, and cleared out. When Komatari got home, he also got up under the roof where the tobacco was stored, but found much of it missing, so he placed what was left elsewhere, and drove away all the marabuntas except one particular kind, a black variety, the oro [= yiseri of the Arawaks], which he made his watchmen. Starting now on his field, he cut it day after day, and after burning it, at last planted his tobacco. When he saw that it was beginning to thrive, he built a piai-house, and going round his field, looked out for a calabash tree; he found one full of gourds. He took one, but on turning round, he saw a Hebu, who, after asking whether it belonged to him and getting "Yes" for an answer, said: "All right. So long as the calabash is yours, you may have the whole tree. I have a name, but will not tell it you. I want to see whether you learn the piai business well. If you do, you will be able to find it out for yourself." On reaching home with the calabash, Komatari started cleaning it out. When cleaned, another Hebu came along and asked him what he intended doing with it, but Komatari would not tell him. You see this particular Hebu was the one who comes to kill people and so was afraid of the power of the maraka [rattle], which is made from this very calabash. After scooping out and cleaning the calabash, Komatari went into the bush and, traveling along, came upon a creek with swiftly-flowing water: it was here that he cut the timber from out of which he next shaped the handle for the rattle and cut the sticks to make his special fire with.1 Returning home once more, he fastened the handle in the gourd, but was not satisfied with the result: the rattle did not look as it should. So he hung it up on the beam of his piai-house, and went once more into the bush, where he again met the killing Hebu, who repeated his question as to what Komatari intended doing with the rattle, but, as before, the latter would not tell him. Passing along, and hearing a noise as of many people talking, Komatari proceeded in the direction whence the sound came, and found a number of Hebus fastening various parrot feathers into cotton-twine. How pretty this ornament would look tied on his calabash left hanging up at home, was Komatari's first thought when he saw what they were doing. On asking, the ornament was given him. The Hebu who gave it to him said: "I have a name, but I will not tell it to you. You can find it out for yourself, if you should ever become a good piai-man." Komatari next asked him for another kind of cotton-plait, with feathers different from those on the one mentioned, to wear as a hat,2 but the Hebu said he had none, though he would get it at the next house. So Komatari went to the next house, saw the Hebu house-master, asked for the cotton-plait for the hat, and in the same manner as before, this Hebu also said to him: "I have a name, but I will not tell it to you. You must find it out for yourself when you are a medicine-man." Komatari went home now, and arranged the feathered cotton on top of the calabash, when who should put in an appearance again but the killing Hebu. When he again asked Komatari what he intended doing with the calabash, the latter refused to tell him, as before. But Komatari was not satisfied even now, because when he shook the gourd it did not rattle. As yet it had no stones in it. So Komatari went into the bush again, and followed creek after creek, and at last came to a big river. There he met another Hebu, who got the proper stones that were wanted. When he had given them to Komatari, he said, like the others: "I have a name, but p. 338I will not tell it to you. You must find it out for yourself when you are a medicine-man." Komatari again made his way home and put the stones into the calabash. Just as he was finishing the work the killing Hebu again appeared, asking him as before, what he intended doing with the calabash. The answer was, "This is to kill you with, and to prevent you killing other people," and as Komatari shook the calabash, which was now a finished maraka rattle, the Hebu began to tremble and stagger and almost fell, but he managed to pick himself up and get away just in the nick of time. He ran to his Aijamo [head-man, chief] and said: "There is a man who has an object with which he nearly killed me and I must get my payment [i. e. my revenge]. I am going back to kill him." "All right!" said the Aijamo, "I will go with you." So they went together, and brought sickness to a friend and neighbor of Komatari's; for they were afraid of attacking Komatari himself. However, his sick friend sent for him. Komatari went, and played the maraka on him, and took out his sickness. So the killing Hebu made another man ill, but Komatari took the disease out of him also. The Hebu next afflicted a third victim, and again Komatari was victorious. But when he attacked a fourth one, Komatari was out hunting. When he returned, the poor fellow was in a bad enough condition: so strong did the sickness come, that Komatari could not cure him—he had "stood too long." The killing Hebu then explained to Komatari that it would always be thus: some patients he (Komatari) could save, and other patients he could not. Of course Komatari had been able to find out the names of all the Hebus that had lent him assistance in the manufacture of his maraka, and it is to these different Hebus whom the present-day medicine-men are said to "sing" and call on when they cure the sick. For instance the name of the Hebu that procured the tobacco seeds for Komatari was Wau-uno [= Arawak Anura], "the white crane."

297.* The apprenticeship of the medicine-man in the olden days was very far from being the proverbial bed of roses. Among other tests, he had for many months to practise self-denial, and submit under a stinted diet to the prohibition of what were to him accustomed luxuries. He had to satisfy his teacher in his knowledge of the instincts and habits of animals, in the properties of plants, and the seasons for flowering and bearing, for the piai man was often consulted as to when and where game was to be found, and he was more than often correct in his surmises. He also had to know of the grouping of the stars into constellations, and the legends connected not only with them, but with his own tribe. He had likewise to be conversant with the media for the invocation of the Spirits, as chants and recitatives, and also to be able to imitate animal and human voices. He had to submit to a chance of death by drinking a decoction of tobacco in repeated and increasing doses, and to have his eyes washed with the infusion of hiari leaves (Sect. 169); he slowly recovered, with a confused mind, believing that in his trance, the effect of narcotics and a distempered mind, he was admitted into the company of the Spirits, that he conversed with them, and was by themselves consecrated to the office of piai priest-doctor (Da, 285). Bancroft (316) says that the novitiate "is dosed with the juice of tobacco till it no longer operates as an emetic." Sometimes, as among the Oyambis on the Oyapock River in French Guiana, other things were mixed with the tobacco, for example, a plant called p. 339quinquiva, as well as certain of the drippings from an exposed dead body (Cr, 158). For the same colony Fathers Grillet and Bechamel (GB, 48) record that the medicine-men proffer neither physic nor divination "till they have made divers experiments, one of which is so dangerous that it often makes them burst. They stamp the green leaves of tobacco and squeeze out the juice of it, of which they drink the quantity of a large glassful, etc.; so that none but those who are of a very robust constitution, who try this practice upon themselves, escape with their lives." Brett (Br, 362) also testifies to the severity of the ordeal, for after the novice has been reduced to the deathlike state of sickness to which the fasting coupled with the drinking of tobacco-water has brought him—

His death is loudly proclaimed, and his countrymen called to witness his state. Recovery is slow, and about the tenth day he comes forth from the sacred hut in a most emaciated condition. For ten months after the new sorcerer must abstain from the flesh of birds and beasts, and only the smallest kinds of fish are allowed him. Even cassava bread is to be eaten sparingly, and intoxicating drinks avoided during that period. Meats and food not indigenous to the country are especially tabooed. . . . McClintock states that the "above rules are common to the Caribs as well as the Waraus, but that the former are allowed during their period of abstinence to take a little meat—the flesh of the Acouri. . . . The Akawoios differ in some respects from the other tribes, inasmuch as not less than four, and frequently more, become M. D.'s at the same time."

Gumilla (II, 25), on the Orinoco speaks of the apprenticeship of the Piache in the following terms:

In the forest of Casiabo, there was a medicine-man named Tulujay, so celebrated that Indians flocked to him from all quarters, but they did not all come to learn, nor subject themselves to his teaching, because this cost them very dear. For besides adequate payment, he imposes such a rigorous 40-day fast on them, that few dare to undertake it: of those that do, the majority leave the Master weakened with the fasting: he who completes it is made to swallow, without chewing, three pills, manufactured of different herbs, of the size of a cherry-stone. These pills are said to be an antidote for every kind of poison, and so render the disciple secure from all his rivals and enemies. The credulity of the Indians is so simple that none of them will meddle with any individuals so treated (curados).

Most of the above accounts are concerned mainly with the drinking of the tobacco, an ordeal to which the old-time missionaries and travelers seem chiefly to have devoted their attention. Though it would have been of course more or less practised beforehand, the tobacco ordeal in its entirety was reserved for the grand day when the public installation took place. During his course of training, in addition to his other instruction, the apprentice was taught to suffer the pangs of hunger and thirst, and to experience the martyrdom of pain without complaint or murmur. To teach him the latter, he was either bitten with ants or cut on various portions of the body. Among the Islanders "his body is scraped with acouri teeth" (BBR, 236). The ants were fixed into the interstices of plaited diamond-shaped p. 340mats or girdles and these were held or tied on the neck, breast, stomach, or legs (WJ, 91). In some cases, during their period of probationership, the prospective medicine-men must not come into contact with Europeans, as this would destroy forever their influence over the spirit world (ScR, I, 423). West of the Orinoco, "they submitted to a seclusion of two years in caverns, situated in the deepest recesses of the forests. During this period they ate no animal food; they saw no person, not even their parents. The old Piaches or doctors went and instructed them during the night" (FD, 50). Magic stones are alleged to be placed in the novitiate's head (KG, II, 154). Crévaux, among the Roucouyennes of the Yary River, French Guiana, speaks of the "many years of probationership" (Cr, 117). "Takes some years: the novice returns more like a skeleton than a man among his people" (ScR, I, 423-4). The only account of a public installation of the would-be piai, actually described as such, comes from Cayenne:

At the public installation to which the neighboring piais are invited, the aspirant has to swallow at one draught a calabash containing about two pints of tobacco-juice. Most often he falls into a swoon, whereupon he is carried to his hammock: if he does not vomit directly after taking this powerful emetic, he dies, or at least he is seized with horrible convulsions and breaks out into cold sweats, etc., which all tend to bring him to the grave. But if he survives, he is acclaimed Piai. [PBa, 211.]

In the Island practices, the novitiate is made to drink tobacco-juice until he faints, and, when they say that his Spirit has gone to the Chemeen, they rub his body with gum, and cover it with feathers to allow him to fly to the Chemeen (BBR, 235). Among the Pomeroon District Arawaks and Warraus it would seem that the aspirant wore a special cotton headdress at the time of installation. Pitou mentions the piai installation as taking place on the night before the marriages (LAP, II, 266).

298.* Mention has already been made (Sect. 297) of the knowledge, of which the medicine-man had to give proof, concerning the instincts, habits, etc., of animals. Seated on his professional stool, with maraka in hand, he might be observed studying where game is to be found by the morrow's daybreak. He lights up his fire, and igniting some tobacco, he invites by invocation the spirits of the game he desires (Sect. 116). In his enthusiasm he speaks to them and answers for them in their supposed peculiar tones, modulated as in ventriloquy; for he believes that, being possessed, they answer through him, he being at the same time the humble earnest inquirer and the sufficient aswerer of his own inquiries (Da, 287). This belief in the interdependence of the priesthood and animal life is well illustrated in an example (Ti, II, 1883, p. 348) given by McClintock: "I had an Accawoi huntsman who was a sorcerer (peaiman) and considered that he had certain birds and animals so completely under his control that p. 341no inducement would have tempted him to kill any of them; among them were powis . . . maroodies, and the Arua tiger. . . . The latter he always told he could put his hand upon any time he went out."

Another apt illustration is furnished by Schomburgk: "In our peregrinations in the savannahs we frequently met with the nests, of wild bees. They belonged to a species which the Makusi Indians called wampang; the Wapisiana camuiba. The hives or nests are generally fixed to branches of trees, and are from 2 to 3 feet in length. . . . It stings severely; and in order to secure nests, the Indians kindle fires under them, when the insects abandon their fabrics en masse. I have, however, seen an Indian who was the conjurer or piaiman of his tribe, merely approach the nest, and knocking with his fingers against it, drive out all the bees without a single one injuring him. I noticed him drawing his fingers under the pits of his arms before he knocked against the hive" (ScT, 40). The piai system made a secret art of hunting; from the priest-doctor the hunters learned to hunt for the particular game they required, and received at his hands charms—maklar and bina—to insure their success (Da, 251). Among the Indians of the Uaupes River, the piais are believed to have power to destroy dogs or game and to make the fish leave a river (ARW, 347). The medicine-man furthermore could transform himself into an animal (Sect. 154); if his wife becomes pregnant she may bear him a tiger, an animal into which he himself may be transformed at death (KG, II, 154).

299.* Certainly among many of the tribes the "doctors" were believed to be endowed with such power over their own spirits as to render themselves invisible. At a Makusi village on the Karakarang River, a branch of the Cotinga, Barrington Brown (Bro, 119) was told that many of their people had gone to Roraima to see an Indian sorcerer there who had the power of making himself invisible at will. At Mora village, on the upper Rupununi, the same traveler (Bro, 139) explains how the piai's absence for the night was unavoidable, owing to his having to go up among the mountains to roam about for the night, while his good spirit remained in one of the houses to cure a sick man.

Not only could the medicine-man invoke Spirits generally, as well as those of particular birds and beasts, but he could also play tricks with his own and other Indians' Spirits. Thus, im Thurn (339): "He is able to call to him and question the spirit of any sleeping Indian of his own tribe, so that if an Indian wishes to know what an absent friend is doing, he has only to employ the piai-man to summon and question the spirit of the far-away Indian. Or the piai-man may send his own spirit, his body remaining present, to get the required information."

300.* The piai's reputation as an interpreter of dreams was second to none: he was both dreamer and seer (Sect. 298), but this is only what p. 342 might have been expected, considering the powers he possessed over other people's Spirits (Sect. 299), and dreams are really but people's Spirits (Sect. 86).

*SAVED BY A DREAM (W)1

A certain man had two wives, but unfortunately they did not agree, the elder being jealous of the younger. At last there was so much contention, that the husband was obliged to send the younger one away, and she took her baby with her. He had no bad mind toward her, but he could not stand the continual quarreling. When taking her departure, he gave her a sharp knife with which to protect herself on the road. The poor woman wandered on until nightfall, when she came upon a fine ite [Mauritia] palm; cutting a forked stick, she planted it against the tree, and climbed on it. Taking the youngest as-yet-unopened leaf, she spread it out and made a sort of temporary basket of it, into which she coiled herself together with her baby, and there she tried to sleep. Now, upon this particular palm, the fruit was plentiful—some seven or eight bunches—and around the stalk of each bunch she had taken the precaution of cutting a little ring, so that with the slightest touch, any bunch would fall to the ground. Somehow or other, the unhappy mother could not sleep, and late in the night she heard the growling of the tigers who had been attracted by her scent. One of these brutes climbed the palm and jumped on one of the fruits, but no sooner had he touched it than it gave way and he fell with a crash into the very midst of his fellows below who, believing him to be the woman they were in search of, promptly tore him to pieces. Another tiger made a similar attempt, climbed the tree, jumped on the fruit, and ended in the same disastrous manner. And so with a third, fourth, fifth, and sixth tiger—all were similarly destroyed. By this time the dawn had broken, and the carcasses were left rotting at the bottom of the tree. What a sight for the terrified mother nestling up above! She could see all the tigers lying still and quiet, but was afraid to come down lest they might still be alive. She therefore waited a little and when, after the rising of the sun, she recognized a wasp settling on each of their protruded tongues, she knew that the tigers must all be dead and could now do her no harm. As soon as she got down she continued her journey, and wandering along all day, she arrived about nightfall at a big manicole tree, which she climbed, with the baby fastened on her back. Tigers were likewise very prevalent here, and scenting her presence, they started digging around the roots with the result that by and by, the tree fell with a crash, but fortunately into an immense spider-web, where its living freight became stuck. Now the woman's father was a celebrated piai, and while the first night's occurrences were taking place, he was dreaming all about her and the tigers. Next morning he started to search and came upon her while resting in the spider-web. It was owing to the baby making water that he had cause to look up and discover his daughter. By daylight he had shot the tigers that were prowling around, and then helped down the woman and his grandchild. Both daughter and father cried; the former had been so strongly punished, the latter was so glad to have her home again.

301.* Among other duties that the medicine-men might be called on to perform was to fix the time most propitious for the people to attack their enemies (HWB, 244). They were supposed to be gifted with the power of prophecy: they foretold the issue of battles (BBR, 234), whether there would be war or peace; similarly, they could prophesy as to the crops—whether these would prove scanty or abundant (FD, 51).

302.* The Pomeroon Arawaks appear to credit the piai with being able to influence the Yawahus in bringing the as-yet-unborn babes to the mothers (Sect. 284A). In some districts, as on the Berbice, the piais were said to be professional poisoners, but it must be remembered that the charge of poisoning was one made against an Arawaks as a habit (Da, 16). Among the wurali-poison-making tribes, for example, the Makusis, Bernau's statement (Be, 36) that the "conjurers alone are conversant with the art of compounding it" does not seem to be borne out by the facts. At one place on the Orinoco, as already stated (Sect. 297), the sorcerers were alleged to be rendered poison-proof (G, II, 25). Waterton's statement (W, 223) that "he is an enchanter: he finds out things lost" is only a further example of the piai's supposed versatility. I remember on one occasion unconsciously giving great offence to my old doctor-friend, Bariki, now alas! gone to his long, last rest, by asking him if he knew so-and-so: he gave me a withering glance, and after a few moments, silence, said, "I know all things." Taking the hint, I subsequently invariably sought information from him by putting my question in the form of "Tell me this, or that," with the result that, pleased with my appreciation of his mental superiority, he was always ready to impart all he knew, and perhaps more.

303.* The following legend is another good example showing that there was very little that the medicine-man could not do in the natural or supernatural sphere: it is apparently a variant of the stories given in Sects. 137 and 142.

*THE MEDICINE-MAN AND THE CARRION CROWS (A)

Makanauro was a very clever medicine-man; we call such an one a semi-chichi. Setting his traps out in the bush, he was always certain of catching something, be it bird or beast. But for some little time he found to his annoyance on going to his trap, that some one had forestalled him and had stolen the meat inside. It puzzled him how this could have been done, because there were no footprints or broken bushes about, to show the advent or departure of any stranger. So he one day climbed a tree in close proximity to one of his traps, and watched from his elevated position. He saw some game caught in the trap and by and by a black Carrion-crow [Cathartes burrovianus] came swooping down, and try to cut it up with a knife, so as to remove it the easier. The Crow's knife, however, was too blunt, so he flew away and fetched the Vulture [Sarcorhamphus papa], who brought a sharper knife with him, and cut up all the meat nicely. And then a lot more Carrion-crows came down, and between them they cleared every particle of the meat away, leaving the trap as empty as before. Makanauro watched all this quietly from under cover of the tree branches, and on several other occasions subsequently saw them play him the same trick, the Vulture being invariably the ringleader. He made up his mind to catch this bird, and disguising himself with cotton, which he stuck all over him, including eyes, nose, and head, he laid himself down on the ground quite close to one of his traps that had game in it, and remained perfectly still. As usual, the Crow came down first, but his knife was still too blunt to cut up either Makanauro or the meat inside the p. 344trap, and so he went, as before, to fetch the Vulture. And when the Vulture came quite close, Makanauro seized him, and held him fast; this made all the other common Crows frightened and they flew away. The bird himself thought that his captor must be a piai, because no one else could have secured him so simply. Now, I have made a mistake talking about "himself," "his," and "him," because it was a hen-bird, as Makanauro speedily found out. Indeed, she was a very fine woman, and he married her there and then. And thus they lived comfortably together for many years, all the Carrion-crows having returned to live in the vicinity as friends and companions. One day, the wife sent him for some water, and gave him a quake to bring it in. He took it down to the riverside, but couldn't "catch" any, of course, because as fast as he poured it in, it flowed out through the meshwork. He tried several times, until at last some muneri ants, noticing his extraordinary movements, asked him what he was trying to do, and when they learnt how anxious he was to oblige his wife, they offered to patch up all the interstices of the basket with "ant-bed," When they had finished the job, the quake retained the water, and Makanauro brought it home full up to the brim. On seeing this, his wife said to herself, "Yes, indeed. My husband must be a real semi-chichi to be able to bring water in a quake for me." And yet she had her doubts about the matter, so she thought she would try him a second time. She accordingly sent him to cut a field for her, but on returning each morning he found that all the timber and bushes that he had cut down the day before were growing again and thriving in their original positions. As a matter of fact, the Carrion-crows had flown to the field each night, at the bidding of the Vulture, and set up again the trees and bushes that had been felled. But poor Makanauro did not know this. All he could do was to ask the kushi ants to eat up the wood, branches and leaves, as fast as he could cut them down; these, knowing the facts of the case, made up their minds to help him, and did so. The Carrion-crows could not fight against the kushi ants, and so Makanauro managed to complete the clearing of his field. And though his wife was inclined at heart still more to believe that her husband was a medicine-man, considering the circumstances under which, as she believed, he had cut his field, she was yet in doubt about it, and determined to try him a third time. She therefore sent him to make a chair-bench for her mother-in-law; he had to carve the head at each extremity into the exact likeness of the old woman. This task she thought was practically impossible;1 and Makanauro thought so, too, because as yet he had never set eyes on his mother-in-law. However, he tried to find out, but every time he even looked in the direction of the old woman, she immediately covered her face with her hand, or turned it aside, or downward. How to make her turn her face upward so as to get a good look at it, was what puzzled him. At last he hit upon an idea. Without her knowing it, he climbed into the roof, and throwing down a centipede so as to fall "flop" into her lap, made her extend her arms and look up for a second, just as he wanted. Then starting to work, he cut up the log, trimmed it into the necessary shape, and finally carved excellent likenesses on the two heads. When completed, his wife took the bench to her mother-in-law, who laughed when she saw her two portraits; certain it is, that both women wondered greatly how Makanauro had managed to obtain a sufficiently good view to enable him to make so exact a likeness. The wife now became quite proud of her husband, and fond of him, too, because he always carried out her wishes. If she asked him to bring her some fish, he would fetch her some wrapped up in a small parcel: and when as usual she would pout her lips and hint that it was not a large quantity, he would tell her to open it, and then the fish would come tumbling out, one after the other, in immense quantities, filling the whole house [cf. Sect. 28] And he would laugh, because being a piai, he could do extraordinary things. A fine boy had long blessed their union, and the p. 345 mother was beginning to feel homesick: anxious to show off her husband and child to her own people, she told him that they must all leave his place, and go to her father's, up and beyond the clouds. And there they remained with her relations, the Carrion-crows, for many a long day. She, however, was always telling her folk what a clever man her husband was, and that whatever she asked him to do, do it he did. So these Crows asked him to perform a number of seemingly impossible feats, and not one did he fail in executing. But this only made all the Crows jealous of him, and they determined to put him to death. Makanauro, being a medicine-man, however, knew that they proposed doing so, and said, "All right. Let me get back to my place, and fetch my friends, and we will fight it out." So, taking his wife and son, he returned to his old home, and collecting all the birds in the neighborhood, he told them to prepare for the onslaught with the Carrion-crows. Now, when these arrived and saw the hosts of other birds ready to receive them, they determined to secure by stratagem a victory which they recognized they could not obtain by force. Their idea was to burn up the whole world, together with Makanauro and his friends in it. For this purpose, the Crows started fires here, there, and everywhere around, but Makanauro saw his friend the black kurri-kurri [Harpiprion cayennensis] flying high, and told all his other friends to curse her, he joining in their imprecations. This made the rain fall, and so the fires were extinguished.1 Now that his wife became angered with him for having frustrated her own people, the Crows, in their design of burning up the world in general, Makanauro left her and went his way. She then sent her son to waylay and kill him, but whether he effected this wicked design I do not know.2

304.* In some cases the piais were recognized to a greater or less extent as the guardians of the tribal traditions. Thus in the "Archivos de Indias; Patronato. Rodrigo de Navarrete: An account of the Provinces and Nations of the Aruacas" [Arawaks], written some time during the last quarter of the sixteenth century, a work quoted by Rodway, in Timehri (for 1895, p. 10), there is the following interesting reference:

These Indians have a meeting-place or school where they assemble, as in a manner for preaching. There are among them old and wise men whom they call Cemetu [compare the usual form Cemi, Semi, etc., Sect. 93]; these assemble in the houses designed for their meetings and these these old men recount the traditions and exploits of their ancestors and great men: and also narrate what those ancestors heard from their forefathers; so that in this manner they remember the most ancient events of their country and people. And, in like manner they recount or preach about events relating to the heavens, the sun, moon, and stars.

305.* The medicine-men not only gave names to the children, as with the Arawaks (Sect. 264), but under certain circumstances would change them. Thus, among this same nation, if a piai is called on to treat a sick child, and is successful in effecting a cure, he may give his little patient a new name, and thus enable it to make a fresh start in life.

306.* The chief business, however, of these doctors is centered in counteracting the evil designs of certain Spirits, Kanaima or other, p. 346who cause disease of such a nature as to baffle the ordinary home treatment and household remedies of the average Indian, though I know of one instance in which a woman in labor was brought by her husband to seek remedial measures from one of this fraternity. The home treatment just referred to might consist in the use of ordinary herbs, vapor baths, and in other measures known to the average Indian. But occasionally, as with the Dakinis, to obtain such an herbal remedy, the piai's assistance may have to be invoked (Sect. 168B). As a matter of fact, all disease which does not respond readily to treatment is ascribed to various Spirits acting directly or indirectly, by means of thorns, pointed bones, etc., maliciously inserted into the body of the patient. When once invoked, the medicine-man is able to learn the cause of the trouble, and how to combat its effects.

307.* Disease or death is not a "natural" phenomenon, so to speak, but is usually due to one of two agencies. It may be the work of some Spirit, perpetrated either judicially or of mere malice, as some affirm, or through the importunity of a votary. An evil Spirit, one who causes an evil, might send an animal to bite or sting a person, or cause a tree to fall upon him, his ax to cut him, water to drown him, or some other calamity (Da, 289). Now, except through the agency of the piai, the influence of this Spirit causing the evil can not usually be counteracted. Berman alone for the Mainland makes the statement, which I must regard as confirmed by the practice of a similar custom on the Islands, that "when sickness assails them, they [laymen, Sect. 89] present a propitiation to the Evil Spirit, consisting of a piece of the flesh of any quadruped. If recovery follows, they suppose the Evil Spirit to have regarded and accepted the offering," but if no recovery, the conjurer is called in, etc. (Be, 51-54). The piais are undoubtedly believed to have the power of influencing the Spirits not only in removing the causes of the disease which they (the Spirits) have inflicted, but also in sending sickness elsewhere (Sect. 319) In the spring of 1907 the Ojanas (Cayenne) suffered from an epidemic of bronchitis, or "galloping consumption," from which many died; this was ascribed to the piais (Go, 14). It is possible, however, that the medicine-men, independently of Spirits, and certain old people, can inflict sickness on folks at a distance; for instance, the Apaläi Indians of the upper Parou, Cayenne, when they can not subdue their sicknesses revenge themselves by sending an evil charm to a woman (Sect. 319) of the neighboring tribe (Cr, 299). It is not at an uncommon for one tribe to put the blame of some real or imagined ill on the shoulders of another. For example, the Wapisianas consider the Makusis the most dangerous poisoners and Kanaimas—every illness is ascribed by them to the wickedness of the Makusis (ScR, II, 387). Similarly, on the Tiquie River (Rio Negro) the Makus p. 347 are blamed for everything (KG, I, 270). There is a certain skin disease, believed to be a vitiligo, which the Piapocos of the lower Guaviar (Orinoco River) call sero: it is always contracted by drinking the yocuto (couac mixed with water) of an enemy affected with this trouble, who has mixed in the brew a few drops of his blood (Cr, 527). Death and other evils may be due also to some human enemy more or less disguised, modified, or influenced by a peculiarly terrible Spirit known as Kanaima, against whose machinations the power of the piai avails nothing. To this belief in Kanaima I propose devoting a separate chapter (Sect. 320).

308.* In the Pomeroon District, the present-day Arawak procedure of the piai, for the treatment of disease, is as follows: Suppose the patient visits the "doctor," the latter will sling the sufferer's hammock in the special out-house already mentioned. In those cases in which the person is too ill to bear removal, the doctor will visit him, and there erect a closely plaited conical-shaped cage of manicole leaves, with a low door only just large enough to crawl in and out by. Nothing further can be done now until the sun sets, but as soon after sundown as convenient the medicine-man will start a new fire, by twirling one stick upon another. The fire once kindled, he rolls tobacco to make the usual Indian cigarette, and proceeds to examine the patient. He then asks what the pain is like, and where it is—as, in stomach, head, chest,—and talks to his kickshaws, especially the manikin, or doll, to learn whether the patient is going to be cured. The method of employment of this doll has already been given (Sect. 290). Seated on his special chair, the doctor next lights and smokes his cigarette, and finally rubs his hands with haiawa wax. This done, he proceeds to massage the painful spot, and smokes on it through his hands placed funnel-wise. This part of the treatment may be viewed by the public, there being nothing secret or mysterious about it, and may of itself effect a cure, in which case, as the Creoles would say, "Story done." With the next procedure, however, provided the illness prove stubborn, the females are all sent away from the place, men have to keep at a respectful distance, quiet must reign, and all lights have to be extinguished. The alleged reason for putting out the fires is that the various Spirits whom he is now about to invoke may not be afraid to come. (If the treatment is being carried out at the patient's residence, the medicine-man will crawl into the cage when the invocation takes place.) In the meantime, the medicine-man cleans and polishes his maraka, which he pieces together, and ties the feathers carefully on, smoking on it all the while: he sings and shakes his rattle. Leaving his bench, he touches the painful spot or spots with the maraka, circling it in the air, smoking and singing all the while, altering his voice from bass to alto and vice-versa according to the voice of the Spirit which is presumed p. 348to be conversing with him. Apparently two voices are often heard. When it is remembered that the Spirit may be anything from a tiger to a powis, even another piai, the various modulations of voice and speech which he has been trained to reproduce can be better imagined than described. He does not know beforehand which one has wrought the mischief; hence he has to invite and interrogate each one. This manner of invocation, according to the fee given, may continue until two or three in the morning—there is a limit to the doctor's powers and endurance—when all the kickshaws will be put away in the specially constructed pegall. Our medicine-man, seated on his divining stool, will proceed to smoke and dream, and in his dream he will discover at whose instigation the sickness has been sent, and whether the illness itself is due to a dead person's Spirit (as a Bush Spirit), to a living one's Spirit (a Kanaima), or to the Oriyu, or Water Spirit. At the same time he also learns the mode of cure. Next morning he will retail this information either to the patient or to his friends, as soon as he is paid something over and above the fee (as cloth, beads, money), which he has already received. The cure may be such as can then and there be carried out, as the extraction of the evil by suction, or the disease may prove of so serious a nature that it is a matter for the Spirits alone to deal with. At any rate the medicine-man then gives careful directions as to how the patient and his relatives are to be fed—with bird, fish, or otherwise, as the case may be—but there is always the stipulation that whatever is ordered (a) must never be added to, or taken away from, for example, no salt, peppers, seasoning, etc., and no "trimming off;" (b) must be cooked with the doctor's own fire, or with another specially made for the purpose by means of two pieces of stick, care being taken in both cases that it is not touched by a stranger; (c) must not be allowed to boil over the edge of the pot. If during the course of the day the patient should not improve, the doctor will repeat the treatment the same night—smoking, singing, and dreaming— but on this occasion, addressing the Spirit which has caused the mischief, he implores it if possible to restore the health which it has impaired. He may even repeat all this the third night if the patient's grave condition warrants so doing, and he is paid an adequate fee. At any rate, when he finally completes the treatment the doctor invariably tells the patient, unless the latter is actually moribund, that he will recover, but that both he and his family must be very careful as to the foods prescribed, for should the sufferer unfortunately die it is always because one or other of the stipulations regarding diet has not been properly obeyed. When, during the course of the treatment, rain happens to fall, the proceedings are immediately postponed to the following evening.

309.* Among the Pomeroon Caribs I have been present on several occasions on the Manawarin River at the procedure adopted by a piai to affect a cure. It has always been at night, with the doctor seated in a small temporary cone-shaped structure roughly made of manicole leaves, and the rattle brought into requisition. Operations invariably commenced with the invocation of four particular Spirits by "singing" to them, each with a different song, by tobacco smoke, and by shaking the maraka. As a matter of fact the medico is said to call up only the first Spirit; the latter, however, invokes the second, and so on. The names of these four Spirits, in the order in which they are summoned, are Mawari (Sect. 122), Makai-abáni, Iakai-a, and Aturaróni. All except the second live somewhere in the bush, but they come when summoned by the rattle. Makai-abáni, on the other hand, remains in the maraka, coming out only when shaken, and then he envelops himself in the tobacco-smoke. All these four are good Spirits and friends of the piai; they are male and female, like people, and come from the bodies of old-time medicine-men; they tell the celebrant whether the disease from which the sick man is suffering has been sent by another Spirit or by another piai at the instigation of some enemy. The three evil Spirits who send sickness, ill-luck, and other calamities to mankind, belong to Cloud-land, and to Water; Kwamaraka lives in the sky below the clouds and is something like a "gaulding" bird (Pilerodius); Tokoroi-mo has his home below the clouds, and resembles the "doraquarra" bird (Odontophorus); while Oko-yumo is the "water-mamma" (Sect. 177). These three have a master, called No-séno, who lives somewhere above the clouds; he is a man, a very bad one, is always for killing somebody, and is his own master. But to return. If the disease has been sent by one or other of these bad Spirits, the piai gets Mawari to take it far, far away, away to the Orinoco River; but if by another piai, the present celebrant will send it back to him, and woe betide the latter if he is not smart enough to avoid it, for unless he takes very great care he is sure to die from it. Should, however, the sickness prove stubborn, "Tiger" is finally called on; directly his voice is heard the disease comes out to be speedily devoured by him. But if Tiger should prove unsuccessful, nothing now can possibly save the patient.

310.* The Galibi piai of French Guiana practised similar methods, according to the accounts left us by Barrere: After placing the maraka below the patient's hammock, the piai starts sucking at those parts of the sick person's body where the pains are greatest, afterward passing both hands over the patient; he then strikes his hands together and blows on each palm (Sect. 85) so as to drive away the "Devil" [spirit] that has attached itself there (Sect. 74); the piai will sometimes pinch up pieces of his own skin, and thus extracting corpulency (embonpoint) and good health, will apply these in handsful to the patient while making the passes over him. p. 350 These Indians also employed the little hut specially constructed in the karbet, in which, after all the lights have been extinguished, the medicine-men "sings" and shakes the rattle. He often comes out of his little cabin and would pretend that it is the Devil [Spirit] that has got out. He will then run right round the karbet and tug at the hammocks in which the Indians are lying. He sometimes says that he is going up into the skies, but will soon return, and he will then mimic the distant voice, etc. (PBa, 213-215).

311.* In remote parts [of French Guiana] and toward the sources of the River Oyapok, the Indians [? Oyampis] practise another method, with the figure of a Devil [Spirit] made of a very soft and resonant wood. This statue, which is three or four feet high, looks frightful with its long tail (queue) and big claws with which they provide it. They call it Anaan-tanha (literally, Devil-figure). After having blown on the sick person, the piais carry the statue out of the hut. There they talk to it, and thrash it unmercifully with sticks, so as to force the Devil [Spirit], in spite of itself, to leave the sick person. These exorcisms are carried out at night, after the fires have been extinguished (PBa, 216). Very interesting in this connection is the maize-straw manikin, found by Crévaux, among the Apaläi Indians of Cayenne (Cr, 301), which may have been employed for a similar purpose; it represented a warrior ready to let fly an arrow, fixed on two sticks arranged crosswise like a gallows.

312.* It is not always necessary, however, to use the maraka, it being quite possible to invoke the Spirits with a couple of bundles of leaves. Thus, Schomburgk gives the following account of a Makusi performance at Nappi, on the Canuku Mountains:

The old man came into my hut with two bundles of leaves in his hands, and with them he drove out the other occupants. He then put out all the fires, sat near my hammock on the ground, which he whipped with the bundles, and started howling, only now and again broken by short pauses. After this had gone on for a quarter of an hour, I recognized a second voice by the side of my hammock, and question and answer went on between the two. The conversations with the evil spirits are unintelligible even to the Indians: it was next morning that the piai took care to make them aware of its contents. After the double conversation was finished, the magician placed himself at the head-end of my hammock, howled close to my forehead and, after lighting a cigar, blew strong clouds of tobacco-smoke into my face which almost suffocated me, and pressed the bundle of leaves (which I recognized by the smell as tobacco leaves) onto my forehead. This went on for quite half an hour and got me into a good sweat: at last his voice failed him, and he left the hut. He did not use the maraka. [ScR II, 145-146.]

313.* Westward of the Guianas a particular kind of wood apparently played the same rôle as the rattle or the leaf-bundle, if we accept the statement of Depons in his description of the Captain Generalship of Caracas:

The practice of these professors of the healing art consisted in licking and sucking the affected part, in order, according to them, to eliminate the peccant humour. p. 351When the fever or pain increased, suction of the joints, as well as friction over all the body with the hand, was employed. During the performance of this operation, some unintelligible words were pronounced, with a loud voice, commanding the evil spirits to depart out of the patient's body. If the malady did not readily yield, the Piache or physician had recourse to a particular kind of wood, known to himself alone, with which he rubbed the breast, throat, and mouth of the patient; a practice which seldom failed to produce sickness and vomiting. In the meantime the Piache on his side uttered dreadful exclamations, howled, shook, and made a thousand contortions with his body. If the sick person recovered, everything contained in the house was given to the Piache; if he died, the fault was imputed to Destiny, never to the physician. [FD, 50.]

314.* Among the Island Carib Indians the piai procedure was of the simplest kind:

They say that the Chemeen [Sect. 90 et seq.] always comes on scenting the odor of this incense [tobacco] and, being interrogated, he answers with a clear voice, but sounding as from a distance. The sorcerer then approaches the sick person repeatedly, feels, presses, and manipulates the suffering part, always blowing on it, and extracts something from it, or rather appears to extract, some thorns, or small pieces of cassava, wood, or bones, making the sick person believe that this was the sole cause of the pain. Very often he sucks the painful part, and immediately goes out of the house to vomit what he calls the poison. [BBR, 234.]

The following are further particulars of the Island practices as reported by Rochefort and Poincy:

The Boye . . . consults his Familiar Spirit who tells him that it is the [Familiar] Spirit of such an one who has done it [who has brought the mischief] [RoP, 473]. . . . Then the devil [Familiar Spirit] whom he has invoked . . . violently shakes the ridge of the roof, or with some other noise immediately appears, and replies distinctly to all the questions asked by the Boye [ibid., 563]. . . . If the devil assures him that the illness is not mortal, both the Boye and the accompanying phantom approach the sick person to assure him that he will soon be cured: and to encourage him in this hope they touch gently the most painiul parts of his body, and having pressed them a little pretend to extract from them thorns, broken bones, splinters of wood and stones which these wretched doctors say were the cause of the ill. They also moisten with their breath the weak spot and having repeatedly sucked it, they persuade the patient that by this means they have extracted the poison which was in his body and kept it in languor. They finally rub the sick person's body with junipa fruit. . . . But if the Boye has learnt from the communication which he has had with his demon that the sickness is a fatal one, he contents himself with consoling the sick person by the statement that this God, or rather to say, his Familiar Devil, having pity on him, wishes to take him into his company, so as to be freed from all his infirmities. [RoP, 564.]

315.* With regard to the nature of the Spirits specially invoked, Barrington Brown (Bro, 140) when describing the performances of a Makusi piai at Mora Village, upper Rupununi, remarks that—

In some instances the good spirit for the time being brought with it the evil one that was supposed to have had some hand in producing the man's malady; and then the wife asked it how it could come and injure a being who had never harmed it, begging it to desist and leave her husband alone. The only answer she obtained to this appeal was a most diabolical, mocking laugh. The Makunaima, or great spirit, p. 352 was never called upon by the sorcerer to assist or cure the sick man, but only the subordinate inhabitants of spirit-land.1

316.* As to the extraordinary variety of visible objects inserted into the body of the victim by the invisible Spirit and similar agencies, and subsequently extracted by massage and suction, the following will give some idea: Fangs of the much-dreaded Lachesis mutus, "bushmaster" snake (McClintock, Ti., June, 1886, p. 94), grass-roots (G, II, 27), gravel-stone, fish-bone, bird's claw, snake's tooth, or piece of wire (Br, 364-5), a worm (HWB, 244), a miniature bow and arrow (Cr, 526). The last-mentioned is very interesting in view of the Arawak Indians' belief (Br, 361) that all pain is due to the Evil Spirit's arrow (Sect. 330). The medicos of the Otomac nation suck with such force as to extract blood from the patient, and when this is spat out on a cleared space, minute stony particles are to be seen in it (G, II, 27). Fathers Grillet and Bechamel apparently gave approval (GB, 48) to this method of cure: "Besides divers sorts of Plants, Gums, and Woods they use to cure diseases and wounds, they have a way of sucking their patients in that part of the body in which they feel their pain, and this method is most commonly very successful."

317.* The idea that not only the patient but also his relatives and others should abstain from certain diets was very widespread: "The Piache's first prescription is to impose a general fast on the patient and all his kinsfolk: the majority of the Piaches demand that no one belonging to the house should eat anything hot, anything cooked, or peppers" (G, I, 210). With the Caribs, Arawaks (Sect. 308), and Warraus, the whole family—father, mother, brothers, and sisters—is dieted on exactly the same lines as the invalid. "If a man [Carib Islander] gets wounded or ill, he will ask his brother, sister, or some relation to abstain from eating such or such a thing. This would make their pain worse even if they were fifty miles off" (BBR, 250). So also other observances may be incumbent on the whole family as well as on the patient (Sect. 180). Among the Roucouyennes of the upper Yary, Cayenne, besides the diet, the only license which the doctor allows the patient is to throw himself into the river when the fever is very high (Cr, 117). As a matter of fact, when death ensues in spite of the treatment, this was usually ascribed to disobedience as to food-restrictions, though other causes were occasionally held accountable. Thus, the implacable inveteracy of the Spirit causing the mischief may be too powerful for the doctor to contend against, or some rival sorcerer, whom the sufferer has unhappily made his p. 353enemy, and who is supposed to have employed the Yawahu in destroying him (Br, 364-5), will at times come in for a share of the blame.

318.* Crévaux (250) states that when consulted, the piai is offered a cigarette: if he accepts it, this means that he undertakes to visit the sick person. He will not receive, however, certain gifts (in this this case a comb, child's hammock, and sifter) offered him until the sick person is completely cured. "A young girl is sometimes given as payment for the professional services of the piaiman during sickness, which may account for the scale of his domestic establishment" (Br, 320). So great is his influence among the women that his wives are always the choicest (ScR, I, 423-4). With the Carib Islanders it was customary for the person cured to express his gratitude by a big feast, where the

Boye, who had helped in the cure, held first rank among the guests: furthermore, it was incumbent on the convalescent not to omit the Anakri (Sect. 89) for the devil [Familiar Spirit] who did not fail to find a place among the assembled company (RoP, 564).

319.* There is said to have been on the Islands a class of men and of women who, though in a large measure alleged to be playing the rôle of piai, can not quite correctly be classed as such; references to them may conveniently be given here. Besides the Boyes or Magicians, there are sorcerers (sorciers), at least the people believe so, who, according to what they say, send charms on them, of very dangerous and fatal kinds, and these sorcerers they kill when they can catch them; their presence often serves as a pretext for getting rid of one's enemies (RoP, 474).

They believe themselves never to get ill, but to be bewitched; and, simply for a headache or stomach-ache, they kill or cause to be killed those whom they suspect to have given it to them. It is generally a woman (Sect. 307), since they dare not openly attack a man. But before killing her, they ill-treat this unfortunate person most cruelly. Their parents and friends go and fetch her, and she is then made to search in the earth in different places, and ill-treated, until she finds what they believe her to have hidden; and very often, the woman, in order to deliver herself from her executioners, confesses what is not true, picking up some pieces of shell . . . or fish-bones. . . . When the women who are accused as witches pick up these different shells they say that it is the remains of what the bewitched had eaten, which the pretended witch had buried in the ground. Many incisions are then made on her body. She is hanged by the feet; a kind of very strong pepper (Sect. 255) called Piman is then rubbed in her eyes, and she is left for some days without food, until a drunken executioner arrives and puts an end to the unfortunate being by breaking her head with a club. [BBR, 232-234.]

With regard to the celebration of the anniversary of a Guahibo chieftain's death on the mainland, there is a record by Crévaux (548) of the medicine-man casting, or rather blowing, a spell over (souffle pour jeter un sortilège à) the individual who caused the death [compare Sect. 85]; the others, men and women, then following his example.

Next

Footnotes

p. 336

1 For further account of the relationship between hummingbirds and tobacco, see Sect. 350.

p. 337

1 The timber always employed for the two purposes has a milky sap, and is found in places such as described, that is in the forest, along the banks of swiftly flowing creeks.

2 That is, the headdress with the cotton "pompons" wom by the medicine-man when initiated.

p. 343

1 For another Warrau version of this story, see Sect. 136A.

p. 344

1 Before contact with European influences, it was strictly taboo for any Indian either to enter his mother-in-law's apartment, to remain in the same room, to talk with her, or even to look at her.

p. 345

1 The belief is still prevalent among the Pomeroon Arawaks that if one hears the black kurri-kurri "calling" in early morning, and thereupon curses the bird, rain is certain to fall during the day (Sect. 213).

2 Compare Makona-ura, a youth famous for his skill as a fisher, and credited with inventing the maswa, or fish basket-trap (Da, 259).

p. 352

1 This observation is quite correct because, from personal inquiry among the Mainland Caribs (Sect. 309) and from the records left to us of the Island Caribs (Sect. 90), the Spirits invoked were undoubtedly of the "Familiar" class (Sect. 314).—W. E. R.

CHAPTER XVIII
KANAIMA; THE INVISIBLE OR BROKEN ARROW

Expression of the Law of Retaliation: Kanaima may appear as a human being or Spirit (320), and perhaps can be satisfactorily explained (320A), or as an animal (321). Kanaima's handiwork, when fatal, can be recognized as such only by the piai (322). Discovery of the individual under whose influence Kanaima has acted (323); search for this individual by one of deceased's relatives, or by a hireling (324); avenger proceeds to get into touch with his victim (325); mutilates him with poison, club, or arrow (326), but only to such extent that death will not ensue until third day after (327-328), when he will complete the mutilation of the corpse, and so obtain his own purification (329).
The Invisible or Broken Arrow (330-331); the Misson of the Arrow (331A).

320.* An individual becomes exceedingly ill. All the ordinary everyday remedies have been resorted to, the piai has invoked his Familiar Spirit, yet the patient dies; or he may sometimes expire without warning. The very fact of the medicine-man's inability to effect a cure serves only to confirm the belief held in certain tribes—Akawaios, Makusis, Arekunas, for example—that the victim's condition is the work of some human agency more or less disguised, modified, or influenced by a peculiarly terrible Spirit known as Kanaima (Sect. 307). The word itself is said to be Akawaio; the Arawak term is Mahui, which thus comes to be applied by this people to all Akawaios in general. According to inquiry made of the Arawaks, who, like the Caribs and Warraus, do not appear to know very much about the subject, and that only at second-hand, Kanaima is said to be the name of a certain tree growing in the savannahs, of which the sap has remarkable properties. After rubbing himself with it a man will go mad and become changed into some animal, as a tiger or a snake, and do people harm. The sap can also be thrown over other folk with similar results. But the word mentioned has really a very extended meaning; it is the expression of the law of retaliation, which is sacredly observed among the Indians of Guiana (Da, 16), at least, certainly among the Makusis, Akawais, Wapisianas, and Arekunas. Though applied to the man who has devoted himself to perform a deed of blood, it seems more properly to belong to the murderous Spirit under the influence of which he acts, and which is supposed to possess him (Br, 373); it indicates also the person whose rights have been injured (ScR, I, 322-3) as well as the whole mode of procedure, including the means, poison, etc., employed. Thus, the audacity of the Akawais "in these predatory excursions is astonishing. If a party can muster eight or ten stand p. 355of fire-arms it will fight its way through all the mountain tribes, though at open war with them; and by the rapidity of their marches and nightly enterprises, which they call Kanaima, they conceal the weakness of their numbers, and carry terror before them" (HiC, 234). Schomburgk says it was impossible to learn clearly how Kanaima is regarded, because he appears not only as an evil invisible Being (dämonisches Wesen) and, in many cases, as a particular personality (individuelle persönlichkeit), but always as the avenger of a known or an unknown injury. Who and what Kanaima was, they could not tell us, but they reckoned that every casualty (Todesfall) was due to him. I had already observed the thirst for vengeance among the Warraus which often overcomes and tortures an Indian to the point of madness, as soon as he considers himself injured in his reputation or in his wife; a thirst which is but quenched with the death of the offender, or in the annihilation of his whole family (SCR, I, 322).

The same author gives an account of a certain waterfall on the upper Cotinga which his terrified Indians tried to get past as quickly and as quietly as possible. Kanaima, the hereditary enemy of the human race, was being followed by a powerful Spirit: the pursuer was close at hand, escape seemed impossible, the steep bank preventing further flight over level ground, but in this opening it was possible: he burrowed in here, and came out again on the opposite shore of the river bank about ten or twelve miles farther on, whence he emerged to continue afresh his torments upon mankind (ScR, II, 182).

320A.* And yet again it is quite possible that the term Kanaima may have an easily intelligible origin based on the bloody exploits of certain of the Rio Branco tribes, whose reputation, through the avenues of exchange and barter, could easily have reached the Indians of British Guiana. As a matter of fact, I can not recall at present a single instance of Kanaima culled from the literature dealing with Cayenne, Surinam, or the Orinoco region. At the head of the River Jauapiry and River Taruman-Assu (streams flowing into the Rio Negro to the eastward of the Rio Branco) are a series of wild tribes. These tribes are not wild in the sense of making war on civilized and quiet peoples (mansos), but are Kanaima tribes (tribus canaémés), as the Indians of the upper Rio Branco call them, that is, they are tribes of cut-throats by profession, educated from generation to generation in murder and theft, killing for the pleasure of killing, not even eating their victims but utilizing their tibias for flutes and their teeth for necklaces. Indians of a dozen tribes have assured me, says Coudreau, that there exists among the canaémés an association of piais who exert great influence. What makes the thing appear very probable is that it is known that these various Kanaima tribes are allied and more or less united (solidaires). [Cou, II, 235-6.]

321.* As already hinted, the Kanaima may just as often be in the form of an animal. "Many of the Indians believe that these 'Kanaima' animals are possessed by the spirits of men who have devoted themselves to deeds of blood and cannibalism. To enjoy the savage delight of killing and devouring human beings, such a person will assume the form, or his soul animate the body, of a jaguar [Sects. 146, 147, 148], approach the sleeping-places of men, or waylay the solitary Indian in his path" (Br, 373). One can tell, by the effects, the particular animal whose characteristics Kanaima have assumed. Does he give a blow that stretches his victim on the ground? Then he is a "tiger." Does he in wrestling find his arms encircling the neck of him devoted to destruction? Then he imbibes the spirit of the camudi, and like the constrictor, strangles (Da, 277). He may appear also in the form of a bird, and may even enter a person's body in the form of an insect, a worm, or even an inanimate object.

322.* When a person dies it is only the piai who knows whether the death is due to an evil Spirit, or to the "poison" [blood-revenge] of another Indian. If to the former, he is buried with the usual ceremonial, but if the verdict is that he was sacrificed for some offence the corpse is carefully examined, and should only a blue spot or something unusual be found on it, the piai will show that here the victim was wounded with the invisible poisoned arrow (ScR, II, 496).1

323.* Once the handiwork of Kanaima has been recognized, the piai's powers, as such, are not brought into further requisition, in the way of retaliation or revenge on the particular individual with whose connivance this terrible Spirit has wrought the mischief. It is not the Kanaima but his human agent who is sought for punishment. The retaliation and revenge are matters for the victim's relatives and friends to deal with, and various measures are adopted by them to discover the particular individual specially concerned. [Among the Arawaks] in order to ascertain this a pot is filled with certain leaves [and water] and placed over a fire: when it begins to boil over they consider that on whichever side the scum first falls, it points out the quarter from whence the murderer came (Be, 57). Among the Makusis, above the Waraputa Falls, Essequibo River, Schomburgk relates the following striking instance: "A Makusi boy had died of dropsy, and his relatives endeavored to discover the quarter to which the Kanaima, who was supposed to have slain him, belonged . . . the father, cutting from the corpse both the thumbs and little fingers, both the great and the little toes, and a piece of each heel, threw these pieces into a new pot which had been p. 357filled with water. A fire was kindled, and on this the pot was placed. When the water began to boil, according to the side on which one of the pieces was first thrown out from the pot by the bubbling of the water, in that direction would the Kanaima be" (ScR, I, 325). A consultation is thereupon held, the place is pointed out, and the individual whose death is to atone for that of the deceased (Be, 57). If any one—man, woman, or child—has incurred the hatred of the all-powerful piai, or should the latter be desirous of the wife of some Indian, this or the other would be the cause of the death (ScR, II, 496).

324.* A near relative is charged with the work of vengeance: he becomes a Kanaima, is supposed to be possessed by the destroying Spirit so-called, and has to live apart according to strict rule, and submit to many privations until the deed of blood be accomplished (Br, 357). If the individual can not be found, or rather if the favorable opportunity for committing the deed does not present itself, although it will be sought for years, any other member of his family will suffice. Sometimes the near relative will charge himself with the duty: a little Warrau boy of about 12 years of age avenges his father's and mother's death by smashing in the piai's skull with a club when the latter lies drunk in his hammock (ScR, I, 158). Formerly, the Indians at the Great Falls of the Demerara were employed by the Arawaks of the lower district to work their vengeance as Kanaima mercenaries (Da, 277). The Indians of Itéuni, Berbice River, sent a deputation to the Arekuna tribe with presents, to induce them to come and exterminate Mekro and his settlement. These Arekunas, chosen for the deed of blood on account of the remoteness of their habitation as likely to baffle all trace of the originators (Da, 16), came over from a great distance. Some Indians, who are adepts in the art of making subtle poisons, hire themselves out to rid their employers of any obnoxious individuals, and these are called Kanaimas (Bro, 141). These examples serve to show how the work of vengeance could be deputed to strangers and mercenaries.

325.* But whoever it may be that is charged with the duty of avenging the death, he suddenly disappears from the settlement: no one knows where he is. He wanders now as Kanaima through the forests, valleys, and heights, and does not return until he has slain his victim or shot him with the poisoned arrow. Half a year or more [even years] may thus be spent, during which time he avoids all contact with other Indians. From the moment he leaves the settlement, he is outlawed—he has cut all the ties which bind him to his family and his tribe—and it is the business of any Indians who may meet him in the bush, to kill him (ScR, I, 322-3). Nor is he allowed to speak with any he may meet in his way, says Bernau (57), but Hilhouse makes the statement for the Arawaks, that an Indian who is deputed to revenge a murder will follow his enemy p. 358for years, publicly avowing his purpose, which he will relinquish only with life (HiC, 231). He has to abstain from meat and live on what the forest supplies, a fact which will account for his usually emaciated appearance. As for ornament, he is credited with wearing a curiously wrought cap (Be, 57), but it is the bodily decoration which gives him his distinctive features. He paints bright red spots on his skin, to show that, changing into a jaguar at night, he can thus slay his victims. A set of jaguar's claws hung up in a sorcerer's hut have the same threatening signification (BrB, 154). In describing two such Kanaimas, Dance says that their emaciated bodies were painted in lines: they were tigers or [boa]-

constrictors (Da, 276). Schomburgk talks of the avenger being painted in a peculiar manner, and clothed with an animal skin (ScR, I, 324).

326.* The longed-for opportunity arrives at last; the Kanaima finds his victim alone, and slays him by poison, the arrow, or the club. Among the Akawaios especially, but also among the Makusis, Wapisianas, and Arekunas, a frightful poison known as wassi is brought into requisition. This is extracted from the bulb or tuber of a plant which the Indians refused to show him, says Schomburgk, in spite of entreaty and rich reward, on the score that if the Paranaghieris [Europeans] knew it, they would immediately discover its antidote. They cut the bulb into thin shavings, dry in the sun, and then crush to the finest powder, which has quite the appearance of arsenic. Should the alleged delinquent be caught asleep, some of this powder is strewn upon his lips or under his nose, so that it is inhaled. A sharp burning sensation in the bowels, a raging fever, and a tantalizing thirst, with no means of obtaining relief, are the symptoms of the poison, and convince the victim that his days, even his hours, are numbered. Within four weeks he becomes reduced to a skeleton and dies in fearful torment. (ScR, I, 323.) Thus, among the Makusis at Mora on the Rupununi River, was met an unfortunate woman whose attenuated body was a most shocking sight: she was a living skeleton, being nothing but skin and bones, with the exception of the face, which was not reduced in proportion with that of the rest of the body: they told me, says Brown, that this woman had come to them from the Ireng River district, where she had been poisoned by Kanaimas, and that this accounted for her wasted condition (Bro, 258). Another account I am able to quote, from the Mazaruni River, where a white powder is employed by inunction. It appeared that the murdered man had been induced to join a fishing party, and then had been set upon by a number of men, who had forced his limbs out of joint, rubbed his body over with a white powder made from a species of wild tannier, and then pulled them into their sockets again: he managed to reach home with great difficulty and take to his hammock, where he was seized with vomiting and died in a few hours (Bro, 55). p. 359 Further reference to this poison was obtained from the upper Pomeroon Caribs, who speak of it as massi, and tell me of its being put to use by the Akawaios as follows: Massi is a weed which is rubbed on a thin stick and the latter is pointed at the individual it is wished to injure. The person so pointed at must come to the one holding the stick, and as he walks along, he falls down in a sort of fainting fit: While thus unconscious, Kanaima covers him with trisel (Pentaclethra filamentosa) and thus makes him wake, but by this time Kanaima changes himself into an acouri or a deer. As the victim limps along, he startles either one of these animals, and by this sign or token recognizes that Kanaima has been giving him "medicine."1

327.* Now, whichever means—as, poison, arrow, club, visible or invisible—the Kanaima agent may employ to carry out his design, he especially refrains from causing the immediate death of his victim for the reason that at least a three days' respite or interregnum has to be observed before he can complete, on his victim's body, those particular rites (Sect. 329) without the due observance of which he can not obtain his own purification. If circumstances should prevent him thus being purified, he must become demented and die raving mad. Hence, after assuring himself that the actual death will not take place before three days shall have passed, he makes equally certain of the sufferer in the meantime holding his tongue in more senses than one, thus preventing him giving any definite clue to his assailant's identity or existence in the immediate neighborhood. To effect this, the Kanaima devotee accordingly slits his victim's tongue with the fangs of a most poisonous snake. Schomburgk tells us from his own experience (ScR, I, 324) how the Indians collect the fangs of such snakes. Of course accidents will often happen, and even after taking the precaution of shooting an arrow into his back, the victim may be killed on the spot: in such a case the Kanaima agent will bury the corpse at once superficially in the spot where the man fell, taking care to remember the place, that he may find it when he returns, after the third day, to complete the final ceremony. Even should the wound fail to prove immediately fatal, before the poor creature can reach home the tongue has become inflamed and swollen, so that he (or she) is unable to tell who did the deed. Dance speaks of another method of impairing speech, by twisting the tongue, and inserting poisoned pills into the mouth. These pills are composed of the parings of a macaw's bill, parings of cowhorn, dog's hair, scrapings from the bulb-root of the dhu turu, and another poison, the name of which was not ascertained (Da, 278). p. 360 Brett thus talks of an Akawai murdered on the banks of the Manawarin, a branch of the Moruca: "The deed was perpetrated by a 'Kanaima' devotee in the usual manner, and close to the Indian settlement: A loud shout was heard in the forest, and when the friends of the victim ran to the spot, they found him on the ground with his back and neck bruised, but not bleeding. He had been deprived of speech by the murderer according to the cruel system followed in those crimes" (Br, 269).

328.* If the sufferer is found by his friends and carried home, the perpetrator of the deed, the Kanaima, is obliged to hover near, to discover the place of burial (Br, 357-60), for reasons already stated (Sect. 327). But the victim's friends are equally shrewd in burying the corpse so secretly that its whereabouts shall not be known to him, hence every precaution is taken to insure this object. Should the site of burial be ultimately discovered by the Kanaima, however—and the friends of the victim will take no chances—they will either poison the corpse or stick "pimplers" (palm-spines) into it. Thus, a man having been killed by Quio, the corpse was laid out naked, with a basin of water under it, into which the pimplers of the parepi palm were placed. The body was then washed with the water, and a portion of the spines were broken, and forced into the body. When laid in the grave, the remaining spines were strewn over his body: this, they said, would kill the man who tasted of the juice of the dead body (Da, 278). Or again, so as to make certain of revenge on Kanaima, if the grave is molested by him, some of the deceased's friends will open the body, take out the liver, and put a red-hot ax-head in its place. If after that is done, the Kanaima should disturb the corpse, the intense heat which was in the ax-head, when placed there, will pass into the Kanaima devotee's body, consuming his vitals and causing him to perish miserably. An Akawai told Brett of another plan that is sometimes followed, namely, wurali poison is placed on the dead body (Br, 359-60).

329.* On the third night the Kanaima visits the grave and sticks a pointed staff into the body: upon drawing this out, if there is blood on it, he will lick it off, and all the dangerous consequences of his act are paralyzed for him, with the result that he returns contented to his settlement (ScR, II, 497). He has undergone purification, so to speak.1

He cannot be released from the power of the evil Spirit which possesses him until he has performed this act. If this, which is an offering to the Kanaima Spirit within him, be accomplished, he becomes like other men, and can return to his family, but if not, he wanders on till madness or some other dire consequences, through the agency of the disappointed Spirit, are believed to come upon him p. 361(Br, 359). The Arawak is firmly convinced that if the Kanaima, on the third day, cannot taste any of his victim's blood, he will become mad and die mad (ScR, II, 497); he can be freed only if he succeed in leaving behind his two distinctive death-marks—the swollen tongue and the damaged entrails. The original doctrine of Kanaima would almost seem to have constituted a special cult, the inner working of which it is now hard to unravel. Brett says that, among the Akawais, the whole system of Kanaima is taught by father to son in many families (Br, 358).

330.* It has been already stated (Sect. 322) that Kanaima's handiwork may be recognized in the blue spot due to the invisible poisoned arrow employed by him. On the Napo River (Amazon), the Indians will "attribute many of their ills to the puffing of invisible darts into their bodies by evil, designing persons—an idea no doubt suggested by the mysterious and silent operation of their own instruments of offence" (AS, 155). A similar belief is current in the Guianas. Caribs ascribe children's sicknesses (Sect. 110) and Arawaks otherwise unaccountable illness in general, and any sharp sudden agonizing pains in particular, to an invisible arrow. The latter tribe will often describe it as the Bush Spirit's arrow (Yawahu-shímara). Interesting in this connection is the fact that a miniature bow and arrow may be extracted by the piai from the patient's body by means of massage and suction (Sect. 316). There are further beliefs about certain mysterious arrows which it is worth noting. Where the arrow sank into the water, there lurked the danger in the shape of submerged rocks, but where it floated, there the passage was clear for the corial to pass (Sect. 151). Owing to an invisible fungus growing upon the arrow in the one case (Sect. 145) and upon the bowman's arm in the other (Sect. 144), the missile does not hit its mark. When either is properly cleaned, however, the arrow is made to split a fishing-line and a distant hanging-vine rope, respectively. It has been claimed for the Spirits, and medicine-man—and after all, the powers of these agents were identical—as almost one of their perquisites, so to speak (Sect. 30), that they alone can hit an animal by shooting the arrow up into the air and letting it fall from above on the quarry. As a matter of fact this was once a more or less common practice among the turtle-hunters of the Amazon and Orinoco.[1]

331.* A few words on certain ideas concerning broken bows and broken arrows must be given place here. The term "broken" would seem to represent almost the normal condition in which certain of the Bush Spirits employed bows, for which reason some of these denizens of the forest were known as Shimarabu-akaradáni (Sect. 95). The same p. 362 Beings were also evidently not averse to using broken arrows, subsquently spliced (Sect. 144), but it is certainly difficult to trace the raison-d'être of the self-castigation with the two halves of a broken arrow to insure strength and courage (Sects. 139, 221B).

331A.* The idea of invisible poisoned or broken arrows noted in the two next sections preceding may possibly bear relation to one of the procedures adopted in the declaration of hostilities on the outbreak of war. Thus, the call to arms may be noiseless, the emissaries silently announcing the fact that the tribe is at war without even saying a word, for it suffices to leave in passing a barbed arrow in a public place for all to take up arms. This notice is called the Mission of the Arrow (correr la flecha) and is tantamount to a declaration of a state of war (G, I, 134). Martius recorded a similar procedure among the Caribs, Yuri, Miranya, and others (Beiträge, I, 97); the practice is also observed with the Guariua of the Yapura at the present day (KG, II, 316).

Next

Footnotes

p. 356

1 For further information concerning this particular arrow, see Sects. 330, 331.

p. 359

1 On the Rio Içana (upper Rio Negro); maraka-imbára is the secret magic poison to which every death is ascribed (KG, I, 45, 207, 214).

p. 360

1 Compare the licking of the switch by the girl at puberty (Sect. 171).

p. 361

1 I have observed and since recorded the same method among the natives of North Queensland.—W. E. R.

CHAPTER XIX
MISCELLANEOUS INDIAN BELIEFS CONCERNING MAN AND ANIMALS

Dwarfs, People with their Feet Turned Backward, Touvingas, White and White-haired Folk, Acephali (332); Amazons (333-334). Orang-Utang, etc. (335-336); Warracaba "Tiger" (337); "Tigers" in general (338); Tapir (339); Armadillo (340); Bush-hog and "Skunk" (341); Anteater (342); Sloth (343); Turtle, etc. (344); Alligator (345); Gecko (346); Snakes in general (347); Camudi (348); Frogs (349); Birds (350); Fish (351); Insects (351A).

332.* What more natural from the primitive man's point of view than that lake people and river people, more often in the water than out of it, should come to be looked on as fish; that men invariably wearing their headdress in a manner usually considered appropriate only for the opposite sex, should be regarded in the light of women; and that monkeys, grown in imagination to man's size, should come to be the dread of unprotected females? We have our Fish folk (Sects. 152, 178), our Amazons (Sects. 157, 296), our

Orang-utangs and the like (Sects. 138, 140A) in Guiana folk-lore. But there are other peculiar people to be reckoned with also. The Toupinambous, inhabiting a large island in the River Amazon below the Rio Negro, told Father Acuña (158) that on the south side near their island—

there are two Nations among others upon the Continent that are very remarkable; one of them are Dwarfs as small as little children, and are called Guayazis, the other is a Race of people that come into the world with their feet turned behind them, so that those that are unacquatnted with their monstrous shape, and should follow their Track, would run from them instead of overtaking them. They are called Matayus, and are tributary to the Toupinambous, whom they are obliged to furnish with Hatchets made of stone to fell great trees with, when they have a mind to clear a piece of ground; for they frame these Hatchets very neatly, and it is their whole business to make them.

According to the idea current among the Trios, people were originally like wood and stone, and had no faces (Go, 12). On the upper Parou, French Guiana, Crévaux (284) passed a small stream up which the Ouayanas never venture, owing to the reputed presence of white-haired Indians who sleep by day and walk by night. History does not say whether it was the unusual coloration or the nocturnal perambulation that rendered them so uncanny to his native companions. Brown (Bro, 281), when at the Orindouie Falls on the Ireng, saw on distant ridges to the eastward Indian villages, the inhabitants of which, his Cumumaring guide informed him, were p. 364turning white, and in time would be white people. The association with white people of the idea of life everlasting in this mundane world, an idea which the Indians themselves possessed, has already been referred to (Sect. 66). In a work by J. J. Hartsinck (II, 810) occurs the following passage concerning certain negroes at Saramacca;

Regarding the "Touvingas" or Two-fingered Negroes [pl. 7] it is observed that they are a people who had only two large fingers on their hands and two large toes on their feet, similar to those of a crab, as is figured in the illustration. The wrist is somewhat larger than that of the average man: the thumb and little finger are more than twice the usual size, and stand out from the limb, have a bend at the tip, and appear as one piece of flesh on which there is something like a nail. The palm of the hand has no bends, but appears as a solid mass, yet the divisions can be felt. . . . After the declaration of freedom, these negroes of Saramacca walked publicly through Paramaribo. . . . Many argue that they are not a distinct tribe or nation, but just a family who by accident or freak of nature have been thus deformed. These people are becoming very rare indeed, probably through intercourse with others, fast bastardizing.

The forests of the River Sipapo, Orinoco, are altogether unknown and there the missionaries place the nation of the Rayas, whose mouths are believed to be in their navels; they were so called on account of the pretended analogy with the fish of this name, the mouth of which seems as if forced downward below the body: an old Indian at Carichana, who boasted of having often eaten human flesh, had seen these acephali with his own eyes (AVH, II, 317). Mianiko, one of the three tribal Kobéua heroes, had no head, but eyes in place of nipples (KG, II, 162).

333.* Particularly interesting among all the extraordinary folk coming under our ken are the Amazons, whose existence is believed in among the Indians even up to the present day. Several legends, of which I have given example (Sect. 157), bear reference to them. Like many another, I have striven in vain to discover the exact whereabouts of these valiant females, who, though cast sufficiently in the Spartan mold to amputate the right breast with a view to insuring greater freedom of movement for the arm in battling upon the Field of Mars, were nevertheless women enough to be occasionally caught napping under the canopy of Venus. The Jesuit Father Acuña (164) gives the accompanying account of them; he appears to have been more fortunate than I.

Up the River Cunuris on the north side of the Amazon, to the east of Toupinambou Island, live the Apotos [? Apautos], the Tagaris [? Tagua-us], and lastly the Guacaras, who are the people that have the Privilege to converse with these valiant Women and enjoy their favors. They dwell upon huge mountains: one that lifts its Head a great height above all the rest is Yacamiaba. These women (as has been said) are very courageous and have always maintained themselves alone without the help and assistance of men; and when their neighbors come into their country at a time concerted with them, they receive them with weapons in their hands, which are Bows and Arrows, and which they exercise as if they were going against their enemies; but p. 365knowing well that the others do not come to fight, but are their friends, they lay down their arms, and all run into the canoes or other little vessels of these Indians, and each Amazone takes the Hammock (a cotton Bed they hang up to sleep in) which she finds next at hand; this she carries home [Sect. 275] and hangs up in a place where the owner of it may know it again when he comes; after which she receives him as her guest, and treats him those few days they continue together. These Indians afterward return to their own dwellings, and never fail to make this voyage every year at the appointed Time. The girls which they bear are brought up by their mothers. As for the male children, it is not certain what they do with them.

Father Acuña saw an Indian who told him that when he was a child he was with his father at such an interview, and assured him that they gave the male children to their fathers the next time they came subsequent to the birth. But the common report is that they kill all their males as soon as they are born. Schomburgk gives us the following particulars:

334.* According to the statements of Mahanarwa, the last Kazike of the Caribs, they [Amazons] live at a place on the River Wara, quite enclosed by mountains, to which there is but a single entrance: he also mentions the tribe which the Amazons annually visit—it is the Teyrous or Tairas in Cayenne. . . . Among the Makusis and Arawaks, we found the accounts of the Amazons to be widely scattered . . . each tribe, however, gives a different locality to where these women are to be met with. . . . An Arawak chief told me that his brother, who lived on the upper Mazaruni, had visited them on one occasion, and that he received one of those green stones as a present from the Wirisamoca, as he called these Amazons. [ScR, II, 330.]

There are three opinions worth considering as to the origin of the myth, those of Wallace, Schomburgk, and Humboldt. In describing the Indians of the River Uaupes, Wallace says:

The men, on the other hand, have the hair carefully parted and combed on each side, and tied in a queue behind. In the young men, it hangs in long locks down their necks, and, with the comb, which is invariably carried stuck in the top of the head, gives to them a most feminine appearance: this is increased by the large necklaces and bracelets of beads, and the careful extirpation of every symptom of beard. Taking these circumstances into consideration, I am strongly of opinion that the story of the Amazons has arisen from these feminine-looking warriors encountered by the early voyagers. I am inclined to this opinion, from the effect they first produced on myself, when it was only by close examination I saw that they were men; and, were the front parts of their bodies and their breasts covered with shields, such as they always use, I am convinced any person seeing them for the first time would conclude they were women. [ARW, 343.]

Schomburgk bases the fable on the "warlike reputation of the women of certain tribes, namely, the Caribs. Columbus in his second voyage gives proofs of the courage of the women folk of Guadalupe—and Peter Martyr d'Anghieri says of the inhabitants of this island that both sexes possess great strength and skill in the use of the bow and other weapons. . . . Columbus had already on his first voyage found fighting women, and in them recognized Amazons: what had been told him in the old world, he believed to find again in the new" (ScR, II, 330). Humboldt recognizes a motive p. 366 that prompted exaggeration on the part of those writers of the sixteenth century who have given most reputation to the Amazons of America, in their tendency to find among the newly discovered nations all that the Greeks have related to us of the first age of the world, and of the manners of the barbarous Scythians and Africans (AVH, II, 400).

335.* The orang-utang of Guiana, as we are told with all due solemnity by Bancroft (Ba, 130), is much larger than either the African or the oriental, if the accounts of the natives may be relied on. He does not find that any specimens have been seen by the white inhabitants on this coast, who never penetrate far into the woods. These animals, in all the various languages of the natives, are called by names signifying a wild man. They are represented by the Indians as being near five feet in height, maintaining an erect position, and having a human form, thinly covered with short black hair; but Bancroft suspects that their height has been augmented by the fears of the Indians, who greatly dread them, and instantly flee as soon as one is discovered, so that none of them has ever been taken alive, much less any attempts made for taming them. The Indians relate many fabulous stories of these animals, and, like the inhabitants of Africa and the East, assert that they will attack the males and ravish the females of the human species. It is to be noted that this author's description nearly agrees with that of the Spirit of the Forest, the Tukuyuba of the Arawaks, etc. (Sect. 95).

Humboldt also makes mention, on the Orinoco, of a—

hairy man of the woods called salvaje, that carries off women, constructs huts, and sometimes eats human flesh. The Tamanacs call him achi, and the Maypures vasitri or "great devil." The natives and the missionaries have no doubt of the existence of this man-shaped monkey, of which they entertain a singular dread. Father Gili gravely relates the history of a lady in the town of San Carlos, in the Llanos of Venezuela, who much praised the gentle character and attentions of the man of the woods. She is stated to have lived several years with one in great domestic harmony, and only requested some hunters to take her back, "because she and her children (a little hairy also) were weary of living far from the church and the sacraments." [AVH, II, 270.]

With regard to the black monkey, the Arawaks have the following proverb: Ka´to hure bobaldi; kenna titina kebeldi; bowajilida (lit. "When black monkey shot; and blood licks; lively, active"), referring to a man working hard (pulling a paddle, etc.) all day, a hint that a little stimulant (paiwarri) will revive him.

336.* The Maroon negroes of the Maroni, when they kill a howling monkey, preserve the vocal apparatus, out of which a cup is made; if a child is given its drink out of this cup for some months, it will be cured of stammering (Cr, 159). Humboldt was told by his guides [? Indians] that to cure asthma it is sufficient to drink out of the bony drum of the hyoidal bone of this creature (AVH, II, 70).

337.* I am afraid that the existence of a Warracaba tiger, like many another quaint conceit, must be consigned to the oblivion of superstition. The belief is of somewhat local origin and of comparatively recent date, no references being met with in all the old literature available. It is very probably akin to the many other mythical "tigers" with which the Indian folk-lore is so replete: for example, the Kanaima (Sect. 320) of the natives generally, the Tobe-horoanna (Sects. 144, 146, 148) of the Warraus particularly, for which it fulfills a somewhat similar purpose. On the other hand, it is possible that the myth has its origin in certain indigenous wild dogs which hunt in packs. On the Quitaro River, some Wapisiana Indians stated that the journey to the Ataraipu Rock and back would have to be accomplished in one day, as it would be impossible to spend a night near the rock, on account of a pack of Warracaba tigers that inhabited the district (Bro, 149). The most vivid description of the creature comes from the pen of Barrington Brown (Bro, 72, 73, 74) when on the Mazaruni:

I eagerly inquired what were Warracaba tigers, and was hastily informed that they were small and exceedingly ferocious tigers, that they hunted in packs, and were not frightened by camp-fires or anything except the barking of dogs. To water they have a special aversion, and will never cross a stream which is too wide for them to jump. . . . As we stopped, a shrill scream rent the night air. . . . This was answered by another cry coming from the depths of the forest, the interval between them being filled by low growls and trumpeting sounds which smote most disagreeably on the ear. . . . The call of these animals resembles that of the Warracaba or Trumpet-bird (Psophia crepitans) . . . and hence they have obtained the name of Warracaba tigers. The Ackawoise Indians call them "Y'agamisheri," and say that they vary in size as well as in color. As many as a hundred are said to have been seen in one pack. . . . They are said to frequent the mountains, but when pressed by hunger . . . they descend to the lowlands.

Schomburgk states that this tiger is so named after the peculiar coloring of the breast, which is exactly like the feathers of the trumpeter bird (ScR, II, 85).

338.* Speaking of "tigers" generally, it is almost traditional among the Indians that each of the various kinds of tigers and tiger-cats hunts one kind of animal in particular, the call of which it can imitate. The Arawaks have a saying, Hamáro kamungka turuwati (lit. "everything has tiger"), as a reminder of the fact that we should be circumspect, and on our guard, there always being some enemy about. It is a general belief among the Indians and the white inhabitants of Brazil that the onça (jaguar) has the power of fascination (ARW, 317).

339.* The tapir has between its eyebrows a bone so strong as to enable it to break down the undergrowth in the forests; with this means of defence it can protect itself from a tiger by crushing the latter against the rugged timber, and so tearing it to pieces (G, I, 265). The same animal, the Rio Negro Indians say, "has a peculiar p. 368 fancy for dropping his dung only in the water (Sect. 162B), and they never find it except in brooks and springs, though it is so large and abundant that it could not be overlooked in the forest. If there is no water to be found, the animal makes a rough basket of leaves and carries it to the nearest stream and there deposits it" (ARW, 154). On the upper Essequibo the men removed the hoofs from a tapir for the purpose of using them, when occasion required, as charms for bites of snakes, stings of ray-fish, and fits of all kinds: they said that the hoofs are first singed, and then placed in water, which is drunk (Bro, 240). The same belief was current on the Orinoco: tapir hoofs crushed to powder, and one hung on the neck of a patient, constitute an excellent and well-known cure for epilepsy (G, I, 265). The remedy is still employed, to my own knowledge, by creole residents in Georgetown.

340.* The smaller armadillo (Dasypus villosus Desm.), the jassi of the Makusis, and other tribes, according to the Indians, is met with only on the savannahs and lives chiefly on carrion. Hence, in certain festival songs of the Wapisiana and Makusi this creature plays an important rôle, in that almost every refrain ends with the words, "And when I am dead, put me in the savannah; the jassi will come and bury me." According to Von Martius a similar song is common among the Indians of the Rio Negro (ScR, II, 97-98). The last joint or bone of the armadillo's tail has been found an efficacious remedy for earache (G, II, 263), but whether by Indians or by Spaniards unfortunately is not stated. The real interest of the connection between the animal and the complaint lies rather in the creature's ears being so distinctive a feature, a fact to which attention has already been drawn in dealing with its bina (Sect. 233). Explanations have been given as to the bush-master snake (Lachesis mutus) being always found in armadillo holes (Sect. 7).

341.* Well into the eighteenth century the musk-gland on the dorsum of the bush-hog (Dicotyles) was believed to be its navel by Creoles and Europeans, from the Orinoco to Cayenne, though the idea does not seem to have been shared by the Indians. There is one particular animal, seemingly of a skunk-like nature (? Conepatus) which thus far has baffled me in the way of identification. Father Gumilla (II, 272) describes it as follows:

A little animal, very scarce, and the most detestable of any that I have hitherto seen. Amongst the whites of America it is called mapurito: and the Indians call it mafutiliqui: it is like one of those very elegant little mongrel curs which ladies breed in their mansions. All its little body is spotted white and black: its tail proportionate, uncommon (hermoso), and much covered with long hair: very active and flighty in its manner of walking, and daring beyond measure. It waits for its enemy, tiger, man or animal, face to face: and so soon as it is approached close enough, it turns its back. The atmosphere is rendered so pestiferous that the enemy remains stupefied, and requires a long time before he can get away.

342.* The Rio Negro Indians declare that the great anteaters (Myrmecophaga jubata) are all females and believe that the male is the Curupira, or demon of the forest (Sept. 117): the peculiar organization of the animal has probably led to this error (ARW, 314).

343.* With regard to the sloth, there would seem to be but few references to the animal in Guiana folk-lore. I have already mentioned him in the light of a girl's sweetheart (Sect. 134), and the smaller species in connection with a death omen (Sect. 222). Arawaks say Káto awaduli fudi: hau akonaka (lit. when wind blows, sloth walks), that is, people are going to exert themselves only when they are obliged to.

344.* Among the Island Caribs the tortoise bore a reputation for being "smart." One of the most offensive things they could say when chaffing one another was, "You are as wide-awake (adroit) as a tortoise" (RoP, 453), though the same authors elsewhere refer to its clumsiness (lourdise) and stupidity (RoP, 465).

345.* To account for the rough stones invariably found in the belly of the alligator, the Otomac Indians were of opinion that, as the creature increases in size it finds a corresponding difficulty in sinking "to the bottom of the river on the sands on which it sleeps, covered with all the weight of the waters; and that, guided by instinct, it proceeds to the banks, where it swallows as many stones as may be necessary to weigh it down; whence, it may be inferred that the bigger it grows, the more stones are required for its ballast and counterpoise (G, II, 215). But in those rivers where there are no stones, to effect its purpose of sinking to the bottom the alligator retains the bones of the animals which it has devoured (G, II, 218). According to Indian accounts the seat of life (der Sitz des Lebens) is situated in the animal's tail. That the tail is the most sensitive part is shown by the fact that with every blow thereon the creature rears up, though it will hardly respond to a cudgeling on the head and back (ScR, II, 177).

346.* Indians and colored people consider the gecko, the "wood-slave" of the colonists (Hemidactylus Mabouia Cuv., and Platydactylus Theconyx Dum.), as poisonous as their snakes. They believe that if a gecko fall from the roof or beams on the bare skin of a person, the latter will be seized with convulsions, which will soon be followed by death (ScR, II, 116).

347.* Throughout many races of mankind the snake has played a very important rôle in connection with sexual matters. Several references on this score are to be met with in the animism of the Guiana Indian, but a few will suffice for present purposes. The snake appears as the husband or lover (Sects. 23, 47, 56, 363), is especially fond of the women at their menstrual periods (Sects. 55, 188, 274), and not infrequently may be found actually inside the p. 370 female (Sects. 31, 55, 56). He is also the progenitor of the human race (Sects. 54, 55), the source of origin of all the binas (Sect. 235), and his skin has given their natural color to all the birds (Sect. 162). For reasons already given (Sect. 64), he is symbolic of everlasting life. Certain snake dances have been referred to (Sect. 47). There is also a connection between snakes and rain (Sect. 213).

348.* There are one or two curious beliefs concerning the camudi snake, or buio, of the Orinoco. The Jirara Indians designated it aviofa, but other tribes, and the Indians of Quito, named it "water-mamma" (madre del agua) because it ordinarily lives in the water. This is how, a couple of centuries ago, the camudi was believed to capture its prey:

As soon as it hears a noise, it raises its head, and a yard or two of its body, and when it sees its prey, be it tiger, calf, deer, or man, it takes aim, and opening its terrible mouth emits so poisonous and foul an exhalation as to fix the victim, stupefy him, and render him unable to move. For this reason, no one dares to travel alone by himself, either for fishing or hunting, no matter where the journey may be: at least two have to go in company, so that in case the buio, hidden or discovered, should take aim at one of them, the other, either with his hat, or with a tree-branch, will shake and cut the air intervening between his friend and the monster. [G, II, 148.]

With regard to the foul exhalation just referred to, it is curious to note Schomburgk's remark concerning the coulacanara [kole-konaro (Sect. 235)] boa-constrictor: "If anyone approaches the creature when hissing, he is met with a musky kind of stench" (ScR, II, 250). Bancroft tells us that the white inhabitants of the colony spoke of the camudi by the name of Sodomite Snake owing to the peculiar manner in which it was believed by the Indians to kill its prey when larger than a duck or goose, namely, by inserting its pointed tail into the creature's rectum (Ba, 205); this extraordinary belief I have found existing among the present day Pomeroon Arawaks.

349.* Mention has been made of the frog being regarded in the light of a divinity by the original Carib tribes in the way of sending rain or fine weather, of its being kept as a domestic animal, and whipped when the wishes of the votaries were not fulfilled (Sect. 46). The frog is very generally spoken of as a female (Sects. 12, 24); she it was who brought fire out of her mouth (Sect. 34), food-starch and cassava out of her neck and shoulders (Sects. 34, 37), taught music (Sect. 12), and showed folk how to hunt (Sects. 12, 144, 145). As a preparatory charm for hunting, she is accordingly employed, either by being swallowed or by being rubbed into the incisions made on the hunter (Sects. 228,

229). She is depicted on the neck-ornament of the medicine-man (Sect. 292). One particular frog is used by pregnant Arawak women as an omen (Sect. 222).1

350.* The búnia, or "stinking bird" (Ostinops spp.) is believed to produce the aerial roots of the kofa tree (Clusia grandifolia), an epiphyte, which are supposed to be its castings turned into wood (Sects. 138, 168): the natural "stench" of the bird's feathers may have had something to do with the origin of the idea. The same bird is represented as removing the snake from out of the plum-tree woman (Sect. 31), and also as a transformed medicine-man (Sect. 154). The tiki-tiki is a fabulous bird mentioned by Humboldt as the enemy of the human race, which causes the deformities of newly-born children (AVH, II, 249): it is also referred to by Schomburgk as tigtitig (Sect. 82). Macaws are believed to advise and assist the Water Spirits in upsetting the canoes (Sect. 179). There is a Pomeroon Arawak belief that the tiriliana, the "corn-bird," is too lazy to look after its own, and therefore lays its eggs in the nest of the mockingbird (Cassicus), which does the hatching for it. A similar remark applies, among these same people, to the werebekwa, a very small creature that deposits its eggs in the nest of a hummingbird, which it thereupon drives away. The caution of the goat-sucker (Caprimulgus) makes the Wapisianas declare that this bird carries another pair of eyes on its back (ScR, II, 61). Goat-suckers are always birds of ill-omen (Sect. 223). The vulture is very reasonably known as the "boss, or governor," of the carrion-crows (Sect. 137). Among the Indians hummingbirds are proverbially exceedingly quarrelsome (Be, 11). There are several allusions in the literature to the natural association of hummingbirds with tobacco, not only because these little creatures nest in this particular plant (RoP, 114, 178), but also because they possess a peculiarly pleasant smell (ibid., 177). It is quite common to hear the hummingbird spoken of by Arawaks and Warraus as the "doctor's bird," for a similar reason, the tobacco plant having been brought into great prominence by the medicine-men, and having been introduced among these tribes by the little creature just mentioned (Sect. 296).

351.* The curbinata, so named by the Spaniards, is a fish found in the Orinoco, but it is not so much as an article of subsistence that it is valued, as on account of two stones in its head, exactly in the place which is usually occupied by the brain. These stones, which are regarded as a specific in cases of retention of urine [? by Indians or Spaniards], sell for their weight in gold (FD, 150). I have known of Arawaks sticking a sting-ray (Raja) barb into the aching hollow, to relieve toothache.

351A.* Spider-webs must evidently have been formerly of immense size to allow of people climbing down them (Sect. 142), and strong enough to support a fallen tree (Sect. 300).

Next

Footnotes

1 With the Gran Chaco Indians the frog is also represented as stealing the fire, and bringing it away in its mouth (Nor, 254, 314).

CHAPTER XX
ANIMISM AND FOLK-TALES OF RECENT INTRODUCTION; MIXED FOREIGN AND INDIGENOUS BELIEFS

The Story of "Brer Rabbit" (352-362), and other Tales (363-364).

352.* There are many stories current of undoubted foreign origin, chiefly African, modified more or less by local conditions. Among these are the celebrated adventures of Brer Rabbit, who, through the Spanish form of the word (conejo) is here known as Koneso (Arawak), or Konehu (Warrau). The Warraus apply the term to any "smart" man, indeed to any knave or rogue who is always outwitting his neighbors. Both nations claim the hero as their own, the Arawaks even crediting themselves with his long ears, and it was from these two sources that I was able to glean the details given here.

*THE STORY OF KONESO (BRER RABBIT)

353.* There was once a Koneso; but although he was a rabbit, he had short ears just like any other person. He traveled about all over the country, and he had plenty of children everywhere. Yes; he gave a lot of trouble to the single girls, and upset the harmony of many a married man's home. If the other men aimed at him with a club or with an arrow, it would either glide off or break, and Koneso would laugh. They found they could not kill him, and he continued doing just what he liked. But at last he himself got tired of everybody, and went away to another country. Now, the country he went to was ruled by a nafudi,1 who was celebrated as having a very beautiful daughter. Koneso happened to see this lovely woman one day, and forthwith went and asked the father to give her to him for a wife. But the nafudi told him he must first of all bring him two quakes full of alligator and camudi eyes. So, Koneso retired to make the quakes, and spent some days in arranging for the manufacture of cassiri. With the cassiri he filled plenty of jugs and brought them down to the waterside, close to the river bank. He next took his bone flute and played pretty music—it was such pretty music that all the alligators and camudis came out of the water to listen to it. He then handed the drinks round in a calabash, made them intoxicated, and while they were all lying dead drunk there, he gouged their eyes out with his finger. Having filled his quakes with their eyes, he hurried back with them to the nafudi, but the latter said, "I can not let anyone like you have my daughter. Hang your impudence!" And with this, he pulled sharply at Koneso's ears.2 But with the pull, Koneso's ears got stretched and hung down a good way over his neck. When Koneso found that he had now got long ears, he became very angry, and told the nafudi he would show him what he could do. Whereupon, he began attempting to take liberties with the pretty daughter, but the more she screamed, the more he laughed; and every stick that the nafudi beat him with got broken immediately it touched his skin. When the nafudi saw that he could not hurt Koneso this way, he told his men to seize him, p. 373to tie him up against a tree, and shoot him at close range: but every arrow that was shot either got broken or glanced off. The men thereupon put Koneso in a corial and tied him on to the benches, put up an its sail, and let the vessel drift out to sea: but Koneso soon released himself, sailed back again, and went to the nafudi and told him that he had brought the boat safe into port. The men thereupon seized Koneso a third time; they tied him hand and foot, fixed around his neck a long vine-rope with a heavy stone attached, took him out to sea, and threw him overboard; but as soon as Koneso touched ground, he "loosed himself," and resting the heavy stone on his shoulder walked along the bottom of the sea until he reached shore, when he reported himself again to the nafudi; and told him that he had brought back the stone quite safe. To make a long story short, the nafudi recognizing his helplessness, gave Koneso his daughter.

354.* Koneso after a time got homesick, and came back to his own country. He went one day deep into the forest and began to pull the big vine-ropes from off the trees. Tiger heard him, and coming up, asked him what all the noise was about. "Nothing," said Koneso, "except that there will be a big wind blowing the day after tomorrow, and as I don't want to be blown away, I intend tying myself up to a tree with one of these vines." Tiger became much frightened at hearing all this, and begged Koneso to tie him up before he fixed himself in safety. After Koneso had accordingly bound him up tight against a tree, he went away and started cutting down some more vine-rope, making plenty of noise over it, just to make believe that he was going to treat himself in the same manner. But instead of that, he just quietly walked home again. In the meantime Tiger waited patiently for the three days to pass, and no wind came at all, and he began to feel hungry, but tug and pull as hard as he could, he was unable to loose himself. Many animals passed by, and though he begged each and every one to undo the ropes, they were all afraid lest, once freed, Tiger might eat them after so long a fast. At last, on the fourth day, a carrion-crow came hopping along, and Tiger promised him that if he untied him he would in future always give him some meat to eat. Thereupon the bird released him, and this is why, whenever Tiger kills game, he always leaves behind something for the carrion-crow to peck at.

355.* Some time after, Tiger met Koneso and told him that he was going to kill him for playing such a trick. But Koneso begged so hard, saying that he was only skin and bones, and that even if he ate him, he would not satisfy his hunger, that Tiger spared his life, but all the same was determined upon catching him again in another manner. Now, Tiger knew the pond where Koneso used to bathe, so without saying anything to anybody, he climbed up into the branches of an overhanging tree, and patiently waited for his prey to come along, when he would jump upon his back and kill him. But Koneso had been to a drink-party, and, decked with flowers over his head, around his neck, his chest and waist, came sauntering leisurely along. With all these flowers he looked like some other animal, and Tiger did not recognize him. As Koneso came out of his bath, however, he happened to look up and noticed Tiger crouching along one of the upper branches at the same time that Tiger, seeing his face, recognized him. Tiger then made a spring, but not quite fast enough, because Koneso was already off. For a long distance they thus ran, one after the other, and just in the nick of time Koneso escaped into an armadillo hole. This hole was too small for Tiger to chase him, so he made up his mind to close it altogether. Near by there was a hawk: one of those hawks which cry tau-a tau-a in the early morning before the sun shines. Tiger called to the bird and asked her to watch at the armadillo hole while he went home to fetch a digging-stick. While Tiger was gone, and the hawk was keeping watch, Koneso came up to the mouth of the hole and started whispering sweet nothings to her, flattering her with honeyed words, and among other things said: "You are indeed a pretty woman. p. 374Do bend your face down a bit. I would so love to see it closer." And when the silly hawk bent her face down, Koneso immediately threw a handful of sand into her eyes, and so blinded her, which gave him the opportunity of getting away from Tiger.1

356.* There was once a celebrated Konehu, walking along the bush, when he met a female Tiger. The latter, who was hungry, wanted to go out hunting, but did not like to leave her three little cubs at home without anyone in charge of the place. So Konehu agreed to look after the youngsters while Tiger searched for game. Things went on very well for some time, Tiger returning home each evening with meat which she shared with Konehu. But on a certain day, one of the cubs bit Konehu, so he killed it, threw the body away, and said nothing to the mother when she returned. In fact, Konehu as usual brought from out of the hollow log one cub after another for the mother to suckle, but on this occasion he brought out the same cub twice, and the mother was none the wiser. Next day, another cub bit Konehu. So he killed it, threw the body away as before, and said nothing, but in the evening brought out the remaining cub three times to be fed, and its mother was none the wiser. Next day, however, the surviving whelp bit Konehu. So he killed it, left its carcass close by the hollow log, and made tracks elsewhere.2 He knew that Tiger would follow him, so he traveled a long, long way before he rested. He next built a house on very high posts, posts too high for anyone to climb up, and then started making the roof which was just as high up again. Indeed, to get up all that way, he built a long ladder. And he started tying on the thatch. In the meantime, Tiger, on her return home, found her one dead cub but no signs of the other two. There was also no Konehu. She therefore was vexed much, and determined to follow and kill him. She traveled night and day, and went on and on until she came to the house which Konehu was building, and there she saw him on top thatching the roof. "Hullo!" she growls, "What are you doing up there? I am come to eat you." But Konehu does not worry himself. He only says: "You had better look out for yourself, because there is a big sea coming. I am building this house to save myself. You had better join me. Come up the ladder." Tiger thereupon clambers up the ladder and gets close to Konehu who is tying on the thatch with the itiriti strand. As soon as she got too uncomfortably close to him, he suddenly exclaimed: "Oh! What a pity! I have just dropped a piece of the tying strand. Wait up here a minute, while I go down and fetch it." This was a lie, for directly he reached the ground, he removed the ladder, leaving Tiger helpless on the roof. Again Konehu made tracks and walked about. He walked so far that he got tired. He then sat down and started making a quake, an openwork basket. Now, what did Tiger do? When she found the ladder gone, she scrambled up and under the roof, over and among the beams and rafters, but she could not get down. At last, hunger compelled her to say, "I must live, or I must die." So she made a big jump and reached the ground safely. She was vexed much, and determined upon following and killing Konehu. She traveled night and day, and went on and on until she reached the spot where Konehu was seated, busily occupied in making his quake. "Hullo!" she growls, "What are you doing? I am come to eat you." Konehu however remained quite cool and quiet. He stuck to his story about the big sea coming, and swore that he was making the quake so that when completed he could get inside and haul himself up to the top most branch of a big mora tree that was close by. Silly Tiger then believed what he told her, and said she would like to get into the basket also. Konehu therefore took her measure and increased the size of the basket. When finished, he told her to get inside, but no sooner had she comfortably fixed herself, p. 375than he drew the sides of the quake together, and sewed them up. Tiger was now prisoner. Fixing a long vine-rope to the basket, Konehu threw it over the topmost branch of the mora tree, pulled on its free end, left his victim dangling in mid-air, and made tracks. Tiger was now in a bad way, for the more she roared the more did all the other animals get frightened and run away. At last, one of the most inquisitive, a little monkey, wanting to know what all the noise was about, climbed down the vine-rope and opened the basket. No sooner had he done so, than out jumped Tiger and both fell to the ground, where the monkey's only reward was to be eaten. Yes, Tiger was vexed much and determined upon following and killing Konehu. She wandered on and on, and at last met him upon the banks of a river. Directly he saw her coming he commenced looking down into the water very hard, as if he was examining something very carefully. "Hullo!" growled Tiger. "What are you looking at? I am come to eat you." "Nonsense, woman," says Konehu. "Look, look down there. Don't you see that beautiful yellow stone [gold]? If you could only fetch it you would be a rich woman. You would have a new husband, and get new cubs."1 Now what he was pointing at in the water was only the reflection of the sun overhead. Tiger, however, being both silly and greedy, dived in, and quickly came up to the surface to breathe. "Oh!" he tells her, "you must go down deeper." So she jumps in again, and stays under much longer. When she again appears on the surface, Konehu reiterates "You haven't gone deep enough." And so the game goes on, she being fooled every time about not having stayed below long enough. She makes a last effort to dive under a very long time, when Konehu takes the opportunity of making good his escape. Tiger now sees that she has been tricked. She is vexed much and is more than ever determined to follow and kill Konehu, who by this time knows what to expect. So he travels far, far until he comes to a high hill on the top of which he balances a big rock, and at the bottom of which he digs a deep pit. By and by, Tiger comes along, and seeing Konehu on top of the hill, looks up at him and says: "Hullo! What are you doing up there? I am come to eat you." But Konehu puts his arms around the rock, and says it is a large piece of meat, which he will throw down to her if she lies quietly in the pit. And the silly, greedy Tiger believes him again, does just what he tells her, and waits for the meat to come. Soon, bumpty, bumpty, down the hill comes the big rock, faster and faster it speeds, until falling on Tiger, it kills and buries her.2

357.* Konehu was a lazy man, and would not labor for his living. He was hungry. One fine morning he sat at the foot of a high overhanging cliff, waiting for some one to come along. By and by he saw a company of men approaching. They had been out hunting, and were bringing along a quantity of game. Konehu then picked up a long wooden pole, and placing it against the side of the cliff after the manner of a brace, began pressing it into position just as the huntsmen came up. In reply to their inquiry as to why he was pressing so hard upon the pole, Konehu said: "Can't you see that the mountain is falling over, and that if I don't brace it up, it will come down and destroy all of us? Look up and see it moving! Come, take my place, and let me have a little rest. I have been shoving at it all the morning." The huntsmen accordingly gazed up the wall of the precipice, and seeing the clouds moving over the top of it, indeed thought that the cliff was about to fall. So dropping their quarry on the ground, they all together started pressing on the timber, and continued pressing, and pressed harder, until by the time the sun was about to sink, they were so exhausted that they could press no longer. They satisfied their conscience by saying that whether the cliff overwhelmed them or not, it would not be their fault. They therefore p. 376 let go the timber and turned around to pick up all their game and provisions. But these had all disappeared. And so had Konehu!

358.* On another occasion Konehu was again hungry, but the people all about knew what a tricky man he was, and refused to give him anything to eat, unless he paid or worked for it. He had nothing to give, so he had to work. He asked for food at a certain house, and the house-master told him to pound some rice. He pounded away until late in the afternoon. The master came to see how much rice had been cleaned, but was astonished to find so small an amount resulting from the large quantity that had been handed over in the morning. The master gave Konehu the same quantity to pound next day, and in the afternoon there was again a marked shortage, so he became very angry and sent Konehu away. That very night, Konehu cooked rice for supper. Instead of a solid heavy-wood pounder, he had used a hollow-bamboo one, and the more he pounded the rice with it, the quicker it became filled.1

359.* An exploit next takes place wherein our friend Konehu fools a fellow-traveler over some kokerite seeds (Maximiliana regia). He was sitting on a rock one day eating kokerite nuts. Holding them in close proximity to his crutch, he was breaking them on the hard surface with a stone. While eating the kernels, a traveler passed, and the latter was invited to taste them. He ate with great gusto, and asked Konehu what they were.2 "Eheu, edo testiculos meos. Quare nonne edes tuoes," inquit. Itaque hostes, testiculos suos prehens, lapide pulsavit, atque tanto modo se vulneravit ut morietur.

360.* One day Konehu met a man carrying two quakes of yams. The yams looked just splendid, and Konehu, not having any of his own, determined on possessing himself of them. "Those are fine yams," he said, "what are you going to do with them?" On learning that they were being taken up the river for sale at the next settlement, Konehu said that he knew of another settlement where such beautiful yams would fetch a far higher price, and that if they were handed over to his care he, Konehu would negotiate the business to the better advantage just for friendship's sake. Once they were in his possession, however, Konehu said good-by to the stranger, and brought them home for his wife to cook. All that he had said about selling them at a big price was a lie. Soon after the very same man whom he had cheated came up to the house and threatened to kill him. But Konehu managed to talk "sweet-mouth" and soothed his anger by telling him that if he waited a while, he would give hin some nice pepper-pot. Going into that portion of the logie which was screened off for the women-folk, he told his wife to shriek and scream as if he were killing her. She did what she was bid. Konehu brought out some pepper-pot, which he placed before the stranger. The man tasted and was enchanted with it. "That is a fine pepper-pot. What did you make it from?" he says. "Just out of my wife's breast," replied Konehu. "Didn't you hear her yell when I cut it off?" The foolish man went back to his own home, and seizing his wife, gashed her breast to pieces, but the result was that she bled to death, and he recognized only too late that he had again been tricked.

361.* The way in which Konehu managed to get the advantage of everybody soon spread abroad. Among others, it reached the ear of a head-man at one of the settlements. This man had a big field and several wives: he was indeed a rich man. He prided himself on being very clever and knowing everything: he knew all about the history of his tribe, and by looking at a certain star he could tell the proper time to visit the coast when the crabs were "on the march." In fact, he knew he was shrewder than Konehu, and publicly said so. Now, Konehu heard of this, and p. 377taking up a position on the path leading to this individual's cassava field, waited for the owner to come along. As soon as he heard footsteps appreaching, he loosed his bowels, and tearing a "cap" from off the shoot of a "troolie" palm, carefully placed it point upwards on the ground, over the dung, at the same time pressing his palms around the edge just as if there was some live animal underneath.1 When a few feet distant, the owner saw Konehu in this extraordinary attitude, he asked him what he was doing. "I have just caught a bird here," says Konehu, "and am afraid of it getting away. Do you happen to have a quake with you?" Not suspecting any trickery, the man told him that if he liked to go round to his house, he could have the quake which he would find hanging up on one of the posts. So he puts down his bow, arrows, and pegall, and Konehu shows him how to hold the troolie cap tightly down and prevent the wonderful bird escaping. Konehu takes up the bow and arrows, marches off to the logie, and makes himself quite at home with both the eatables and the women: indeed, he spends a gloriously happy time there. But as for the man watching over the wonderful bird, hour after hour passed and he finally felt so weary that he tipped up one edge of the troolie cap, and saw that he had indeed been outwitted by the very man he had boasted to despise.

362.* The time at last arrived when mere mention of Konehu's name made everyone spit. All had been fooled by him at some time or another, and now left him strictly to himself. His wife went off with another man. Poor Konehu did not know how to clean the house, which became more and more dilapidated; he knew nothing about cooking, he had no cassava, and when he did manage to go out hunting with bow and arrow, he invariably met with poor success. One day, however, he managed to shoot a fine big deer. He ate all of it except one leg, which he barbecued and slung up to one of the beams of his house. Next day, he again managed to secure some game, and so things went on, his luck, day after day, not only continuing but increasing. More than this, every time he reached home in the afternoon, there he found the fire lighted, the pepper-pot already boiled, everything tidied up and cleaned, and yet not a soul was to be seen. He became curious. So instead of going hunting out back one morning, he hid himself behind a big tree whence he could observe everything taking place in the house without himself being seen. He waited and waited. By and by he saw the deer leg (Sect. 98) change into a beautiful woman, and he then knew who it was that had been minding him so carefully. He rushed forward and held her fast. He wanted her to be his wife, but she resolutely declined, though she promised to remain and continue as his benefactress. He therefore built another house, adjoining his, just for her especial use. After a time, she changed her mind about becoming his wife. She had only refused his offer before, because she was afraid he might tell his friends and relatives who she was—the offspring of a deer's foot—the shame and disgrace of which she felt she could never face. The bargain was accordingly struck that so long as he held his tongue about her antecedents, she would remain with him as his spouse: if he betrayed her, she would punish him. They were happy together for a long time, and everything prospered. Konehu's luck in hunting and fishing, as well as his abundance of provisions, became now almost proverbial, but whenever questioned as to how he managed to secure such luck, and what binas (Sect. 233) he employed, he always remained silent. The neighbors' envy and curiosity were not to be baffled by his silence. They said, "Let us ask Konehu to a paiwarri, and make him drunk. Then he will tell us!" So they held a big feast, and they had many jars of drink, and Konehu, getting beastly intoxicated, told the whole story. When he woke next morning out of his debauchery, he turned his steps homeward: His astonishment was indeed great to find his old house, without any additions, just as dirty and untidy as in his grass-widower days—and, yes, there was the deer-leg still hanging on the cord. In his anger he determined on eating p. 378the venison, but when he struck his knife in, all the blood gushed forth. This sobered him, and he left the house to become a wanderer. He may be here today, and gone tomorrow. Yes, indeed, there are so many Konehus [i. e. rogues and vagabonds] wandering about the world now, that it is very difficult to recognize which one is our old friend.

363.* THE WOMAN AND THE SERPENT OROLI

Long ago there was a girl who had many offers of marriage from among her own people, but who always refused them. One day a stranger came, dressed in fine style. Directly she saw him she exclaimed, "That is the man for me. I want him for my husband." He married her, built a house in one day, and prepared all the furniture—as the stools, paiwarri trough, the mortar—all at the same time. By this token (everything being made so quickly) the girl knew that something was wrong, but she could not say definitely what. As a matter of fact it was really the terrible snake Oroli (Sect. 235), who had come disguised as a man, decorated with boar's teeth and beautiful feathers. And when at the wedding feast the bridegroom did not want to eat with the others, and could be prevailed on to do so only on the condition that he should be provided with an uncooked duck, which he swallowed all by himself, the girl was still more certain that his actions were a token of some impending evil. After the feast was over she accompanied her husband to their new home, where she remained in his hammock for three days, but he did not even once play the part of a husband. He was really starving himself preparatory to making a meal of her. At the end of this time he told her to turn round, so that her head rested at his feet. When she had obeyed him, he started swallowing her foot first. "Mother! Mother!" she cried, "something is swallowing me." "No! No!" screamed the man, "I am only acting as a good husband." Her mother rushed into the house, but found only a great fat serpent in the hammock. Her daughter was nowhere to be seen, and the mother knew what had happened. She then ran to the priest who had married them, and begged him to kill the snake, but the good Father said, "No. I can not do so, because he is a Catholic." So the girl was punished for having preferred the stranger to an Indian.

364.* THE PIAI AND THE EARTHQUAKE PEOPLE (C)

A party of Caribs were out shooting birds in the forest when an earthquake (tutulu) took place: this made a great noise and the ground opened. Many people were inside the earth, and one of the Caribs, Aiyobanni by name, jumped in to join them. His mother, not being able to find him anywhere, commenced weeping. The head-man of the Earthquake People heard her crying, and told Aiyobanni how she was mourning his absence. "You must stay a little longer with us," he added, "but by and by we will carry you back to her, after we have taught you all about piai." They taught him the practice of the profession, and all the time Aiyobanni was down beneath the ground with the Earthquake People, the girls made him amatory overtures, but he wanted none; he was so anxious to get back to his poor old mother. Many years passed. There was another earthquake, the earth opened, and Aiyobanni approached his mother. "Don't cry, mother," were his first words to her. He slept that night under her roof, but complained next morning of the great number of dog fleas about. On proposing to wet the ground, his mother said, "All right," and every minute expected to see him go to the boat-landing to fetch the water. Instead of this he knocked at all the house-posts, and water flowed from the base of each until it covered all the ground and rose above their ankles. His mother was indeed frightened now and thought he was going to sink the earth altogether. After doing this and several other wonderful things, his fame as a piai spread far and wide. At last the Missionary p. 379came to visit him. "Aiyobanni," said the visitor, "you are a piai and must stop doing these things. The Government pays me to be piai, so you must not interfere with my work." "But I can not stop," replied Aiyobanni; "bad Indians taught me, I might perhaps be able to oblige you, but as the Earthquake People trained me, I dare not now give up my work." About a month later the Missionary was taken ill. He tried many medicines without success; hence he was obliged to send for Aiyobanni. Although the Missionary sent for him with a letter and a big tent-boat, for some time he would not go; finally, after being sent for five times he went. When he reached the Missionary's house after making his patient take off all his clothes, he anointed him from head to foot, whereupon a large number of quartz crystals came out from all over his body and fell to the floor. The Missionary was so much pleased because of the cure effected that he paid Aiyobanni one hundred dollars; but the latter took good care never to tell him that he himself had caused the crystals to enter his body long before he had been sent for to give treatment.

Next

Footnotes

p. 372

1 Nafudi is the Arawak term for the head of a settlement, for a "boss," and used to be applied to a chieftain or cacique, in the same sense that it would be and still is applied to the King or to the Governor.

2 It is a common trick for the Indians to give a sharp downward tug on their children's ears when the youngsters are naughty or disobedient.

p. 374

1 The rest of this story is fairly similar to the following Warrau version.

2 In the Arawak version of the story as told on the Pomeroon, the slaughter of all three youngsters is wilfully done on the one occasion by throwing them into boiling water in a pot, which the miscreant covers with a baking-stone.

p. 375

1 The exploit of the yellow stone in the water has been met with only in the Pomeroon Warrau version of the story.

2 From Cayenne comes a variation of the story of the Tiger in a pit, covered over with a stone (Cou, I, 272-3).

p. 376

1 Although Father Gumilla, upward of two centuries ago, speaks of indigenous rice growing luxuriantly on the Orinoco, thus far I have not met with any records of its having been cultivated by the Indians previous to the Conquest.—W. E. R.

2 The Arawaks on the Essequibo have the same story.

p. 377

1 The spathe of this palm (Manicaria sp.) was used as a hat by the Warrau and Arawak males.

CHAPTER XXI
MISCELLANEOUS FOLK-LORE, INDEPENDENT OF ANIMISM

Various Tales and Legends (365-370).

365.* HOW THE LAZY MAN WAS CURED (W)

This is another crab story (Sect. 278); but the hero of it was distinguished by his laziness, and not by his ignorance. A large party of people went out in a big boat to catch crabs: every one of them had twenty quakes aboard, and as they rested at each stopping-place, they still continued plaiting them. You see, they had nothing to distract their attention, having left their wives at home to make the paiwarri ready for their return. At one of the inlets where they put in for a rest on the way down, they saw growing close to the banks a small kokerite palm, with a large bunch of ripe fruit. Having cut off the bunch, they put it into the boat, shoved off, and then started eating. The hero of this story asked them to save all the seeds, after they had removed the fruity parts, and let him have them. This they did, and on the night before their arrival at the place agreed upon for catching crabs, he filled all his quakes with them. Next morning the others landed to hunt, but this fellow refused to join them, and remained in the boat, not even putting his feet into the water. He knew well enough how to hunt the crabs, but was too lazy, and counted on receiving contributions from all his companions. These, on the contrary, were equally determined that he should not have any: they filled all their own quakes, returned to the boat, and finally reached home. It was night when they got there, and they turned into their hammocks. Next morning, they called their wives to fetch the crabs from the place where they had left them at the water-side. The wife of the individual who had brought back the kokerite seeds, asked him where his crabs were: he told her that she would find them at the bottom of the heap and that she would have to wait until all the other women had cleared away theirs. She did as she was instructed and, carrying the quakes to her mother, let her know that these were the kind of crabs that her husband had brought home with him. The old woman thought much, but merely said, "Put them into a big pot and boil them on the fire, till the shells crack." In the meantime, each of the other women gave the naturally diaappointed wife one quakeful of crabs each, but conditionally, on her promising that she would give none to her husband. And thus, with one exception, they all started on a hearty meal of crabs and paiwarri. The old mother took a calabash full of the cooked kokerite seeds, and placing it before her good-for-nothing son-in-law, bade him eat. This was obliged to do, even if only out of mere shame, because he was so hungry, and knew that no one would give him of their crabs. At any rate, the lesson cured him of his laziness, and on the next occasion that he went out hunting, he brought home to his poor wife crabs and not kokerite seeds.

366.* ALWAYS BE CONTENT (W)

An expedition was arranged by a house-master for his relatives and friends, who were to come and join him on the coast and hunt sea-birds. Before starting, they all made quakes for collecting the birds' eggs, it being then the proper season, and eggs p. 381 always good to eat.1 After they had gathered sufficient eggs to fill their baskets, they proceeded with their bows and arrows to shoot birds, and were very successful. The old house-master's son-in-law, however, went off by himself in quite another direction, where there was plenty of dry timber and shot only woodpeckers, of which he brought back plenty. When they got home again, the wives made cassiri for them. The old man and his friends gave to the son-in-law of their big stock of various sea-birds, and the latter gave them woodpeckers in exchange. In the course of conversation, they asked why he had shot only land-birds when he was supposed to have come out to shoot sea-birds. He replied that he did not mind whether they had come from land or sea, so long as they were birds, and that he was quite content to eat one or the other.

367.* THE OLD WOMAN WHO DIED OF SHAME (W)

A very old woman once took her little grandson with her into the bush to gather honey. She looked up at a tree, and, seeing some bees coming in and out of a hole, told the boy she was going to climb it. Now, as these were biting [stinging] bees, she told him also that she intended blowing into the hole so as to keep the insects quiet. When, however, she reached a convenient height, and commenced blowing, she soon recognized that she was dealing with wasps, not bees. She got terribly stung, and in beating a hasty retreat, her foot slipped, her kuyu [apron-belt] caught on a small projecting branch, and she fell naked to the ground. Of course, she did not dare go home in that state, and so her grandson shot an arrow into the apron, hanging a long way up on the tree, and brought it down for her. They went back home, and the old woman told the child on no account to tell his parents what had happened, because she was so afraid of being laughed at. Thus it was that she always kept the little boy near her, lest he should talk about the incident. One day, however, the youngster slipped away to his father and mother, and told them of the old grandmother's adventure with the wasps, and how she had come down the tree without her clothes. They roared with laughter as the little boy mimicked the old woman's actions. The poor old soul heard them both laughing, and began to cry for very shame; and she cried so long that she died.

368.* THE MAN WHO INTERFERED WITH HIS BROTHER'S WIFE (A)

There were once two brothers. The elder went one morning to the field to clean up, leaving his wife at home to grate cassava. The younger, who lived at a distance, had a habit of visiting his brother's house always at a time when he knew full well that he would not be at home. So it happened on this very occasion. He asked his sister-in-law where her husband was, and she told him quite truly that he had just gone to the field. "And when is he coming back?" to which she replied, "In the evening." He thereupon asked her whether she would like him to take liberties with her, an offer which she indignantly refused. So he tried to obtain his desires by force: she repelled him: they wrestled with one another: she ran away into the bush, he following her closely. She only got back home again late in the p. 382afternoon just before her husband arrived. When he saw the grated cassava lying in the trough he asked her what she had been about; surely she had not taken all day to grate that little bit of cassava! She was forced then to tell him, how his brother had come to visit her during his absence, how he had chased her into the bush, and what had happened there. The husband said, "All right! I will wait for him tomorrow, when he will be sure to visit you again." the next day, sure enough, the brother came once more. "Where is your husband?" He inquired. "Yonder in the maraka-bakruru," she told him.1 The husband purposely made a noise with his massi [club] to attract the attention of the visitor: the latter heard it, and thinking that drink must be the cause of the row, went over to see if that really were the case. But as soon as he got inside, the aggrieved man gave him a good beating, told him what he had heard from his wife's own lips, chased him into the bush, still beating him, and ran on until he could run no farther. When the husband finally got home again, he told his wife to sling up their hammock close to the roof, on the runner (to which the thatch was tied), because his brother would certainly return that night to kill the pair of them. There, close to the roof, they went to sleep, and in the middle of the night the brother came. They heard him say, "I will show you what I will do for your trying to kill me." They saw him take a stick and strike in all directions. They saw the cudgel knock against the beam and break, part rebounding on the would-be murderer's head. Half dazed with the blow, the latter thought it was the injured husband who had struck him, because they heard him scream out, "Oh! instead of me killing you as I had intended, you have killed me." The husband now descended from his hammock and chased the worthless fellow out into the bush, saying, "I will indeed kill you if you dare come here again." But the scoundrel never returned to molest his sister-in-law.

369.* THE OLD BLIND MAN WHO WANTED A WOMAN (W)

There was once an old blind man and the young fellows were always making fun of him. One day they asked him if he would like to have a woman. He said "yes," and told them to find him a fine young one. It was therefore arranged for that very evening, that they would tie a rope to his hammock and attach its other end to the hammock of a young girl, so that, as soon as everyone was asleep, he would have merely to feel his way stealthfully along the rope. Now, instead of attaching the rope's end as originally promised, the young rascals tied it to a tree overhanging the river bank, with the result that on obeying the instructions given, the poor old blind man floundered into the chilly waters of the stream, and just managed to save himself from drowning by holding onto a ho-aranni tree.2 When the young men saw that their joke had gone too far, they became frightened, and, getting into a corial, went to bring him back. "Grandfather! we have come to fetch you;" but the old man was much vexed and they were obliged to return without him. One of the youngsters, dressing himself up as a girl, with an apron-belt, and putting the basket-strap over his forehead, just as the women carry it, now went to get the old man home. "No!" he said, "I am not coming home any more;" but when he heard the young man say, "I am a girl," he felt her cotton anklets, her bangles, and her basket, and was accordingly satisfied; he then jumped into the corial and saved himself.

370.* HOW WE BEAT THE CARIBS (A)

I give the following almost word for word translation of the account told me by an old Pomeroon Arawak; it is well worth comparing with Brett's version (BrB, 35):

An Arawak and a Carib were very friendly: this must needs be so, because each had taken the other's sister to wife. They regularly used to go hunting together. After living in harmony for a long time, they went out hunting, but on this occasion they did not go in company, and they both stayed away longer than usual, and their friends wefe beginning to wonder what had happened to them. The Arawak, having finally returned, went to see after his brother-in-law, followed his tracks into the bush, and came on the babracote upon which he found the dried body of his sister whom her husband had evidently killed. He went home, but did not speak for some time. He them told his wife, the Carib's sister, to come into the bush and hunt with him: when he got her away, he killed and babracoted her. The Carib next came along to see what had happened, and he soon saw. He also went home again, but did not speak for some time. Finally, he expressed a wish to fight and kill the Arawak, but the Nafudi said "No. All the Caribs together must fight the Arawaks together." So both sides cut a big field and planted plenty of the particular canes required for making arrows, and when these canes were full grown, they cut them down and completed their weapons, and both sides erected a strong house, Waiba, to store them in. Up at Jack Low, on the left bank of the Pomeroon, is still to be recognized the site of the old settlement and fortress, the place itself even to this day being known as Waiba-diki. Furthermore, it was arranged by both parties that as they intended fighting their battle at sea, and not on land, they would allow themselves time to build a large number of canoes. This being done, they filled their boats with arrows: twenty canoes were paddled by Arawaks, and forty by Caribs. They all went down the river, out to sea, at the Pomeroon mouth, each taking up such position as would permit of the intervening distance being just sufficient to allow of the arrows thrown from one side reaching the other. The Arawaks, however, were shrewd. They made themselves cork-wood shields [nonabokuanna].1 The Caribs let fly their arrows first, but these stuck in the shields, when the Arawaks broke them off with their mossi, the now almost obsolete club. None of the Arawaks were slain, and it was now their turn to shoot. This they did, with the result that they killed all their enemy, except two, whom they purposely spared in order that they might go home and tell their friends what had happened, and what to expect should they ever dare to fight the Arawaks again. The two who had been spared went away to the Cuyuni, to the Barima, and to the Waini, and remained three months gathering together all their people, who clamored that they would never rest until they had destroyed all the Arawaks. The Arawaks were waiting for them at Waiba-diki, their stronghold, and stretched a vine-rope across the river; and as the hosts of Caribs approached up the stream, the steering paddles of their canoes became entangled in this rope, and broke away; and while the occupants were looking after them, their canoes all tossed one against the other in dire confusion, and the Arawaks shot showers of arrows into the wavering multitude. Half the Caribs were destroyed; the other half effected a landing. But around their fortress, the Arawaks had already built a palisade, with just a few chinks in it to permit of arrows flying through; they were all well under cover, and though losing a few of their own people, massacred as before all their enemy, leaving but two to give the news to their friends. These two went to the east, to Surinam, and started collecting the remnants of their own tribe from those parts. p. 384About three months passed. The Arawaks could wait no longer, so they traveled over to Surinam, and came upon the Carib forces, collected in a fortress with enclosing palisade, similar to what they themselves had constructed for their own preservation at Waiba-diki. The Caribs were in overwhelming numbers. So the Arawaks hid themselves, and sent in one of their number to reconnoiter. This man, who could talk Carib, painted himself like one of that nation, and boldly entered the enemy's camp, where he found them all drinking. He said he was a Carib, and that he had just come from the Pomeroon looking for his family; he accepted a little drink and then took his departure, but not before discovering that very early on the following morning, long before daybreak, a crab whistle (i. e. made from a crab claw) would be blown as a signal for them to prepare for battle. The scout returned to his people, with all the information that he had gleaned. That night, every one of the Arawaks made a crab whistle, and surrounding the Caribs while they were still drinking, blew their whistles, surprising the enemy, and slew them all, save one man and woman, who begged so earnestly for their lives that only their legs were speared. It is from this couple that all the present day Caribs are derived, and this is why there are comparatively so few of them. It was we Arawaks who broke their power.

Next

Footnotes

1 I am well aware of the statement often made (for example, by Boddam-Whetham, p. 250; im Thurn, p. 265) about Indians not eating birds' eggs; this, however, applies only to eggs of domesticated birds, as noted by Schomburgk in his visit to the Takutu (Sc.T. 70): "Fowls are the only animals which the Indian of Guiana domesticates . . . ; but he raises them only for his diversion, as he makes neither use of their eggs nor of their flesh." Crévaux (164), in French Guiana, speaking of fowls and eggs, says that these are not eaten by the Oyambis, nor by the Roucouyennes. On his asking the chief for the reason, the latter told him that, in spite of his advanced age, he still wished to have children and that the eggs of all species of birds were preserved for the old people of both sexes. I am given to understand that the aboriginal Guiana receipt for cooking eggs is as follows: Break a number into a pot over the fire, stir with a wooden spoon, add salt, when procurable, to taste, and then serve.—W. E. R.

p. 382

1 The maraka-bakuru is a small detached house, in which in the olden times the Warru house-master would keep his arrows, clubs, tools, and implements, and other knickknacks.

2 Any snag or tree growing from out of the river-bed above the water is believed to have been planted there by the Water People, or Ho-aranni (Sect. 177), and hence is given this name.

p. 383

1 Although we have historical evidence of the use of shields from the Orinoco, Cayenne, and the Amazon, this is the first reference that I have come across concerning these weapons in British Guiana.—W. E. R.

GLOSSARY

ACOURI or AGOUTI, ADOURI. Species of Dasyprocta; small game animals of great food value.

BABOON. The almost invariable Creole term applied to the Howling Monkey (Mycetes seniculus).

BABRACOTE (a corrupted form of Barbecue). A small three-legged or four-legged wooden staging upon which meat is laid to be smoke-dried.

BANAB or BENAB. A temporary shed built of sticks and leaves for shelter from sun, rain, or dew.

BARBECUE. To smoke-dry.

BELTIRI. A fermented drink, made from cassava, essentially for home consumption.

BUCK (feminine, BUCKEEN). A term originally applied by the Dutch to any aboriginal Indian.

BULLET TREE. The Mimusops globosa, a timber tree with excellent fruit and valuable "milk."

BUNIA. The "stinking-bird" (Ostinops spp.).

BUSH-COW. Another name for the tapir.

BUSH-HOG. Dicotyles sp.

BUSH-MASTER snake. Lachesis mutus.

BUSH-RAT. The name applied in the Pomeroon District to the opossum. There are, however, several bush-rats proper (Muridæ).

CAMUDI, CAMOODIE. The land (Boa constrictor) or water (Eunectes murinus) boas.

CASSAVA bread. The Indian's "staff of life," made from the Manihot.

CASSIRI, CAXIRI. A fermented drink, similar to beer, made from cassava; drunk in large quantities to intoxicate.

CHIGOE. A species of flea which, penetrating the flesh, may cause great irritation.

CORIAL. A dug-out canoe.

CREOLE. A British Guiana term applied to any person born in the colony, of parents other than aboriginal Indians.

CURARE (known also as URALI, WURALI). The well-known deadly poison of which the chief ingredient is derived from Strychnos toxifera.

GILBACKER. A food-fish (Sciadeicthys parkeri).

HAIAMARA. A food-fish (Hoplias macrophthalmus).

HAIAWA, HAIOWA. The Incense tree, from which a very fragrant resin is derived.

HARRI-HARRI. See YARRI-YARRI.

HOBU. The Hog-plum (Spondias lutea).

HOWLING MONKEY. See BABOON.

HURI. A food-fish (Hoplias malabaricus).

IGARIPE. A water-channel.

ITABO. A water-channel.

ITE (written also ITA and ETA). The Mauritia palm; of immense economic value to the Indians.

ITIRITI. A plant (Ischnosiphon) with a reedlike stem, which is split down to form strands for plaiting.

JIGGER. See CHIGOE.

KESKEDEE. The onomatopœic term for a certain bird (a species of Lanius).

KOKERITE. The Maximiliana regia palm.

KURAUA (written also CROWA). A species of Agave from the fibers of which very strong cords are made.

KUSHI. A leaf-cutting ant; very destructive on the plantations.

LABARIA. An exceedingly poisonous snake (Lachesis lanceolatus).

LABBA. One of the most savory of the rodents (Cœlogenys paca).

LUKUNANNI. A food fish (Cichla ocellaris). The Pomeroon Indians sometimes speak of it as "sunfish," owing to its brilliant coloration.

MAAM. See SCRUB-TURKEY.

MAIPURI. The Indian name for the tapir.

MALOKA, MALOCCA. A large house in which several families live a more or less communal life.

MANICOLE. The Euterpe edulis palm.

MARABUNTA. The Creole term for several species of wasp.

MARAKA. The Calabash-gourd rattle.

MARUDI. A black fowl (Penelope sp.) with a scarlet neck.

MATAPI. The plaited snakelike press for squeezing the poisonous juice out of the cassava.

MORA. One of the giants of the forest trees the wood of which is very hard.

MOROKOT. A food fish, something like the pacu (Myletes).

"NANCY"-STORY. One of the many African stories having the mythical spider, or anansi, as hero; hence applied by the Creoles to any legend, myth, or fairy tale

NEGROCOP. "Crane" or "stork" (Mycteria americana).

OPOSSUM. See BUSH-RAT; YAWARRI.

OÜICOU. A fermented drink, or paste, made from cassava and potatoes.

PAIWARRI. A blackish fermented drink made from cassava used on occasions of feasting and sport.

PARIPI or PEACH-PALM. Guilielma sp.

PECCARY. The kairuni or abuya, two of the bush-hogs.

PEGALL. A basket having a plaited body and cover, much like a European woman's traveling dress basket.

PEPPER-POT. A meat stew containing capsicums and cassareep, kept good by daily sterilizing (boiling).

PIMPLER PALM. From "pimple," meaning a thorn; species of Bactris.

PIRAI. A very voracious carnivorous fish (Pygocentris sp.) with exceedingly strong and sharp incisors.

POWIS. An excellent bird (Crax sp.) for the table.

PURPLE-HEART. A strong timber (Copaifera sp.) used in making dug-out canoes house posts, etc.

QUAKE. A term applied indiscriminately to all open-work Indian baskets.

QUATTA. A monkey (Ateles paniscus).

QUERRIMAN. A food fish (Mugil brasilianus).

SALAPENTA. The Creole term for the larger lizards.

SAWYER BEETLE. A beetle (Macrodontia dejani) which "rings" branches of trees.

SCRUB-TURKEY or MAAM. Tinamus subcristatus.

SEA-COW. A Creole term for the Manatus.

SILK-COTTON TREE. A large deciduous tree (Eriodendron, Bombax).

TIGER. The Creole term applied to practically all the members of the feline tribe—jaguar, puma, wildcat, and others.

TRULI or TROOLIE. The Manicaria palm, the leaves of which are used for thatch.

TRUMPETER. The Warracabba bird (Psophia sp.).

URALI. See CURARE.

VULTURE. The carrion-crow "governor," or "Boss" (Sarcoramphus papa).

WATER-DOG. The Creole term for otter.

WOODSKIN. A canoe made of a single sheet of bark.

WURALI, URALI. Other forms of the word CURARE.

YACKMAN. The Jagd-man's, or Huntsman's, Ant, which comes at regular intervals and clears out all the other ants.

YARRI-YARRI. The Indian flute.

YAWARRI. Species of opossum (Didelphys).